HISTORY
OF THE BRITISH RESIDENCY
IN BURMA
1826 - 1840

By the same author

India and Burma. Orient Longmans, 1952.

A Pageant of Burmese History. Orient Longmans, 1961.

Deposed King Thibaw of Burma in India, 1885–1916. Bharitya Vidya Bhavan, 1967.

The Reconquest of India : Pre-British Period. Delhi, 1950.

Bombay and the Marathas up to 1774. Munshiram Manoharlal. New Delhi, 1970.

HISTORY of THE BRITISH RESIDENCY IN BURMA

1826-1840

BY

W. S. DESAI, M.A. Bom. & Cantab.

Burma Educational Service

Lecturer in History

University College

Rangoon

Published by:

The University of Rangoon

1939

ISBN 0 576 03152 6

Republished in 1972 by Gregg International Publishers Limited
Westmead, Farnborough, Hants, England

Printed in England

CONTENTS

APPENDICES

PREFACE

This work constitutes the first attempt yet made to describe Anglo-Burmese relations from the close of the First Anglo-Burmese War (1824-1826) up to the early years of the reign of Tharrawaddy (1837-1846). Its object is to furnish the student as well as the general reader with the story of the British Residency in Burma up to its withdrawal in 1840. During this period of nearly 15 years, the British Indian Government made great attempts to maintain, without resort to war, diplomatic relations with the Government of Burma by means of a permanent Residency at the Royal Capital. The Burmese monarch was, however, interested in the Residency only so far as he could make use of it for his own purpose. The Residency was looked upon as a humiliating badge of the defeat in the War which had cost the King considerable territorial losses; so that every possible effort, other than war, was made to remove the Residency at least from the capital, and confine it to Rangoon. Tharrawaddy ultimately succeeded in this attempt; but the Indian Government was not prepared to retain the Residency in the country unless it was honourably entertained at the capital. In the absence of this the Residency was withdrawn, and and during the period between 1840 and the outbreak of the Second Burmese War in 1852, diplomatic relations between the two governments were at a standstill. In the reign of Mindon they were resumed and the Residency was re-established at the capital in 1862.

Besides supplying the history of the British Residency in Burma and the course of Anglo-Burmese relations during these 15 years, this work throws considerable light upon the internal history of Burma, giving to the reader an altogether new insight into the reigns and times of the two monarchs Bagyidaw

vii

PREFACE

and Tharrawaddy. Henry Burney, Resident in Burma, 1830-1838, who hitherto has been just a name in Anglo-Burmese history, emerges as an outstanding and honourable personality. Many other interesting characters, hitherto lying buried in the record room, have come to light. Besides the Residents, Burney and Benson, there are their assistants, Bayfield, Blundell, Hannay, McLeod and Edwards; the scholarly Woongyees, Maung Za and the Prince of Mekkhara; Lane the writer of the Burmese dictionary in collaboration with the Prince of Mekkhara; Lanciago the Spanish trader and Shahbunder of Rangoon, and many others.

A special introduction to this book is not necessary. A preliminary idea of the discourse may be obtained from the list of Contents. The first two chapters will provide all the introduction required even by the uninitiated. The reader will have no difficulty in understanding the footnotes. The abbreviations used are self-evident: they are also explained in the Bibliography. Whenever a letter to the Government of India, by any of its officers is cited, the writer alone is mentioned, such as " Burney's Letter."

In the composition of this work, I have attempted to describe history pure and simple as supplied by the original sources. It has not been the intention either to support or to oppose any particular theories or opinions, but to present history without fear or favour. This, I believe, is the true function of history.

It only remains now to express my thanks to those who have helped me: — My grateful thanks are due to Principal U Pe Maung Tin, University College, Rangoon, for ready help granted on special points: explanations of Burmese terms and phrases in the text, some of them of an obscure nature, have been made available owing to his readiness to help at all times and seasons. Special thanks are also due to G. H. Luce, Esq., Reader in Far Eastern History, University of Rangoon, for help and advice rendered on doubtful points and answers to queries; to my colleagues, Professor A. Brookes, University of Rangoon, and B. R. Pearn, Esq., Lecturer in History, Univer-

viii

PREFACE

sity College, Rangoon, for reading the manuscript after its completion, and making useful suggestions; to N. R. H. Iyer, Esq., of the English Department, University College, Rangoon, for answers to enquiries; and to my former student, U E Cho, now Tutor in History, University College, Rangoon, for translating portions of the Kone-baung-set Mahayazawin into English. The staffs of the Library and Record Department at the India Office must not be forgotten: I have experienced nothing but courtesy and help at their hands. Thanks are also due to the Manipur Durbar and to the Secretary to the Governor of Assam for supplying information concerning Raja Gumbheer Singh. I wish also to thank the printers of this book for their earnest desire to meet my wishes at all times, and for the carefulness shown by them in the execution of their work. I feel reluctant to close this section of the book without acknowledging the encouragement, sympathy and support that I have received from my wife during the composition of this work, in the midst of discouragements and earthly disappointments. Thanks are also due to her and to our two daughters for help rendered in the reading of the printer's proofs.

Finally, I wish to express my gratitude to the University of Rangoon for its interest in this work, and above all, for generously financing its publication.

W. S. D.

STILL WATERS,
    University Avenue,
        Rangoon.

———

Genealogical Table of the Kings of the
Alaungpaya Dynasty, 1752 — 1885

Capitals —

1752 — 1765 Moksobo (Shwebo).
1765 — 1783 and 1823 — June 1837 Ava.
June 1837 — December 1837 Kyauk - Myaung.
1783 — 1823 and December 1837 — 1857 Amarapura.
1857 — 1885 Mandalay.

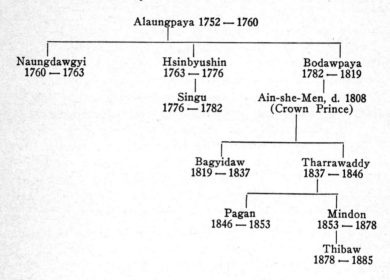

Alaungpaya 1752 — 1760

Naungdawgyi 1760 — 1763

Hsinbyushin 1763 — 1776

Singu 1776 — 1782

Bodawpaya 1782 — 1819

Ain-she-Men, d. 1808 (Crown Prince)

Bagyidaw 1819 — 1837

Tharrawaddy 1837 — 1846

Pagan 1846 — 1853

Mindon 1853 — 1878

Thibaw 1878 — 1885

List of the Governor - Generals of
British India, 1823 - 1856

Amherst	.. ..	1 August, 1823 — 13 March, 1828.
		13 March, 1828 — 4 July, 1828, W. B. Bayley, Acting Governor-General.
Bentinck	.. ..	4 July, 1828 — 20 March, 1835.
		20 March, 1835 — 4 March, 1836, C. Metcalf, Acting Governor-General.
Auckland	.. ..	4 March, 1836 — 28 February, 1842.
Ellenborough	.. ..	1842 — 1844.
Hardinge	.. ..	1844 — 1848.
Dalhousie	.. ..	1848 — 1856.

List of British Residents in Burma, 1826 - 1840

J. Crawfurd, 1826 — 1827.

Henry Burney,[1] 1830 — 1838.

Ava, 24 April, 1830 — 10 April, 1832.
Rangoon, May 1832 to October 1833.
Calcutta, January-March 1833.
Moulmein, May and June 1833.

10 April, 1832 — 6 November, 1833, in charge of the Residency at Ava:—Blundell April to September 1832; H. Macfarquhar September 1832 to August 1833; Wm. McLeod August to November 1833.

Ava, 6 November, 1833 — 16 April, 1834.
Rangoon, 1 May 1834 to 20 June 1835.
Calcutta, February to April 1835.

16 April, 1834 — 27 July, 1835, G. T. Bayfield in charge of the Residency at Ava.

Ava, 27 July, 1835 — 17 June, 1837.
Rangoon, July to October, 1837.
Calcutta, November 1837 to 8 March, 1838.

On 8 March, 1838, Col. Burney relinquished the duties of Resident.

12 October, 1837—16 July, 1838, G. T. Bayfield in charge of the Residency at Rangoon.

R. Benson, 1838 — 1840.

Rangoon, 16 July, 1838 — 29 August, 1838.

Amarapura, 5 October, 1838 — 14 March, 1839.
Rangoon and Moulmein, March and April 1839.
Calcutta, April 1839 — 1 May, 1840.

On 1 May, 1840, Col. Benson relinquished the duties of Resident.

14 March, 1839 — 7 January, 1840, Wm. McLeod Officiating Resident:— At Amarapura, March to July 1839; at Rangoon 31 July 1839 to 7 January, 1840.

---

[1] Major, 1830.
Lt. Col. 17 January, 1834.
Colonel, 1835.

Modern Spelling of Burmese and other Place - Names which occur in the text

In the Text		Modern
Aeng	.. ..	An
Amarapoora Umarapura Umerapurah Umarapoora Umerapoora	..	Amarapura
Aracan Arracan	..	Arakan
Bamau	.. ..	Bhamo
Beeling	.. ..	Bilin
Bilugum Pulogyon Pullogyon	..	Bilugyun
Erawadi Irawadi	..	Irrawaddy (River)
Enbay	.. ..	Enbe
Hookoom Hookoung Hookum	..	Hukawng (Burmese name, Payendwen)
Kendeam Kendream Kyendwin	..	Chindwin (River)
Kekkha	.. ..	Ketka
Kendat	.. ..	Kindat
Khyouk Myoung Kyouk Myoung	..	Kyauk-Myaung
Kubo Kubboo	..	Kabaw
Kuwai Khyan	.. ..	Kywegyan
Kyoukphyoo	.. ..	Kyaukpyu
Kyouk-taloun	.. ..	Kyauk-ta-loun
Letweyin	.. ..	Le-ywa

PLACE — NAMES

Manipoora Munnipore Munnipur	} ..	Manipur
Maingkhown Maingkhon Moongkhoom	} ..	Maing-Khwan
Mouttshobo	.. ..	Moksobomyo (Shwebo)
Mone Moneh	} ..	Mong-Nai
Myit-ngay	.. ..	Myitnge (River)
Ningthee	.. ..	Ningtee (same as the Chindwin)
Padoo	.. ..	Padu
Paghan	. ..	Pagan
Shain Maga Shin Moga	} ..	Sheinmaga
Takaing Tsagain	} ..	Sagaing
Tsinguh	.. ..	Singu
Samoo Tamoo Tummoo	} ..	Tammu
Toung-ngoo	.. ..	Toungoo
Tsa-ye	.. ..	Saye
Yandaboo	.. ..	Yandabo
Yathea	.. ..	Ayuthia (old capital of Siam)
Yeh	.. ..	Ye
Yeoo	.. ..	Yeu
Yunan	.. ..	Yunnan

Modern Spelling of terms other
than place - names

Gan-bee-ra-shing Gumbhir Singh Gambhir Singh	} ..	Gumbheer Singh (Raja of Manipur)
Hlutdau Hluttau Lhwottau Lootoo	} ..	Hlutdaw (Great Council of State)
Kakhyens	.. ..	Kachins
Kheyns	.. ..	Chins
Kodau	.. ..	Kạdaw (Homage; to do homage)
Myodau	.. ..	Myodaw (Royal City)
Talain Talien	} ..	Talaing (Mon in modern usage)
Tharawadee Tharawadi	} ..	Tharrawaddy (King of Burma)
Thugyee	.. ..	Thugyi (Headman)
Youndau Youn-dau	} ..	Youndaw (Court-house)

N.B. — The following old forms which occur in the text are used in preference to their modern equivalents (shown below in brackets), for the sake of convenience and uniformity:—

Atwenwoon (Atwinwun); Interior Minister or Privy Councillor.

Bo Mhu Woon (Bo-hmu Wun); General officer (military); Secretary of State for War.

Ken Woon (Ken-wun); Governor of the Castle.

Kubo (Kabaw); The Valley between Burma and Manipur.

Kyeewoon (Kyiwun); Overseer of the Granaries.

Men (Min); Ruler or King; also Meng.

Menthagyee (Minthagyi); Great Prince; also Menthagyeh, Menzagyee.

Myowoon (Myowun); Governor of a city or district.

Tsakyamen (Sakyamin); The Sakya Prince: Bagyidaw's son's title.

Tsaredaugyee (Sayedawgyi); Royal writer or Clerk of the Council.

Woon (Wun); Minister or Governor.

Woondouk (Wundauk); Assistant Minister or under Secretary of State.

Woongyee (Wungyi); Great Minister.

CORRECTIONS

Page 33, line 1 and page 489, index: for "Major A. D. Maingy" read "A. D. Maingy".

Page 62, 2nd paragraph, last line: first bracket is missing.

Page 212, last paragraph, line 7: for "Bruney" read "Burney".

Page 325, 2nd paragraph, line 3: for ". . . thought in . . ." read ". . . thought it . . ."

Page 444, paragraph 2, line 10: for ". . . not a proper . . ." read ". . . not proper . . ."

Page 490, index: for "Nagrais" read "Negrais".

HISTORY OF THE BRITISH RESIDENCY IN BURMA
1826-1840

CHAPTER I

ANGLO-BURMESE RELATIONS FROM THE TREATY OF YANDABO TO THE ESTABLISHMENT OF THE RESIDENCY, 1826-1830.

On 24 February, 1826, the First Anglo-Burmese War was brought to an end by the Treaty of Yandabo.[1] By this treaty, Bagyidaw, King of Burma, agreed, to renounce all claims upon, and abstain from all future interference with Assam, Cachar and Jaintia; to recognize Gumbheer Singh as Raja of Manipur; to cede to the British Government the conquered provinces of Arakan, Ye, Tavoy, Mergui and Tenasserim, taking the Arakan Mountains and the river Salween as the lines of demarcation on the western and southern frontiers of Burma respectively; to pay to the British Government the sum of One Crore of rupees in four equal instalments, to be completed by 24 February, 1828; to treat British subjects in Burma, whether European or Indian, according to the universal law of nations; to abolish all exactions upon British ships in Burmese ports that were not required from Burmese ships in British ports; to deliver over all prisoners, and to cultivate and improve the relations of amity and peace between the two governments by means of accredited ministers from each residing at the Durbar[2] of the other, and by a commercial treaty, upon principles of reciprocal advantage, to be contracted between the two powers.

It gradually became evident that the Treaty was very ill-defined; and especially did it fail in fixing the frontier lines of

[1] See Appendix I.
[2] The Government or Royal Court.

demarcation, which raised untold complications in the negotiations between the two states.   In conformity with Article 7 of the Treaty[1] and to effect the Commercial Treaty, John Crawfurd was deputed as Envoy and Resident Minister at the Court of Ava.[2] Besides the Commercial convention, to be contracted on terms of absolute equality, Crawfurd was instructed to discuss the adjustment of the boundary questions on the Assam, Manipur, Arakan and Martaban frontiers, as well as any other points arising out of the Treaty of Yandabo.

On 2 September, 1826, Crawfurd left Rangoon on the steamer *Diana* (about 130 tons).   He arrived at Henzada on 8 September, and was well received by the Chief Officer[3] of the place, who, however, tried his best to detain the Mission, the Burmese Court, having, as Crawfurd says, " from the first shown much reluctance to admit the residence of a permanent diplomatic agent, and especially to the military guard of fifty men, by which such agent in the terms of the treaty was to be accompanied......He said that he was authorised to treat with us upon any subject whatsoever, even to the conclusion of the commercial convention provided for in the treaty of peace, and ' what need, therefore,' added he, ' is there for our going to Ava?' ".[4] The Burmese Officer's construction of Article 7 of the treaty in respect of the residence of accredited agents appeared " singular and unexpected " to Crawfurd.   In the English copy of the treaty the words were " at each other's Durbars ", in the Burmese version " the Burman Royal City " or Myanma Myodaw.[5] The Officer contended that Rangoon

---

[1] " In order to cultivate and improve the relations of amity and peace hereby established between the two governments, it is agreed, that accredited ministers retaining an escort, or safeguard of fifty men from each, shall reside at the durbar of the other, who shall be permitted to purchase, or to build a suitable place of residence, of permanent materials, and a commercial treaty upon principles of reciprocal advantage will be entered into, by the two contracting parties." (Art. VII *Aitchison:* A Collection of Treaties etc.)

[2] Bengal Secret and Political Vol. 345, 6 April, 1827, Government Resolution No. 30.

[3] His name Maung Kain.

[4] Crawfurd's Journal, p. 16.

[5] မြန်မာပြည်တော်။

was intended by this, not Ava, and that according to Burmese notions Rangoon was a Myodaw or Royal City.

Crawfurd, however, proceeded up the river, and on 30 September, reached Ava. He was well received by the central authorities, and one large house and five smaller houses were assigned to him and to his party. The general effect on arrival of the Embassy may be described in Crawfurd's own words: — "The appearance of a British Mission at Ava, although specifically provided for by the Treaty of Peace, had excited a good deal of uneasiness on the part of the Court, and much alarm among the people. Our little party of less than thirty Europeans had been magnified by rumour into some hundreds, and from such a force the capital itself was scarcely thought to be safe — so deep an impression had the superiority of European arms produced upon the nation at large!"[1]

On 20 October, Crawfurd had an audience of the King on a Kadaw day,[2] and between 12 October, and 24 November, no less than thirteen conferences were held between the British Agent and two Atwenwoons[3] deputed by the Burmese Court to negotiate the Commercial treaty. Crawfurd at first drew up a treaty of twenty-two articles; but this copious sketch was soon discovered to be impracticable, and so was reduced to seven before it was proposed to the Burmese Government. The Burmese Commissioners objected to two articles as not being strictly of a commercial nature, so that Crawfurd's final draft of the treaty consisted of only five articles which sought to stipulate for, (1) freedom of trade for British merchants in Burma and for Burmese merchants in India, (2) free exportation of gold and silver from the two countries, (3) fixed port duties on vessels according to their size, (4) freedom of movement for merchants in the two countries, and permission

[1] Crawfurd's Journal p. 97.
[2] "Beg pardon day": the Durbar day when the vassals and dependents of the King appeared as suppliants, craving pardon for their faults supposed or unknown.
[3] The Kyi-Woon and Maung M'ha; the Atwenwoons were Ministers of the Interior or Privy Councillors.

to take away their families [1] with them on leaving the country, and (5) assistance and protection for shipwrecked vessels.

After a good deal of discussion the Burmese Commissioners finally refused to agree to the exportation of precious metals from Burma or to allow the families of merchants to quit the country. Crawfurd laboured hard to secure these two concessions, but the Burmese Government looked upon them as dangerous to the existence of Burma, and so refused to concede them. Crawfurd ultimately agreed to the terms presented by the Burmese Commissioners, and on 24 November, 1826, the Commercial Treaty was signed and sealed. Crawfurd sums up the treaty in the following words:—

"The first article of the Convention stipulates generally for a free commercial intercourse between the subjects of the two Governments, and for protection to the persons and property of those engaged in trade. It in fact, however, makes no alteration in the circumstances under which that trade has been long conducted; but it may be said to secure, by the formalities of a public instrument, a branch of British commerce which had hitherto existed only by sufferance.

"By the second article of the Treaty, all British vessels, not exceeding fifty tons burthen, or thereabouts, are exempted from the payment of tonnage duties and port charges. This places our trade in the ports of the Burman Empire nearly on a footing with that of its own subjects and of the Chinese, whose boats and junks seldom exceed the tonnage now mentioned, and who have always been exempt from the payment of such charges. The stipulation makes no change in the state of the Burman trade at British ports. The privilege thus secured to us may, it is hoped, give rise to a coasting trade of some value and extent between the Burmese ports and our various settlements in the Bay of Bengal.

"The third article secures some advantages to British merchants resident in the Burman dominions, although far short of those required by the justice and necessity of the case.

"According to the Burman laws, all vessels shipwrecked upon the coast are forfeited, and become the property of the King. This arbitrary and unjust law is cancelled by the fourth and last

---

[1] The Burmese Government did not permit women to leave the country, for fear it might do damage by leading to a depletion in the population.

article of the Convention, which stipulates for British property shipwrecked, the same immunity and protection as under civilized governments." [1]

The Burmese Commissioners also brought up the following questions and claims for discussion:— First, they claimed, that although according to Article 4 of the Treaty of Yandabo, the Salween river was mentioned as the boundary between Burmese and British territory, yet, it was also stated that only the districts of Tenasserim, Tavoy, Mergui and Ye were to be ceded to the British; however, that Moulmein and certain other places to the east of the Salween were parts of the district of Martaban, and so the British had no right to them and ought to return them to the King.[2]   Second, they represented, that since one-half of the indemnity had been paid, and a firm and "grand friendship" had been formed between the two countries, and since "Aracan, Ramree, Sandoway, Cheduba, Ye, Tavoy, Mergui, and Tenasserim, have always belonged to the royal country," these ceded territories should be returned to the King, so that a kind feeling between the two countries might be secured in perpetuity.[3]   Third, they claimed, that according to Article 2 of the Treaty, Raja Gumbheer Singh had been allowed to return to Manipur in peace, but that he had encroached upon Burmese territory which lay on the right bank of the river Ningtee.[4]   They also objected to the presence of British officers in Manipur, and held that Gumbheer Singh being an independent ruler, neither Burmese nor British officers should be stationed there. [5]   Fourth, they desired that the payment of the third and fourth instalments of the indemnity be remitted or deferred, because of the poverty of the country.[6]

[1] Crawfurd's Journal, Appendix pp. 8, 9.
[2] Ibid. pp. 149, 150, 216-224.
[3] Ibid. pp. 180-182.
[4] The Chindwin River. At the end of the War in 1826, the British had confirmed the Kubo Valley to Gumbheer Singh, Raja of Manipur, since as an ally of the Company he had occupied it during the War and had also claimed it as a part of his ancestral property.
[5] Crawfurd's Journal, pp. 182, 208-213. The British officers stationed in Manipur were Grant and Pemberton.
[6] Ibid. pp. 201-205, 261-264.

Crawfurd, however, did not feel justified by his instructions from his Government to arrive at a final decision in the discussions on these political questions, and looked upon his embassy as pre-eminently a commercial one. He sought to meet the arguments of the Burmese deputies, and tried to explain the British view, but left the questions for future negotiation. After the Commercial Convention had been agreed to, therefore, he conveyed his position to the Burmese Commissioners in the following words:— " For my own part, my business is now done. I have no favours to ask......My business is now concluded, and I wish to return......It is my intention to leave Ava, if possible, in about seven days."[1] In assuming this attitude Crawfurd, undoubtedly, committed a grave blunder: his instructions did authorise him to discuss any questions arising from the Treaty of Yandabo.

A few days before his departure, however, Crawfurd demanded the release of Manipuree and Assamese captives, according to Article 11 of the Treaty. Several thousands of these prisoners were kept as slaves in Burma, and Crawfurd made a vigorous attempt to obtain their release. The Burmese deputies held that they were bound to give up all prisoners of war, and had accordingly released all soldiers and sepoys, but that the Manipurees and Assamese, who once were subjects of the King, were not covered by the treaty. They further checkmated Crawfurd by reminding him of his own words, that he had come to negotiate a commercial treaty, and that his business was "now done," and they added, "we do not think it proper to call these people[2] before you."[3] The subject was discussed a second time, but nothing was gained by it. The final outcome of the Crawfurd embassy was merely the Commercial Convention of four articles: all the other questions that were raised and discussed were left for future adjustment.

---

[1] *Ibid.* p. 257.
[2] *i.e.* the slaves in question.
[3] Crawfurd's Journal, pp. 283, 284.

On 12 December, 1826, the Mission quitted Ava, and on 22 February, 1827, Crawfurd submitted his report to his Government. In the absence of Lord Amherst, the Governor-General, in Simla, Lord Combermere, the Vice-President-in-Council at Calcutta, in a resolution, dated 6 April, 1827, most severely criticized the procedure and conduct of the embassy.

As regards the Commercial Convention, the Vice-President-in-Council disapproved of Crawfurd's attempts to press the Burmese Government to permit the exportation of precious metals and to allow European and Indian merchants to take along with them their families on quitting the country. The Government held, that although these objects were desirable of attainment, the envoy was not instructed to insist upon them; that he laboured perseveringly to attain these two objects, while losing sight comparatively of the other objects; that time was wasted fruitlessly, and the Burmese deputies stuck to their guns, thinking these were the greatest objects before Crawfurd. In the words of the Government resolution, " The result was.... attended with the humiliating circumstance of the British Envoy being foiled in his object after proposing various concessions to the Burmese with regard to the payment of the instalments still due...." [1] The Vice-President-in-Council held that Crawfurd should have occupied much higher ground, and negotiated a treaty for which purpose he was sent; and that it would have been better if he had come away without a treaty, rather than have accepted the terms of the Ministers.

As to the Manipur boundary question, the resolution expressed regret that so little of this subject was effected by Crawfurd, and that he did not persist in his offer of deputing his assistant Lieut. Montmorency to that quarter with Burmese officers. " In fact," says the resolution, " he has left the question just where he found it, and has done nothing more than point out to the Burmese deputies what was already known to be the fact with respect to the terms in which the independence

[1] Bengal Secret and Political, Vol. 345, Consultations 6 April, 1827, No. 30.

of Rajah Gumbheer Singh was recognized in the Burmese version of the Treaty." The resolution avers, that Crawfurd should have earnestly urged the point, and exerted his utmost to settle the Manipur boundary question, and adds, that "had the Burmese Court ultimately refused to comply with so reasonable a proposition, the envoy would have been warranted in declaring, that as it would not agree to the fair proposal he had made, the Burmese Government must expect that the British Government would settle the question for itself."

The Vice-President-in-Council further expressed surprise, that the question of the release of prisoners was not brought forward for discussion till on 2 December, previous to which the Envoy had told the Burmese deputies (on 24 November) that his business was done. That since he made such a gratuitous declaration, the Burmese Government naturally did not give much consideration to the Envoy's drawing attention to a distinct breach of Article 11 of the treaty, viz., the retention of the prisoners — about 7000 of them forcibly detained and in a state of slavery; that it did not matter if the vast majority of them were from Manipur, Assam, Cachar, and Sylhet: they belonged to British territory, and their detention was a breach of the treaty, and should have been taken up seriously and early in the discussions. According to the Government view, Crawfurd had on the spot the opportunity of identifying the unfortunate men and of appealing to the King.[1]

The resolution also disapproved of Crawfurd having allowed himself to be presented to the King on a Kadaw day, knowing it to be so, and that he should have made an attempt to secure a better presentation, in keeping with the dignity of a great and independent power, whose representative he was.

His Lordship the Vice-President-in-Council further criticized Crawfurd's doings in Ava by observing, "that throughout the whole course of his proceedings at Ava, the Envoy appears to have considered that he had sufficiently performed

---

[1] This was by no means as easy a task as the Government considered it to be. The slaves were not all in Ava, but scattered all over the country.

his duty in agitating the several points, and when opposed, in leaving them to be settled by the Burmese Embassy [1] to be sent to Bengal. Such a procedure evidently rendered nugatory any object which the Government had persuaded itself, would be best accomplished by the ability, judgment, firmness and address of its Political Agent in immediate communication with the Lootoo [2] and the King himself."

Crawfurd had quitted Ava without first communicating with his Government. This step was also disapproved of: " With regard to the Envoy's departure from Ava, without first communicating with his Government respecting his future movements, the Vice-President-in-Council is decidedly of opinion, that as the period for demanding the payment of the third instalment [3] was approaching, and as the Treaty of Yandaboo provided that it should be paid to a British officer in Ava, Mr. Crawfurd ought to have remained somewhere within the Burmese territories until the receipt of further instructions from Government. Had he remained at Rangoon, he would have relieved Lieut. Rawlinson the officer left in temporary charge of political affairs there by Sir Archibald Campbell,[4] and Government would have taken into its consideration, after the perusal of Mr. Crawfurd's report and journal, whether it was expedient permanently to station a Resident Minister at Ava or to appoint a Consul at Rangoon. His Lordship-in-Council is satisfied that at the present moment, at least, the return of Mr. Crawfurd to Ava in the former capacity would not be desirable, and with regard to the latter arrangement, namely, the appointment of a consul, the subject will be resumed when a dispatch lately received from the Deputy Secretary to Government in attendance on the Governor-General relative to the employment of Mr. Crawfurd as Com-

---

[1] The Burmese Embassy to Calcutta and later to Moulmein, 1827. The Burmese Government was arranging for this at this time.
[2] The Hlutdaw or the Great Council of State consisting of the Woongyees or the highest Ministers of the King.
[3] Of the Indemnity of One Crore of rupees.
[4] He was the Commander-in-Chief of the British Army in Burma during the War, 1824-1826.

missioner in the Tenasserim Provinces now in circulation
comes to be discussed."

Lord Amherst, the Governor-General, then in Simla, confessed himself unable to concur in the tone of general disapprobation which pervaded the Calcutta resolution of censure upon
Crawfurd.   In his Minute, dated Simla, 12 May, 1827, he
wrote:—

> " Mr. Crawfurd was perhaps wrong in assuming that as the
> Envoy and Resident at the Court of Ava, appointed under that
> article of the Treaty which provided for the maintenance of ac-
> credited agents in either country, he was deputed to that Court
> for the accomplishment of one single object, viz. the negotiation
> of the Commercial Treaty, which finished, he had no further duty
> to perform.   It seems to me clear, no less from the tenor of his
> instructions than from the general sense of the thing, that the
> Government in deputing him looked at least as much to the poli-
> tical advantages of having an Agent at the Court of Ava ready
> to enter upon the discussion of all doubtful questions arising out
> of the Treaty, and to bring such matters into the train of adjust-
> ment under the orders which he would from time to time receive,
> as to the formation of a Treaty of Commerce.   The Envoy would
> therefore, I think, better have conformed to the spirit of his in-
> structions, if when he had ascertained the existence of many sub-
> jects of discussion between the two governments and the appar-
> ently impracticable humour of the Burmese on two very mate-
> rial questions, viz. the Munipur Boundary and the Release of
> Prisoners, he had reported on these matters to his own Govern-
> ment and awaited its farther orders.   But, in resolving to come
> away, under the circumstances stated in his journal, I am by no
> means prepared to admit that Mr. Crawfurd exercised the dis-
> cretion necessarily vested in him, injuriously to the public inter-
> ests.   A considerable expense has been saved; after all that had
> passed, no farther advantage was to be expected from his stay;
> and under the jealousy evinced by the Burmese Government and
> the restraints placed on the Envoy's freedom of intercourse and
> correspondence, irritation, collision and positive embarrassment
> might have resulted from his prolonged residence at the Capital.
>
> " I cannot attach blame to Mr. Crawfurd, either for urging
> the formation of the Commercial Treaty and the concessions
> therewith connected as the main object of his Mission, or for not
> assuming a more decided tone regarding the settlement first of
> the Munnipur Boundary and the liberation of the Prisoners; be-
> cause the negotiation of such a Treaty was distinctly set forth

in his Instructions as the principal and indeed the only *precise* and *specific* duty assigned to him. Second, no authority was given him to settle questions of boundary, farther reference to Government being expressly prescribed in the case of Munnipur; and his orders regarding prisoners, founded apparently on his own suggestion, and which did not reach him till a very late period, empowered him only, if he and Sir Archibald Campbell were clearly of opinion that their case came within the 11th article of the Treaty, to demand their release, otherwise influence and good offices were alone to be made use of. I must further add, that in my judgment, it would neither have been justifiable in our Envoy to urge with pertinacity the deputation of an officer of his suite from Ava to Munnipur, nor reasonable to expect that the Burmese would consent to such an exposure of that route, in return for any equivalent or consideration which Mr. Crawfurd was empowered to offer.

"I do not concur in the opinion that under the circumstance of the case, the Envoy would have done well to decline executing a Commercial Treaty at all. Nothing has been lost with the Burmese by his agreeing to sign the instrument actually negotiated, and something has been gained thereby; little, it is true, and far short of the necessities of the case, which would otherwise have been forfeited. The Treaty, should, I think, be formally ratified and promulgated for general information." [1]

The Governor-General further goes on to say, "I must declare my conviction that our Mission was in many respects received with marked attention, and at all events with higher honours than had been shown to any former Embassy from Bengal.......I do not estimate lightly the value of the points virtually conceded by the Burmese Ministers during the course of the Conferences, and which may be considered as established by the results of Mr. Crawfurd's Mission, viz., the recognition by the Government of Gumbheer Singh's perfect independence, and of our rightful occupation of the country beyond the Salween River and the Island [2] at its mouth...."

Crawfurd also made a vigorous defence [3] of his Mission and sought to reply to all the points of criticism raised by the

---

[1] Bengal Secret and Political, Vol. 346, Consultations 15 June, 1827, The Governor-General's Minute, dated, Simla, 12 May, 1827. No. 4.

[2] The Bilugyun Island.

[3] Bengal Secret and Political, Vol. 346, Consultations 15 June, 1827, Crawfurd's defence, dated Calcutta, 17 April, 1827.

Vice-President-in-Council. Subsequent events made it clear that the Supreme Government expected far too much from Crawfurd, which, neither his instructions nor the difficult situation in which he was employed, justified. Crawfurd had frankly confessed in his report,[1] "that much has not been effected in respect to our commercial relations with the Burmans." All questions, commercial as well as political, could have been settled with greater dispatch, and to the satisfaction of the Supreme Government, had negotiations been opened and concluded without removing the British Army from Yandabo.[2] The withdrawal of the Army under the shadow of a defective treaty, drawn up by British military men, was a blunder, when it was considered to be of the highest magnitude to establish English influence in Burma and protect British trade in that country.

By Article 5 of the Treaty of Yandabo, the King of Burma had agreed to pay to the British the sum of One Crore of rupees; and by an additional article it was stipulated that upon payment of the first instalment of 25 lacs of rupees, the other articles of the treaty being executed, the British Army would retire to Rangoon; upon payment of a second instalment within 100 days of the date of the treaty, the Army would evacuate the dominions of His Majesty, "leaving the remaining moiety of the sum total to be paid by equal annual instalments in two years, from this Twenty-fourth day of February 1826 A. D. through the Consul or Resident in Ava or Pegu, on the part of the Honourable the East India Company." The first instalment was soon paid and the Army withdrew to Rangoon. The payment of the second instalment was completed by 8 December, 1826, and on the following day the Army under Major-General Sir Archibald Campbell evacuated Rangoon; but Lieut. Rawlinson was left behind to act as British Agent

[1] Crawfurd's Journal, Appendix II, p. 9.
[2] The author of "Two Years in Ava, 1824-1826", a British Military Officer, who was present at Yandabo, says on p. 395 of his book, "......the premier Woongyee, lord of Laykaing, and Atwenwoon Shwaguin, had been sent with full powers by the King, to concede every point we demanded".

for the protection of British trade, and to receive from the Burmese authorities the remaining instalments of the indemnity.

The Burmese Government soon discovered its inability to pay off within time the third and fourth instalments, and fearing the British would take drastic measures to enforce the claim, expressed a willingness to pay interest on the debt[1]; but finally it was decided to send an embassy to Bengal, no doubt in imitation of the Crawfurd Mission. Two envoys were deputed, Thandozein Radanatazendau Moo Meng Hla Raja[2] being the senior, and Yewoon Nemyo-nanda Thoo[3] his junior. The two envoys with followers proceeded from Rangoon on board the *David Malcolm,* and arrived at Calcutta on 5 April, 1827. A complimentary message was sent to them from the Right Hon. the Vice-President, and on landing they were received by Mr. Grant, an assistant to Mr. S. Fraser, Deputy Persian Secretary.. The Burmese Mission was accommodated in a commodious house specially rented[4] for the purpose, and the envoys expressed themselves satisfied with the arrangements made for them. Since the envoys preferred money to provisions, each of them was given an allowance at the rate of Rs. 6 per diem, and just over Rs. 200 a month for their followers. A carriage, horses, and palanquins were placed at their disposal, and orders were issued to purchase articles necessary for their comfort and convenience.[5]

On 11 April, the Envoys submitted a paper of requests.[6] First, they desired that the payment of the third instalment of the indemnity may be delayed by 2 or 3 years, and the fourth instalment by a year longer. The reasons they gave for craving this indulgence were, that the people of Burma were poor

---

[1] R. B. *Pemberton:* The Eastern Frontier; *Dr. Bayfield's* Supplement on British political relations with Burma, pp. xlviii-xlix.
[2] He was one of the private secretaries of the King, occupying a fifth grade position at Court.
[3] He was an ex-Yewoon, one step below a Governor, and had once before visited Calcutta.
[4] Rent Rs. 250 per mensem.
[5] Bengal Secret and Political, Vol. 345, Consultations 28 April, 1827, Note by the Persian Secretary, 6 April, 1827. No. 3.
[6] *Ibid.* No. 6, 11 April, 1827.

and destitute, and that after Rangoon was evacuated by the British, the Talaings rose in rebellion, in consequence of which the King had to spend about 25 lacs of rupees to subdue them.[1] Their second request was stated as follows:—" By the 2nd article of the Treaty of Yandaboo concerning Manipoora, if Gumbheer Singh wishes to return and govern his own country, the Burmese King shall not prevent or molest him. Not only Gumbheer Singh remains there, but also English officers having arrived at Manipoora have entered the Royal Country of the Burman Shans and traverse and inspect the country. They have arrived below Samoo[2] where the Burman Shans reside. It is not proper they should come there. Although it is not meet that the people stationed at the boundary should quarrel, we represent that such may be the case." The third request was that the British had taken Kwagyoung in Bassein district and to the north of it Manoungdee with its villages, contrary to the treaty, these not being a part of Arakan, so that commissioners should be appointed to fix the proper boundary.

On 23 April, the Envoys were presented to the Vice-President, Lord Combermere, in Durbar, and they produced their credentials under the Royal Seal as well as a letter from the Woongyees to the Indian Government; the Royal gifts to the Governor-General were also presented.[3] The Government, however, found it impossible to discuss and settle the questions at issue with the envoys, because the latter had not been empowered to commit their Government to any conclusions that might be arrived at.[4] Their credentials simply stated, that " in order that the two countries may remain in amity," they " have permission and are appointed to speak on all subjects before the English Governor." The letter of the Woongyees also gave them no such powers, and simply stated, that " in order to pro-

---

[1] This rebellion did break out at about the time stated.
[2] Tammu, in the Upper Chindwin district. The territory in dispute was the Kubo Valley considered in a subsequent chapter.
[3] Bengal Secret and Political, Vol. 345 Consultations 28 April, 1827, No. 5, I. The presents consisted of silk cloths, gold and lacquered boxes, cups and basins, ponies and ruby rings.
[4] Ibid. 6 April, 1827, No. 30.

mote the friendship of the two countries," they "have permission to hold all communications, and are sent as ambassadors with the Most Excellent Royal Order. These ambassadors are appointed for mutual benefits. Let them return with all dispatch."[1] On 28 April, therefore, the Government gave to the Envoys a written reply[2] to their paper of requests. In this letter a hope was expressed that the King of Burma will punctually fulfil the spirit and letter of the stipulations of the Treaty, and release all prisoners; and that the British Government would consider meanwhile the question of postponing the payment of the instalments. As regards Manipur, the Envoys were reminded of Campbell's answer to the Burmese plenipotentiaries at Yandabo, that Burmese troops should not cross the Ningtee, which river was declared to be the boundary between Burma and Manipur; and that the southern boundary of Manipur could only be satisfactorily settled by commissioners from both the governments. As to the third proposition, the reply was, that the 3rd article of the Treaty of Yandabo clearly defined the Arakan boundary, and that if there was any dispute, it would be settled by commissioners as provided for by the treaty itself.

The Envoys were then referred to Sir Archibald Campbell[3] in Moulmein for further particulars,[4] and the latter was invested with full powers to discuss and settle all questions that might be raised by them and by their government. It was at the same time left to the option of the Envoys, either to remain in Calcutta as the accredited agents of the Burmese Government provided for by Article 7 of the Treaty, or to return to Rangoon. Detailed instructions[5] were also issued to Campbell, to guide him in his conversations with the Envoys, so that he

---

[1] *Ibid.* 28 April, 1827, No. 5, I and II.
[2] *Ibid.* No. 10.
[3] After the war he was appointed Senior Commissioner of Tenasserim, and Crawfurd the Civil Commissioner.
[4] Bengal Secret and Political, Vol. 345, Consultations 6 April, 1827. No. 30.
[5] *Ibid.* Vol. 346, Consultations 15 June, 1827, No. 8, Letter from Government to Campbell, 15 June, 1827.

might arrive at a final settlement on the questions at dispute with the Government of Burma.

The Governor-General, meanwhile, decided[1] to grant indulgence to the Burmese in the payment of the indemnity. They were to be asked to pay 10 lacs of rupees of the third instalment in cash or jewels or timber by 1 September next, and the balance of 15 lacs was to be postponed to September 1828; the fourth instalment of 25 lacs was to be postponed to September 1829. It was Campbell's opinion that the Royal Family had in its possession treasure enough to pay; but Crawfurd was convinced of the incapacity of the Burmese Government to pay punctually. Lord Amherst was impressed with the language and tenor of the Envoys' letter of requests, as appealing to the liberality and compassion of the British Government, and being free from all arrogance, and containing no trace of bad faith. He also considered, that the port of Rangoon, which was the most important source of revenue, was expected to go to the King in June 1826, but that it did not till six months later, and that soon after its recovery the Talaing rebellion broke out. " I am decidedly of opinion," says the Governor-General's Minute, " that indulgence should be granted to the Burmese in regard to the time of paying the 3rd and 4th instalments; and I feel deeply convinced, that we should ill perform our duty to the Company and to the Nation, were we to incur the risk of a renewal of hostilities by attempting rigidly to enforce a pecuniary demand, which the Government of Ava whilst fully acknowledging the obligation incumbent on it, declares with a fair semblance of truth and probability, it is unable through poverty immediately to discharge." Campbell was instructed to make the following demands upon the Burmese, in respect of questions still unadjusted between the two states, in return for the above indulgence; but the conditions were not to be indispensable:—

First as to commercial advantages, it was decided not to press questions such as the exportation of precious metals and

[1] *Ibid.* No. 4 The Governor-General's Minute, Simla, 12 May, 1827.

the right of merchants to remove their families, which the Burmese were repugnant to grant. The Home Authorities were expected to sanction the development of Amherst, and the Governor-General felt that this new town would in time displace Rangoon as a port, so that British imports could be brought to Amherst and all the commercial difficulties of trade with Burma would thus cease.

Second, as to the Manipur boundary, it appeared from reports on the frontier, that the Burmese Government questioned the right of Gumbheer Singh to occupy the Kubo Valley. The Governor-General desired that a matter of so much importance should be definitely set at rest as early as possible. The third article of the treaty of Yandabo did not define the Burma-Manipur boundary, but the Governor-General " felt little doubt that we are entitled in equity, and according to the sense of the negotiators who framed the Treaty, to demand that the Ningtee shall be considered the line of demarcation from north to south, both in virtue of Sir Archibald Campbell's declaration to the Burmese Commissioners during the Conference that the boundary of Munnipur should be its ancient limits, and in consideration of the fact that Gumbheer Singh had actually reconquered this disputed portion of his ancient territory previous to the conclusion of the treaty of Peace...." [1]

With regard to the objection of the Burmese Government to the presence of European officers in Manipur, it was felt, that Gumbheer Singh being an independent ruler was at liberty to employ either British or Burmese officers. Besides at Yandabo the British Commissioners had been interrogated by those of Ava as to British intentions regarding Assam, Cachar and Manipur, and the reply was distinctly, " It is nothing to you what we intend to do respecting them. We take them from you." [1] The Burmese Government felt very jealous of British relations with Manipur, but the Indian Government held, that it had the full right to maintain a Political Agent at the Court of Gumbheer Singh, with his consent and concurrence, as at the court of any other independent prince.

[1] *Ibid.*

2

The third question to be settled was regarding the prisoners detained in Burma. In Crawfurd's opinion, the Burmese version of the Treaty excluded from release those of Buddhist persuasion belonging to Arakan, Assam, Manipur, and Cachar. The Governor-General refused to accept this view, and upheld the right of release "on principles of general and natural equity, to see justice done to our subjects and the inhabitants of protected states carried off by hostile incursions into a condition of bondage and captivity......the interests of humanity as well as our honour and character demand that we should make the most strenuous effort for their liberation." [1] Campbell was, therefore, instructed to ask for their release at least as a concession in return for the indulgence of postponing the instalments.

Finally, there was the question of the Arakan frontier. Crawfurd had come away from Ava with the impression that the Burmese Government had no complaint on this frontier; but the Envoys now claimed the district of Kwagyoung. Campbell was instructed to settle this dispute through commissioners from both sides.

The various questions for settlement were placed by Amherst in the following order of importance [2]: — The release of British subjects; the Ningtee to be the eastern boundary of Manipur; the liberation of the slaves in question; and last, the adjustment of the frontier disputes.

The above instructions, however, did not reach Campbell till after he had seen the Envoys and come to an agreement with them, so that the indulgence granted by him fell far short of the Governor-General's Minute. The Burmese ambassadors arrived on 1 June, at Amherst in the Company's ship *Errand,* and on 3 June, at Moulmein in the *Diana.* Campbell had made arrangements for their residence and comforts. On 3 and 6 June, they held conferences with Campbell, and asked for a postponement of the two remaining instalments of the indemnity by 2 or 3 years. Campbell told them that their request was

---

[1] *Ibid.*
[2] *Ibid.* No. 8. Letter from Government to Campbell, Fort William, 15 June, 1827.

inadmissible, and made a peremptory demand for an early payment of the third instalment, fixing his ultimatum to 5 September, 1827.[1] The following is a sample of the conversation [2] between the two parties:—

> "Ambassadors:—We went to the Supreme Government to ask for a postponement of two or three years for our next payments.
>
> "Campbell:—You know my wish to come at once to the point in question, and therefore I tell you, instead of the two or three years, I shall only give you as many months, and consequently I trust you will instruct your Government accordingly, as I assure you that the next instalment must be forthcoming in three months.
>
> "Ambassadors:—We came to you and were happy in the idea of your meeting our wishes, but instead of this you only give us three months. How can this be settled?
>
> "Campbell:—I only go by the Treaty; when we make treaties we keep them, and if others break them we take our measures for vindicating the insult.
>
> "Ambassadors:—We come to throw ourselves upon your friendship.
>
> "Campbell:—This is a Public transaction, and it behoves me to do justice in my Public character to the country I serve. Why did your King and Ministers sign a Treaty that they thought they could not fulfil?
>
> "Ambassadors:—They did from the fear of your guns which came very near us.
>
> "Campbell:—And what will be the consequence of your taking our guns much nearer? You ought to be ashamed of yourselves in acknowledging that your King and His Government lent themselves to an act of duplicity from fear; however, assure yourselves that unless the Treaty is adhered to, you will probably see and hear our guns much nearer than you have hitherto done; I, therefore, demand your answer as to whether you intend to make the payment of the third instalment at the period I have stated."

After a good deal of further conversation, the Envoys finally agreed, in behalf of their Government, to pay the third instal-

---

[1] *Ibid.* Vol. 347 Consultations 27 July, 1827, Nos. 7 and 10, Letter from Campbell to his Government, Moulmein 11 June, 1827.
[2] *Ibid.* No. 8, Moulmein 3 June, 1827.

ment between 4 September, 1827, and 15 November, 1827, and
the fourth instalment between 31 August, 1828, and 19 October,
1828. The following is an extract from the statement signed
by the envoys:—

> "We, therefore, jointly and severally, solemnly promise and
> bind ourselves in the name and on the behalf of our Government,
> to commence paying the third instalment of 25 lacks of sicca [1]
> rupees on the 88th day from this date, viz. the 4th day of Sep-
> tember, 1827, and to finish the payment of the same within the
> period of 50 days from the above date...... We also in like
> manner bind ourselves as aforesaid, that the fourth instalment
> due by the said Treaty of Yandaboo on the 15th day of March
> 1828, shall be paid on the 31st August, of the same year, or in
> other words, at the expiration of 448 days from this date, in like
> manner as the Third Instalment aforesaid, viz. within fifty
> days." [2]

Thus Campbell reduced by one year the period of indulgence sanctioned by the Governor-General in the payment of
the two instalments. He also upbraided the Envoys with non-
conformance on the part of their Government to article 11 of
the treaty of Yandabo on the general release of prisoners and
slaves.[3] The Envoys at first agreed to make every possible
enquiry into the matter, and to bring about a release of all such
prisoners who were willing to leave the country; [4] but when
the agreement was presented to them on 7 June, for their
signature, they refused to commit themselves to such an undertaking. On the day of this refusal they came to dinner with
Campbell, and there was further conversation.[5] The Envoys
expressed their inability to affix their signatures to the document, binding their Government to release the prisoners in
question, because it made particular mention of prisoners of
states not mentioned in the Treaty of Yandabo. Campbell took

---

[1] Sicca in India is weight for gold or silver, equivalent to nearly
    180 grains Troy. It was a term applied to the Bengal rupee
    which contained more silver than the Madras rupee.
[2] Bengal Secret and Political, Vol. 347, Consultations 27 July, 1827,
    No. 10, Moulmein 8 June, 1827.
[3] Ibid. No. 10.
[4] Ibid. No. 7, Letter from Campbell to his Government, Moulmein,
    11 June, 1827.
[5] Ibid. No. 11.

them severely to task for agreeing to it in conversation on the previous day and later shifting away. He tried to convince them that article 11 of Yandabo covered the prisoners of those states as well, but they positively refused to sign the document. The following is an extract from the conversation:—

> "Ambassadors: — Oblige us by leaving out the enumeration of the different states, and insert generally all *Kulas*[1] as in the Treaty of Yandaboo.
>
> "Campbell: — What is the meaning of all this?
>
> "Ambassadors: — We are afraid to sign any document mentioning those states.
>
> "Campbell: — Then you intend to retract all that you have hitherto agreed on relative to this subject.
>
> "Ambassadors: — No, but we doubt whether the release of the prisoners of those states came strictly under the Treaty of Yandaboo.
>
> "Campbell: — What can be more explicit than the wording of the Treaty of Yandaboo, expressly mentioning 'all English, American, and all other white and black Kula.prisoners.' Do you mean to say that the prisoners of the states in question do not come under denomination of the words, 'all other white and black prisoners'? Remember, I only demand those taken during the War, as already agreed upon, and fully acceded to by yourselves.
>
> ....
> ....
>
> "Ambassadors: — We think, as you did not particularize those people (in the Treaty of Yandaboo) you have no claim to them, and we are afraid to sign.
>
> "Campbell: — Now I see what you aim at, nothing less than to cover an act of injustice, duplicity, and breach of Treaty by having recourse to miserable quibbles. You know you have not only the prisoners of the states in question, but several actually English subjects; but which you may rest assured we shall take other means of having released from your tyranny and oppression, even if you send them (in order to their concealment) to the remotest part of your kingdom.
>
> "Ambassadors: — We never intend to oblige you to that necessity; we shall adhere to the Treaty of Yandaboo, and again we beg you as a favour, to leave out the clause we object to; we are afraid; don't be angry with us."

---

[1] Foreigner: lit. ကူး = cross, လာ = come, *i.e.* one who has crossed over and come into the country.

Much extraneous conversation took place, " in the course of which," says Campbell, " the Burmese Ambassadors had recourse to every species of low and mean subterfuge, the burden of which evidently emanating from personal fear in giving their signature to an act that would deprive the principal great men about Court and others of a large retinue of slaves." [1]

It must be remarked that it would have been futile for the the Burmese Envoys to bind their Government to the requirements demanded of them by the British Commissioner, because they had not been empowered to enter into any such agreement. Besides, the situation of the Envoys cannot be properly appreciated without recognizing the peculiar nature of the government whose servants they were. They were actually risking their lives in respect of any agreement they might make, or even if they failed to accomplish that for which they had been deputed. It is impossible, therefore, to judge them and their doings by standards applicable to Campbell and to his government. In many respects, and especially in the matter of uncertainty of life for government officials, Burma at that time approximated to Europe of the Dark and Middle Ages.

On 8 June, the Envoys sent Campbell a message to the following effect, which truly expresses their precarious position as ambassadors:—" That they spent the night and were still in the most distressing state of perplexity, so much so that they could not eat their breakfasts, pointing to the rice, etc., cold in their plates; that they were aware of the awful state of responsibility in which they were placed, convinced, if they signed the document I sent them they would lose their heads, and on the other hand if they did not, the misery they would in all probability draw upon their country, would in like manner insure their being sacrificed; but if I (*i.e.* Campbell) would leave the clause out of the paper, specifying the prisoners of Munnipore and other states, they would come to a private or

---

[1] Bengal Secret and Political, Vol. 347, Consultations, 27 July, 1827, No. 11.

secret agreement to use their influence to the release of the said prisoners." [1]

Campbell sent a threatening reply [2] to the above, and further warned them that their monarch might meet with the fate of Tipu [3] who persisted in his opposition to the British, and " again sought war, which ended by the taking of his capital, himself killed in the assault, and his dynasty not allowed to reign." Campbell also declined to come to a secret agreement with them, and declared, that he demanded justice in virtue of the Treaty Yandabo.

The Ambassadors replied, " We beg to entreat, you will not urge us to say anything more on the subject; we are already committed. We have thrown ourselves upon your consideration and pity; if not granted, it will be much better for us to remain with you altogether than return to certain death at Ava." [4] Campbell then asked them to give him a written statement that they were not authorized to treat with him on the subject of the prisoners. This they did [5]; " and you may rest assured," they told him, " of our good offices on our return to Ava to the accomplishment of all your just demands; we have too great a regard for our King and Country to endanger its tranquillity in not doing so. We now see matters in a different light to what we have hitherto done."

On 10 June, the Envoys raised the question of the Arakan boundary, and claimed that the British were not entitled to Kwagyoung and Manoungdee occupied by them. It was mutually agreed, that according to the 3rd article of the Treaty, British and Burmese commissioners be appointed to settle the question. [6]

[1] *Ibid.* No. 15.
[2] *Ibid.*
[3] Sultan of Mysore (1782-1799). He was defeated and slain at Seringapatam in 1799. Wellesley, the Governor-General, set aside the dynasty of Hyder Ali, and restored to the throne a representative of the ancient family of the Royal Wodeyars, the rulers of Mysore.
[4] Bengal Secret and Political, Vol. 347, Consultations 27 July, 1827, No. 15.
[5] *Ibid.* No. 12.
[6] *Ibid.* No. 16.

The business of the Envoys was now concluded, and they desired to return to Ava as soon as possible, but they had no other means to do so than small boats, which would at that season of the year have taken them at least a month to get through the inland creeks and waters. " I was therefore compelled," says Campbell in his letter to his Government, " although reluctantly, to hire the *Bombay Merchant* for the sum of sicca Rs. 2785, to send them and their suite to Rangoon, a measure I beg may be approved of, considering that by incurring this expense we avoid that of feeding them here, besides which we show them that nothing has been left undone by us to forward them in the accomplishment of what they have undertaken to perform." [1]

The Embassy had for its main object the postponement of the two instalments of the indemnity by two or three years; but relief was granted by only about six months for each instalment. From the point of view of the British Government, the money payments were brought to a determined issue, the Envoys having accepted fixed dates within which to discharge the obligations; but nothing was achieved as to the general release of prisoners and the settlement of the Manipur boundary. In his letter to his Government, Campbell flattered himself by saying, that " although the ambassadors retracted their agreement on the former (i.e. the Prisoners), yet I think they carry with them such a conviction of the necessity of its being immediately acceded to, that their pledged remonstrance at Court upon that head will have the desired effect." [1]

It is strange that the Envoys did not plead poverty before Campbell, in connection with the money payments, as they did in Calcutta, for the latter goes on to say, " Upon this subject I am happy to say, the ambassadors did not attempt, beyond a simple effort or two, at which they themselves laughed, to plead anything like poverty or their inability to meet our demand, nor did they once hint at the expense into which they were led by

[1] *Ibid.* No. 7.

the Talien[1] insurrection, as stated in the paper they gave at Calcutta, well knowing its absurdity."[2]

After the departure of the Envoys, Campbell sought to follow up the matter of the prisoners with the Governor of Rangoon, who had previously informed the British Commissioner, that he had been fully empowered by his government to discuss and settle all points that may be at issue between the two countries.[2] On 9 June, therefore, he made a demand upon the Governor in the following words:—" My being also invested by my government with a similar authority, I now in virtue thereof peremptorily demand of you the immediate release of all prisoners and captives, in conformity to the true spirit and intent of the Treaty of Yandaboo, and I have too high an opinion of your discernment and judgment to think you will for a moment attempt to screen a non-compliance by such vague subterfuges, as I have mentioned to have been had recourse to in another quarter."[2] Campbell also called upon the Governor to nominate Burmese officers as Commissioners to settle the Burma-Manipur boundary in collaboration with British officers, as soon as the fair season arrived.

The Woongyee-Governor of Rangoon replied without much delay. He emphasised the friendship subsisting between the two countries, but studiously avoided enumerating the states whose subjects were held captive in Burma; yet he admitted in general terms British right to claim all prisoners taken during the War, should there be any yet unreleased; and declared, that his Government had sent repeated orders to officers all over the country to release all such. He also agreed to appoint commissioners to settle the boundary questions.[3]

Campbell's letters to his Government show that he was very sanguine of settling all the questions at issue between the

---

[1] Talaing; in modern usage, Mon.
[2] Bengal Secret and Political, Vol. 347, Consultations 27 July, 1827, No. 14, Letter from Campbell to the Rangoon Governor, Moulmein 9 June, 1827.
[3] *Ibid.* Consultations 17 August, 1827, Nos. 34 and 36, Campbell's letter to his Government, 19 July, 1827, and Translation of the Woongyee's letter Rangoon, 18 June, 1827.

two governments. He even wrote on 16 July, that the Burmese Government was making every effort to fulfil the engagement into which the Envoys had entered touching the indemnity. Later events made it clear, however, that these hopes were not easy of realization merely by diplomacy, and that Campbell had failed to take into consideration the factor of Burma being under an ignorant autocracy, the most intelligent officers of which were at the mercy of the whim of the King or his favourite.[1]

The Woongyees at Ava, members of the Hlutdaw, expressed much displeasure at their envoys signing the engagement with Campbell, binding their government to pay the two instalments within stated periods. The Rangoon Woongyee declared, that they had exceeded their powers; but the whole of their proceedings was not disclosed to the King, for fear His Majesty in a fit of passion might order their execution. They were presented to the King, and His Majesty was informed that the Mission had not entirely failed, as it had gained a delay of six months, from March to September. The envoys, on the other hand, pretended, that they had been intimidated into signing the engagement, and that they signed it to save their country from another visit of the British Army.[2]

Capt. Henry Burney, who was at Rangoon in August 1827, reported that "opinion prevails throughout the country that it [3] will be attacked and reoccupied by Sir Archibald Campbell, if the 3rd instalment be not punctually discharged. Great exertions are therefore making to raise the money from the people and particularly at the Capital, where some of the chiefs and reputed rich men have been tied to enforce large contributions."[4] Attempts were also made to raise money in the Lower Provin-

[1] Ibid. No. 32.
[2] Ibid. Consultations 21 September, 1827, No. 18, Letter from Major Henry Burney to Government, September 1827.
[3] Rangoon.
[4] Bengal Secret and Political, Vol. 347, Consultations 21 September, 1827, No. 18, Letter from Henry Burney to the Government of India, September, 1827.

ces, but not with the same vigour, for fear the people might migrate into British Burma. Burney goes on to say, " My observations and enquiries at Rangoon convince me, that the Government of Ava is just now deeply impressed with a sense of our superiority and great power, and that any manifestation of liberality from us......would still further humble the pride of the Burmese Ministers, and convince them that their best policy is to cultivate amicable relations with us."

The Government of India now issued orders to its officers in Assam, Manipur, Arakan, and Tenasserim, to prepare lists of prisoners and captives detained in Burma. It was generally thought, on Crawfurd's report, that there were about 7000 such unfortunate people living in a state of slavery under Burmese masters. In spite of the attempts of the officers concerned, it was found impossible to ascertain the names or the number of persons detained in Burma.[1] Henry Burney also reported that Crawfurd's figure no longer held good, as many had been massacred while the Burmese were on the retreat during the War; also many of the prisoners were kept as slaves by great Chiefs and high officers of state, who would not easily part with them.[2] The Governor-General, ultimately, called upon the Burmese Court, through Campbell, to give an assurance, that the natives of Assam, Manipur, Cachar, Sylhet, Chittagong, and Arakan, who had been carried off during the War, would not be prevented from returning to their own homes, and that the English had the right to demand the release of any British subjects detained in Burma. The Burmese Government agreed to the proposal, and declared that there was no objection even to a British officer proceeding to the capital to receive the prisoners if any.[1]

Lieut. Rawlinson was accordingly deputed to Ava to receive the prisoners, and he arrived at the capital on 22 Feb-

[1] *Pemberton:* The Eastern Frontier; the Supplement by *Bayfield,* p. (1).
[2] Bengal Secret and Political, Vol. 347, Consultations 21 September, 1827, No. 18, Letter from Henry Burney to the Government of India, September, 1827.

ruary, 1828. It was, however, never the intention of the Burmese Government to lose any of its population which was already sparse. It had been an immemorial custom with the rulers of Burma to populate their country by bringing over prisoners from their vanquished neighbours. Rawlinson made a strict search for the captives, but was unable to discover a single individual: every one of them had either been conveyed into the interior of the country or kept concealed. The project of having the captives released failed completely.

The Burma-Manipur boundary dispute was also still to be settled. During the War, Raja Gumbheer Singh, an ally of the British, drove the Burmese from the Kubo Valley lying between the Chindwin or Ningtee river and a Manipur range of mountains. At the termination of the war, he retained possession of his conquest as part of ancient Manipur. The Burmese Government, however, claimed that the Treaty of Yandabo did not oblige them to cede Kubo, which was in their possession when hostilities broke out in 1824. Under the advice of Major F. J. Grant and Lieut. R. B. Pemberton, British Commissioners and advisers to the Raja of Manipur, the Supreme Government fixed the boundary confirming Gumbheer Singh in his possession of the Valley, and declared the Chindwin to be the line of demarcation between the two states. The Burmese Government strongly objected to this decision, and as has been noticed before, represented the matter to Calcutta and afterwards to Moulmein through envoys. Finally, in keeping with the agreement between Campbell and the Governor of Rangoon, the Indian Government appointed Grant and Pemberton as the British Commissioners to meet Burmese Commissioners on the Chindwin, and settle the boundary dispute. Lieut. Montmorency of the Madras Army was deputed to Ava with dispatches from Campbell to the British Commissioners, and he was to accompany the Burmese Commissioners to the Chindwin, the Conference being fixed to take place early in February 1828.

Montmorency arrived at Ava, and in company with the Burmese Commissioner, Woondouk[1] Maha Min-sa-Raja and his secretary Nemyo Su Zoo, set out for the meeting place, which, however, the party did not reach till at the end of March, nearly two months after the appointed date.[2] Grant and Pemberton, meanwhile, who had been waiting for them all this time, finding the spot becoming unhealthy, retired to a more healthy place two days journey from the Valley. Montmorency, not finding the British Commissioners at the appointed place, and being dissatisfied with the way the Burmese Commissioner was treating him,[3] left him to shift for himself and returned to Rangoon without waiting for Grant and Pemberton. The Commissioners finally succeeded in coming together, and the Woondouk produced a Burmese map in which was shown a large river to the westward of Kubo: this he maintained was the Ningtee river, and so the true boundary between Burma and Manipur. He also denied that the Chindwin, in any part of its course, bore the appellation of Ningtee. Pemberton, who was well acquainted with the frontier in that region, having been at one time engaged in the survey of the North Eastern Frontier of India, immediately pointed out the inaccuracy of the Burmese map, and said that there was no big river to the west of Kubo, and that the Ningtee and the Chindwin were one and the same. It was now, however, too late to enter more deeply into the matter by touring the area in order to fix the boundary, because the fair season had almost come to a close. The Commissioners, therefore, decided, and agreed to meet again in January 1829.[4]

---

[1] *Lit.* Prop of the Woon: Woon = Governor or Minister, *lit.* burden; douk = prop. Woongyee = Great Woon. The Woondouk was an Under Secretary of State, and in rank was immediately under the Woongyee.

[2] Bengal Secret and Political, Vol. 355, Consultations 10 July, 1829, No. 27 Letter from the Woongyees to the Government of India.

[3] *Pemberton:* The North Eastern Frontier; Supplement by *Bayfield*, p. li.

[4] Bengal Secret and Political, Vol. 354, Consultations 10 April, 1829, No. 14, Letter from Lieut. Rawlinson to the Government of Burma.

When January 1829 arrived, the Burmese Government failed to depute commissioners as arranged, and the British authorities threatened to fix the boundary without them. The Woongyees wrote, that " in the month of January the officers were so deeply engaged in money transactions that they could not abide by their agreements." [1] They also announced that their Commissioners would most certainly meet the British Commissioners in January 1830, and requested the Indian Government not to fix the boundary without mutual consent, so that friendship might increase. One of the Woongyees writing to Calcutta said, " To distinguish things in a proper way both parties should be present, or how is it possible the boundary line can be properly defined and fixed, and unless such a procedure is adopted, nothing can come to a proper termination, for by the adjustment of this point it will save us both future misunderstanding and trouble." [2] He also claimed the Kubo Valley in the following words:—" The village of Shan stands in the south of Munnipur and on the north of Kulla Mu, from generation to generation it belonged to His Majesty, and as a boundary line a pagoda was erected by some former King........Place no reliance on what Gumbheer Singh may report. Between the two great countries there should be continuance of friendship, and our respective desires must be equal in promoting it." [2]

The Indian Government had, however, by now decided to permit Manipur to retain possession of Kubo. This is clear from Rawlinson's letter to the Hlutdaw as well as from the letter of the Chief Secretary, Mr. G. Swinton, to the Woongyees. Rawlinson wrote on 30 March, 1829, after Burmese commissioners had failed to turn up for the conference, " The two officers [3] have been ordered to proceed to the banks of the Ningthee the place agreed on last year, and if the two Burmese Commissioners are not there the English officers will fix to the northward of Kullah (the southern part of Kubo)

---

[1] *Ibid.* Vol. 355, Consultations 10 July, 1829, No. 27.
[2] *Ibid.*
[3] Grant and Pemberton.

or the southern boundary, and the Ningthee Kendeam[1] or Thulawuttee by whatever name the Burmese call it, the Eastern boundary. This boundary the Court of Ava will know as the proper one and that the Kendeam River has ever in its course through the valley of Kubboo been called the Ningthee "[2] The Chief Secretary's letter says, " When the Burmese Commissioners shall meet the English officers at the time appointed in the Burmese year 1191 (i.e. 1830 A.D.), they will be satisfied that the country to the northward of that boundary line has been clearly and uninterruptedly in the possession of Raja Gumbheer Singh since the conclusion of the Treaty of Peace in the year 1187 B. E. at the village of Yandaboo, and nothing will remain but to visit the spot together and fix the posts on each side of the boundary, so that in future no room for doubt or dispute may exist."[3]

In January 1830, the chief Burmese Commissioner, Woondouk Maung Khan Ye, met the two British Commissioners on the Manipur frontier. He claimed, that the disputed territory lying between the Muring hills and the Chindwin river, called by the British " Kubo Valley " and by the Burmese " Thoungthwot," had been in the possession of Burmese Kings for a period of 2000 years. Claims of the same nature were advanced in favour of Raja Gumbheer Singh. The British Commissioners were, however, bound by their orders from the Supreme Government to fix the Chindwin as the boundary; so that in spite of all the protests and threats of the Burmese Commissioners, they planted flags, and fixed that river as the dividing line between Burma and Manipur. There was much excitement in Ava when the news of this decision was received. The King and Court looked upon the action of the British Commissioners as unauthorized, and decided to dispatch envoys to Calcutta to complain of their conduct, and to substantiate the claim of Burma to the Valley.[4] Meanwhile intelligence was received

---

[1] The Chindwin.
[2] Bengal Secret and Political, Vol. 354, Consultations 10 April, 1829, No. 14.
[3] *Ibid.* Vol. 355, Consultations 10 July, 1829, No. 28.
[4] *Pemberton and Bayfield, op. cit. p. lv.*

of Major Henry Burney's appointment as Resident at the Burmese Court, and it was considered advisable to await his arrival. The Supreme Government at Calcutta, however, fully approved of the action of their Commissioners in Manipur, and accepted the boundary fixed as the final answer to Burma.

Since 1785, when Burma conquered Arakan and became an immediate neighbour of British India on the Chittagong side, there had been endless frontier disputes between the two countries, particularly in connection with outrages committed by the subjects of one or the other in the opposite territory. The Burmese War (1824-1826), far from putting an end to this trouble, greatly intensified the opportunity for outrages, because the Burmese and the British were now neighbours along a greatly extended frontier — from the northernmost point of Burma, along Assam, Manipur, Bengal, and the Arakan Yoma. However, the most serious outrages occurred on the Martaban-Moulmein frontier demarcated by the river Salween. The Burmese Central Government was not particularly interested in the suppression of frontier outrages, if they did not mean more than plunder and murder, be they enacted on their side or the neighbour's side of the frontier. Burmese officers in general did not receive salaries, so that the frontier officers found it necessary to derive some profit for themselves, either by conniving at such outrages or even by privately supporting them. Again, the river Salween being used by the subjects of both the governments, very often dacoits from the Burmese side had opportunities of attacking boats belonging to British subjects.

These depredations had been occurring more or less from the first occupation of Moulmein by the British, but they had not been brought seriously to the notice of the Supreme Government.[1] Early in 1829, Major-General Sir Archibald Campbell, Agent to the Governor-General and Senior Commissioner for the affairs of Tenasserim, retired from service. His

---

[1] Bengal Secret and Political, Vol. 354, Consultations 10 April, 1829, No. 2, Letter from Maingy to his Government, 27 March, 1829.

place was taken by Major A. D. Maingy. Soon after the arrival of Maingy, two serious cases of aggression occurred. The first took place in February 1829, when a party of men issued from the Burmese side in two boats and attacked the station of Natman, killing one man and severely wounding four others. Maingy immediately brought this affair to the notice of the Governor of Rangoon, who sent an officer to Martaban to institute an enquiry; but the culprits were not apprehended. On the other hand, according to Maingy, this officer "allowed the principal delinquent, who was pointed out to him at Martaban, to escape from thence".[1] The second outrage occurred about a month later when four Burmans of Moulmein were attacked and murdered by a party in a boat, which then retired towards Martaban. Maingy strongly suspected the Burmese officers in Martaban of being privy to these outrages. Similar outrages also occurred on the Arakan frontier.

In March 1829, the Governor-General, Lord William Bentinck, visited Moulmein, and determined upon a definite policy in respect of the outrages. Maingy accordingly was instructed,[2] first, to make representations to the Burmese Court through the Governor of Rangoon, "regarding the support given to the robberies of Arracan by the Burmese local officers." Second, the Governor-General was very unwilling to believe that the outrages and acts of violence committed had been sanctioned by the Burmese Government, or that the latter would not bring to justice the criminals, if their guilt was proved; but he laid it down that "no reliance can be placed on the honour and integrity of the inferior officers of the Ava Government, and that on the part of the Government itself, provided that the amount of the revenue due to the state be collected, little attention is ever paid to the conduct of its subordinate authorities." Bentinck, therefore, argued that it

[1] Bengal Secret and Political, Vol. 354, Consultations 10 April, 1829, No. 2, Letter from Maingy to his Government, 27 March, 1829.
[2] Ibid. No. 4. Letter from Secretary to the Governor-General to Maingy, Moulmein, 27 March, 1829.

was incumbent upon the British Government " to act upon the principle of self-defence, if the Court of Ava should be either unwilling or unable to control its own subjects," and thus protect its subjects as well as uphold its own authority and dignity.

Thirdly, the Governor-General announced, that he was thoroughly convinced, " that decided language and decided measures can alone keep a Court like that of Ava in check," so that Maingy should proceed in person to Rangoon and represent to the Woongyee the British complaints against Burmese officers and subjects on the frontier,—" that you should report the sentiments herein expressed to have been communicated to you directly by the Governor-General, and that you will inform him of the positive orders you have received, if such outrages again occur, and if the authors of them are not immediately delivered up, to proceed with a force sufficient to seize them......" [1]

Maingy accordingly arrived at Rangoon on 1 April, and on the following day the Woongyee and all his officers received him with the most marked respect.[2] At the conference, Maingy pointed out the views of his Government on the frontier outrages in very plain language: he charged the Burmese frontier officers with want of desire to grant satisfaction, but declared that the Governor-General wished to cherish and maintain the existing friendship, and finally informed the Burmese Governor, that if the authors of those outrages on the Tenasserim and Arakan frontiers, were not handed over to the British authorities, " it is His Lordship's positive orders that the British officers shall proceed into the Ava territory with a force sufficient to seize the robbers and plunderers, and having seized them, try and punish them immediately." [2] The Woongyee heard Maingy with attention, and said, that he would punish the offenders himself, and further hoped that Maingy would not

[1] *Ibid.* No. 4. Letter from Secretary to the Governor-General to Maingy, Moulmein, 27 March, 1829.
[2] *Ibid.* Consultations 1 May, 1829, No. 11 Maingy's letter to his Government, Amherst, 12 April, 1829.

be hasty in taking any steps towards seizing the offenders. Maingy, however, complained that all his representations had up till then proved fruitless, and to use his own words, he " took great pains to let the Woongyee clearly comprehend the nature of my instructions from the Right Honourable the Governor-General, assuming as high and firm and decided a tone as I could command when I apprised him of my determination to execute these instructions to their fullest extent." [1] This threat, however, did not produce the desired effect, for he goes on to say, " But I regret to state that the Woongyee and his surrounding officers displayed much less emotion than what the nature of my communication had led me to expect from them, and I saw at last that they considered my declaration as little better than mere foam, and that they have been of late so much used to threats of all kinds to induce them to accelerate the payment of the 3rd and 4th instalments, [2] that they cannot believe the Right Honourable Governor-General now means anything by the communication which I made, except to show his Lordship's dissatisfaction at these instances of plunder and murder. They seemed to entertain little fear of my doing what I told them I was ordered to do in the next case of our people being attacked or plundered by persons from within the Ava frontiers." [1]

His visit to Rangoon having failed to produce immediate results, Maingy wrote a strong letter [3] to the Hlutdaw at the capital, appealing to the Ministers to stop the outrages, but at the same time threatening to enter Burmese territory with a force. In October 1829, however, no less than three villages on the British side were attacked and plundered by bands of robbers from Martaban and the Burmese ports on the right bank of the Salween. [4] In these attacks three British subjects were killed and four desperately wounded. The vigilance of

[1] *Ibid.*
[2] Of the Indemnity of One Crore of rupees.
[3] Bengal Secret and Political, Vol. 354, Consultations 1 May, 1829, No. 11 Amherst, 12 April, 1829.
[4] *Ibid.* Vol. 355, Consultations 20 November, 1829, Maingy's letter to his Government, Moulmein 19 October, 1829.

the Moulmein police boats defeated several other attempts of freebooters to plunder more villages; at one time their increasing insolence emboldened them to attempt to land a party of 60 men within a few yards of the Commissioner's residence.

Maingy now determined to adopt some measure of severity in order to chastise the inhabitants of Martaban; but before embarking upon such a drastic step, he gave one more opportunity to the Governor of Rangoon to grant satisfaction. Having ascertained the names of seven of the leaders of the late outrages, he directed his assistant Major Henry Burney, who was then on his way from Tavoy to Calcutta, to touch at Rangoon, and demand of the Woongyee the surrender of these ringleaders, and to warn him, that in the event of a refusal on his part, Martaban would be chastised.

Burney had an interview with the Woongyee (October 1829), and the latter agreed to send one of his principal secretaries to first visit Maingy and then proceed to Martaban, seize the seven ringleaders and hand them over to the British Commissioner.[1] The Secretary with 43 followers arrived at Moulmein, and on 4 November, with all his followers, and accompanied by some of the Company's servants, crossed over to Martaban. The Burmese Chief of Martaban, however, showed very little respect to the Woongyee's Agent and was disposed to disobey the orders of the Governor, expressing his determination not to deliver over the offenders to Maingy, but that he would send them to Rangoon, and pretended that the men were not to be found. The Company's servants, however, saw some of the offenders and apprehended one named Nga Shwe Lu.[1] The same day Burney too crossed over and saw the Martaban Chief. He asked him if he was prepared to disobey the orders of the Woongyee, and the Chief replied in a tone of great indifference that he was searching for the men; but to Burney it appeared that he was secreting the offenders, or giving them an opportunity to escape. He, therefore, warned him, that if the seven men were not immediately handed over to Maingy,

---

[1] *Ibid.* No. 25, Burney's letter to his Government, 11 November, 1829.

a British force would cross the river and seize them as well as the Chief himself, who would be looked upon as setting himself up in opposition to the orders of his own Government, and placing himself at the head of a band of robbers. Burney reported, that " the Chief seemed to care very little for my threat, and confirmed my former suspicions, that he is too much interested in the existing system of plundering our villages and inhabitants, to be willing to put a stop to it." [1]

The whole company together with their captive, Nga Shwe Lu, returned to Moulmein, and the Woongyee's Agent frankly owned to Maingy, that his impression was that the town of Martaban was nothing but a nest of robbers and plunderers. He also advised Maingy to apprehend the Martaban Chief and send him to Rangoon. Maingy came to the conclusion that the Chief was in league with the robbers, and so decided to punish him and his town. His hands were further strengthened, because early in November another robbery took place on the river, and when men were sent to the Chief for the recovery of the property, they were treated with insolence. [2]

Maingy directed his acting Assistant, Lieut. McCally, to accompany Lieut. Col. H. T. Shaw and two companies of British troops to Martaban. Their instructions were to proceed with the troops in the steamer *Diana* and other boats to Martaban, seize the robbers as well as the Chief of Martaban, and bring them to Moulmein; but the troops were not to penetrate beyond three or four miles inland from the bank of the river. [3]

Shaw and his troops, consisting of a detachment of His Majesty's 45th Regiment, accompanied by McCally, disembarked at 6-30 a.m. at the southern entrance of the Martaban stockade, which was found abandoned. The troops immediately advanced through the stockade to the Chief's house, but found it evacuated,

---

[1] *Ibid.*
[2] *Ibid.* Consultations 19 December, 1829, No. 6, Maingy's letter to his Government, Moulmein 13 November, 1829.
[3] *Ibid.* No. 9, Maingy's letter to McCally, Moulmein 7 November, 1829.

and soon it was discovered that all the male population of the
town had fled into the jungle and long grass with which
Martaban was then covered; small parties, however, of the
armed adherents of the Chief were occasionally seen retreating
precipitately before the troops through the jungle.   Having
failed in the first object, Shaw marched the troops to Kywegyan,
a village about 3 miles to the north of the stockade, but failed
to apprehend any person of consequence.   The detachment even
moved two or three miles beyond the village, until the guides
led it into an almost impassable jungle, when it was decided to
return to Martaban whence the troops embarked at 4-30 p.m.[1]

A large number of the inhabitants of Moulmein had followed the troops to Martaban, and these set fire to the huts in
the town as well as in the villages of Kywegyan, Kudien and
Maphee, as a result of which all four places were totally burnt
to the ground.   McCally, in his report to Maingy, says, that
these places " were destroyed by fire, and thus fell a sacrifice to
the just indignation of our incensed native subjects suffering
under a long series of outrages committed on them by the preda-
tory bands who occupied those places." [1]   Maingy thoroughly
approved of the measure: " It is to be regretted," he wrote,
" that we have failed in apprehending any of the robbers.   I am
satisfied, however, that the measures of beating up their quarters
is not only the best way of checking their depredations, but
that in doing so there is no chance of a rupture with Ava, but
on the contrary every chance of facilitating our pending negotiations." [2]

Maingy had received definitely the permission of the
Governor-General to march troops into Martaban, if need be,
for the apprehension of the robbers, but now one town and three
villages had been burnt to the ground as a result of such action.
However, neither Ava nor Rangoon took any serious notice of

[1] *Ibid.* No. 10, McCally's report to Maingy, Moulmein 8 November,
1829, and No. 14, Scott's report to Brigadier Vigoureux, 9 November, 1829.
[2] *Ibid.* No. 6, " pending negotiations " refers to the Burney Residency which was at this time getting ready to proceed to Ava.

these occurrences. Maingy was well aware of the safety of his measures, for in his report just quoted, he says, " The Court of Ava will see that they are liable to such attacks from us, and we are as good as our word, and this conviction will make them listen with more attention to the high tone Major Burney may be directed to assume, and make them more disposed to enter into arrangements by which they may preclude such attacks from us."

The destruction of Martaban did produce a salutary effect upon the hives of frontier robbers, but only for a season. It was not till 1852, when the Province of Pegu was annexed by the British, that these outrages ceased. In a later report to his Government, Maingy goes even further, and accuses the Ava authorities of complicity in the outrages: " I am fully satisfied," he says, " that in sending a force against the robbers at Martaban, I have pursued the only effectual method of checking their outrages, being more than ever convinced that the opinion which I expressed on a former occasion, regarding the conduct of the late Talien Chief Oozinah, may with safety be applied to all the Burmese authorities in this quarter, viz., that they are secretly instigated by the Court of Ava to prove themselves as troublesome as possible, in order to make us consider our position in this territory one full of difficulty and inconvenience." [1]

The Chief of Martaban and his followers had taken refuge with the Chief of Bilin a few miles up the river. After the retirement of the troops, the fugitives began gradually to return to the ruined town. Maingy, meanwhile, had secured the person of another of the seven leading robbers, and decided to arrest the other five as well. On 12 November, therefore, he sent McCally to Rangoon to explain to the Woongyee in a friendly manner the causes that had led to the attack upon Martaban, to show him documentary evidence of the Martaban Chief's complicity in the robberies, and finally to request him to take immediate measures to deliver over to the British Commissioner the remaining five robbers, and to warn him, that in the event

[1] *Ibid.* Consultations 26 December, 1829, Maingy's letter to his Government, 5 December, 1829.

of his not apprehending and sending them over to Moulmein, the Commissioner would send a force in search of them.[1]

McCally had an interview with the Woongyee at Rangoon on 13 November, and communicated to him the message from Maingy. At first the Woongyee showed surprise at British action in Martaban, and said, that those proceedings and the language of the communications seemed to breathe the spirit of hostility instead of friendship, which, he said, he had been endeavouring to cultivate and cement. Finally, however, he agreed that the Martaban Chief was implicated in the robberies, and ought to be severely punished; he also undertook to do all in his power to capture and punish the culprits.[2] " In short," says McCally, " the whole tone of the Woongyee's conversation, during my interview with him, impressed me to believe that there was no disposition to make our late proceedings the foundation of any serious rupture, which, there can be no doubt, must be dreaded by the Court of Ava, and that the specimen we have given of our determination to procure redress, when his own officers have been unable to afford it to us, will induce the Woongyee to take the most active steps to prevent any future cause of complaint, and will be attended with more real benefit to our subjects than whole years spent in fruitless representations."[2]   The supine attitude of the Woongyee towards the destruction of Martaban is further evident from his own words to McCally: " I would not have minded if you had only sent the Kulas to Martaban, but you have sent our enemies the Taliens[3] there."[2]

The Woongyee said, that he would require over a month's time to capture the culprits; but Maingy had learnt privately, that the Woongyee had already secured four of the principal robbers as well as the person of the Martaban Chief, and was waiting for orders from Ava, as to whether he should surrender them to Moulmein or not. Meanwhile Maingy had apprehended

---

[1] *Ibid.* Consultations 19 December, 1829, Maingy's letter to McCally, 10 November, 1829.
[2] *Ibid.* Consultations 26 December, 1829, No. 17, McCally's letter to Maingy 16 November, 1829.
[3] Alluding to the parties of Moulmein Talaing Town Police which accompanied the troops to Martaban.

another robber, so that there were now three of them in the lock up.

While negotiations were proceeding for the surrender of the robbers, arrangements were being made for Burney to proceed to Ava and reside there as the British Resident. It followed, therefore, that all disputes between the two countries would now be settled by negotiation between the Burmese Government and the Resident. Although the Governor of Rangoon did not hand over to the Moulmein authorities the four robbers in question, the action taken by the Commissioner did produce some desirable results. Writing to his Government on 12 January, 1830, Maingy said, "I feel sincere pleasure in assuring your Lordship-in-Council, that the greatest quiet and tranquillity prevail in the southern provinces, and also in being able to apply the same observation to this province, in which not a single robbery has occurred since the period of my sending a force against the robbers at Martaban. I am further happy in being able to state, that our inhabitants are again settling on the banks of the Salween, and that our trading boats are moving about in every direction without fear or molestation, and that the commercial intercourse which formerly passed between Moulmein and the territory to the north, and along the western bank of the Salween, are enjoying more comfort and greater security of person and property than they have ever known since our first occupying Moulmein." [1] The Government of India fully approved of Maingy's action in connection with Martaban and the robbers. [2]

Finally, among the questions outstanding in the Anglo-Burmese relations, there was the problem of disputes between the Burmese Customs authorities and British traders resident in Rangoon. By the Crawfurd Treaty of 1826, merchants were not to be made to pay extras or bribes besides the customary duties; also port duties were fixed according to the size of ships; but it was against Burmese law for merchants to export precious

---

[1] Bengal Secret and Political, Vol. 357, No. 1.
[2] *Ibid.* Vol. 355, Consultations 26 December, 1829, No. 21, Letter from Government to Maingy, Fort William 26 December, 1829.

metals. As already noticed, Burmese officials did not receive salaries from their government, so that they did make attempts to secure something for themselves from merchants. Besides, British and other foreign traders in Rangoon were generally of a very doubtful character,[1] and attempted not only to elude payment of duties, but tried to export precious metals from the country as well. The Governor of Rangoon had often to resort to desperate measures, which generally amounted to fines and detention in the ordinary prison. In February 1828, some British merchants of Rangoon petitioned Sir Archibald Campbell against alleged extortions of the customs and port officers; but on enquiry it was discovered, that their complaints had not much of a foundation. Bayfield in his Historical Review of the Political Relations between the British Government in India and the Empire of Burma, says, " One of these merchants went to the Rangoon Woongyee's house, treated him with disrespect, and used indecorous language also towards the Supreme Government. Rangoon has long been notorious as an asylum for fraudulent debtors and violent and unprincipled characters from every part of India; and the only way of keeping this description of persons in order, and preventing them from disgracing the British character, impairing British interests, and disturbing the good understanding which now subsists between the British and Burmese Governments, would be by the Supreme Government maintaining always a British officer at that port, and conferring upon him the same judicial powers as are entrusted to British Consuls at Constantinople and in the Barbary States."

---

[1] *Pemberton and Bayfield*, op. cit. p. lii.

CHAPTER II

THE ORIGINS OF THE BRITISH RESIDENCY IN BURMA AND THE APPOINTMENT OF MAJOR HENRY BURNEY TO AVA, 1830.

The development of the office of a British Resident in Anglo-Burmese relations was by no means a new idea in the history of the East India Company. Soon after the Company acquired Bombay (in 1668), it realized the necessity of keeping in touch with Maratha affairs through envoys and residents at the Royal Capital. After the Peshwas had established their authority at Poona early in the 18th century, the Company learnt to maintain a representative at the Maratha Durbar with the object of preserving friendship, watching the movements of the Maratha Imperialists, and extending British trade. The second stage in this policy was reached as the Subsidiary system developed and it became necessary to watch and control the subsidiary states like Hyderabad, Mysore, Oudh, etc. Regular Residents were appointed to the capitals of such states, and as the representatives of the suzerain power they sometimes exercised enormous influence over the Princes.

A new phase in the "Residency" idea was reached at the conclusion of the Nepal War in 1816. A British Resident was now stationed at the Court of an independent Prince on the right of the Treaty of Sigowlee. Gardner, the first Resident in Nepal, was well qualified to soothe the bitterness of defeat felt by a noble foe, and succeeded in reconciling the Gurkha Government to the presence of a British representative at the Royal Capital.

In the relations with Burma the idea was of slow growth, not only because she was considered to be outside the pale of Indian politics, but also because there was want of interest in the Burma trade. Finally, however, when by Article 7 of the

Treaty of Yandabo, the privilege of appointing a British Resident to the Myodaw was extracted from the Burmese King, the right of maintaining a Burmese Resident at the Indian capital was conceded to the Burman Government. This article 7 was strongly objected to by the Burmese plenipotentiaries who negotiated the treaty, but the Company's authorities insisted upon it under influence of the Nepal Treaty. The Treaty of Sigowlee had succeeded in establishing amicable relations between the two states through a resident; the same results were hoped for in the relations with Burma. It is interesting to notice, however, that no steps were taken to appoint a permanent Resident to Ava till 1830. The reasons are not far to seek:—the Burmese military power was not considered to be dangerous; British and Indian merchants were expected to quit Burma and settle in British Burma; and the Commissioner of Tenasserim was expected to maintain diplomatic relations with Ava if necessary.

The Supreme Government very soon realized that it was mistaken in these expectations. The Burma problem became not by any means dangerous, but proved to be very annoying indeed. It was soon discovered, that the Treaty of Yandabo had failed to secure for the Company the many gains due from a vanquished foe, and that it was so defective, that the two parties interpreted it differently complicating matters still further. There was dispute concerning the frontiers towards Manipur, Assam, Arakan, and Tenasserim. The article on the release of prisoners was disputed by the Burmese, who held that only military prisoners belonging to the Company were meant by it, and not the subjects of the Company's allies detained in the country. To these difficulties may be added the unwillingness of the Burmese to pay the two remaining instalments of the Indemnity; the frontier dacoities and murders committed by Burman subjects in British Burma; the problem of the protection of British subjects in Burma, and particularly of British and Indian merchants and their trade in Rangoon; and finally the possible danger of a foreign European power obtaining a footing in Burma.

It was realized in 1830, that the non-enforcement of article 7 of the Treaty was a mistake. This is most clearly confessed by Bentinck in his Minute of 30 December, 1829. He says:—

> "It is to be regretted that at the close of the Burmese War, we had not adopted the same measures as those we did at the close of the Nepal War, for gradually removing from the minds of our opponents the sore and angry feelings left there by defeat, assuring them of the sincerity of our desire of cultivating friendly relations and keeping our government well informed of the real view and state of parties at the capital of Ava. I say, *gradually*, because it was not to be expected that a mission like Mr. Crawfurd's which remained at Ava but for a few weeks and which was avowedly deputed to make a treaty, the conditions of which ought to have been included in the Yandaboo Treaty, could accomplish all that was required. The very sound of the word treaty appears to have excited all the fears and suspicions of the Court of Ava, and the King himself, when told the object of Mr. Crawfurd's Mission, is said to have cried out, What! is he come to make another Yandaboo Treaty with us?

> "There is every reason to hope that if an officer possessing some portion of the judgment, conciliation, and talent of the late Resident of Khatmandu [1] had been fixed at the Court of Ava at the close of the war, our relations with that Kingdom might have been rendered as satisfactory as those which Mr. Gardner has established with the Nepalese under similar circumstances of defeat and humiliation and territorial cession on their part. It is remarkable too that the 7th article of the Treaty of Yandaboo distinctly provided for accredited Ministers residing at the Durbar of each in order to cultivate and improve the relations of amity and peace established between the two governments, and every person qualified by long residence in Ava and experience of the character of the Burmese, Mr. Gouger, [2] Mr. Laird, [3] and above all the worthy missionary Dr. Judson, gave it as his decided opinion.....that the permanent residence of a British Resident at the Court of Ava was very desirable." [4]

[1] The capital of Nepal.
[2] Henry Gouger was a British merchant who resided in Burma from 1822 to 1826. His interesting history may be read in his book, "The Prisoner in Burmah."
[3] John Laird, a ship captain, was before the War (1824-1826) agent to the Prince of Tharrawaddy for the sale of timber. See Gouger's book for Laird's history.
[4] Bengal Secret and Political, Vol. 357, No. 29.

Bentinck then goes on to consider in the same Minute, the objections advanced to such an appointment, founded chiefly upon the circumstance of the distance and jealousy of the Court. In reply he says, " Indeed, one of the principal objects of such appointments is to remove this very jealousy and distrust, and to bring about a more frequent and amicable inter-communication between the two states......

" In our present situation, then, I think the most prudent and advisable measure will be for us to fulfil the stipulation in the 7th article of the Yandaboo Treaty, and to invite the Burmese Court to do the same on their part......"

It was this decision of the Supreme Government under Bentinck that led ultimately to the appointment of Major Henry Burney as the first regular Resident to the Court of Ava in 1830.

The appointment of Burney in 1830, as Resident in Burma, was an important landmark in the history of Anglo-Burmese relations. A number of British envoys had in the past visited the Golden City, but the genesis, nature, and history of the British Residency in Burma from 1830 onwards, although distinctly a development of the historic past, stands out as a new departure, heralding an almost revolutionary change in the history of the relations between the two states. Before 1757, when the British in India were merely a trading body and not a sovereign power, the Presidents of their factories both in Bengal and Madras occasionally sent deputations to Burma with the object of discovering trade conditions in that country. In the year 1757, the Chief of the Negrais Factory deputed Ensign Lester to the Burmese capital. Lester had an interview with Alaungpaya the founder of the Konbaung dynasty. Most probably Lester obtained for the East India Company an " Akhwen dau " or royal license to trade in Negrais and Bassein. It was contrary to Burmese usage for kings to bind themselves down by contracts, and more so with foreign traders who were not supposed to have any political or royal standing. In 1759 took place what is sometimes called the " Negrais Massacre," and in 1760 Capt. Alves was sent by the Governor of Madras to procure compensation and redress, as well as the release of English prisoners. He had a prompt audience of King Naungdaw-gyi (1760-1763) at Shwebo, the then capital, but although he succeeded in securing the liberation of the captives, he failed to obtain any compensation for the damage suffered.

In 1795 the Governor-General sent Capt. Symes as Envoy to Ava, with the object of preventing the French from obtaining a footing in Burma. This was the first attempt of the British towards direct political intercourse with Burma. Symes succeeded in obtaining merely a royal order, permitting a British Commercial Agent to reside in Rangoon " for the purpose of trade, and to forward letters or presents to the King." [1]   In October 1796, Capt. Cox arrived in Rangoon as Agent, and proceeded to the capital, but was not well received, and so returned to Bengal by the end of 1797.

In 1784 Arakan was conquered by Bodawpaya,[2] and soon after there arose frontier disputes with the British authorities in Chittagong district. In 1798 the Burmese Governor of Arakan demanded that Arakan fugitives should be given up to him. The Governor-General, the Marquis of Wellesley, sent Symes again in 1802 to the Burmese King, but he was not well received, and Bodawpaya refused to enter into any new engagement with him. The British, however, feared the Burmese were evincing friendly feelings towards their enemies the French, hence in 1803 Capt. Canning was sent to Rangoon to obtain reliable information on the state of French interests in Burma, and to observe the general conduct and feelings of the Burmese Court towards the British Government. At first he was well received by the Governor, but soon he came into conflict with the Ye-woon [3] who directed all English letters to be opened before delivery. Canning refused to submit to this measure and left for Calcutta.

---

[1] *Aitchison*, Treaties etc., Vol. I, p. 265, The Royal Order, Clause 2.
[2] He was King of Burma, 1782-1819.
[3] *Lit.* Water Chief *i.e.* in charge of the shipping; he ranked next to the Governor.

In 1809 Canning was again sent to Rangoon to explain to the Burmese authorities, that the Isles of France [1] had been blockaded by orders from England, and that all vessels, whether from Burma or elsewhere, detected in communicating with them, would be confiscated. He was also instructed to watch closely the position of French interests in the country. Canning proceeded to the capital as well, and had an audience of the King. In September 1811, Canning was for a third time deputed to the Court of Ava because of the Chittagong frontier troubles, to explain that the Arakanese insurgents were neither instigated nor supported by the British Government, and to complain of outrages perpetrated by Burmese authorities in Arakan upon British subjects. Canning was able to accomplish nothing, and returned to Calcutta in August 1812.

These were all the embassies sent to Burma before the outbreak of the first war: from being of a commercial character at the start, they soon came to acquire a marked political complexion because of the British struggle with Napoleon.

After the War, Crawfurd was the first envoy to be deputed (1826) on the principle and right of the Treaty with the Burmese King. He was appointed " Envoy and Resident Minister " at the Court of Ava on the ground of Article 7 of the Treaty of Yandabo. The immediate object of the Mission was to contract a commercial treaty, but it was also the desire of the Government of India to discover through Crawfurd, " the feelings and deportment of the Burman King towards the British Mission," [2] which useful purpose would " be accomplished by a temporary residence at the capital of a few months." [2] Crawfurd, however, looked upon his Mission as merely meant to contract a commercial treaty, so that when this was accomplished he left Burma. Capt. Henry Burney was also appointed Envoy and Resident Minister under

---

[1] Mauritius and the neighbouring islands east of Madagascar which belonged to France. In 1810 Minto the Governor-General of British India captured these islands.

[2] Bengal Secret and Political, Vol. 345, Consultations 6 April, 1827, No. 30, Resolution of the Vice-President-in-Council in the Secret Department.

Article 7 of the Treaty of Yandabo, but his appointment was meant to be of a permanent nature, and it was intended to settle all questions at issue between the two states through the Resident.

The fact that Article 7 of the Treaty had been insisted upon by the British at Yandabo, shows, that the Government of India counted upon solving any difficulties arising with the neighbouring country of Burma by diplomatic means. Between 1826 and 1830, however, no measures were adopted to take permanent advantage of this article. When Campbell evacuated Rangoon in December 1826, he left behind him Lieut. Rawlinson as Agent to watch over British interests in general, and to receive from the Burmese Government the instalments of the indemnity due from the King. Rawlinson, however, in this capacity was not an accredited Consul or Resident of the British Government, and could not undertake the duties of such an officer, neither was he appointed under the Treaty of Yandabo.

Before his departure for Burma, Crawfurd had expressed his opinion to his Government that the permanent residence of an envoy at Ava was inexpedient. The Government of India did not think it necessary to determine whether such a measure was expedient or not, but wished to discover first, Burmese attitude towards Crawfurd's temporary Residency at the capital.[1] Crawfurd, while in Ava, had impressed upon the Burmese Government British right by treaty to maintain a Resident at the Court, and in his report to Calcutta had stated that this privilege ought not to be abandoned, " because some contingency may possibly arise to make its exercise expedient."[2] But at the same time he added, " In the meanwhile, I am decidedly of opinion, that the maintenance of a permanent Political Agent at Ava would be a measure more likely to

[1] Bengal Secret and Political, Vol. 345, Consultations 6 April, 1827, No. 30, Resolution of the Vice-President-in-Council in the Secret Department.
[2] Crawfurd's Journal, Appendix II.

3

impair than support our interests at that Court." In the following words he gave his reasons for this his decided opinion:—

> "I may here repeat, that a British Resident at Ava, distant
> by a navigation of 1200 miles (nearly 500 of it within the Burman
> territory, where every species of communication is placed under
> the most rigorous and vexatious restraint) from the authority
> he represents, and an object of perpetual jealousy to a Govern-
> ment indescribably ignorant and suspicious, could exercise little
> useful influence upon the councils of that Government, would have
> no means of furnishing his own with useful intelligence, and
> would, in a word, be placed in a situation amounting to little
> better than an honourable imprisonment.

> "The circumstances which attended the residence of the
> present Mission [1] at Ava afford confirmation of this opinion.
> During nearly a period of two months and a half, although a
> British force was still at Rangoon, I found myself compelled, by
> the temper of the Government [2] to abstain from all correspond-
> ence.[3] The same feeling was evinced at every station of our
> route, up and down; so that, in a period altogether of four months,
> and a half, no communication could be made to the Government [4]
> of our proceedings, with the exception of the casual and precari-
> ous one which was made by the route of Aracan." [5]

Crawfurd also did not support the proposal of maintaining
a resident Agent at Rangoon. "This would," he said, "no
doubt, be an arrangement most agreeable to the vanity, preten-
sions, and jealousy of the Burmese Government; but I do not
hesitate in pronouncing it as open to still more cogent objections than the other. The Agent of the British Government, in
this case, would be inevitably shut out from all communication
with the Court of Ava, and become virtually and practically the
representative of the Supreme Government of India to the
Provincial Government of Pegu. His services would be of
some value for the protection of British commerce at the port
of Rangoon, but jealously and narrowly watched, he would be
possessed, in his political capacity, neither of influence nor of

[1] The Crawfurd Mission of 1826.
[2] of Burma.
[3] Because the Envoy's mail was censored by Burmese authorities.
[4] of India.
[5] Crawfurd's Journal, Appendix No. II.

utility."[1] In spite of these views, Crawfurd held that political relations between the two states should be most effectually maintained. In his opinion, "all our future intercourse with the Government of Ava ought to be conducted through the military or civil officer vested with the chief political authority on the Salween frontier; that little direct communication should be held between the Supreme Government and the Court of Ava, and certainly none at all between it and any subordinate Burman authority."[1]

The Government of India did not endorse Crawfurd's views. Even before Crawfurd's departure for Ava, although the Government did not favour the immediate establishment of a permanent resident at the Burmese Court, it did consider the wisdom of having such an officer at Rangoon. Government resolution, 6 April, 1827, says:—"His Lordship-in-Council deems it sufficient to observe that under the present impression of the inexpediency of maintaining permanently a Resident at the Court of Ava, it is not considered of any importance whether or not the Burmese Court consent to recognize a second local authority in Rangoon. The principal British authority, under whatever designation of Resident, Agent or Consul, may himself generally reside at Rangoon, and on the occasion of his proceeding to the capital on any special duty, some subordinate authority may be left to officiate at Rangoon, an arrangement to which His Lordship-in-Council does not imagine the Court of Ava can have any possible objection."[2]

The Government of India was thoroughly dissatisfied with the fruits of the Crawfurd Embassy, and although it disapproved of Crawfurd's action in leaving Burma, it did not consider it desirable to send him again to Ava.[2] In the meantime the expediency of having an Agent or Resident at Rangoon began to be seriously considered, and finally Lord Amherst the Governor-General approved of such a measure, and decided to appoint Capt. Henry Burney as Consul.

[1] *Idem.*
[2] Bengal Secret and Political, Vol. 345, Consultations 6 April, 1827, No. 30.

"Believing," wrote Amherst in his Minute dated Simla, 12 May, 1827, "that the creation of the office of Consul at Rangoon is necessary and expedient as a temporary measure for the protection of the interests of British commerce at that Port, and to ensure the due observance of the Commercial Treaty,[1] as also that the officer so employed may act as Political Agent in subordination to the Principal British authority on the Tenasserim coast, I concur in the proposed appointment and in the selection of Capt. Burney for the situation of Consul with the allowances he at present enjoys, *viz.* Rs. 1,200 per mensem, and some consideration on account of a House or Office."[2]

This appointment at Rangoon was not proposed to be of a permanent nature, because the Supreme Government hoped, that the trade of Rangoon would ultimately shift to Amherst, where traders would be more secure under a comparatively stable government. Under the rule of the East Indian Company, three great ports, Bombay, Calcutta, and Madras, had already sprung up, and traders from all parts of India and the neighbouring world had drifted to them. Kyaikkami, renamed Amherst, was therefore also expected to develop into a great port and thus displace Rangoon. It was with this object in view, that Crawfurd the first Civil Commissioner of Tenasserim selected this station and named it after the Governor-General, as the site for the capital of the new territory. In 1827, however, when Sir Archibald Campbell became Chief Commissioner, he transferred the headquarters to Moulmein for strategical reasons.[3] Another reason, why the appointment of the Agent to Rangoon was to be temporary, was, that the Governor-General thoroughly believed that the political and commercial relations between the two countries would in time become properly understood and consolidated, so that there would not be sufficient employment for an officer in the above capacity.

In August 1827, Maingy, the Tenasserim Commissioner, deputed Burney to the Presidency of Bengal to lay personally before the Government certain questions at issue with Burma, amongst which was the proposition of " the maintenance of a

[1] The Crawfurd Treaty of November, 1826.
[2] Bengal Secret and Political, Vol. 346, No. 4.
[3] Burma Gazetteer, Amherst District, Vol. A, p. 11.

British Agent in the Burmese dominions, and the best mode of preserving our influence and improving our commercial relations with that state."[1] While on his way to Calcutta, Burney broke journey at Rangoon, and made a stay of ten days in order to study local conditions. On his arrival in Calcutta, he made his report[1] to the Government on the questions outstanding with the Burmese Government. As to the appointment of a Resident, he differed from Crawfurd, and thought that such an officer would be very useful, inasmuch as he would be able to give to the Burmese "a proper impression of our character and power," also that it was possible for the Supreme Government to maintain communications with the Resident.[1]

Burney also suggested that the British officer to be stationed in Burma should be designated "Resident," because as such he would not be liable to Burmese law, he would command consideration on all hands, and he would have the right of direct correspondence both with the Supreme Government as well as with the highest authority in Burma. In the English copy of the Treaty of Yandabo the words "Resident or Consul" were used, but in the Burmese version, "Ayashi"[2] or "Government person" and "Governor." To the Burmese Government these terms meant "Accredited Minister." Burney suggested that the term "Consul" be not adopted, because it was wholly unknown to the Burmese, and was not mentioned in their version of the Treaty; also that much difficulty would be experienced in making the Burmese Court comprehend the nature of the office, and it might also be difficult to obtain from it the necessary written declaration recognizing him and authorizing him to exercise his functions.

Caution was necessary in giving a proper designation to the new officer and in clearly defining his official position, because in the past much embarrassment had been experienced by Symes and Cox, due to the circumstance of the Burmese considering them in the inferior light of "Commercial Agents."

---

[1] Bengal Secret and Political, Vol. 347, Consultations 21 September, 1827, No. 18.

[2] အရာရှိ။

While pressing a point, Symes had even at one time been stopped by the Burmese Commissioners, who remarked, that he had been deputed merely for the purpose of negotiating a commercial treaty only.

While the Tenasserim authorities were intently waiting for final orders in connection with the dispatch of Burney as Resident, the Supreme Government suddenly changed its mind, and decided to wait. Burney was ordered to return to Tenasserim [1] and in January 1828, was posted to Tavoy.[2] It appears that in the cause of economy, the older and cheaper arrangement of a Political Assistant in Rangoon, appointed by and under the control of the Tenasserim Commissioner, was allowed to continue for the time being. During the year 1827, Campbell the Chief Commissioner had two Political Assistants at Rangoon, Rawlinson and Ware, and it was his desire too, that some better means of diplomatic relations with Burma be established, in order especially to obtain the release of prisoners detained in the country. Writing to the Chief Secretary to Government on 28 October, 1827, he said, " I have at present two officers at Rangoon, both from experience possessing a good deal of insight into the Burma character; either of them (if the employment of any is thought necessary) might be entrusted with that duty, or perhaps it may be deemed more desirable that Capt. Burney should make his debut in Burmese Diplomacy on so charitable an errand." [3] The Government allowed Campbell to depute Rawlinson to Ava to effect the release of British and allied prisoners, but expressly laid down, that " It is not intended that the deputation of Lieut. Rawlinson should be placed on the footing of a Political Mission from the Supreme Government, but merely on that of an officer sent by yourself to receive the prisoners on the spot......" [4]

[1] Bengal Secret and Political, Vol. 348, Consultations 28 September, 1827, No. 41, Government letter to Maingy, 28 September, 1827.
[2] *Ibid.* Vol. 350, Consultations 8 February, 1828, No. 19, Maingy's letter to his Government, 23 January, 1828.
[3] *Ibid.* Vol. 348, No. 34.
[4] *Ibid.* No. 42, Letter from Government to Campbell, 28 December, 1827.

Rawlinson accordingly proceeded to Ava, and returned to Rangoon in May, 1828, with the report that there were scarcely any prisoners, and not one of those settled in Burma was willing to quit the country.[1] While Rawlinson was away, a dispute arose between the Woongyee of Rangoon and the European merchants of that town on the equity of port charges. A few merchants, under the leadership of Capt. Crisp had an interview with the Woongyee and demanded a reduction of the port charges, and on his refusal to do so exhibited a highly improper conduct. " On the Viceroy producing the Commercial Treaty, and explaining that no more than the customary duties were demanded, Mr. Crisp said that that Treaty may be binding to you and the Company, but if we do not get justice we will go to the Company's Master,[2] and other words so offensive to the Woongyee that he got up and quitted the hall." [3] The merchants next memorialised the British Political Assistant and complained of exactions. Ware enquired into the matter and discovered that Crisp was to blame for the whole affair, in trying to arrogate to himself the duty of discussing with the Woongyee the intents and purposes of the Treaty of Yandabo and Crawfurd's Commercial Convention; that the complaints in the main were unreasonable and unfounded; and finally, that the more respectable of the merchants were not a party to Crisp's action. Ware also had an interview with the Woongyee, and " gave him to understand that in future whenever the British Residents and Traders of the place wished to represent any matter to him, it would be proper that it came through the constituted officer residing on the spot. With this assurance he was very well pleased, and said, in future he shall not receive any representation touching the relations between the two countries but through this regular channel." [4]

The Supreme Government on hearing of this occurrence condemned the attitude and behaviour of the authors of the

---

[1] *Ibid.* Vol. 352, Consultations 8 August, 1828, No. 4.
[2] Meaning thereby the British Government in England.
[3] Bengal Secret and Political, Vol. 351, Consultations 23 May, 1828, No. 16, Letter from Ware to Campbell, 10 March, 1828.
[4] *Ibid.* Nos. 16 and 18.

memorial, and instructed Campbell "to notify to all parties concerned that unless they regulate their conduct according to the advice of the constituted authority on the spot, and appeal through him in all cases of difference or dispute with the Burmese officers or subjects, they will not be considered entitled to the protection and assistance either of the Supreme Government or local Representative at Rangoon."[1]

In February 1829 Ware was recalled,[2] and Rawlinson alone was ordered to discharge the duties of Political Agent in Rangoon. Thus the appointment of a regular Resident was allowed to lapse on the ground of economy and for fear of ruffling the temper of the Burma Government, which looked upon such an appointment humiliating in the extreme to the Majesty of the Burmese Crown. This state of affairs, however, did not last for long. The question of the retention or disposal of the Tenasserim province had been under discussion between the Home Government and the Supreme Government in India since the signing of the Treaty of Yandabo. The great difficulty with Tenasserim was its inability to meet its military expenses. The financial figures were as under:—[3]

Revenue Receipts for 1826	Rs.	165,000
Civil Disbursements	„	122,000
Surplus	Rs.	43,000
Military Charges (Two Regiments)	Rs.	160,000
The Expense for two Cruisers	Rs.	34,000
Total Military Charges	Rs.	194,000
Receipt, Surplus	„	43,000
SURPLUS CHARGE	Rs.	151,000

Thus every year the Government of India had to bear an expense of over 1½ lacs of rupees for Tenasserim, and this charge was expected to increase since buildings, barracks, forti-

---

[1] *Idem.* No. 18.
[2] *Ibid.* Vol. 354, Consultations 13 February, 1829, No. 7, Letter from Government to Campbell, 13 February, 1829.
[3] Home Miscellaneous, Vol. 680, pp. 243-283.

fications, etc., were required.   In 1826 the Court of Directors
had suggested the retrocession of the province to Burma, but
the measure was not insisted upon, on the expectation that large
numbers of the Burmese subjects would migrate into the ceded
provinces.   This migration was considerable at first, amounting
to about 12,000 persons, but later no more arrived, and some of
the original emigrants returned to Burmese territory.[1]

In 1828 the Directors again recommended the retrocession
of the province, and on 25 November, 1828, Lord Ellenborough,
President of the Board of Control, drew up his memorandum [1]
in which he pointed out at some length, " that the Tenasserim
provinces are an undesirable possession, and regret may be
expressed that we insisted upon their cession."   But the problem
was how to get rid of them without disparagement to British
power and diplomacy.   Among the expedients suggested were:
(1) To sell the province to the Siamese; but during the War
Martaban had been offered to them, and they had refused it;
(2) to create an independent state in Tenasserim; but this
would have entailed the difficult problem of its protection especially against Burmese aggression; (3) to return it to the King
of Burma: this would have been the easiest course, but there
was the question of the inhabitants, who protested against the
measure.   It was felt above all, that the Burmese Government
should in no wise be given to know, or allowed to suspect the
anxiety of the British to get rid of the province.

The Supreme Government decided, first to discover
through an Agent the attitude of the Burmese Government
towards the retrocession of the province in exchange for
Negrais or Bassein district, or money or both; the Envoy,
however, was not to reveal the real object of the mission, but
seek for an opportunity to get rid of the troublesome districts
on the best terms, while discussing with the Burma Government other questions at dispute, such as, the Manipur frontier,
Dacoities, the Indemnity, etc.   Major Henry Burney, Deputy
Commissioner of Tavoy, was selected for this task; but he was

[1] *Idem.* pp. 319-343.

not to be sent as a representative of the Governor-General:
Maingy the Commissioner was instructed to send him to Ava
as his agent.   Maingy, however, considered it unwise to depute
Burney, from his side and in his name, to the Court of Ava,
which might look upon such a measure as an insult.   He, therefore, sent Burney to Calcutta, to explain, "that it would be
impolitic for any British officer proceeding to the capital of Ava
to go except in the name and under the direct authority of the
Governor-General." [1]   The Supreme Government thoroughly
agreed with this view, and on 30 December, 1829, appointed
Burney to be the British Resident at Ava in fulfilment of
Article 7 of the Treaty of Yandabo.   By this decision it was
meant to establish a permanent Residency in Burma, and the
Burmese Government was in turn invited to establish a Burmese Residency at Calcutta.

Burney was eminently qualified for the appointment.
Bentinck, the Governor-General, in recommending him to this
office, recorded in his Minute, that it was impossible to find an
individual better qualified than Burney: "indeed I might say
without the least fear of exciting envy, equally qualified to be
employed on the Mission." [1]   Henry Burney was a son of
Richard Burney, Second Master of the Calcutta Military
Orphan School, and was born at Calcutta on 27 February,
1792.   He joined the Company's service as cadet at the age of
16.   The Military Service List is full of praise for Burney in
respect of every official position filled by him. He was soon
marked out as a man of superior talents, and possessed of an
attractive personality.   Between 1823-1825, he was deputed on
missions at different times to Kedah and Prince of Wales Island,
and finally as Political Agent to Siam, a service for which he
earned high praise from the Supreme Government.   In the
middle of 1829, he crushed a most dangerous rebellion which
broke out in Tavoy.   His appointment as Resident at Ava was
more than justified by the manner in which he conducted

---

[1] Bengal Secret and Political, Vol. 357, Bentinck's Minute, 29 December, 1829.

himself, compelling even the admiration of the Burmese Government which hated the presence of a British Resident at the Royal Capital.

The objects of the new Residency to be established at Ava are to be clearly seen in the letter of Government instructions to Burney:—

> "......it is the desire of His Lordship-in-Council that you should make no proposition but encourage the Burmese to disclose their views and make first overtures in all occasions, and that you should quietly make it your study to ascertain and report for the information of Government the state of parties at Ava and the real views of the King and Courtiers, and endeavour to obtain some influence over the Court, and above all to establish a free intercourse between yourself and our possessions both in Aracan and Tenasserm.
>
> "But your first duty on your arrival at the capital of Ava must be to remonstrate against the delay in the payment of the 4th instalment, and against depredations....in Aracan and on the Salween." [1]

On the subject of Manipur, the instructions were to inform the Burmese Government the determination of the Governor-General to fix the Chindwin as the boundary between the two states:

> "Should the Burmese Ministers object to the presence of British officers in Manipur, and desire to enquire what may be our ulterior views with respect to that state, you will explain to them what has already been told them by Major-General Sir Archibald Campbell, that the Treaty of Yandaboo binds the King of Ava not to molest Gambhir Singh, but does not prevent the British Government from sending its officers to that Chief or affording him any other aid which he may require, and that on this point the Governor-General in Council will pursue whatever measures may appear to him expedient, without admitting the right of the Burmese monarch to make any objection."

As to the Burmese claim to Moulmein, that it was a part of Martaban district, Burney was instructed to

[1] Bengal Secret and Political, Vol. 357, Consultations 8 January, 1830, Government Letter of Instructions to Burney, 31 December, 1829, No. 32.

> "inform them, that....our possession of it for so many years must preclude the possibility of our now consenting to relinquish any portion of it or even of allowing it to become the subject of negotiation."

Particular instructions were given as to the projected return of Tenasserim for a consideration, and more so, because the Atwenwoons had been endeavouring through one Mr. Lane, a British merchant, to obtain the return of the province:—

> "It is important, however, that you should endeavour to make yourself well acquainted with the real views and wishes of the Burmese Court with respect to our territory on the Coast of Tenasserim, for the retrocession of which you are aware that an overture has lately been made by the Burmese Interior Ministers through Mr. Lane a British merchant residing at Ava."

Burney was carefully to refrain from expressing any opinion on any such proposition formally made, but endeavour to ascertain and report for the information of the Governor-General,

> "what equivalent the Burmese Court is able or willing to give in exchange for a portion or whole of the Tenasserim provinces, and also whether the Burmese Court could be disposed to cede the island of Negrais with some part of the neighbouring country, including or otherwise the town of Bassein in exchange for a portion of our Territory on the Tenasserim Coast."

The interests of trade were not omitted: Burney was asked to

> "take the earliest measures which you may find it practicable to adopt, without exciting the jealousy or dissatisfaction of the Court of Ava, to open and establish a free intercourse between yourself and this Government by the way of Arracan as well as Rangoon....Your attention should be given to the trade of Ava [1] with a view of reporting to his Lordship-in-Council the practicability of extending and facilitating British Commerce and the consumption of British manufactures."

The instructions also dealt with the desirability of good relations being maintained between the two governments:

> "His Lordship-in-Council is convinced that you will use your best endeavours to satisfy the Court of Ava, that your appoint-

---

[1] The Calcutta authorities called Burma by the name of its capital, Ava.

ment has originated in no other view than that cited in the 7th article of the Treaty of Yandaboo, namely, to cultivate and improve the relations of amity and peace established between the two governments. You will use such arguments and reasoning as your own reading and experience may suggest to you for showing to the King and Court of Ava the advantage and convenience of the relations between the two states maintained unimpaired by means of Resident Ministers, a principle of policy which has been adopted by every civilized state, and you will make known the desire of the Governor-General-in-Council to afford a suitable reception to any Burmese officer of rank and consideration whom the King of Ava may be pleased to depute as his Resident at Calcutta."

Provision was also made in case it became necessary to retire from the Royal capital:—

"If contrary to the expectations of the Governor-General-in-Council, the Court of Ava manifest an invincible repugnance to a British Resident permanently stationed at Ava, and notwithstanding your explanations, observe towards you a line of conduct to which it may be unbecoming in your situation to submit, you will consider yourself authorized to quit the capital and return to Rangoon, taking care, however, to adopt such a step without committing your Government or giving unnecessary umbrage to the Court of Ava. But it is understood that the Court of Ava, although likely at first to view your arrival with considerable jealousy and uneasiness, will soon come to acknowledge the presence of a British officer at Ava as a satisfactory pledge of our pacific intentions, and His Lordship-in-Council confidently relies on your approved talents and address for promoting such a good understanding between yourself and the Burmese Ministers, as may not only divest them of all alarm and jealousy, but show them the utility and convenience of having a British officer near them as a certain channel of acquiring authentic intelligence of the views of the British Government and other general information." [1]

When Cox was appointed Resident at Rangoon in 1796, he was empowered to protect the interests of British subjects residing in Burma; Burney was also invested with the same authority in his letter of credentials:— [2]

---

[1] Bengal Secret and Political, Vol. 357, Consultations 8 January, 1830. Government Letter of Instructions to Burney, 31 December, 1829, No. 32.
[2] Ibid. No. 33.

"And I hereby authorise you to receive complaints from all British subjects residing in the dominions of the King of Ava, in the subject of injuries sustained by them from the Government or subjects of Ava, and to make such representations thereon to the King and Ministers as you may judge advisable."

It was, however, made clear, that "it is not the desire of the Governor-General-in-Council that you should interfere in any such matter whenever the established laws of the country are adequate to afford the parties redress." [1]

Besides his letter of instructions and the credentials, Burney was also armed with a letter [2] from the Governor-General addressed direct to the King of Burma, as well as letters [3] from the Chief Secretary Swinton to the Burmese Ministers at Ava. In these letters the objects of Burney's appointment to Ava were fully elucidated. All the letters were drawn up in the third person, so as to avoid mention of the first personal pronoun, such as, "I the honorific" (အကျွန်ုပ်။) "I the equal rank" (ကျွန်တော်။), and "I the servile" ဘုရားကျွန်တော်။) [4]

Early in February 1830, Burney left Calcutta by the Company's steam vessel the *Ganges* accompanied by the following escort and suite :— [5] One Indian officer, two Havildars, two Naiks, two Drummers, and thirty Sepoys, all volunteers from the 38th Bengal Native (Indian) Infantry. Lieut. George Burney, a brother of the Resident, was appointed to command this escort, as well as to act as Assistant to the Resident. Apothecary Bedford of the Madras service was appointed to the medical charge of the Residency. On his arrival in Rangoon, Burney was authorized to employ an interpreter as well as one Clerk, one Munshi, and four Peons. The presents for the King consisted of "two brass 6 pounder guns complete for the purpose of Horse Artillery, which you will present to the King of Ava in the name of the Governor-General; and

[1] *Ibid.* No. 32.
[2] *Ibid.* No. 34.
[3] *Ibid.* Nos. 35 and 36.
[4] *Ibid.* No. 37.
[5] *Ibid.* No. 32.

you are authorized to incur an expense not exceeding Rs. 1500 in providing yourself with the same suitable present to be delivered to the Queen of Ava from the Governor-General as well as with certain small articles of Muslins, Pen knives, Scissors, and Essences for present." [1] The Resident's office was thus recognized as one of an exalted nature: the same military honours were to be paid to Burney as to Maingy, including a salute of 11 guns.[2]

On 12 February, Burney arrived in Moulmein after touching at Akyab and Kyaukpyu. From Moulmein he was unable to proceed immediately to Rangoon and Ava, since he was detained as a defence witness in the court martial of Lieut. Sandys at Mergui.[3] Finally, however, late in the evening of 18 March, Burney arrived at Rangoon, and landed on the following morning. The Woongyee received him with every token of respect and consideration, and with unusual celerity promised to supply boats and men for the conveyance of the Royal presents and the Residency baggage to Ava.[4]

Soon after his arrival in Rangoon, the British merchants of the town complained to Burney against certain unjust measures of the Yewoon: "It appears," says Burney "that of late the difficulty of collecting debts here has greatly increased in consequence of the Raywoon [5] taking bribes to release debtors before they came to some understanding with the English Merchants at whose suit they may be confined. I conceived that my instructions justified my remonstrating on this subject with the Woongyee, to whom I explained that we sought to introduce no new law or custom, but merely that the Burmese law, which requires that a debtor if arrested shall give some security, or come to some arrangement with his creditor before he is released, shall always be allowed to take its course.

"The Woongyee and Yewoon promised fair and pledged themselves to give redress to the parties who particularly com-

[1] *Ibid.* No. 32.
[2] *Ibid.* No. 38.
[3] *Ibid.* Burney's letter, Moulmein, 13 March, 1830.
[4] *Ibid.* Letter, Rangoon, 22 March, 1830.
[5] Same as Yewoon or Water Chief.

plained to me, but I much fear that no reliance whatever can be placed on such promise or pledge. The truth is that the administration of justice in Burmah is one of the principal sources of emolument to Burmese officers who have no regular salaries, and as long as a man possesses money he has no difficulty in diverting the course of justice. The British merchants are of opinion that their best chance of security against the fraudulent debtor in future will be my residence in Ava, an arrangement upon which they all congratulate themselves much." [1]

On 1 April Burney arrived at Prome, after a passage of 9 days from Rangoon. His observations and the information collected by him *en route* are interesting. As to the condition and treatment of the people by the King's government, he says, " I must own I have seldom met with more poor and miserable looking people or their habitations than those which we have seen between Rangoon and this place.[2] Everything would assure one that the country had not yet recovered from the desolating effects of the late war......" [3] In Prome Burney found a Mr. Marowly, a native of Denmark, doing business as agent for some British merchants in Rangoon. He informed Burney, that he had been in Prome for 13 months, and that some time ago he was able to sell from Rs. 10,000 to Rs. 12,000 worth of British piece goods in the month; " but of late the Burmese officers have oppressed the people so much in order to collect money for the purpose of paying the instalment [4] due to us, that he cannot sell anything......He further states that scarcely a day passes in which he does not see 10 or 12 of the poor inhabitants tied up and threatened until they make some payment, and that of the money thus collected here, a fourth is taken by the petty officers and only a half of the remainder is

---

[1] Bengal Secret and Political, Vol. 357, Burney's Letter, Rangoon 22 March, 1830.
[2] Prome.
[3] Bengal Secret and Political, Vol. 358, Burney's Letter, Prome 6 April, 1830.
[4] of the Indemnity.

sent to Rangoon for us, the other half being always sent up to the Queen." [1]

In his *Journal*, Burney gives an interesting description of his approach to and reception at Ava. On 23 April, at "about 11 we reached the village of Lebanyeen, where we found 3 horsemen deputed from the Hlutdaw to inform us that a deputation was coming down to receive us according to Burmese etiquette......We passed on towards Pouk-tau, but before we arrived there we were met by two war boats with a Tsaredaugyee [2] from the capital........about 4 p.m. we arrived at Lettshoungyoo about 2 miles below the walls of the town (Ava) ......Here about 5 o'clock, a Woondouk and another Hlutdaw Tsaredaugyee with 3 or 4 more war boats came down to us. The Woondouk was the same young and goodlooking Burmese who had met Mr. Crawfurd. He came immediately on board ......he proposed that we should wait where we were for the night, and proceed to the house prepared for us at the capital at an early hour on the following morning...." [3]

On 24 April, at about 7 a.m. Burney's boats accompanied by the Woondouk and the Tsaredaugyees with 5 or 6 war boats "arrived off a neat looking pucca built house situated close to the river side on the left bank." [4] This house had been built by Lanciago [5] a Spanish merchant, and had specially been purchased by the King for the British Resident. It was situated between the King's Elephant Palace and the north-west angle of the wall of the outer town. [6]

[1] Bengal Secret and Political, Vol. 358, Burney's Letter, 6 April, 1830; Prome as well as many other districts between Ava and Rangoon formed a portion of the Queen's Jagir. *(Idem.)*
[2] *Lit.* "great royal writer" *i.e.* Clerk of the Council.
[3] Burney's Journal, Bengal Secret and Political, Vol. 358.
[4] *Ibid.*
[5] He was later appointed Akoukwun (*i.e.* Customs Officer) of Rangoon by Bagyidaw. He had also filled this office before the War.
[6] *Yule* says in his Narrative, p. 185, "The site of the Residency, long occupied by the respected Colonel Henry Burney, to whose MS. official journals and published papers I have been so repeatedly indebted for illustration in the course of this narrative, has been long swept into the river".

Burney was now invited to land, but he was cute enough to discover that only the Woondouk, who had joined him the previous evening, was present to receive him, and that no arrangements had been made to pay him the same compliment as had been paid to Crawfurd upon his first landing, when a Woongyee, an Atwenwoon and other officers had received him. Crawfurd had come to Ava in a steam vessel, and was accompanied by a European escort, while Burney had changed over at Prome from steamer to Burmese boats,[1] and had an Indian escort. These circumstances, he feared, had created an impression that his office was inferior to that of Crawfurd's. With the object of dispelling this impression, Burney refused to land, until officers of similar rank to those who had paid Crawfurd this compliment were in attendance to receive him. " I knew," he says, " that everything depended upon the first position which I might take up, and the Burmese Court ought not to be allowed to form any opinion that I was an officer subordinate to Mr. Crawfurd and not entitled to the same honours and consideration. If this opinion were once adopted......the difficulty of my situation would be greatly increased, and the chance of my obtaining any influence over the Court very much reduced." [2]

Burney's firm attitude was crowned with success. When the King was informed of the situation, " he gave instant orders that not only a Woongyee and Atwenwoon, but a second Woondouk, and 2 or 3 more Tsaredaugyees and Thandauzens [3] should attend to receive me on shore." [4] At 11-30 a.m. therefore, a Kyeewoon [5] and an Atwenwoon came on board Burney's boat and invited him to land. Burney accompanied them on shore, and on entering the house was welcomed by a Woongyee. After sitting with Burney for about half an hour the Burmese officers took their leave. In the demeanour of all these Burmese

[1] This arrangement was prescribed by the Calcutta authorities, undoubtedly in the cause of economy.
[2] Bengal Secret and Political, Vol. 358, Burney's Journal, par. 3.
[3] *Lit.* " receiver of the royal voice " *i.e.* writer attached to the Royal Household or Secretary of the Palace.
[4] Burney's Journal, par. 3.
[5] Overseer of the Granaries.

functionaries there was one marked feature: " When they met Mr. Crawfurd they confined their enquiries entirely to the King of England's health, pointedly making no mention of the Governor-General's; on the present occasion they asked readily and very civilly the state of the health of the Governor-General and his family, and appeared to have no notion of such a personage as the King of England."[1] The reason was that the Burmese were anxious to have the Kubo Valley question settled in their favour, and they knew that it lay within the power of the Governor-General to restore the Valley to the King. Although they did not relish the presence of a British Resident at the capital, they decided to make use of him in the endeavour to recover the Valley from Manipur.

The house assigned to Burney looked neat from a distance, and undoubtedly its situation was good, being immediately outside the town and close to the river; but it was far from being comfortable.   Burney describes it as follows:—" The house is a dwelling of 2 stories with a brick wall everywhere 3 feet thick and with only three small windows......The lower floor is now unfit for anything but a godown.   The upper storey is divided by a plank partition in 2 rooms one small and another a large one, and covered with a plank roof over which a layer of mortar is placed.   By piercing the wall with 5 or 6 more windows, putting up a verandah and bed room one side, improvements which the Burmese officers immediately consented to make, the house which in its present state is certainly very like a jail, the 3 windows even having iron bars, may be rendered more comfortable.   The compound is limited and within it all the buildings required for our escort, servants and followers having been constructed, there is scarcely 10 sq. ft. of open space."[1]

Until presented to the King, according to the custom of the country, distinguished visitors were expected to avoid going about the town or country to any distance from the house. Burney, however, gives some of his early impressions of Ava:— "......the appearance of Ava is very inferior to that of

[1] Burney's Journal, par. 4.

Bangkok. There all was bustle and animation, numerous boats and junks and people passing to and fro. Here we see very few boats on the river, and scarcely any traffic going on. The streets of the town, as far as we have been able to see them, are broad and regularly laid out, but with the exception of the pagodas all is poverty and misery, and listless and quiet like a deserted city; many of the houses appear to be unoccupied and in ruins. The market also makes a poor appearance — saltfish, betel-nut, and betel pumpkins, love-apples, green mangoes and marians are the only articles for sale. The supply of vegetables and fruit is most contemptible in comparison with that even. There are no yams or the mealy potato called by the Malays Ubitoopong, nor any description of greens in all of which Tavoy market abounds at that time of the year. The plantains are of a poor badly cultivated kind. . . .

" I must not, however, in justice omit to state that the contrast between the demeanour of these Burmese officers and that of Siamese officers in the same circumstances is very much in favour of these people. We are not tormented with questions as to the number and value of the presents we have brought, nor are we subject to importunities for gifts. All we ask those in attendance to bring or do is immediately promised, and much is not only promised but fulfilled." [1]

As to food supplies for the Residency, the Burmese Government arranged to send daily at its own expense all kinds of provisions required, so as to give no occasion to any member of the Residency to visit the market. Burney objected to this arrangement, but was obliged to submit to it for the time being: " The Burmese officers approve of it," says Burney, " as it gives them an opportunity of patronage in appointing some of their friends as Athoun-zares,[2] stewards, Mehmandars,[3] etc., and enable them to commit extortions upon the poor inhabitants for contributions of money and everything else they may pretend we require." [1]

---

[1] *Ibid.*
[2] Controllers of expenses.
[3] Those in charge of distinguished guests to look after their comforts; it is a Hindustani word.

CHAPTER III

THE ESTABLISHMENT OF THE RESIDENCY AT AVA AND THE KUBO PROBLEM.

The British Residency having now been stationed at Ava, it became the great object of Burney to get into personal touch with the King, the Royal Household, the Ministers, and men of rank at the capital. He thought that if he could develop personal friendship with those in control of the government, he would the more easily be able to settle 'the questions at issue between the two neighbours, and simplify diplomatic relations between Calcutta and Ava. It will be seen how far Burney was successful in his efforts.

The Burmese Government, as well as the people, looked upon the Residency as one of the humiliating results of their defeat in the War. The King was in no mood to accept a permanent residency. The Resident, it was feared, was really a spy, and it was generally believed that the Company's ambition was to conquer the whole country. This attitude, however, did not plainly become evident during the first few years of the history of the Residency. The Resident was welcomed, and on the whole treated with respect.[1] The King was anxious particularly to recover the Kubo Valley, and if possible also Tenasserim and Arakan; the presence of the Resident, therefore, was taken advantage of, and much consideration was shown to him. The Kubo Valley was ultimately recovered through Burney, but later when it was discovered, that no more concessions were forthcoming, the Residency was severely neglected, especially under Burney's successors. Burney, besides, was a man of masterly personality, so that he was able to command respect — the human side of his character making a particular impression upon the King, his officers, and people.

[1] Bengal Secret and Political, Vol. 358, Burney's Journal, par. 11.

Before entering upon the business transactions of the Resident it is necessary to sketch the character of the King and Court, so as to obtain a view of the state of parties at the capital.

Bagyidaw (1819-1837) was an absolute monarch, but he was dependent upon his Woongyees and Atwenwoons for the conduct of government. Dr. Adoniram Judson gives the following account of him: " Mild, amiable, good natured and obliging; active, restless, impatient of restraint or close application; playful in his manners, addicted to favouritism; but fickle in his attachments except to the Queen of whom he is passionately fond, and who maintains over him the most controlled influence; fond of shews, theatrical exhibitions, elephant catching and boat racing; not devoted to his religion, not avaricious or irritable, but sometimes carried away by a violent gust of passion which though transient is generally fatal to the offending party; possessed of very moderate talents yet quick in catching an idea, forming an opinion, and making a decision; partial to white foreigners,[1] desirous of encouraging intercourse with them and of improving his country by the introduction of foreign arts;[1] has a high regard for Brahmins, but rather averse to Muselmans, and not much under the influence of Buddhist priests; inordinately devoted to technical researches and experiments, and particularly desirous of discovering the secret of rendering himself invisible at will and also remedy for certain disabilities of system occasioned by early excesses." [2]

Burney gives the following description of Bagyidaw:—

"The King is a poor weak fool, incapable of comprehending any rational argument, and prone to adopt the suggestions of any silly or mischievous courtier rather than the advice of a sensible minister. He is very much led by several of his personal attendants who are called Loobyos — young men — although some of them are as old as the King himself, having been his playmates and companions from infancy." [3]

---

[1] This was so before the War; later he became suspicious of them.
[2] Bengal Secret and Political, Vol. 341, Consultations 5 August, 1826, No. 19.
[3] Ibid. Vol. 358, Consultations 20 August, 1830, Burney's Journal, par. 43.

Burney goes on to say, that the Ministers feared these Loobyos, and bribed them because of their influence over the King; that these men often urged the King to risk another war and recover the lost territory; that the Mahomedans in Ava gave him the same advice; and that the Bos or military officers boasted before the King of their achievements and desired a second war.   Burney further corroborates Judson's evidence, that the Queen's influence over the King was most extraordinary.

"Since my arrival here," continues Burney, "I think I have acquired much better information regarding the real character of this King and his Ministers than what I have heard many of our officers declare that the King himself is a man of good intentions, well disposed to maintain peace and friendly relations with us, but that his ministers are very hostile to us, and that they conceal the truth from him and take every opportunity of inciting him against us.   It is quite the reverse.   All the Ministers of any respectability are most anxious to keep the King quiet, and to preserve peace between the two countries; but the King, who from his very infancy was taken away from his father, and bred up in the palace by his grandfather [1] for a despotic sovereign, is full of the most ungovernable pride and arrogance, and is most unwilling to admit the British Government as equal to his in power or military strength.   More than any other man in his empire he feels and broods over the disasters of the late war, and of all his subjects that war has left the least impression of our superiority upon his mind.   The real truth is, that the King is a spoilt child and his ministers are cowards; they have no power to move him when he entertains a capricious whim and he becomes obstinate, and in the most important affairs of state they have no certain influence over him.   They seldom tell anything that is disagreeable, and whenever they are forced to bring any subject to his notice which they think will displease him, they contrive to cover it up with falsehood...." [2]

As to the powers of the King, Burney says that even the consent of all the ministers is not enough to any proposition: that the King could upset all their decisions even in points of minor importance; "....that there is very little chance for the representations of any British officers situated at a distance

---

[1] Bodawpaya 1782-1819.
[2] Bengal Secret and Political, Vol. 358, Burney's Journal, par. 69.

being ever properly reported to the King if they are likely to
be unpleasant to him.   Had a Resident been sent here from
Yandaboo, whilst the fear of Sir Archibald Campbell's army
prevailed, he could easily and promptly have settled all points
of punctilio and ceremony......

"Now next to the demonstration of a British force
against the capital the best mode of succeeding here is to conciliate the King, to enter into his little amusements, and to
seek every opportunity of seeing and conversing with him....
If the King is won the whole of the ministers and people will
be easily won.   Under existing circumstances it will be a work
of many months before I shall be able to secure the favour of
the King and through him a proper influence over his Government." [1]

Lánciago's opinion as to the feelings of the King towards
the British, was, "that before the late war and even from
infancy the King was always very partial to Europeans, and
took delight in seeing and conversing with English Traders and
in entertaining them in his palace, but that since the war His
Majesty's feelings are quite altered.   His Majesty now accuses
the English of great ingratitude, and often refers to all the
marks of kindness and attention which he used to show us
formerly, and in return for which, he says, we have ruined his
country and robbed him of half of it......" [2]

The Queen, Mai Nu, was "raised from low life, and therefore tenacious of her acquired rights, proud, haughty, bigoted,
avaricious, utterly implacable, dignified in her manners and
capable of assuming an amicable and condescending deportment, possessed of rather superior talents, given to intrigue,
fond of power, averse to all foreigners, and displeased at the
favour which the King is disposed to shew them." [3]

The Queen and her brother Menthagyee [4] were the two
richest persons in Burma and were supposed to be making

[1] Bengal Secret and Political, Vol. 358, Burney's Journal, par. 69.
[2] Ibid. par. 69.
[3] Ibid. Vol. 341, Consultations 5 August, 1826, No. 19.
[4] Lit. The Great Prince.

enormous additions to their wealth.   These two during 1824 —
1826 were at the head of the war party, and " are said to be
amassing wealth from a conviction that in the event of the
death of the King they will be thrust back to the low rank
from which they have risen, unless they have the means of
purchasing a party......She (the Queen) fulfils her duties as
a wife admirably; she uses opium freely and it promises soon
to put an end to her existence." [1]   But after the conclusion of
the War, " they are no more hostile to us than what might be
expected from persons in their situation who are more intimately acquainted with the real sentiments of the King and
most desirous of adopting the line of conduct which they know
will gratify His Majesty." [1]   Since the Queen had an extraordinary influence over her husband, the Ministers often mentioned unpleasant news or business first to her, so that she
might prepare the King before audience was granted to them.

The heir-apparent was Tsakyamen, the King's only son by
his former queen.   He was about 18 years of age and not
possessed of much talent or energy. [2]   But Judson describing
him in 1826, calls him " a fine lad......sprightly, active,
peremptory, severe, high-handed...." [3]   The Princess Theit-
zoophra, 9 years of age, was the only daughter by Mai Nu.
It was the Queen's plan to marry her daughter to the Heir-
apparent.

The Queen's brother, Menthagyee, was " Superintendent of
Privy Councillors, acting Public Minister of State, *factotum* of
the Empire; in character similar to his sister; in person all
favoured; in manners austere; repulsive without one point to
recommend him except some capacity for managing the affairs
of Government after a fashion; illiberal, narrow-minded, no
friend of foreigners and their improvements; avaricious,
dreadfully cruel." [3]

---

[1] Bengal Secret and Political, Vol. 358, Consultations 28 August,
1830, Burney's Journal, pars. 42, 43.
[2] *Ibid.* par. 164.
[3] Judson's Account, Bengal Secret and Political, Vol. 341.

The Prince of Tharrawaddy, who in 1837 rebelled against his brother the King, deposed him and reigned in his stead, was not possessed of any wealth. In character he was about the same as his brother, but addicted to gambling and excessively profligate.[1]

The Woongyees or Ministers of state were known, according to Burmese custom, not by personal names, but by the name of the town or district assigned to them as jagir, and which they were supposed to "eat."[2] When Burney arrived in Ava (1830), there were six such Ministers:—

(1) The Rangoon Woongyee: he was the Governor or Viceroy of Rangoon, and so was unable to take active part in the deliberations of the Hlutdaw. (2) The Queen's Woongyee or Min-ma-daw:[3] his duty was to attend to the interests of his Royal Mistress. (3) The Le-gain Woongyee, also called Padein Woongyee: he was one of the two who signed the treaty of Yandabo, and it was he who received Burney when the latter arrived in Ava. (4) The Kyee Woongyee: he was an old man of very pleasing and prepossessing character, with extremely mild and good humoured manners. Judson describes him to be "intelligent, brave and prudent — the best general in the Burmese service." He commanded the Burmese army during the greater part of the War, but he constantly recommended peace, "until at length a Longyee or woman's petticoat was sent down to him."[4] He had suffered many indignities from the King, and so interfered as little as possible in public affairs. In Snodgrass' account of the Burmese War there is a portrait of this minister, but it is not true to life: Burney describes him to be flat nosed with a scanty grey beard, while the portrait presents Roman features. (5) The Kyouk Tshoung Woongyee: Burney says, he was "a very feeble dull old man." (6) The Myawadi Woongyee Maung Za: He was only lately created

---

[1] Judson's Account, Bengal Secret and Political, Vol. 341.
[2] *i.e.* enjoy the revenues of.
[3] ပင်မှာတော်။ See Appendix II, for note on Min-ma-daw and Nagarané.
[4] Burney's Journal, Bengal Secret and Political, Vol. 358, par. 23.

Woongyee before which he was an Atwenwoon. Judson says that during the War he was Lieutenant-General in Arakan, and that he was " one of the most sensible, intelligent, liberal mind-ed men in the country; in religion a free thinker, but insists on the existence of one eternal God; fully sensible of the superiority of white foreigners, and desirous of encouraging the introduction of their arts and sciences into his own country." Burney speaks of him as being one of the most intelligent men he had ever seen, that he took the lead in official conversation, that he had associated a good deal with Europeans, and partic-ularly with Judson, and had a much greater knowledge of English character and manners than any other Burmese Chief in Ava.[1]

" The Ministers dined with me," says Burney in his Journal par. 107, 9 June, 1830, " and became very familiar and intimate. Maung Za especially took me aside, and pointing to the oppo-site side of the river said that he recollected, what is now all waste and unoccupied, was once full of houses and inhabitants, that the country had suffered dreadfully from the late war, and that he would entreat me to pity the poor inhabitants and pre-serve them from another such calamity. Maung Za is clearly a very extraordinary character. He writes the Nagree [2] charac-ter very well, speaks a little Hindustanee,[3] and surprised me by singing 2 or 3 lines of a Latin hymn which he must have learnt from some of the Roman Catholic Christians here. He informed me that he was in command of the Burmese force which defeated Capt. Norton's party at Ramoo in the begin-ning of the war, declaring that his own force did not exceed 6500 men, at the same time estimating Capt. Norton's party at 7000. He assured me that he had not directed nor authorised any cruelties to be committed towards our European officers, who, he said, were fairly killed in the action. Upon showing

[1] Burney's Journal, Bengal Secret and Political, Vol. 358, par. 23.
[2] The Sanskrit alphabet.
[3] He also possessed some knowledge of the Manipuree language.
    (Burney's Journal, par. 214.)
    N. B.— In the records of this period the term " U " is never used
        even for the highest officers of state: it is always " Maung."

him Wilson's historical account of the Burmese War, he said that they had made a similar collection of their official documents, and gave me hopes of being able to inspect so curious a work."

These Ministers were not each in charge of certain departments of state as was the case in Siam at that time.[1] They all deliberated together in the Hlutdaw on any matter ordered by the King. Sometimes the meetings were presided over by Menthagyee. The decisions of the Ministers were taken down by the Royal Secretaries and delivered to the Atwenwoons to be submitted to the King.[1]

Besides the six Woongyees, there were six Atwenwoons styled Eka-maha-Thenapadi.[2] They did not attend the Hlutdaw, but three of them in rotation always remained near the King. Officially their position was of a subordinate nature, but sometimes individually they exerted enormous influence over the King. " I must not omit to add," says Burney, " that although the Woongyees are much bolder than the Atwenwoons, whenever it is necessary to represent anything to the King, yet even they are sometimes obliged to be cautious........Whenever they have anything disagreeable to submit they pledge themselves to stand by and support each other......The King being at a loss whom to punish, but if much enraged, he takes up his spear and hurls it at the whole set. I am happy to say that His Majesty has not thrown his spear at the Woongyees during the last four months." [1]

There were two noteworthy European merchants in Ava — Lanciago and Lane — who often visited Burney, and kept him informed of conditions at the Court and in the country in general. They frequently appeared at Court before the King and were looked upon as men of influence. Lanciago was a Spaniard and had a very defective knowledge of both English

[1] Burney's Journal, Bengal Secret and Political, Vol. 358, pars. 23, 24.
[2] i.e. Lord. The term is a corruption of the Sanskrit, Eka = Chief, Maha = Great, Sena = Army, Pati = Master: i.e. The Commander-in-Chief; but the Atwenwoons were not Commanders-in-Chief.

and Burmese, but he was a successful business man. Lane
being a Britisher was able to fill a more important role: " I
see," says Burney, " that whilst our Government has been dis-
pensing with a Resident here, Mr. Lane has been taking the
place of such political officer with a view only towards further-
ing his own commercial pursuits. He has succeeded in acquiring some influence over the King and Court, who at the same
time appear to have been considering him as a secret agent from
our Government." [1] Lanciago always accompanied the Ministers when they visited the British Residency, and his duty was
to keep the Woongyees within the safe side of the law in the
discussions. He was educated in France, and in heart and soul
was a Frenchman; he had also given an impression to the Burmese Government that France was superior to England both
on sea and land. Both these men received Bengal newspapers,
relevant parts of which they translated for the King and Ministers. From these newspapers the Burmese Government had
already learnt, before Burney's arrival into the country, that
the Tenasserim province was financially a dead loss to the
Company's government, and that the Governor-General was
anxious to return it to the King.[1] Under these circumstances
there was scarcely any chance for Burney to negotiate the
return of the province for a monetary consideration from
Bagyidaw.

Before Burney could be recognized officially as Resident,
it was necessary for him to be presented to the King in open
Court. He found two humiliating obstacles in his way: the
Kadaw Day and the Shoe question. It was custom with the
Burmese to present foreign agents to the King on a Kadaw
day, so as to impress the people with the superiority of His
Burmanic Majesty over all monarchs. Even the envoys of the
Emperor of China were subjected to this indignity. The Bri-
tish envoys, Symes (in 1795) and Crawfurd (in 1826), had
also submitted to this treatment. Under instructions from

---

[1] Burney's Journal, Bengal Secret and Political. Vol. 358, pars. 37,
    118.

Calcutta, Burney was now determined to resist by all means this humiliation to himself and to his Government.

The Shoe question, which loomed so large in the relations between the two governments, down to the reign of Mindon, Burney found much more difficult to tackle. During his sojourn in Siam as political agent, the King of that country had been pleased to dispense with this ceremony of removing shoes in the case of Burney, and the latter in his conversation with Burmese officers had thrown out hints, that a like indulgence should be granted to him by the King of Burma. He even prepared an address to the King on this subject, and fondly hoped for a favourable reply.[1]

On 4 May, 1830, Burney left in state with his suite, escort and three elephants in the procession for the Youndaw,[2] where the Woongyees and Atwenwoons had assembled to receive him, in order to arrange the procedure and programme of his presentation to the King. When he came within 20 yards of the building a Tsaredaugyee met him, and politely told him, that he hoped Burney would comply with all the Burmese customs. " I now saw," says Burney, " that this matter regarding the shoes was suddenly brought forward with the Burmese cunning under the idea that I might be taken by surprise and induced to comply, and if I once complied all difficulty as to my presentation to the King would be set at rest." [1] Burney, however, took no notice of the Tsaredaugyee, walked into the Youndaw, and sat down in the midst of the Woongyees and Atwenwoons on the floor. ".......The moment I was seated I pulled off my hat and put it down on the floor near me, and I then took great pains to explain to the Woongyees through Mr. Cotton (the interpreter) that I had not removed my shoes because such a ceremony was considered as degrading by most Englishmen, but that I had uncovered my head and done as much as I was in the habit of doing before the Governor-General, and that I would further take care, whilst I was seated

---

[1] Burney's Journal, Bengal Secret and Political, Vol. 358, par. 22.
[2] The Royal Court House where the Hlutdaw assembled.

near them to place my feet so as to prevent my shoes being offensively brought to their view." [1]

After producing the various letters with which he had been armed by his Government, together with translations into Burmese, Burney expressed to the Woongyees his objection to removing his shoes at his presentation to the King. " Do as the King of Siam had done," pleaded Burney, " allow me to appear before him in the same manner as I would appear before my own sovereign." " The Myawade Woongyee, Maung Za, replied that the Burmese do not care much for such a country where the women wear their lower dress in the same manner as the men, taking it between the legs and fastening it up behind. I answered that it is very true that the Siamese women do wear their clothes in this manner, but that Siam is a great and a very rich country, so much richer than Ava that I believe the Siamese would have paid the instalment due to us many months sooner than what the Burmese had been able to do. This last observation the Burmese Ministers did not appear to relish, but I made it purposely, as I am convinced that I cannot urge and taunt the Court too much to force it to complete the payment of the instalment due to us — a vast deal more than what would be sufficient for us has been long ago collected from the poor inhabitants of the country, but the Queen and the Burmese officers have appropriated much of it for themselves." [2]   Burney delivered to the Atwenwoons his memorial to the King on the Shoe question, and they promised to read it to His Majesty and wait upon his orders.

It is strange that the Woongyees took no objection to Burney's Escort accompanying him to the Youndaw as they did when Crawfurd was in Ava in 1826. Burney's Escort even went up on the steps of the Youndaw. [3] Lane was in the habit of taking off his shoes even on visiting subordinate Burmese officials, and advised Burney to do the same at his presentation to the King; but the British merchants at Rangoon, " since

[1] Burney's Journal, par. 25.
[2] *Ibid.* pars. 27, 28.
[3] *Ibid.* par. 30.

the late war, have taken pride in declining to remove their shoes when visiting the Woongyee of that place."[1]

"My objection," says Burney, "to removing my shoes is formed on the fact that the Burmese require it not as the fulfilment of a mere custom, but as a means of exalting their King and gratifying their own pride and vanity by humiliating and degrading the British character. Besides, the Mussalmans of this place have persuaded the Burmese to carry the etiquette regarding the shoes of Europeans much farther than what it is I believe at any other court in Asia. Even in the streets and highways a European, if he meets with the King or joins his party, is obliged to take off his shoes. Dr. Price[2] always walked and ran barefooted along side of the King's litter, and Mr. Lane on one occasion, when he was invited to see the ceremony of the King ploughing the land,[3] which is annually performed here as well in China and Siam, was obliged to remove his shoes and walk a mile or two over a burning sand until he was quite lame. When Sir Archibald Campbell deputed Lieut. Rawlinson and Montmorency to this place in 1828, he prohibited them to take off their shoes, and they did not, therefore, see the King."[4]

On 19 May, the Woongyees and the Atwenwoons visited Burney at the Residency, and the latter accommodated them with chairs. They tried to persuade him to agree to remove his shoes at his presentation to the King. Burney said that he would do it at a private interview with the King, but not at a public presentation. "I would rather let His Majesty cut me to pieces," he declared, "than consent to go barefoot." "As a

---

[1] *Ibid.* par. 31.
[2] A Christian medical missionary.
[3] "Like every other king, Bagyidaw performed the sacramental ploughing of the fields in June each year, wearing his crown, riding the Lord White Elephant from the palace to the field, and using a gilded harrow drawn by milk-white oxen which were harnessed in gold trappings studded with rubies and diamonds." *Harvey,* History of Burma, p. 295. The underlying idea was the "Blessing of the Fields." See Harvey's note on Lehtunmingala in his Appendix, p. 362.
[4] Burney's Journal, par. 32.

suppliant I begged," he wrote in his Journal, "that my sentiments and objections might be properly made known to His
Majesty."[1]

Burney also told the Ministers that as a soldier he should
be allowed to keep his sword, but since this was not the
practice at Royal courts for fear of assassination of the king,
he waived the matter. He offered to do obeisance as he did
to the Siamese King —" to raise my hands joined to my forehead. I then showed that I had already conceded one point
in their favour in consenting when I visited them to sit with
them upon the floor and not to insist upon chairs, and that I
had now conceded two other points, namely, to leave my sword
at home and to perform the Burmese obeisance, and that what
the Ministers wanted I positively would not yield. Their reply
to this was remarkable, as displaying forcibly the Burmese
character and their notion of concession. They said that because I had conceded 3 points *therefore* I ought to concede the
fourth. I am convinced that if our Government restored the
Tenasserim provinces to the Burmese, they would ask for
Arracan; if we granted that, they would ask for a remission of
the balance due to us, and if we granted even that, they would
ask us to return to them what they have already paid to us.
This is the certain and only effect of concession to them, unaccompanied by conditions in our favour. It is sure to urge
and encourage them to look for further concessions."[2]

The Ministers tried for three hours to persuade Burney
to agree to their unshoeing proposal, but he refused.[3] The
Woondouk Maung Khan Ye, who was the principal Burmese
envoy to Calcutta in 1827, was present at this interview.
Burney appealed to him to tell the Ministers how differently
he had been treated in Calcutta. He was afraid to speak out,
but on being cross-questioned he admitted that he had a better
house to live in than any he had seen in Ava, but that he liked
a wooden house just as well. He complained, however, that

[1] *Ibid.* pars. 51, 52.
[2] *Ibid.* par. 53.
[3] *Ibid.* pars. 54, 55.

4

" he was made to stand up before our great men contrary to Burmese ideas of respect which consists in sitting or squatting down upon the ground......"[1]

On 21 May, the Royal Treasurer and Lanciago called upon Burney in order to persuade him to unshoe, but failed in their mission.   It is doubtful if the Atwenwoons read to the King Burney's memorial on the Shoe question, but the Resident was informed that His Majesty was adamant on this point.   Burney even proposed that he be allowed velvet or linen slippers, but the proposition was summarily rejected by the Ministers.[2]   The Resident now found himself in a difficult position; if the situation were allowed to worsen he might miss the opportunity of conciliating the King and his Court, and the project of establishing the Residency at Ava might prove abortive.   He, therefore, decided to surrender on the Shoe question, on condition that the presentation did not take place on a Kadaw day.

" Could I evade the Kodau day, however," he wrote, " the point respecting the shoes, considering that all my predecessors submitted to this ceremony, and that my instructions are wholly silent upon it, is not one of such importance as to justify my breaking with this Government on account of it.   I have now stood against this measure for a whole month and I should have wished to resist it for 3 months more, did I not see the chance now that the King has got into an angry mood of his being led to do or say something that might force me away from the capital on bad terms, an event against which my instructions especially caution me, and the mischievous and embarrassing consequences of my going away with the public presents and without having an audience of the King, will be obviously much greater than if I depart after seeing the King and remaining here a little while.   I shall, therefore, endeavour to persuade the Court to enter into the discussion of the points, and allow me to go before the King without shoes on any other than the Kodau day......"[3]

[1] *Ibid.* pars. 54, 55.
[2] *Ibid.* pars. 59, 65.
[3] *Ibid.* par. 63.

While this tug-of-war was going on, the Burmese Government was arranging to establish a Burmese Residency at Calcutta. In the bitterness of his mind, Burney advised his government to treat the Burmese Residents also in the manner he was being treated in Ava. He wished, he wrote, that they " may meet with something like the treatment which we are receiving here, and that at any rate they may not be granted the same liberal allowances and establishment which were granted to the Burmese envoys in 1827, who enjoyed greedily all they could from us, saved money, and returned to Ava with means to purchase higher appointments and become more efficient enemies to us. I would strongly recommend that they should be made to wait as long as possible before they are honoured with an audience of the Governor-General, and that they should be told and desired to report the same here that they cannot be heard on any subject of business until the payment of the 4th instalment is completed, and proper measures taken by this Court for putting a stop to the incursions of banditti into our territories in Aracan...." [1]

Within a month of his arrival in Ava, Burney's health began to decline owing to the heat of the weather, privations, and anxiety over the questions under discussion. Besides, all kinds of rumours were being spread and also rehearsed to the King detrimental to the Residency. " Every act and speech of mine," says Burney, " or of any person attached to me that can be distorted or magnified into a charge against me is being written down." [2] One complaint was that Bedford the Residency Surgeon shot a pariah dog which used to come every night under his house. " Another complaint is that I [3] destroyed a jar of ghee which also is true. It was bought for the use of the sepoys who were told by Mr. Lane's servant that the Burmese had mixed hog's lard with the ghee. It certainly looked

---

[1] *Ibid.* par. 64.
[2] *Ibid.* par. 75.
[3] *i.e.* Burney.

very suspicious, and to pacify the sepoys [1] I threw away the suspected ghee." [2]

Under these circumstances, and feeling that there was no hope of escaping the Kadaw day, Burney threatened to leave Ava on the score of ill-health. The threat, he thought might induce the Burmese Government to spare him the Kadaw humiliation. On 27 May, therefore, he wrote the following letter to the Woongyees:—" Major Burney came to Ava in the hope, that as he had cemented friendship between the Siamese and English nations, he might do the same between the Burmese and English. Major Burney addressed a respectful letter to the King and has never received an answer from the Atwenwoons. Major Burney asked the Woongyees to come and see him again, they have refused. Major Burney can therefore be no longer of any use in Ava, and as he is very unwell he begs the Woongyees will ask the King to grant him suitable boats to convey himself and his family [3] and people back to Rangoon." [4]

The Ministers sent neither a reply nor boats; but on 29 May, two Burmese doctors deputed by them examined Burney, and said that his liver had got inflamed, and recommended him to eat citrons and coarse sugar. [5] Burney now sent Lane to remonstrate with the Ministers, and agreed to appear before the King without shoes on any other than a Kadaw day. [5] The Ministers would have, without much difficulty, agreed to Burney's proposal, but they were helpless on account of the King's attitude. Soon, however, an opportunity arrived which enabled them to get out of the deadlock. On 2 June, two Woongyees and two Atwenwoons visited Burney, and the latter definitely gave them to understand that under no circumstances would he appear before the King on a Kadaw

---

[1] They were Indian Mahomedans.
[2] *Ibid.* par. 75.
[3] There is evidence here and in a few more places that Burney had the company of his wife in Ava; but he seldom mentions her, and only once speaks of a child that died at the capital.
[4] Burney's Journal, par. 73: Bengal Secret and Political, Vol. 358.
[5] *Ibid.* pars. 70 and 78.

day. At first they were reticent, but when Burney said that his ill-health would not permit him of a prolonged ceremony as on a Kadaw day, they jumped at the idea, and it was finally arranged, the King agreeing thereto, that the Resident be presented on 17 June, not being a Kadaw day.

On the eve of the presentation, two Woongyees and two Atwenwoons had a conference with Burney at the Residency in order to decide the ceremonial of the presentation. " The Atwenwoon Maung Yeet had the insolence to propose to me to remove my shoes at the gate of the palace enclosure, and to take off my hat and make an obeisance upon first seeing the palace spire. I rose up and told him that I certainly would not remove my shoes in any other place than at the steps leading up to the palace where Mr. Crawfurd removed his, and that as the English did not pay compliments to wood and stone, I would not take off my hat nor make any salutation until I actually saw His Majesty. Maung Yeet said that what he had proposed was the custom......I then declared my resolution of not shutting my umbrella nor dismounting from the conveyance, in which I might be carried, in any other place than that where it is customary." [1] Writing to his Government on the Shoe question, Burney said, " I resisted as long as possible consenting to remove my shoes......I succeeded in persuading the Ministers to relieve me from this act of degradation, but the King was immovable on the subject......I am not sorry for having made a stand against it, as my acquiescence at last has given me the credit here of having undertaken a very heavy responsibility in order to conciliate the King......Indeed, I am convinced that I could not otherwise have evaded being presented to the King on the " Kodau " or ask pardon day upon which occasions, I find that this arrogant Court has always contrived to introduce the Governor-General's representatives among the suppliants." [2]

[1] *Ibid.* par. 114.
[2] Bengal Secret and Political, Vol. 358, Burney's Letter, Ava, 24 June, 1830.

As to the ceremonial of the presentation, it was proposed by the Ministers and accepted by Burney, that the British Resident be treated on the same footing as a Burmese Woongyee. Burney was fully alive to this high rank accorded to him, and made full use of his position with a marked degree of success. It was also mutually agreed to use the following forms in future correspondence:—The King was to be styled "His Most Glorious and Excellent Majesty who rules over all the white umbrella wearers and eastern countries within the empire of Thuna-paranta[1] and Tomba-dewa,[2] the King of the Rising Sun, Lord of the Celestial Elephant, and proprietor of all the White Elephants, Lord of Life, the Great and Just Chief." The Woongyees were "those who bear his[3] two golden feet continually upon their heads like the germ of the lotus and direct all important affairs of state, their Excellencies the Ministers of State and Generals." Burney was to be called "The Woongyee of the English "Men"[4] who rules over India (Bengal) and the great countries to the westward (i.e. the rest of India)."[5]

The presentation to the King took place on 17 June. At an early hour of the morning the Royal Treasurer called at Burney's house and took away the presents for Their Majesties on 24 ponies, a few elephants and 150 coolies. He asked Burney to make as much of the presents as possible, and divide them out among all the trays. The following is Burney's own interesting account of the presentation:—

> "At 9 o'clock I left the house in my Tonjon[6] carrying in my hand the Governor-General's letter preceded by my escort of Sepoys and a large picture of His Majesty the King of England,[7] one of the public presents which two of my servants bore in the most respectful manner. I was accompanied by Lieut. G. Burney, and Mr. Lane, Mr. Sarkies,[8] Mr. Bedford, my interpreter Mr.

---

[1] Sona-paranta = The Golden Land.
[2] Tamba-depa = The Red Land. It signifies Upper Burma east of the Irrawaddy.
[3] the Burmese King.
[4] Ruler, i.e. the Governor-General; ၆င်း။
[5] Burney's Journal, Bengal Secret and Political, Vol. 358, par. 116.
[6] A sedan chair slung on a pole and carried by four bearers.
[7] George IV (1820-1830).
[8] An Armenian merchant of Rangoon.

Cotton, and clerk Mr. Edward and overseer Richardson upon the 6 elephants besides the Tsare-dau-gyee, Treasurer and other Burmese officers upon 5 or 6 other elephants...... Lieut. G. Burney went with a pair of stockings over his shoes and a second pair of shoes,[1] but as I had engaged to remove mine I thought it best to do the thing with a good grace, and I was unwilling to subject myself to any disagreeable discussion in the event of the Burmese officers discovering shoes under my stockings. After ascending the steps we walked a long verandah and then entered the audience hall immediately in front of the King's throne over which stands the lofty spire or Pya Sath. The King had not yet taken his seat, but all who were to attend this day had arrived and taken their seats in front and on each side of a space which was left vacant for us. Carpets were here spread for us to sit upon, and six paces in front was a golden salver upon which I respectfully placed the Governor-General's letter and then walked back and sat down, still retaining my hat upon my head. The guns[2] were taken into another part of the palace enclosure, but all the other presents were placed before and on each side of me. When the Prince of Tharawadi and Menzagyee were pointed out to me, I took off my hat and made a bow to each. They both only smiled — no Burmese ever returns a salute. Mr. Lanciago was seated near me and dressed very ridiculously, wearing with a European hat covered with tinsel a Burmese gown and chain. All the princes and officers were dressed in their civil robes of ceremony consisting of a crimson or scarlet robe — something like our dressing gown with a large border of tinsel gold lace and a cap of the same coloured velvet, fashioned something like a bishop's mitre with the front part turned back a little having tinsel ornaments around it...... The Prince of Tharawadi was dressed in Kin Khaub[3] and Muslin like a Siamese Chief and next to the King looked by far the best dressed man in the Hall of Audience.

"I own I was much disappointed at the appearance of the Palace. The gilding is very paltry, indeed all the gold used by the Burmese in gilding is so much alloyed that it seldom looks well for more than a year or two. Probably the gilding looked better when Mr. Crawfurd was here, for at present the palace certainly does not correspond with his favourable representation. The pillars were partly gilt and partly covered with red paint.

---

[1] This second pair only was removed at the doorway by Geo. Burney.
[2] These were a part of the presents from the Government of India.
[3] A heavy silk with gold or silver thread-work.

> The floor of the verandah was a rough and coarse terrace like the steps; the floor of the hall was a little better, the chunam [1] having the appearance of having been polished, but it was uneven and irregular............
>
> "About 6 minutes after we had been seated we heard a loud rumbling noise like distant thunder, when folding doors at the back of the throne were thrown open and the King made his appearance. All the Burmese present joined their hands and lowered their heads to the floor; we simply removed our hats. The King advanced and descending one or two steps took his seat upon the throne which was about 6 feet higher than the floor of the hall of audience and without any canopy. He wore a crown resembling a Burmese war helmet richly set with jewels and a gown of the same pattern as his officers, only a gold cloth and apparently studded with jewels." [2]

The proceedings opened with several Brahmins on each side of the King chanting a prayer and a song, a part of which meant that His Majesty had always been victorious and had conquered every country. When the chanting was over, the two Atwenwoons Maung Yeet and Maung Ba Youk, who were sitting near Burney, advanced bending as low as possible towards the foot of the throne.[3] "His Majesty moved his lips but we could not hear what he said. Maung Yeet cried out that His Majesty wished to know how many months it was since I had left Bengal? I answered, six months........Maung Yeet then asked, How was the Governor-General when I left Bengal?......the last question asked was whether the wind and rain had been good, that is, whether the seasons had been favourable.

"A set of betel apparatus with a goglet and gold cup......were now placed before myself and my assistant, and the Nakhandau [4] near me then read with a loud voice the Bur-

---

[1] Lime.
[2] Burney's Journal, pars. 121-126, Bengal Secret and Political, Vol. 358.
  The Kone-baung-set Mahayazawin makes mention of Burney's presentation to the King, in Book 2, pp. 477 and 486.
[3] Burney's Journal.
[4] *Lit.* "Royal ear-listener," *i.e.* King's Listener. He was immediately under the Atwenwoons.

mese translation of the Governor-General's letter [1]; we all
watched him attentively and were pleased to see that he read
the whole of the document exactly as I had given it to the
Ministers. He next read out a list of the presents which I had
brought." [2] The King then retired, the Courtiers bowed their
heads, and Burney returned to his house. "The whole time
we saw the King," says Burney, "could not have occupied more
than 10 or 12 minutes." [2] Burney had suggested to the Minis-

---

[1] "From the Governor-General to the King of Ava. Begins with
official address and titles of the Governor-General.
"....This is the first time that the Governor-General, since
his arrival in India, has had occasion to address the King of
Ava. It is the Governor-General's sincere wish to maintain
uninterrupted, and to cement still closer the relations of peace
and amity which have been established between the King of
Ava and the British Government. Both nations, the English
and the Burmese, will derive profit from cultivating peace and
friendship and prosecuting with each other a free intercourse
and extensive commerce. It is the Governor-General's earnest
resolution to maintain most strictly every stipulation com-
prised in the Treaty which has been made between the King
of Ava and the British Government, and as by the 7th Article
of that treaty it is agreed that accredited ministers shall be
fixed at the Durbar of each state in order to cultivate and
improve the relations of amity and peace established between
the two governments, the Governor-General has determined
upon deputing a British officer as his representative to reside
at the Burmese Court near the person of the King of Ava,
and the Governor-General invites the King of Ava to send a
suitable Burmese officer to Calcutta to reside near the
Governor-General. For the situation of the Governor-General's
agent and British Resident at the Burmese Court, the
Governor-General has selected Major Henry Burney an officer
who visited the King of Siam, established friendship between
the Siamese and the English, and succeeded in releasing
several hundreds of Burmese from the yoke of slavery in
Siam. He has been many years employed in Eastern countries,
he is well acquainted with the language and character and
customs of the Burmese, Siamese and Malayan nations, and
he last served as administrator of the provinces of Tavoy and
Mergui. This official will assure the King of Ava of the
friendly disposition of the British Government, and he will
soon become the instrument of establishing between the
English and the Burmese nations a good understanding which
no tales of evil disposed men or other cause will ever again
be able to disturb or impair...... The Governor-General
requests the King of Ava and the Royal Queen will accept of
certain gifts which Major Burney will present to their
Majesties as tokens of the Governor-General's friendship."
(Bengal Secret and Political, Vol. 357).
[2] Burney's Journal, par. 123, Bengal Secret and Political, Vol. 358.

ters that the King should put some sensible questions and not
" absurd ones " about the seasons, etc., but there was no departure from the usual procedure during the ceremony. Giving
his impressions of the function, Burney says, " the King was
as fixed and unmovable as a statue excepting when he took
some betel. He never once smiled nor looked interested as the
King of Siam did at his audience. He was wearing, I was
told, the true Burmese countenance of official dignity.

"But the whole ceremony was far inferior and less imposing than that at Bangkok.[1] Although the audience chamber
there has not so much gilding as the one here, yet the throne
is far more rich and tasteful, and the dresses of the officers
being of Kinkhaub and gold and silver flowered muslins, are
much more splendid and showy. The King himself too there
appeared much more intelligent and more richly habited. Here
the whole scene was naked and exposed to view at once;
whereas at Bangkok the light near the throne and the entrance
into the audience hall were so managed that upon admission
it was sometime before the eyes could distinguish anything but
a dazzling flood of gold and jewels."[2]

Now that Burney had been presented to the King, and so
officially recognized as British Resident in Burma, he was at
liberty to go about the capital. He made it a point to get into
touch with men of importance, and by developing friendship
with them make his residence in Ava a success. On 24 June,
he visited the Heir-apparent, Tsakyamen, who, on seeing Burney felt so nervous that he was unable to speak for 15 minutes.
This prince had not yet been recognized as Ain-she-men[3] or
Lord of the Eastern House, because of the adverse influence
of his stepmother the Queen.[4] Burney made the following
suggestion to his Government concerning this timid Prince:—
" In the event of the British Government ever desiring to
exercise a greater influence at this Court, an opportunity will

[1] Burney was in Siam in 1825 as Political Agent.
[2] Burney's Journal, pars. 125, 126.
[3] Heir-apparent.
[4] Bengal Secret and Political, Vol. 358, Burney's Journal par. 141.

be afforded at the death of the present King, when this Tsakyamen may require our support to enable him to succeed to his right to the throne."[1]   No doubt, Burney thought that such a step would greatly facilitate the smoothness of the relations between the two countries.

On 26 June, Burney paid a visit to the Prince of Tharrawaddy the only full brother of the King.   At the entrance of the hall of audience he removed his shoes and was given a seat within on a carpet.   Here he was made to wait unnecessarily, so that he protested, and declared, " that an Englishman considers it very rude and impolite to be made to wait on an occasion when he visits even a man of the highest rank, at an hour appointed by that man himself; that in my case such a delay was particularly offensive...."[2]   The Prince then appeared and " took his seat on a couch, putting his feet up...... an affable good humoured character with a pleasing and rather intelligent smile. ......He expressed his hopes that I would cement a permanent good understanding between our two countries.   I begged of him to allow me to come and visit him whenever I had any business to transact.   He said he would be always happy to see me as a friend, but that when I had any business to transact I had better communicate with the Woongyees...."[3]

The next person visited was the widow of the late Ainshe-men,[4] an old lady highly respected by the King.   Just as Burney was going to unshoe at the steps of her house, a petty Burmese officer very disrespectfully motioned to him to remove

---

[1] *Ibid.* par. 142.
[2] *Ibid.* par. 147.   It seems it was a Burmese custom to make visitors wait, the time of waiting being determined by the relative positions of the host and the visitor.   Burney says in his Journal, " On the day we visited the Tsakyamen I overheard one of the officers, after we had been made to wait for nearly half an hour, say to another " tau byee," it is suitable or sufficient, meaning that I had been made to wait long enough and that it was then suitable to the Prince's dignity to make his appearance......." (Bengal Secret and Political, Vol. 358, par. 148.)
[3] Bengal Secret and Political Consultations Vol. 358, Burney's Journal, par. 148.
[4] Bodawpaya's eldest son and Bagyidaw's father; he died in 1808.

his socks as well. It had previously been agreed with the Ministers, that the two officers, who had been appointed as Burney's guides, should address him on matters of ceremony, so Burney thrust away the petty officer, entered the hall of audience, and declined to take his seat until the Princess appeared. " This proceeding," says Burney, " effectually put a stop to all further manifestation of Burmese dignity. The gilded shutters of the window looking into her apartment were immediately thrown open and she appeared in view. She asked kindly after my health."[1]   Burney complained to her of the conduct of the petty Burmese officer, and requested her to punish him. He was immediately ordered to be put on the stocks. Burney next complained that he was unable to see her face well enough from where he was, so she asked him to come close to her. This kindly old lady used to send food and clothes to the Europeans and Armenians confined in the Ava jail during the War (1824-1826).

On 25 June, Menthagyee the Queens' brother was visited. His house and attendants bespoke much greater wealth and importance than even those of Tsakyamen or the Prince of Tharrawaddy. His appearance, manners, and conversation satisfied Burney of his reputed superiority over the Prince of Tharrawaddy as well as over most Burmese officers at the capital. Burney asked him also " to let me visit him whenever I had any business to transact, and explained to him that as the ministers here possess no real power and are very timid, much advantage and time would be gained if he would let the ministers and myself always assemble at his house and conduct our negotiations in his presence in the same manner as in Siam where the King's brother presided over my discussions with the 6 ministers or Woongyees. Menzagyee laughed and said that I had already got through a great deal of business with the Burmese Ministers and that he would be afraid to take a direct part in my negotiations, because if he were to say or do any-

---

[1] Bengal Secret and Political Consultations Vol. 358, **The Journal,** par. 149.

thing wrong it could not afterwards be remedied so easily as in the case of any error committed by one of the ministers." [1]

Thus both the Prince of Tharrawaddy and the Mentha-gyee, who were the most important men next to the King, were not willing to shoulder the responsibility of holding official conversation with the British Resident. They feared the King's wrath, in case they failed in anything in which His Majesty was interested; and he was particularly interested in the recovery of the Kubo Valley.

At the desire of the King, Burney was invited on 11 July, to visit his monastery, where His Majesty himself was in the habit of removing his shoes. Burney, however, had no objection to removing his shoes out of respect for religion. " I am sorry to say," he remarks, " whether it is owing to all the missionaries whom the Burmese have seen being either Catholics, Anabaptists or Americans, or whether it is owing to the conduct of some of our troops during the war, the people of this country consider the English as devoid of all religious sentiment." [2] At the monastery, the Nyoung-dau Sayadaugyee received Burney seated in great state, surrounded by about 20 pongyees, and very civilly and politely encouraged him to talk on religious matters.

On 26 July, the King and Royal Family passed by Burney's house in war boats to the Royal Elephant Palace, to see some new elephants that had been captured. A message was sent to Burney, that while the King passed by no one should be seen standing or looking out of the windows above Their Majesties' heads; Burney was at the same time invited to the Elephant Palace. He gives the following account of his fresh experience:—" His Majesty conversed very affably and good humouredly with me, put questions about Siam and the White Elephant there, about my knowledge of the Burmese language and other matters of no public interest." As to the Queen, " I was rather agreeably disappointed with her appearance and manners. I had fancied her to be rather a coarse, low bred looking woman, whereas she really is the best looking Burmese

[1] *Ibid.* par. 150.
[2] *Ibid.* par. 159.

woman of 48 years of age and showed much intelligence......
although according to Burmese etiquette I never spoke, but
when the King asked a question and encouraged me to make an
observation I lost no opportunity of paying compliments and
making civil speeches, and I own I strove very hard to make a
favourable impression on both the King and Queen." [1] Burney
was later informed by officers and others that Their Majesties
were highly pleased with his conduct that day.

On 7 August, Burney was again with the Royal family at
a Rama and Hanuman play.[2] The King presented two valuable ruby rings to him and to his assistant; this was looked upon
by the people as a mark of great favour. " We really deserved
some return of civility for we sat for upwards of four hours
after the Burmese custom with our feet under us until we
nearly lost the use of our legs. Seeing that all my exertions
in this country will be of no avail until I succeed in conciliating the King, and believing that I was deputed here not to pick
a quarrel or to irritate, but to soothe and allay the sore and
angry feelings left by the late war upon the minds of this Court,
I have for some time past resolved upon submitting to many
disagreeable ceremonials and making many sacrifices in order
to win if possible the good will and confidence of the monarch;
but to do him justice his whole deportment and manner were
very pleasing. His affability and condescension were princely.
We heard a song in high flown praise of His Majesty......
composed by Maung Za who appeared, however, to have stolen
the air from some hymn which he must have heard the Catholics
chant." [3] Burney certainly did succeed in making an impression upon the Queen. He praised her personal appearance before some officers who reported it to the Queen. This flattering intelligence so pleased Her Majesty, that a couple of days
after when Burney saw her at a festival and salaamed her, she
honoured him " with a very gracious smile." [4]

[1] *Ibid.* par. 171.
[2] The Ramleela play of the Ramayana, the great Indian Epic.
[3] Bengal Secret and Political Consultations Vol. 358, Burney's
    Journal, pars. 197, 198.
[4] *Ibid.* par. 204.

On 29 July, Burney obtained permission to visit the Ministers in their houses without having to remove his shoes.   He
accordingly visited the Kyee-Woongyee who received him most
kindly and cordially, accommodated him and his party with
chairs, and introduced him to the ladies of his house.   The Kyi-
Woon Atwenwoon also received Burney in the same manner,
and introduced him to the ladies of his house.   In both these
houses Burney voluntarily removed his shoes before entering
the female apartments.   This act of his, says Burney, " is in-
comprehensible to a Burman who has no idea of our treating
the female sex with superior respect.   I am told, however, that
the Queen will be much pleased to hear this." [1]

Next the Myawadi Woongyee Maung Za, the Padein
Woongyee, and the Atwenwoon Maung Yeet were visited.
They also received Burney most cordially and introduced him
to the ladies of the house. [2]   It seems the Ministers had mutually agreed to receive Burney in the manner here described.
Burney speaks at length of one officer that he visited by name
Shwe Loo, his title being Mengyee-maha-thengyan-kheboung
Myo Za.   "......his particular office at the Court is styled
Myauk-wen-dau-hmau, literally the Governor or Commandant
of the Northern Royal Entrance......no person can approach
the King from on that side without this officer's knowledge or
permission.   ......Maung Shwe Loo attended a good deal
upon the King during his infancy and youth, and he is now
described as holding a higher place in the estimation of the
monarch than perhaps any other man in the country.   At
all events he fears responsibility less than any other courtier; at a time when every other officer here dreaded to say
a word in favour of Dr. Judson, this man did not hesitate
to receive him and some of the other prisoners into his
own house and to stand security for their good conduct." [3]
Burney thanked Shwe Loo in the name of his Government for

[1] *Ibid.* pars. 174, 175.
[2] *Ibid.* pars. 178, 181.   Maung Za's wife was a grand-daughter of
    the last King of Pegu. *Ibid.* par. 187.
    Ibid. par. 182.

his noble and benevolent conduct towards the foreign prisoners.
" We were amazed to see hanging *punkhas* [1] in his house, the
only place where we have yet seen them.   He resided for some
time at Rangoon and this accounts for his superior intelligence,
for we have found all those Burmese officers who have mixed
with Europeans at Rangoon most distinguished by good sense,
and freedom from pride and prejudice.   Mr. Sarkies calls Rangoon the Burmese University." [2]

The Ministers objected to Burney visiting the principal
wife of the Rangoon Woongyee, since her husband was absent
in Rangoon.   But her husband had requested Burney to call
upon her, and she herself had sent fruit and civil messages to
Burney.   When she heard of the attitude of the Ministers, she
sent a spirited communication to them, expressing her desire to
see Burney; the Ministers gave in, and on 2 August, Burney
visited her.   She entertained him sumptuously.   He found her
house well fitted with European furniture. [3]

Burney thus succeeded in making much headway, by
coming into touch with the Royal Family as well as with the
great officers of state.   He sums up his achievement in his
letter to his Government in the following words:— " ....Since
I last wrote I have had two interviews with the King both of
which were of a satisfactory nature, as His Majesty and the
Queen who was with him expressed themselves pleased with
me, a circumstance more calculated to improve my situation
here and increase my means of usefulness to my own Government than anything which I could devise.

" It will be seen that I have paid visits in the same manner
as Mr. Crawfurd did to the Tsakyamen, Prince of Tharawadi,
Ain-she-men's widow, and Menzagyee; but in addition to these
I have been allowed to visit the Kyee-Woongyee, Myawadi, and
Padein Woongyees, and Tshan and Kyee woon Atwenwoons at
their own houses and without removing my shoes.   I have now

[1] Fans.
[2] Bengal Secret and Political Consultations Vol. 358, Burney's Journal, pars. 183, 184.
[3] *Ibid.* pars. 185, 186.

free access to the houses of all these principal ministers, and I consider the establishing of this easy and familiar communication with the different ministers as the most important point which I have gained. No foreign envoy appears ever before to have been allowed to visit the ministers in the manner in which I am now permitted to do, and I think much advantage to the public service has already been derived from such an arrangement......" [1]

One notable character at this time residing in Ava must not be omitted. This was Mekkhara-men or the Prince of Mekkhara, an uncle of the King. Judson speaks of him as being a great metaphysician, theologian, and meddler in ecclesiastical affairs. Burney was particularly drawn towards this Prince, and his account of him may be reproduced here:—

"He has been taught to read and understand English by the late Mr. Rogers [2] and he evinces a very laudable desire of becoming acquainted with European science and literature. He obtained from Calcutta through Mr. Lane a copy of Rees's Cyclopaedia, and that gentleman assures me that this Prince has translated parts of some of the most scientific articles in that work. During the last three years Mr. Lane and he have been preparing an English and Burmese Dictionary which is just now nearly completed.

"We found the Prince a very intelligent and inquisitive character. I was with him for upwards of an hour, and he put questions to me as fast as I could answer them, and then observed that he had not asked me one-hundredth part of the questions which he wished to ask. He questioned as to the latitude and longitude of London, Calcutta, Ava, and Bangkok, the cause of the polarity of the needle, the reappearance of the last comet, the properties of the Barometer and Thermometer both of which instruments were hanging in his room, and the nature of Algebra which science, he said, he much wished to learn. Indeed he surprised me with the ex-

[1] *Ibid*. Letter dated Ava, 8 August, 1830.
[2] A British merchant, mentioned by *Gouger* in his, The Prisoner in Burmah.

tent of his knowledge and he seemed to comprehend and admit the correctness of our system of the Universe. We saw in a handsome bookcase with glazed folding doors his library books consisting of Rees's Cyclopaedia, Johnson's Dictionary, the Holy Bible with Dr. Judson's translations, all of which, he said he had read very carefully. On the whole he is certainly the most extraordinary man we have seen in this country. He sent lately to Mr. Lane translations from Rees's Cyclopaedia of two very scientific articles, one regarding the calculations of eclipses and the other regarding the formation of hailstones." [1] This versatile Burmese genius also learnt Logarithms from Lane, and in 1831, when Lieut. Blundell arrived in Ava as Assistant to Burney, he offered to teach him Algebra; but the Prince said that it would be against the established custom of the Burmese Government for any official to call on him without the permission of the Hlutdaw, or be intimate with him: if any such intimacy were to develop he might be charged of being in league with the English. " I never met with an individual who displayed a greater thirst after knowledge than what this Prince does; and it is much to be regretted that he cannot visit Bengal." [2]

Burney was anxious that the Burmese Government should make suitable replies to the letters that he had brought from the Governor-General to the King, and from the Chief Secretary to the Woongyees. He succeeded in obtaining a promise from the Ministers that a suitable reply would be made to the Governor-General in the name of the King, and sent by the hand of the Burmese Resident to be deputed to Calcutta. [3] The Ministers, however, immediately replied to the Chief Secretary's letter. The following is a translation of their letter, dated Ava, 25 June, 1830: —

" The Most Glorious and Excellent Majesty who rules over all the umbrella wearers and eastern countries within the Empire

[1] Bengal Secret and Political Consultations, Vol. 358, Burney's Journal, pars. 208-210.
[2] *Ibid*. Vol. 362, par. 828.
[3] *Ibid*. Vol. 358, Burney's Letter, dated Ava, 24 June, 1830.

of Thunaparanta[1] and Tambadewa,[2] Lord of the Celestial Elephant, and Proprietor of all the White Elephants, Lord of Life, the Great and Just Chief; those who bear his two Golden Feet continually upon their heads like the germ of the Lotus and direct all important affairs of state, their Excellencies the Ministers of State and Generals inform George Swinton the Minister of the English Chief who rules over India and all the great countries to the westward. Major Burney sent with presents by the English Chief....as his representative and Resident Minister in order to improve and cement peace and friendship pursuant to the 7th Article of the Treaty, having arrived with a letter from the English Chief, and another from the English Minister, he was met and received, and a proper brick built house granted for his accomodation.

"In the letter it is stated that the Resident Major Burney will use his endeavours agreeably to the 7th Article of the Treaty, that no malignant nor evil disposed persons shall do mischief, and that friendship shall be cemented and perpetuated, and that he shall here write down and forward to the English Chief whatever His Majesty the King may say. It is further observed that nothing is required from the Burmese Empire and that the Resident Major Burney will soon convince the Burmese Chiefs and remove all doubts as to his having been deputed to promote friendship with truth and sincerity.

"To increase and cement friendship also the Woongyees and Atwenwoons assembled and consulted. But when the presents were to be conveyed within the palace the Resident Major Burney proposed to enter according to English customs. There are customs peculiar to the Burmese country as well as customs peculiar to the English country, and it is written in the Sacred Books that respect should be shown to those of every nation. The Resident is mentioned in the Letter from the English Chief as having been an Envoy to the Siamese, Malay and other eastern countries for many years and as being acquainted with the customs and manners of those nations, as having administered the provinces of Tavoy and Mergui, and as being a man of talents and abilities. When it was mentioned to him that he ought not to break customs recorded in the Sacred Books he said that he did not wish to do so of his own accord, but that the English Chiefs desired him to enter (the palace) according to the customs of the English, and that a letter should be written to settle the matter and

[1] Sonapranta: The Golden Land.
[2] Tamba-depa: *Lit.* Red Land. It signifies Upper Burma east of the Irrawaddy; old Pagan is also known by this name.

save him from blame. The two countries are in amity and it is not right that the matter should remain unsettled. We will write an answer to the English Chief's Woongyee who is a man cf talents and ability and is versed in all manners and customs of both the Burmese and English countries.

" When this point was discussed and settled according to the customs of the Burmese country, elephants and horses were furnished, and accompanied by several Burmese officers Major Burney and the Letter and Gifts were conveyed to the Golden Palace and presented on the 12th day of the waning moon, Nayon in the year 1192 (17th June, 1830).

".......Agreeable to the 7th Article of the Treaty the King of the Rising Sun will appoint persons of rank and depute them to Bengal and they will take an answer from him to the letter which has been received from the English Chief.

" With respect to the money, of the ten parts nine and more have been paid. There remains only one part and a little more which the Resident Major Burney requires may be paid up in the year 1192 between the months of Watsho [1] and the month of Thaden-Kywat [2] (October 1830) within 4 months. If we were obliged to liquidate the amount in the month of Thaden-Kywat (October) it would not be the season to tax the poor inhabitants. We shall be enabled to get the money by the month of Tabodwe [3] ...." [4]

Between June 1830 and April 1832, Burney was continuously in Ava discharging his duties as Resident. On 9 April, 1832, he departed for Rangoon in order to recoup his health. During these two years he carried on negotiations with the Burmese Government on the questions of the Kubo Valley, the payment of the Indemnity, the Arakan and Moulmein frontiers, the retrocession of Tenasserim, and the protection of British subjects and their trade in Burma. Besides, he took every opportunity to study the true state of affairs in Burma, such as the temper of the King and his Ministers, the military strength of the monarch, the possibilities of trade, and general social conditions in the land. Discussions on the various questions were rendered easy, because before

[1] Wazo: June-July.
[2] Thadingyut: September-October.
[3] January-February.
[4] Bengal Secret and Political Consultations Vol. 358, No. 6.

the end of 1830, Burney was able to obtain two unique privileges at the Burmese Court: "....the King has consented to
my request to be allowed to attend his morning levees in
company with the Ministers of his Court once in 8 or 10
days; and the other (privilege) is, I may always, when I have
some business to transact, attend the Hlutdaw, and request
the presence there of five Woongyees and two Atwenwoons
Maung Yeet and Maung Ba Youk to discuss the matter with
me. I have of late repeatedly attended the Hlutdaw, and succeeded in discussing and settling several points in communication with these seven ministers, being seated in the midst
of them and on an equality with themselves." [1]

The problem of Manipur and the Kubo Valley has
already been stated; also that in January 1830 the British
Commissioners, Grant and Pemberton, under the direction
of the Supreme Government and in the presence of Burmese
Commissioners, had declared the Ningtee (*i.e.* the Chindwin)
to be the eastern boundary of Manipur. Thus the Valley
passed to Gumbheer Singh. The Burmese Commissioners
protested against this decision, and when the news reached
Ava the King was highly enraged. He issued orders to use
armed force and remove the flags and landmarks placed by
British officers to indicate the new boundary; the Woongyees,
however, ultimtely succeeded in persuading him to cancel his
orders.[2] It was thought advisable to wait for the arrival of
the British Resident so that representations might be made
through him. There was, however, much tension between
the frontier authorities of Manipur and Burma on the Chindwin, and a few minor clashes also took place. On Burney's
arrival in Ava, he found the King especially sore on the
Kubo question; not that the Valley was desirable from the
revenue point of view,[3] but because it was very humiliating
to lose it to Gumbheer Singh and to Manipur. In one respect, however, Kubo was certainly a useful possession, be-

---

[1] *Ibid.* Burney's Letter, dated Ava, 9 October, 1830.
[2] *Ibid.* Burney's Journal, par. 34.
[3] The Revenue of Kubo was only 100 ticals per anum. (*Ibid.* par.
137).

cause "they (the Casseyars) are considered valuable subjects, being much more industrious and more expert in handi-
craft trades than the Burmese." [1]   Burney bears testimony
to the presence of a large number of Manipuris in Ava and
neighbourhood, taken prisoners both before 1824 as well as
during the war.[1]

On 3 June, 1830, the Ministers informed Burney of serious developments having taken place on the Manipur frontier: that Grant and Pemberton had notified Burmese subjects
residing in the Kubo Valley to the west of the Ningtee to
gather their crops and cross over to the eastern side, and
that if they did not do so by 25 June, 1830, they would be
considered and treated as subjects of the Raja of Manipur.
The Ministers desired Burney to prevent a rupture, because,
they said, that if Grant and Pemberton acted up to their
notification, before the King could appeal to the Governor-
General, a quarrel would certainly take place.[2]   Burney threw
oil over the troubled waters, by requesting Calcutta to send
either Grant or Pemberton to Ava to discuss the Kubo question afresh; at the same time he wrote to these two officers
apprising them of the situation, and advised them not to do
anything that might produce a collision till the King had
appealed to the Governor-General.   Burney was by no means
convinced of the Burmese claims to Kubo, but his object
was, if possible, to settle the problem amicably.   Writing to
his Government he said, "......this Court will never be able
to give us anything more than bare assertions in support of
its claims to the disputed territory; yet I thought it advisable
to give the King the opportunity of adopting the civilized
course, which he proposes, of an appeal to the Governor-
General, and therefore did not hesitate to accede to the earnest request of the Ministers to write to Captains Grant and
Pemberton, not to commit any acts which might lead to collision, until such time as the Governor-General-in-Council could

---

[1] *Ibid.* Burney's Letter, dated Ava, 9 October, 1830.
[2] *Ibid.* Burney's Journal, pars. 85-95.

be put in possession of the report of my proceedings here....." [1]

Burney was at the same time so convinced of the futility of ever being able to come to a just agreement with the King, that he suggested to his Government two alternatives in the settlement of the problem. " My own conviction," he wrote, " is, that no friendly means or argument which we can use will ever be successful in persuading the King of Ava to acknowledge Gumbheer Singh's right to the valley of Kubo. My opinion also as to the utter inefficiency of the measure of settling boundaries with such a state as Ava by means of Commissioners to be deputed by each state, has long ago been submitted to Government, and I am satisfied that the only chance of establishing the line of frontier select- ed by us, is for our Government to support with a high-hand- ed and decided tone Gumbheer Singh's claim to the whole territory in dispute." [1'] The second alternative proposed by him is rather curious: " the next best line of proceeding would certainly be, to divide the disputed tract equally between Gumbheer Singh and the Burmese. Such a measure would be in very exact accordance with the Burmese ideas and with their practice of administering justice." [2]

The Supreme Government directed Pemberton to pro- ceed to Ava and answer the objections of the Burmese Govern- ment to the new Manipuri boundary. He arrived in Ava on 12 August with 70 followers. [3] On 15 August, Burney intro-

1 *Ibid.* Burney's Letter, dated 24 June, 1830.
2 *Ibid.* Burney's Journal, par. 34. " In Tavoy almost every dispute in regard to the possession of lands, which was referred to the provincial officers, they used to decide by recommending the ground to be divided equally between the litigants, and I could never convince those officers of the absurdity of such a decision, and show them that the land either belonged or did not belong to one of the parties. Mr. Lane informs me that the same rule of proceeding is very common here. A short time ago he had a suit against a man who owed him a sum of Rs. 12,000; after some investigation the Prince of Tharawadi proposed that the dispute should be decided by the Burmese paying to Mr. Lane one half of his claim." *Ibid.* Burney's Journal, par. 134.
3 *Ibid.* pars. 206, 211, 212.

duced him to the King. " His Majesty upon our first entrance appeared rather stiff, and disposed apparently to show a little ill-humour towards Capt. Pemberton, but this expression of countenance was soon altered for a more agreeable one, when a very handsome double barrelled fowling piece was laid before him as a present from Capt. Pemberton...... After a little while the King called out to a man to approach a spot where we were seated and pointed him out to me as the young Prince of Siam who was brought away by the Burmese when they took the old capital of that country...." [1] The King also exhibited a prince of Assam and a prince of Arakan specially to produce an impression upon Pemberton.[2] Burney's sepoys performed some wrestling feats, after which one of the King's musicians possessing comic powers mimicked these different feats in such amusing silence and serenity that the King was convulsed with laughter. " I was happy to see," says Burney, " that he and all his Court were in the highest good humour with us...." [3]

[1] *Ibid.* pars. 214, 215. Burney gives the following account of this Prince:—" He told me that his name is Phra-ong-choo-soo-that, that he is 68 years of age, that he was brought to this country 63 years ago, that his father had been King of Siam and had died before the city of Siam (*i.e.* Ayuthia) was captured by the Burmese, that of the different princes who were brought away he is the only one now living, but that several princes are still alive, and that he now resides at Umerapoora and gains a livelihood by selling drugs. I affected to be much pleased with the liberal manner in which this poor prince is treated by the King of Ava, and repeatedly said that the conduct of His Majesty in not confining this prince or putting him in irons as the Siamese always do to Burmese in their power, would when known by highly extolled by every civilized country. This prince was dressed as a Burmese and appeared timid and not very intelligent......To do the Burmese justice, they treat their prisoners much more liberally and kindly than what the Siamese do, who always keep their prisoners and particularly all Burmese in iron. This difference of conduct between the two nations may, however, be owing to the different situations of the two cities — at Bangkok the vicinity of the sea and a number of junks and other vessels afford infinitely more facility to the escape of prisoners than what is afforded at such a spot as this ...." *Ibid.* Burney's Journal, par. 215. The chronology furnished by the prince certainly tallies with the capture of Ayuthia in 1767 by the Burmese in the reign of Hsinbyushin.
[2] *Ibid.* par. 216.
[3] *Ibid.* par. 217.

Burney and Pemberton held a number of conferences with the Woongyees and Atwenwoons on the Kubo question. The Burmese Ministers sought to prove by means of witnesses and written documents that the Valley was a Burmese possession, and desired Burney and Pemberton to acknowledge the same. The two British officers, however, plainly gave them to understand that they had no authority to do so, but that they would forward to the Governor-General all the arguments and evidence adduced by the Burmese Government, and wait upon his orders. " Maung Yeet (an Atwenwoon) then entered into a long argument," says Burney, " to show how advantageous it would be for both countries if we would leave the Munnipuris alone, and let the Burmese and that people settle their own quarrel by themselves. I recommended Maung Yeet and the Ministers as a friend, to desist from this line of argument and to avoid proposing or even mentioning any such thing, as it would tend only to displease my Government most seriously and to injure the Burmese. I explained that the British honour was now engaged to support its ally Gumbheer Singh, and that any proposition on the part of the Burmese for us to desert him, would be treated as a gross insult to my Government. I begged the Ministers, therefore, to remove from their minds all idea of the British Government ever leaving Munnipur to be attacked by the Burmese." [1]

Maung Yeet strove to obtain a pledge from Burney that he would recommend to the Governor-General a decision in favour of Burma. The Ministers also desired some such statement from Burney, so that they might report it to the King and please him. Burney said that he would merely submit the Burmese case, and he himself would not be responsible for the decision. He also ridiculed the idea of pleasing the King in the manner proposed as dangerous, since, if disappointed later, the King would be greatly enraged. Burney asked the Ministers what they would do if the

[1] *Ibid.* par. 220.

Governor-General decided the matter against Ava. They paused, and then said that it would be their duty to join with the British Resident in discovering other methods to please the King, so that the friendship between the two states may not be destroyed.[1]

The King was highly displeased, when he realized, that Burney had managed to render the Governor-General the arbiter in the dispute. " The King's pride is mortified," he wrote, " at the idea of his having to submit his claim to the decision of the Governor-General." [2]   When the Ministers met Burney and Pemberton again (on 25 August), they appeared much perplexed and distressed: " Maung Za's countenance was particularly expressive, and I was induced to remonstrate with him as to his conduct, saying that he was a very high officer, a Woongyee, whose duty it ought to be at all times to prevent the King from being misled by false hopes and flattering tales; and I warned him of the explosion which would take place whenever His Majesty came to hear the whole truth...... Maung Za was over-heard by Mr. Cotton my interpreter to observe, in the bitter-ness of his heart to some of the Burmese officers near him, that my pointing out to him his duty as a Woongyee was very disrespectful, and that if it had not been for the late war he would not have condescended to speak for a moment to one of us." [3]

The Ministers requested Burney to write and ask Capt. Grant not to molest the subjects of Ava. Burney replied that Gumbheer Singh's right to Kubo had been settled by the Governor-General, and that the latter alone could cancel the arrangement; meanwhile, he added, " the Burmese might go over and cultivate (in Kubo), but if they did, they would be considered as subjects of Munnipur. Upon hearing this, the Ministers rose up in anger, and with some rudeness hastily took their departure." [4]

[1] Ibid. par. 228.
[2] Ibid. par. 234.
[3] Ibid. par. 238.
[4] Ibid. par. 242.

The next day, however, the conference was resumed, and Maung Za showed particular concern regarding the fate of Kubo. " I do not think," says Burney, " his fears are anything more than personal. The King, like a child, has for the last 6 or 7 months been bent on the possession of the territory, and in the event of his wish not been gratified, he will impute the failure to the conduct of Maung Za and the other Ministers."[1]

On 1 September, 1830, Burney had one of the happiest conferences with the Ministers: it was decided that Pemberton should go to Calcutta by way of Akyab, and place before the Governor-General the Burmese view and claims in respect of Kubo. On 8 September, the following officers dined with Burney at 5 p.m.: — the Kyee Woongyee, Maung Za Woongyee, the Tshan Atwenwoon, the Burmese Resident-designate-to-Calcutta and his Assistant, the Woondouk Maung Khan Ye, and the Treasurer. Messrs. Lane, Sarkies, and Lanciago were also invited. " They partook freely of our dinner," says Burney, " and seemed anxious to do exactly as they observed we were doing. They all declined wine, although I am assured that two or three of them are rather partial to our wines and spiritous liquors...... The Ministers left us highly satisfied and overflowing with love and affection, so much so indeed as to lead me to fear that the cherry brandy in the Trifle of which they had all eaten heartily without supposing it to contain any such liquor, had tended to exhilarate them not a little...... I consider the measure of persuading these Woongyees to come and dine with me this day in so friendly and unceremonious a style and in a manner in which they had never to any of my predecessors, as one of the greatest advantages I could have secured to my permanent residence here. The ease and absence of all formality attending such intercourse will facilitate in an eminent degree, my public labours here."[2]

[1] *Ibid.* par. 244.
[2] *Ibid.* pars. 255, 267, 269, 270.

The Governor-General had already declared (in January 1830) Kubo to be a possession of Gumbheer Singh; but now, largely due to Burney, the whole problem was in fact reopened. Burney in his letter to his Government, dated Ava, 11 September, 1830, makes clear his own position in the matter: —

" I found it necessary upon Capt. Pemberton's arrival here to call the Burmese Ministers to resume the discussions regarding the disputed territory. For if I had then refused to hear any one of the arguments or witnesses....my refusal would have destroyed all the confidence and good will which I am gradually establishing here, and would have excited such unpleasant feelings against me on the part of the King as would have deprived me of all chance of our being useful here to my Government. At the same time I knew that my refusal would not have precluded the Ministers from further troubling my Government in a matter which their King has taken much to heart, and about which he has been as eager during the last eight months as a spoiled child after some toy." [1]

In the same letter Burney further gave his view of the conduct to be pursued towards the Government of Burma: — " The Governor-General-in-Council cannot maintain too high and firm a tone in all his communications and proceedings. But the British Resident here must affect to be kindly disposed towards the King and Court, and to be willing on all occasions to act as a kind of mediator and pacificator between them and His Lordship-in-Council. He should be always ready to hear and forward their complaints and representations, to advise, offer explanations, and appear anxious to conciliate and soften his own Government, and obtain little boons and favours from it for the Burmese.

" These considerations must form my apology for allowing the Burmese Ministers to assume the discussion after I had been apprised that the Governor-General-in-Council had

[1] *Ibid.* Vol. 358.

approved of the proceedings of our Commissioners in Munnipur. But I took care to treat the subject in the light of an
appeal or complaint which the King and Ministers of Ava
desired to make to the Governor-General against the acts of
our officers, and I warned the Ministers that Capt. Pemberton
was not at liberty to renew the discussions, but that he had
come down simply to afford me aid to explain and to meet
the objections which they had urged against his and Capt.
Grant's proceedings...... As I had anticipated no arguments or explanations which I could urge with the aid even
of Capt. Pemberton, effected any change in the sentiments of
the Ministers, and the question remains as it did before for
the final decision of the Governor-General-in-Council."

Ultimately the Kubo Valley was returned to the King,
and that at the recommendation of Burney, but at this particular time he saw no reason why this territory should go
to Burma. The same letter continues — " I am certainly not
prepared to predict confidently, what course so ignorant and
arrogant a monarch as this will pursue when the decision of
the Governor-General in favour of Gumbheer Singh is made
known. But I hope that the lessons of the last war are not
yet quite forgotten; and it must be my study and duty to
soothe and explain, and prevent an interruption of the existing good understanding." As to the attitude of the Ministers,
Burney says, " I am convinced that all the Burmese Ministers
are sincerely desirous of averting another war, although they
dare not contradict the King or give up any point upon which
he may have set his heart; and I see that the personal safety
and comfort of these poor creatures will be endangered by
the unsuccessful issue of the negotiations which they have
had to conduct with me respecting the territory of Kubo. It
is difficult to describe and equally so not to sympathize in
their extreme anxiety on this subject."

The state of the King's mind Burney describes in the
following words: — " Had our determination regarding Kubo
Valley been communicated to the Court in 1827, at a time
when it sought so much to obtain some delay in the payment
of the third instalment, and at a time when the King's weak

mind had not taken up this subject, I think there would have arisen little or no difficulty. But now (and I consider that I shall not fulfil the whole of my public duty if I omit to enumerate them for the consideration of my superiors) there are some grounds of probability that the determination of the Governor-General-in-Council in favour of Munnipur may ultimately produce a collision between the British and Burmese States.

" The mind of the King is still sore and angry against us, and intent upon resenting the injuries and recovering the losses which the last war inflicted upon him. He is very keen on the subject of Kubo, and is said to have expressed his vexation that we should not only emancipate his slaves the Munnipureans, but desire to give them a portion of his territory. Whilst he is in this humour, he will be more likely to be instigated by his flatterers and the Mahomedans, our bitter enemies at this Court, into ordering measures which may impose upon us the necessity of going to war...... I must not also conceal from Government that both Mr. Lane and Mr. Lanciago have often expressed their fears to me, although I have always ridiculed the idea, that the loss of Kubo may urge the King to order the measures that may lead to war, an event, which they maintain, would certainly have occurred in the beginning of this year but for my expected arrival here.

" All these calculations of probabilities I can only oppose by submitting to Government the settled conviction of my mind, that the present King of Ava will take the first favourable opportunity of engaging in another war with us."

On 13 October, 1830, Pemberton left Ava for Calcutta by the overland route via An in Arakan, his object being to place before the Governor-General the Burmese objections to Manipur's claim to the Kubo Valley.[1] On 9 October, 1830, the King also dispatched two ambassadors to Calcutta with representations to the Governor-General concerning the dis-

---

[1] *Ibid*. Burney's Journal, par. 278.

puted territory.[1]   As a result of the reconsideration of this
question by the Governor-General, finally, in March, 1833,
the Supreme Government decided to return the Valley to
Burma; on 9 January, 1834, this change was put into effect.
During this interregnum of three years (1830-1833) a great
many incidents and minor clashes took place between the
frontier subjects and officers of Manipur and Burma; but
through the good offices of Burney serious developments were
prevented.   Throughout the negotiations and talks on Kubo,
the Burmese Ministers openly declared their hatred for
Gumbheer Singh and his Manipuris.   It was almost a disease
with them to pronounce even the Raja's name with rancour.[2]

On 18 January, 1831, very disagreeable news was received
from the Manipur frontier.   The Burmese Governor of Kendat
had pursued four or five of his runaway slaves across the Chindwin into Kubo, and after capturing them had executed them in
Kendat.   Burney informed the Ministers that this violation
of Manipur territory was a serious outrage, and that the
Indian Government was bound to demand satisfaction.   The
Ministers readily acknowledged the error of the Governor.
Burney had also an interview with the King and conversed
with him in Burmese.   The King disavowed the action of the
Governor of Kendat and said that he had acted on his own
responsibility and would have to answer for it.[3]   Investigation was made, and the frontier officers of the two states
arrived at an amicable settlement in connection with the outrage.   The Ministers also agreed to write and warn the
Governor as to the seriousness of his offence.[4]   On 4 March,
however, Burney discovered, that although the Ministers had
written to the Governor, they made no mention of his action.
Burney warned them that if no notice would be taken of the

---

[1] *W. S. Desai,* History of the Burmese Mission to India, 1830-1833,
in the Journal of the Burma Research Society, Vol. XXVI, Part
II, August, 1936.
[2] Bengal Secret and Political Consultations Vol. 358, Burney's
Journal, pars. 474, 476.
[3] *Ibid.* Vol. 360, pars. 509, 510.
[4] *Ibid.* pars. 570-572.

offence, Grant might appear on the frontier with a force and punish the Governor. The Ministers felt offended at these words. Some of them even said that the Governor had committed no offence, because Kubo was Burmese territory by right. Burney on the other hand maintained that it was Manipuri territory so long as the Governor-General did not revise his former decision. There was much altercation and argument, but finally it was agreed "that offenders escaping within the jurisdiction of Munnipur or Ava must be demanded in a suitable manner by letter, and that either party will deliver up such fugitives if satisfied that they are proper subjects to be so delivered, and not otherwise."[1] This agreement did not put an end to the trouble. Complaints and counter complaints did not cease to come to Ava from the frontier.

[1] *Ibid.* pars. 579, 581-583.

CHAPTER IV

BURNEY AND THE QUESTIONS OF THE INDEMNITY, THE FRONTIERS, AND TENASSERIM.

According to the Treaty of Yandabo, the King of Burma was bound to pay up the fourth and last instalment of the Indemnity by 4 February, 1828. At the representation of the Burmese Mission to Calcutta (1827), the Governor-General proposed to extend the date to 4 September, 1829; but before the concession could be announced, Sir Archibald Campbell was able to induce the Mission to agree to the payment of the third instalment by 15 November, 1827, and the fourth instalment by 19 October, 1828.[1] The Burmese Government was unable to liquidate the indemnity according to this agree-ment. The payment of the third instalment was not complet-ed before the middle of 1828. They began paying the fourth instalment from August, 1828, and by August, 1829, had paid only 10 lacs, leaving a balance of 15 lacs still due.[2] Between August, 1829, and April, 1830, very little had been paid, so that on the arrival of Burney at Ava a balance of about 12 lacs of rupees was still outstanding.[3] It became now, therefore, the duty of Burney to press or induce the Ministers to discharge the obligation without delay.

On his arrival at Ava, Burney found that respectable Burmans disapproved of the delay in the payment of the indemnity, and blamed the officers for embezzling what they collected.[4] The King had given orders to pay off the fourth instalment without further delay, but mere orders could not

---

[1] Vide Chapter I.
[2] Burma Secret and Political Consultations Vol. 357, Minute of the Governor-General, 22 August, 1829.
[3] *Ibid.* Vol. 358, Burney's Journal, par. 80. For an account of the Indemnity see, The Journal of the Burma Research Society, Vol. XXIV, Part III, December, 1934: History of the Burma In-demnity, 1826-1833 by *W. S. Desai.*
[4] *Ibid.* par. 41.

5

be effective, because of the poverty of the people and the empty Royal treasury due to the late war. Only the Queen and her brother Menthagyee were supposed to be wealthy. The Government had, however, already borrowed from the Queen about 20 lacs of rupees towards the payment of the first instalment of the indemnity at the signing of the treaty of Yandabo, and now she was pressing the Ministers to repay the debt.[1] Burney's task was therefore most difficult.

On 19 June, 1830, he called upon the Ministers to fix the date for the payment of the money due. They suggested February, 1831, while Burney stuck to October, 1830. Burney gives the following reason for the attitude of the Ministers:—
" The truth is the Burmese Government are always obliged to watch for the proper time for squeezing the inhabitants. The two most favourable periods are just after the paddy is sown in May or June, and just when it is fit to cut in December and January. If contributions are demanded or exactions levied at any other season the inhabitants escape into the woods, or more into other parts of the country.[2] It is

---

[1] Bengal Secret and Political Consultations Vol. 357, Burney's Letter to his Government 24 June, 1830. *Ibid.* Vol. 358, Burney's Journal, par. 42.

[2] " The financial system of the Government," says Crawfurd, in his report of his Mission to Burma (1827), " is rude, barbarous, and inefficient, beyond what can be easily believed. No regular land revenue, as in other Asiatic countries, is collected on account of the sovereign, the great majority of the lands being given away in Jageer to the members of the royal family, to public officers, and to favourites in the form of pensions or salaries, and a mere trifling being reserved for the King..... No disbursements in the shape of money are almost ever made from the treasury as no money salary is paid to any officers from the highest to the lowest,— all those who have no lands living as they can upon the produce of fees, perquisites and extortions. Even the Government itself does not touch upon its hoard except on very extraordinary occasions, and may be said to support itself as if it were from hand to mouth. If an embassy is to be sent to a foreign country, a contribution is levied for the purpose; if an army is sent upon an expedition, the necessary expenses are raised on the spur of the moment; if a temple is to be built, the same thing is done; and so on in all other cases. When the remaining instalments are to be paid to us, this is the mode in which the money will inevitably be raised.... It may well be believed that under a Government so rude and unskilful, and from a country so exhausted and misgoverned no large accumulation of public treasure can reasonably be expected."

an established Burmese custom that a family is exempt from taxation during the first year of their arrival at a new place."[1]

Burney explained quietly to the Ministers the danger of not paying up the indemnity quickly, and that the Indian Government might take possession of Rangoon; also that the King's claim to Kubo would be inadmissible while the debt remained unpaid. This threat, however, did not produce much effect, for Burney says in his Journal, "after all I am of opinion that unless our Government take some decisive measures the 4th instalment will not be completed until February next."[2]

From June to September, 1830, only two sums of 500 viss of silver each had been sent down to Rangoon in payment of the fourth instalment.[3] "Maung Za complained of the great difficulty which had been felt in raising it. Every officer of Government had been made to contribute, and he and Maung Yeet Atwenwoon had each had to pay 1800 ticals. He said the payment of this 4th instalment pressed very hard upon all the Burmese officers here."[4] In October the Ministers informed Burney that they would not be able to complete the payment till the ensuing harvest. Burney made the following note in his Journal in respect of this communication:—"It is much to be regretted that the British Government cannot resort to some more efficacious negotiations to force open the hoards of the Queen and her brother Menzagyee. The manner in which the money is being levied from the poor inhabitants of the country furnishes a rich harvest for peculation to all the village and subordinate Burmese officers, and the sooner all the money is paid the better it will be for the

---

[1] Bengal Secret and Political Consultations Vol. 358, Burney's Journal, par. 129.
[2] *Ibid.* par. 140.
[3] *Ibid.* pars. 290-293.
[4] *Ibid.* Vol. 360, par. 364. In April, 1831, a boat belonging to an old Armenian merchant was attacked by river pirates near Pagan in broad day light. The robbers, when they boarded the boat, cried out, "You Kalas have forced us to pay plenty of money, we will now retake some of it." They killed the Armenian and plundered his boat. Bengal Secret and Political Consultations Vol. 361, The Journal, pars. 649, 658, 668.

people."[1]   The Government of India was not willing to take
any military action in the matter, since the late war had been
a costly one, so that the unpaid balance of the indemnity was
not worth the candle.

In November, 1830, 500 viss of silver was again sent
down to Rangoon, but in the same month Burney had to face
a new problem which proved exceedingly troublesome.   A
dispute arose over the quality of the silver to be paid.[2]   In
the British version of the Treaty of Yandabo the indemnity
mentioned was One Crore of rupees; but it is not specified
if it was to be the Calcutta or the Madras mint rupee: the
former contained more silver than the latter.   In the Burmese
version of the treaty 75,000 viss of good silver is mentioned;
but there were 36 different qualities of silver current in
Burma, the two main types being Yowetnee and Dain,
the best Dain being 10 per cent superior to Yowetnee :—[3]

---

[1] *Ibid.* Vol. 360, par. 373.
[2] *Ibid.* pars. 429, 448.
[3] "The purest silver current in Burma is called *Bau.*   It contains
three or four per cent of alloy, but not more.   This degree of
purity cannot be given by the pwezas to small pieces of metal
according to Burney.   I believe it is the money in which the
foreign merchants at Amarapoora usually demand to be paid
by the shopkeepers.   The King again receives no payments in
bau; because, as I was told, the value of the lower alloy, called
Dain, is more easily tested.
"The variety next in purity to *bau* is *Khayobat,* so called from
Khayo, a univalve shell, and *pat,* circle or winding, in consequence of the spiral lines or efflorescence on the surface.   It is
said to consist of nineteen-and-a-half parts of *bau* to half a part
of copper.   An expert pweza, however, it is said can make it:
that is to say can produce the necessary marks, with three-
fourths instead of one-half of copper.   Supposing the *bau* to
contain four per cent of alloy, khayobat will, according to the
former proportions, contain 6·4 per cent.
"Next comes *dain,* the purest kind of which is formed of nineteen
parts of *bau* to one of copper, or contains about 9·6 of absolute
alloy.   This used to be the money most extensively current in
commerce with foreigners.   All the China trade is carried on
with *dain.*
"*Dain* and *khayobat* are cast in large disks, weighing twenty tikals
and upwards.
"Yowet-ni (red-leaf), or flowered silver, so called from certain
stars or radiating lines on the surface, is the standard currency
in which accounts are kept, the "current money with the merchant," (Gen. xxiii), and which is understood to be the medium

100 ticals of Yowetnee silver = Calcutta Sicca
  Rs. 126-8-0.
100 ticals of Dain silver = Calcutta Sicca
  Rs. 139-2-0.

Hitherto there had been a tacit understanding that
75,000 viss of Dain silver was to be paid, and the Burmese
Government had so far been paying in Dain, and had already
paid in all 68,716, viss of Dain silver, equivalent to Rs. 95,60,113
at Rs. 139-2-0 per 100 ticals. However, Lieut. Rawlinson at
Rangoon, the officer appointed to receive the indemnity, had
valued the Dain silver paid in to be of an inferior quality,
not 10 per cent superior to Yowetnee, and had fixed its value
at Rs. 133 per 100 ticals.[1]

The Ministers now insisted that the British had no right
to demand Dain silver since the Treaty mentioned 75,000 viss
of good silver, which, they said, was Yowetnee, and which
was also the standard of the country. " They then calculated
that they had already paid 68,716 viss of Dain which are
equal to 75,588 viss of Yowetnee, and maintained that instead
of having to pay us 9 lacs of rupees more, we ought to return
to them 588 viss which they have paid us in excess."[2]

of payment when no stipulation as to the kind of money is
made. It is that in which revenue is assessed. It is cast in
pieces of five to seven tikals in weight. Even about this standard there seems to be uncertainty, for the best *yowet-ni* is stated
to have only ten per cent copper to ninety of *bau,* whilst Burney
states the composition of *Yowet-ni* at fifteen per cent copper
to eighty-five of *bau.* This last appears to be the standard. The
different qualities of *dain* are distinguished by their relation to
yowet-ni. Thus the best *dain* is called ten per cent above
yowet-ni, or simply " ten per cent *dain."* Five per cent *dain* is
the lowest bullion properly entitled to that name.
" There are also many degrees in the scale of current bullion recognized below *yowet-ni,* down at least to what is called eighty
per cent silver; such, that is to say, that 180 tikals of it are
equal to 100 of *yowet-ni.* But all below fifty per cent is by the
King's order liable to confiscation. These inferior currencies
are common in the provinces, but not in the capital. Before
the war of 1824 the currency of Rangoon used to be twenty-five
per cent silver. After the war it was ten per cent silver...."
Yule's Narrative, pp. 259-261.
[1] Bengal Secret and Political Consultations Vol. ·360, Burney's
  Journal, pars. 429, 448.
[2] *Ibid.* par. 429.

Burney argued that in the Treaty the term "One Crore of rupees" was also mentioned, but the Ministers kept repeating that Yowetnee was good silver. Burney's argument was undoubtedly weak, and he himself confesses in his letter to his Government that the Treaty did not say whether the one crore of rupees was to be paid in the Calcutta Sicca[1] rupee or in the Madras rupee: — "I shall here only add," he wrote, "that the expression 'good silver' in the Yandaboo Treaty appears to me to be very vague, and that 75 lacs of 10 per cent Dain are nearly as much in excess of one crore of rupees as the same sum of Yowetnee ticals is below it. It is also remarkable that in the Yandaboo treaty the rupee is not specified whether sicca or Madras which (latter) was the principal currency in our camp at the time."[2]

During the discussions, "the Kyeewoon Atwenwoon observed, 'We do not refuse to acknowledge the debt or to pay the money, and you have no right, and it will be contrary to principles of friendship for you to get angry at our not paying up the balance by February,' and he petulantly added, 'If we cannot pay it in February you must wait another year, and if we cannot pay it then you must wait a second year.' I told him that there was no friendship in money matters, and that I must apprise him of English customs so that he may hereafter not plead ignorance of them: If a debtor forfeited his engagement and was unable to pay we adopted steps for seizing his property and making him pay in some other way than in money."[3]

The Ministers admitted that they had paid the first instalment at Yandabo in Dain, and that they had in fact all along been paying in that description of silver; but, they said, that they had since discovered that they had made a mistake in so doing. They also shrewdly argued, "that our sicca rupees

---

[1] Sicca = a rupee or coin of 180 grains Troy: applied to the Calcutta rupee.
[2] Bengal Secret and Political Consultations Vol. 360, Letter dated 15 December, 1830.
[3] *Ibid.* Burney's Journal, par. 447.

are by no means all of the same standard."[1]   Burney assured
them " that the British Government would not retain one anna
more than what would be equivalent to one crore of rupees,
and that I would write to Bengal and solicit my Government
to supply me with a detailed statement from the Calcutta
Mint of the exact amount and value with reference to the
sicca rupees of the whole of the Bullion received from Ava.
Menzagyee and the other Ministers were perfectly satisfied
with this assurance, and begged of me to write immediately
. . . . . ."[2]   Burney also forwarded to Calcutta a statement of
the Burma Government concerning the payments hitherto
made, but warned the Ministers that they must continue to
pay according to Capt. Rawlinson's statement, and that his
government would retain no more than one crore of rupees.[3]

Burney soon discovered to his dismay, that the Ministers
construed his conduct into an admission that their own statements and accounts were correct, and so stopped collecting
money from the inhabitants.[4]   He made a vigorous protest,
but to no effect.   On the other hand, on 20 June, 1831, they
informed him in writing, that the Indemnity of One Crore of
rupees had been fully paid, and that the Supreme Government in Calcutta might be informed accordingly.   Burney
upbraided the Ministers for their conduct, and after recount-
ing the history of the money due, he said, " Let the Ministers
consider how often they have broken their pledge.   Their envoys agreed to pay up the whole of the 4th instalment by the
month of August, 1828.   They themselves agreed to pay it
up by the month of February, 1831.   They then agreed to
pay 3,000 viss of silver between December and the end of
February.   Have any of these pledges been fulfilled?   No,
they have not only been broken, but the Ministers have now
discontinued raising any more money from the people on
account of the balance which is still due.   Under these circumstances Major Burney can do nothing more than obey

---

[1] *Ibid.*
[2] *Ibid.* par. 571.
[3] *Ibid.* par. 607.
[4] *Ibid.* Burney's Letter, Ava, 8 April, 1831.

his orders. He, therefore, tells the Ministers, that if they ....will not collect money from the people as before, Major Burney will remove himself and the whole of the Mission to Rangoon. Major Burney has all his boats ready to leave Ava immediately, and he only waits for the answer of the Ministers to this letter." [1]

The Ministers bluntly replied, to say, that they had already paid 70,473 viss, 52 ticals of 10 per cent Dain silver which was equivalent to sicca rupees 1,03,36,116, and thus that the British Government had received 336,116 sicca rupees in excess of the stipulated Crore. They also instructed Burney that " as the great countries are in friendship, it is proper that Major Burney should write to the officers in Bengal to say that this is correct." [2] Burney refused to comply with their request. [3]

A whole month passed away, but the Ministers took no measures towards completing the balance of the indemnity. On 6 August, Burney warned them at the Hlutdaw that unless they resumed their collections, he would most certainly quit Ava. This declaration, however, made no impression upon them. There were rumours current of an impending war between Ranjit Singh, the Lion of the Punjab, and the British Government, so that the Ministers felt encouraged to defy Burney. The British Resident, however, was not to be beaten in this game. His opporunity soon arrived. He was drawn into a disagreeable argument with the Ministers over the detention at Kyauk-ta-loun [4] *chokey* of Agha Saadat, a Moulmein merchant, for a breach of a new regulation requiring all merchants leaving Ava to report the quantity of specie they were taking away with them. Burney objected to the proceedings on the ground that the regulation was not in keeping with the ancient laws and customs of the country, and that it had not also been duly proclaimed before the

---

[1] *Ibid*. Vol. 362, Burney's Letter, dated 9 August, 1831.
[2] *Ibid*. Appendix K.
[3] *Ibid*. Vol. 361, Burney's Journal, par. 697.
[4] A Customs station 10 miles south of Ava.

Moulmein trader left Ava. Burney also addressed a letter to the King on the subject.[1]

The Ministers promised to release the trader and to read his letter to the King but failed to do either. Burney now made all arrangements to embark, and threatened to retire to Rangoon. The Ministers did not take these threats seriously; but when they discovered that the Resident really meant to embark, they ordered the release of the Agha and sent Woondouk Maung Khan Ye to confer with Burney. Burney told Khan Ye that unless the Ministers agreed to pay up the balance of the Indemnity within one month of hearing from their Resident in Calcutta (to whom a reference had been made), he would quit Ava.[1]

On 13 August, Burney attended the Hlutdaw and repeated his demand, but failed to bring the Ministers to terms. He, therefore, left them with a declaration that on the following morning he would quit Ava, if in the meanwhile they did not send him a document agreeing to pay up the indemnity as required by him. What followed may be described in Burney's own words: —

"I waited until 10 o'clock a.m. of the 14th instant without any answer from the Ministers; I then saw the whole of my party on board the boats, and embarked myself, and quitted Ava.

"Before I had been two hours [2] absent from the City a war boat with the old Treasurer and another Burmese officer overtook us, and after some discussion I consented to wait until 6 o'clock on the following morning, if they would return by that time with such a document as I required. They begged of me to give them a paper stipulating on my side that if on the receipt of the letter from the Burmese Vakeels at Calcutta it should appear that an overplus had been paid to us, the same would be repaid to Ava in the same period of time, one month, that the Ministers would engage to liquidate any balance which might appear to be due to us. Although I declared that we should not require one day or one hour to refund any such overplus, yet I consented to give them such a paper as I knew that it would

[1] Bengal Secret and Political Consultations Vol. 362, Burney's Letter, dated Ava, 28 August, 1831; also his Journal, pars. 731-736.

[2] *i.e.* 7 or 8 miles down the river. (The Journal, par. 744).

be consolatory to the pride of the Ministers, and afford them a decent pretext for escaping out of the difficulty into which they had got.

"On the morning of the 15th before 6 o'clock, the Treasurer returned to me with the document which I had required from the Ministers.........

"I returned to Ava on the 16th, and on the 21st instant I met all the Ministers at the Hluttaw, and we became apparently as sincere and cordial friends as ever........

"The Ministers never believed, that I would or ever could leave Ava, and I was of course obliged to sacrifice some of my property which I was unable to embark on board the boats...." [1]

In his Journal Burney gives the following further interesting information concerning the episode: — "I now learn from Mr. Lane that the intelligence of my departure came like a thunder-bolt upon the whole Court. The Princes and Ministers were running to and fro with long faces unable to decide what to do until the Treasurer returned with my letter. As I had believed also, the moment the Ministers saw my offer to engage that any surplus should be repaid in one month, they all seized upon it and said, 'Oh! the matter is now quite easy and simple. We can of course agree to his terms. It is just the same on both sides. If there is a surplus it will be repaid in one month, and of course if there is a balance we shall pay it in the same time.'

"The truth is the Ministers never believed that I could leave Ava, and they had no idea I could ever think of sacrificing all my furniture, and departing in the decided and expeditious manner in which I did. My liquors and some of my stock which I gave away of course I cannot recover; but I am happy to find that my furniture is all safe, as orders were issued by the Ministers to guard it the moment they heard of my departure." [2]

The Ministers were alarmed at the departure of Burney from Ava because the Kubo question had not yet been settled,

[1] Bengal Secret and Political Consultations Vol. 362, Burney's Letter, dated Ava, 28 August, 1831; also his Journal, pars. 731-736.
[2] Ibid. Vol. 362, Burney's Journal, pars. 749, 750.

and they feared that in case of a diplomatic rupture, there would be no chance of ever recovering that Valley upon which the King's heart was set. Besides, the Ministers, if not the King, thoroughly understood that there were no prospects of wresting the Valley from Manipur by force.

The Governor-General, however, disapproved of the action of Burney in leaving Ava, and issued fresh instructions in case of similar circumstances arising again: — " ......it appears to His Lordship that in threatening to remove the Residency and in embarking for the purpose on the 14th August, you proceeded further than could be considered proper without specific orders to that effect. Had the Court of Ava not yielded to you in that particular instance by furnishing the written paper required by you, the British Government might have found itself placed in a situation of considerable embarrassment......His Lordship thinks it would have been prudent to have limited your representations to a refusal to hold further communication until the point at issue could be referred for the orders of superior authority, instead of committing yourself to a measure so difficult to retrieve if once carried into effect, as actual retirement from the capital." [1]

Meanwhile on 4 October, 1831, the Mint and Assay Master of Calcutta, after testing Dain and Yowetnee silver in the laboratory in the presence of the Burmese Envoys, declared, that good Dain contained 93·7 per cent of fine silver, and good Yowetnee 90 per cent, the difference between the two being found to be 3·7 per cent, not 10 per cent as before assumed. [2] According to this calculation Rs. 654,232-3-4 was still due from the Burma Government. [3] After the Mint Master had demonstrated to the Burmese Resident the superior methods of assay, the latter made a remark in Burmese. " The Assay Master asked the interpreter what the

[1] *Ibid.* Vol. 363, Chief Secretary's Letter, 2 December, 1831.
[2] *Ibid.* Vol. 362, Consultations 7 October, 1831, Statement, 4 October, 1831.
[3] *Ibid.* Chief Secretary's Letter to Lieut. Geo. Burney, 16 October, 1831.

Vakeel had said, and the reply was, he says, 'it is all non-sense'; or in other words, all this display of chemical science and apparatus is a mere trick to cheat us out of our money ......" [1]

The Indian Government, in keeping with the statement of the Mint Master, instructed Burney to call upon the Ministers to pay up the balance, and at the same time neither to discuss nor to admit the possibility of the Mint statement being wrong, but to demand payment.[2] On 16 December, 1831, accordingly, Burney called upon the Ministers, and advised them of the decision of his Government. There was much talk, and finally on 26 December, at the Hlutdaw Burney said, "that if the Burmese do not immediately pay the balance, the English will be obliged to charge interest on the amount. The Atwenwoon said he would not hear of interest. I replied that there is a way of making people hear with great guns and muskets. This observation produced an uproar among the whole body of Ministers who charged me with loss of temper, and with not talking like a man of sense. When the clamour had subsided, I asked them how they would act, if a private individual owing them money, had repeatedly for 4 or 5 years broken his promises of completing payment, and then prepared a false and absurd account to try and evade payment of a small balance. After much discussion finally the Ministers agreed 'that a balance is really due'" [3]

On 6 January, 1832, the Ministers gave to Burney a written agreement attested with the Royal Seal, that they would pay Rs. 654,232, in Dain silver 4994 viss, within 300 days from 4 January, 1832, and after that interest at 1 per cent per month, and, secondly, that after the Dain silver was refined, if it produced a surplus over Rs. 654,232, it would be returned to them

[1] Ibid. Note by the Chief Secretary, 25 October, 1831.
[2] Ibid. Vol. 365, Burney's Letter, 19 December, 1831; also his Journal, pars. 858, 860.
[3] Ibid. Vol. 366, Burney's Journal, par. 870.

with interest.[1] The Government of India did not appreciate
the further delay of nearly 10 months entailed by this agreement; but Burney issued a serious warning to the Ministers
that if they failed to honour the new agreement, the responsibility of any evil consequences would be solely theirs.[2]

The Ministers now made serious efforts to pay up the
balance, and by 10 April, 1832, were able to remit nearly 2 lacs
of rupees to Rangoon. According to the agreement the entire
balance should have been paid up by 29 October, 1832. This
they were unable to do. The payment was completed in
February, 1833.[3] On a final calculation made by Capt. Rawlinson, it was discovered that the Burmese Government had
paid a surplus of Rs. 14,094 to the One Crore due; this was
ordered to be returned to the Ministers.[4] Thus finally was
this long drawn out question settled. It is doubtful if the
Company would have received the payment in full without
the presence of the Resident in Ava and the services of Henry
Burney.

Besides the Indemnity, the British Resident had to face
the problem of the Anglo-Burmese frontiers. The outrages
committed by the Burmese in British territory on the Moulmein frontier, at the connivance or even the instigation of the
Martaban Chief, have been mentioned in Chapter I. In 1829
troops were sent out from Moulmein, and these burnt down
Martaban and three Burmese villages. While the Moulmein
authorities were negotiating with the Rangoon Woongyee for
the surrender of the culprits, Burney was appointed Resident;
so that it became now his duty to represent matters to the
Ava authorities, and put an end to the outrages not only on
that frontier but also on the Arakan and Manipur frontiers.

On his arrival at Ava (April 1830), Burney found that
the King and his Ministers had felt annoyed at British pro-

---

[1] *Ibid.* pars. 872, 873, 879, 880.
   Ibid. Vol. 365, the Agreement, Ava, 6 January, 1832.
[2] *Ibid.* Vol. 366, Burney's Letter, 30 March, 1832.
[3] *Ibid.* Vol. 371, Burney's Letter, dated Fort William 13 March,
   1833. The sum of Rs. 68,04,305-14-10 was paid in gold, and
   Rs. 31,95,694-1-2 in silver. *Ibid.* Vol. 361, 5 August, 1831.
[4] *Ibid.* Vol. 372, Letter from Government to Burney, 16 March, 1833.

ceedings in Martaban. In Burney's opinion, however, the destruction of that town had been of great service in convincing the King and his Government, "that we are not afraid to carry our threats into effect." Burney discovered that previous to this, the Burmese idea was that the late war had ruined the British financially, and that they would not embark upon another war. Some of the King's favourites had even been referring to history, to prove to the King, that since Burma had recovered from damage suffered due to wars in the past with the Shans and Talaings, she was well able to recover also from the late war with the British, even to the reconquest of the lost territory. On the other hand, the Ministers fully understood the helpless condition of their country, and were bent upon preventing another rupture.[1]

On 2 June, 1830, there was a conversation with the Ministers on the question of the Burmese banditti on the Salween. Burney said that unless the outrages ceased the British would be forced to take measures themselves, as they did in the case of Martaban. The Ministers disapproved of the British action, and said that the conduct of the Martaban Chief should have been reported to the Rangoon Woongyee. Burney replied that in 1828 Sir Archibald Campbell had drawn the attention of Ava to the outrages, and so had Maingy complained to the Rangoon Woongyee, but without effect. He also gave the Ministers plainly to understand that Maingy, in sending out troops, had acted in obedience to the orders of the Governor-General, and finally asked them if the frontier Chief, in harbouring and encouraging robbers and murderers, was acting in obedience to the orders of the Government of Ava.[1] The Ministers did not give an answer to this, but asked, ".......if I considered the friends of the Burmese to be the friends of the English, and the enemies of the Burmese to be the enemies of the English. I said, certainly not, that the treaty of Yandaboo had not been an offensive and defen-

---

[1] *Ibid.* Vol. 358, Burney's Journal, pars. 35, 81.

sive alliance."[1]   The Ministers, however, did not press the
subject, but said, " let bygones be bygones, let us now live in
peace." [1]   They issued orders to their frontier officers warning them to maintain the peace.[2]

By the middle of 1831, Maingy again complained of the
behaviour of the Burmese officer in charge of Martaban, stig-
matizing it to be "litigious, disrespectful and unfriendly."
Burney immediately warned the Ministers of the danger of
reprisals; but the Rangoon Woongyee had already taken
cognizance of the complaint and had attempted to prevent
trouble.[3]   In the month of November, Maingy made charges
in writing against the Martaban officer, and these were delivered to the Ministers: that he had harboured robbers, and
shared stolen property with them.   All the Ministers were
most anxious to avert trouble, and although they also brought
counter-charges against a police officer of Moulmein, they
finally removed the Martaban officer.[4]

Similar complaints were also made by the Commissioner
of Arakan.   In August, 1830, Burney was informed that the
Myothugyi of Kanoung protected and encouraged insurgents
belonging to British territory.   The Resident " hinted plainly
to Maung Za that if the Burmese officers did not forbear protecting or taking part with such insurgents and depredators
as fled to them from our territories in Arakan, some of the
Burmese towns on the frontiers would meet most probably
with a catastrophe similar to that which had occurred last
year at Martaban...." [5]   The King was also informed of the
complaint, and orders were issued to investigate into the
charges alleged against the Thugyi, and to surrender the insurgents to British officers.[6]   As a result of these enquiries
and the orders from Ava, the Rangoon Woongyee summoned
the Myothugyi and put him in confinement.[7]

[1] *Ibid*. par. 82.
[2] *Ibid*. par. 130.
[3] *Ibid*. pars. 772, 773, 778.
[4] *Ibid*. Vol. 362, pars. 831, 894, 898, 930.
[5] *Ibid*. Vol. 358, par. 189.
[6] *Ibid*. par. 191.
[7] *Ibid*. Burney to his Government, Ava, 9 October, 1830.

In October, 1830, the Myothugyi of Maphe was accused of encouraging murders and robberies on the Arakan frontier, and of discouraging trade by various illegal means.[1] At Burney's suggestion the Ministers deputed an officer to Maphe to investigate the charges fully on the spot. " The officer whom the Ministers have ordered to proceed to Maphe," wrote Burney to Capt. Dickenson, Offg. Superintendent of Arakan, " is one of the King's Pages or At-shoung-dau-mya and bears the title of Nemyo-ye-zet Kyan thoo.[2] He is accompanied by an agent Shwe doung Thee ha [3] . . . . . . The instructions delivered to these officers are to receive any testimony which British officers and subjects may be able to produce before them in proof of the same allegations." [4]   In the same communication Burney advised Dickenson to send witnesses together with a British officer to the Burmese Commissioners, and opined that even if there be failure to substantiate the charges, " it will teach the Myothugyi more caution and moderation in future."

The investigation was held as arranged, but the British agents and witnesses failed to establish the charges against the Thugyi.   In order to prevent indifference on the part of the Ministers to any future complaints against their distant officers, Burney offered to reimburse the expenses of the Burmese deputation to Maphe amounting to about 300 ticals.[5]

Early in February, 1831, 22 prisoners escaped from Akyab Jail, plundered the police establishment at Talak, and entered Burmese territory.   The Burmese authorities captured 14 of them.   Burney requested the Ministers to order the frontier officers to hand over the runaways to British authorities.[6] At the Hlutdaw, the Ministers offered to surrender the 14 prisoners, provided Burney agreed that all fugitives demanded

[1] *Ibid.* Vol. 360, Burney's Journal, par. 384.
[2] His name, Maung Bau.
[3] His name, Nga Day.
[4] Burma Secret and Political Consultations Vol. 360, Journal par. 415.
[5] *Ibid.* Burney to his Government, Ava, 4 February, 1831.
[6] *Ibid.* Vol. 361, The Journal, pars, 612, 613, 625.

by either side should in future be surrendered. Burney explained to them that according to the customs of civilized states, it was a point of honour not to surrender persons who fly to them for protection in consequence of any political difference of opinion with their own government, and that only murderers or notorious robbers could be delivered over. Menthagyee said that rebels should be surrendered, and that the King had handed over Chinese rebels to the Emperor of China. Burney explained that the custom of European states was different, and that hundreds of people had been living in England who had fled from Spain, Portugal, and other countries, in consequence of a difference of opinion with their own governments. To this the Tshan Atwenwoon replied very impatiently, " Your and our customs are so completely opposite in so many points. You write on white, we on black paper. You stand up, we sit down; you uncover your head, we our feet in token of respect." [1]

Burney requested the Ministers not to ask for the surrender of political fugitives as it would give his Government a very unfavourable opinion of the intelligence of the Burmese Woongyees. He, however, explained that if the countries were at peace, and rebels attacked the other party, they would be either punished or handed over. The Ministers began to press Burney to agree, that all robbers and murderers be mutually delivered over; but he refused, and said, that every case would have to be examined on its own merits, and that the British authorities would not surrender any fugitives unless they were perfectly satisfied of their guilt. Burney also claimed that the Arakan authorities had proved the guilt of the 14 fugitives who had escaped from their jail, and finally threatened serious consequences if these convicts were not handed over. The Ministers agreed to surrender them, and did so on 1 June, 1831. [2]

The Chief Commissioner of Arakan [3] reported cases of robbery committed by Burmese subjects in Arakan. The

[1] *Ibid.* par. 626.
[2] *Ibid.* par. 627, and Vol. 362, par. 705.
[3] M. I. Halhed.

Ministers took prompt measures to arrest the robbers, but owing to the indisposition of the King, disorders were expected to increase throughout the frontiers. " I know no better mode," wrote Burney to the Commissioner, " of checking this evil, if the King continues unwell, than by our officers being prepared to pursue the offenders into the Burmese territories and apprehend them there."[1]   The Government of India in a slightly modified form approved of this procedure: " The Vice-President-in-Council is happy to learn from your dispatch that the Burmese Government has shown a ready disposition to co-operate with the local authorities in matters of Police. The Vice-President-in-Council would not generally approve sending parties in search of marauders into Burmese Territory, and that course must not be adopted without the special authority of Government being first obtained. Marauders from the Burmese Territory detected in our territory and pursued may at the time be followed beyond the frontier as far as prudence may suggest."[2]   It must be remarked that a peculiar as well as a troublesome situation had been created for both the neighbours, since their respective conceptions of inter-state relations were fundamentally at variance. The Arakan frontier trouble did not cease till all Burma was annexed by the British in the later instalments of 1852 and 1885.

The problem of Tenasserim now remains to be dealt with. It has already been explained in Chapter II, that one of the chief objects of the Burney Residency was to effect the retrocession of Tenasserim to Burma in return for suitable territory elsewhere or a money equivalent. Every year the Government of India had to bear a deficit of $1\frac{1}{2}$ lacs of rupees for this southern acquisition, and this charge was expected to increase. In his letter of instructions Burney was advised to handle the Tenasserim question most carefully, so as not to give the Burmese Government to suspect that the Governor-General was anxious to be rid of the district.

---

[1] Bengal Secret and Political Consultations Vol. 361, Ava, 2 April, 1831.
[2] *Ibid.* Chief Secretary to the Arakan Commissioner, 13 May, 1831.

On his arrival at Ava, Burney was surprised to find that
the King and his Ministers knew " that Tenasserim provinces
are a dead loss to us." This knowledge they had acquired
from Calcutta newspapers received by Lanciago and Lane,
and relevant portions of which they were in the habit of
translating to the King and Ministers.[1] They were even expecting the provinces returned to them, and were surprised
at the delay. A few months before the arrival of Burney in
Ava the Atwenwoons had through Lane informed Maingy,
that the King was prepared to take over the Tenasserim
territory. Lane urged the Ministers to make some specific
offer of money or privilege of trade in return for the coveted
district, but they declined to do so. Burney informed his
Government, that " so long as the Burmese Court entertain
their present ideas, all negotiation regarding this subject is
quite out of the question, and I am satisfied that it will be
very long before the Court will be induced to give anything
in exchange for territory, which they confidently believe, if
they only wait, must ultimately come back to them one way
or another."[1]

Having personal knowledge of the Tenasserim country,
and now also of parts of Burma proper, Burney was able to
explain in the following words the anxiety of the Burmese
Government to recover that province : —

> " It is very necessary for me here to record that none of my
> predecessors had visited Tavoy and Mergui before they came to
> this capital, or it would have struck them as it did me, that there
> is not a single place between Rangoon and Ava to be compared,
> for one moment, with either of those towns. In population, per-
> haps, Prome is equal to Mergui, but neither in the comfortable
> and decent appearance of the houses or inhabitants nor in the
> cultivation of the country, nor in any one thing which raises man
> above the brute, is there a single place between Ava and Ran-
> goon to be compared with even one of the second class villages
> in the provinces of Tavoy. I except only the Pagodas which
> appear to be the work of a former generation, but in regard to
> all other points I really cannot express myself too strongly; although

[1] *Ibid.* Vol. 358, Burney's Journal, par. 37.

the Tenasserim territory may be of little importance to us, there
is no question that it is of very great value to the Burmese
Court, and I am no longer surprised at its eagerness to recover
these provinces." [1]

On 21 May, 1830, Lanciago visited Burney and " urged
me a good deal to allow him to hold out to the Ministers a
hope of recovering the Tenasserim provinces from us.   Of
course I ridiculed the idea of our Government ever restoring
them without an equivalent.....but I could not remove from
his mind the strong impression, an impression which he
owned he and all Ava had received from the Calcutta newspapers that we are anxious to get rid of the Tenasserim territory.   I pretended to him that the Calcutta newspapers publish any nonsense they may hear, and that if a man were to
believe all that they publish he would soon have cause to re-
pent of his folly."[2]

In July, 1830, the King commissioned Lanciago to endeavour to extract from Burney what chances there were of
recovering the territory in question.   Lanciago admitted to
Burney that the Burmese Government was " extremely anxious on this point, but that the Ministers are waiting to find
some good and auspicious opportunity for making an overture to me on this subject, and that their pride debars them
from declaring their wishes to me at once."[3]   Burney requested Lanciago to " lose no time in removing from the mind of
His Majesty and Ministers the foolish notion which they hold
of our anxiety to get rid of these conquests, that he may rest
assured if we do ever relinquish them it will not be without
some equivalent."[3]   Burney also threatened that Siam appeared disposed to grant Queda and some advantage in the Malay
states in exchange for Tenasserim, " and that if the Burmese
really desire to repossess them, they had better not delay
offering us some equivalent which may appear to my Government more advantageous than that held out by the Siamese." [3]   Lanciago, however, declared that the Burmese had

[1] *Ibid.* par. 38.
[2] *Ibid.* par. 59.
[3] *Ibid.* par. 169.

no money to buy back Tenasserim, and " giving us in lieu of
the Provinces a tract in some other quarter would be so opposed to all Burmese ideas that the Ministers could never be
made to comprehend it." [1]   Lanciago also told Burney that
the Ministers confidently believed that one of the principal
objects of the British Residency in Ava was to try and negotiate the retrocession of the Tenasserim territory which had
proved unprofitable to the Company. [1]

The Ministers finally could no longer remain quiet on
the Tenasserim question. All along they had been expecting
Burney to propose its retrocession; now they opened the subject. On 25 August, 1830, a very interesting conversation
took place, reproduced below in the words of Burney: —

" Maung Yeet took me by the hand into another room
and called the Myawadi Woongyee and Maung Ba Youk
Atwenwoon to join us. I was then informed as a very great
secret, that the King of Ava is very anxious to repossess the
Tenasserim provinces, which Maung Yeet hoped I would
assist them to recover as soon as the whole of the 4th instalment is completed." Burney begged " of them to remove
from their minds at once all idea of the British Government
ever restoring those provinces without some equivalent. The
Ministers looked blank, and asked me, whether those provinces were not held by us merely as a kind of pledge or pawn
for the due payment of the instalments, and whether after
Ava had repaid to us all the expenses of the late War, we
could fairly ask for anything more from her. I said....that
one crore of rupees was not a quarter of the amount which
the late war had cost us, and that......at Yandaboo Sir
Archibald Campbell had at first demanded 2 crores from the
Burmese negotiators. I recommended the Ministers to consider the subject well, and to recollect that the Siamese are
anxious to obtain possession of the Tenasserim provinces for
which they are disposed to offer some equivalent." [2]

[1] *Ibid*. par. 169.
[2] *Ibid*. par. 235.

The Ministers, in reply, asked, " What, will the English turn Merchants and sell those provinces to the highest bidder? ....I laughingly answered in the affirmative."[1] Burney also informed the Ministers that his Government was concerned about the safety of the inhabitants of the province in question, and " that the English could not restore the Tenasserim provinces to Ava without securing some asylum for the Talain[2] emigrants and other inhabitants of that territory, whose connexion with us during the war or subsequently had made them obnoxious to the Burmese authorities."[1] The Ministers protested that these men would never be molested. Burney cited the treatment of the Myothugyis of Prome, Henzada, Podaung, etc., who had been put to death because they had helped the British during the war. The Ministers declared that they did not put them to death for that reason. but because after the war they had been found guilty of offences.[1]

Burney finally told them that he was prepared to lay it for the consideration of his Government if money or territory was offered in exchange for Tenasserim. They said they had no money. Burney suggested that they give in exchange some other territory so that an asylum might be provided for the Talaings; " and as we are a nation fond of trade and of possessing ports for our numerous ships, suppose you offer us, but mind I do not vouch for the offer being accepted, Negrais island and some other adjoining territory?"[3] The Ministers expressed themselves very much averse to ceding a single inch of territory in any direction, and said that they had been trying their best to pay up the fourth instalment of the indemnity, in the hope that when this was done, Tenasserim would be returned. Burney adds, " they looked woefully blank and disappointed."[3]

On 25 October, Burney had another talk with the Ministers on Tenasserim. They expressed much dissatisfaction that

---

[1] *Ibid.* par. 235.
[2] Talaing; Mon.
[3] Bengal Secret and Political Consultations Vol. 358, Journal, par. 235.

the British contemplated ceding the province to Siam, " and
asked why their ancient dominions should be given to their
enemies the Siamese. I said that the Burmese seemed not
to be disposed to grant us some equivalent, and that the
Tenasserim country at any rate belonged more anciently to
Siam from which the Burmese had seized it." [1]

Meanwhile, a difference of opinion had arisen in Calcutta
as well as at Home concerning the retrocession of Tenasserim.
Burney, therefore, informed the Ministers that there were
some who thought that the province should not be given up,
believing that it might ultimately become profitable for trade,
and that if it were restored, the Burmese would illtreat the
inhabitants; also that there was a small party which wished
to return the province to the Burmese if the latter paid 1½
crores of rupees; and finally, that the Governor-General was
still undecided in the matter. Burney, however, from his
own side, proposed, that since the Burmese had no money to
give, they should cede instead the island of Negrais and a
portion of territory on the mainland. [2]

Maung Yeet said, " that the Ministers would be pleased
to give to the English whichever they pleased, half a crore
of rupees or Negrais island, but they earnestly hoped that
we would not give them only half a pot of rice but let them
have back their ancient territory of Arakan also!" [3] In reply
Burney told them that such a demand would confirm the
assertion of the party among the British most adverse to the
Burmese, " namely, that they are a nation to whom if you
yield a *thumb breadth* they will demand a *fathom*. I begged
of the Ministers to say not another word regarding Arakan,
and to consider that country as irrevocably lost to Ava." [4]

Maung Yeet now came out with another proposition,
namely, that the Burmese would give Negrais in exchange
for the Tenasserim territory, upon condition that if within

[1] *Ibid.* Vol. 360, par. 378.
[2] *Ibid.* par. 387.
[3] *Ibid.* par. 388.
[4] *Ibid.*

ten years they paid one-half crore of rupees as well, they would be allowed to redeem that island for this sum. Burney laughed at this proposition, and said that the Governor-General would never listen to it.[1] Maung Yeet then retorted that they would have no objection to Tenasserim being given to Siam, because the Burmese could conquer it back. Burney observed that Siam would probably not take the territory without a stipulation that Burma should not be allowed to disturb her possessions.[2]

These long discussions were not devoid of humorous incidents. Burney says, " Finding that Maung Yeet Atwenwoon is allowed by the other Ministers to take the lead in all discussions with me, I naturally look most towards him, and often address my discourse to him. He whispered to me, however, today, to beg of me to turn and look more towards the Woongyees when I speak, as my addressing him alone so much had made them very jealous of him."[3]

The Governor-General, Lord William Bentinck, disapproved of the course taken by Burney in connection with the Tenasserim discussions: " not that the Resident was not warranted, by the instructions he had received on this subject and the intimations given of the views heretofore entertained by Government in making the matter the subject of discussion in the manner reported in his journal and correspondence, but under the decided opinion expressed by Major Burney that the temper of the Court and the feeling of the people is hostile, and that the hope of success, in case of a second rupture, is not yet extinguished, His Lordship cannot look upon it as good policy to take any step, or to encourage any expectation that will bear to the minds of either the appearance of concession."[4] Burney was, therefore, instructed not to discuss for the present the Tenasserim provinces with the Ava Ministers.[4]

---

[1] *Ibid.*
[2] *Ibid.* par. 389.
[3] *Ibid.* par. 390.
[4] *Ibid.* Vol. 360, Secretary to Governor-General to the Chief Secretary, Camp Bareilly, 5 February, 1831.

On 28 August, 1831, Burney wrote to his Government resigning all hope of being able to negotiate any advantageous transfer of the Tenasserim province. " The circumstance which is well known here," he said, " of our annually sending lacks of rupees from India to defray the ordinary expenses of places from which under the Burmese the King was accustomed to realize some surplus revenue, leads all parties here to rest perfectly satisfied that sooner or later, we must restore these provinces to Ava, and that the exercise of a little patience is all that is required on the part of the Ministers of this country to promote the attainment of their wishes." [1]

The Ministers in October, 1831, raised an important question in connection with the interpretation of Article 4 of the Treaty of Yandabo. The Burmese Commissioners, who held discussions with Crawfurd in 1826 in Ava, had raised the same question, namely, that although the Salween was mentioned in Article 4 as the boundary between Burmese and British territory, yet the same article permitted the British to take only the districts of Tenasserim, Tavoy, Mergui, and Ye; but that the British had taken Moulmein and some other places east of the Salween which were parts of Martaban district, and since they had no right to Martaban district they ought to return these.[2] The Ministers opened the subject (1 October, 1831) in an ingenious manner. They " first drew us [3] into a discussion relative to the future state of rewards and punishments; and the Myawadi Woongyee, after explaining that the Burmese do not understand by their Neibban [4] or heaven a place of annihilation or absorbtion as many foreigners interpret it, but a place where they will enjoy a spiritual existence, conscious of being noticed, the place of punishment called by the Burmese Laukandareet Nga-ri or hell of utter darkness lying between three worlds to which those who covet the property of other men are doomed; and

---

[1] *Ibid.* Vol. 362, Consultations 7 October, 1831.
[2] Crawfurd's Journal, pp. 149, 150; 216-224.
[3] to include Blundell who had come to Ava.
[4] Nirvana.

then very ingeniously turned the conversation to the island
of Kanchien in the Salween, which, he said, belonged to the
Burmese, but that the Commissioner Maingy has lately
claimed it." [1]

Burney informed the Ministers that the island in question had been in British possession since 1826, that it was
situated close to the Moulmein side of the river, and that the
main stream of the Salween lay to the west of it.[2] The Ministers then advanced their old claim to all the islands in the
Salween, including Bilu-gyun, and to all the territory lying
between the old boundary of Ye and that river, on the ground
that all this was a part of Martaban, no part of which district
had been ceded by the Treaty of Yandabo.[3] Burney replied
that he was prohibited by his Government from entering into
any discussion on this point, and that his orders were to inform the Ministers " that the Governor-General believes Mr.
Crawfurd satisfactorily settled this point when he was in
Ava in 1826, and that at any rate the circumstance of our
being so long in possession of the territory must preclude the
possibility of our ever consenting to relinquish any portion
of it, or of even allowing it to become a subject of negotiation." [4]

The Ministers handed to Burney a memorandum [5] on
this claim of theirs, and requested him to give due attention
to it. Within a week's time Burney made them a written
reply, in which, after impressing upon them the argument of
" possession," he drew their attention to incidents during the
Yandabo negotiations to show that the Salween had definitely
been fixed to be the boundary irrespective of the limits of the
Martaban district: " Let the Ministers ask the Padein Woongyee (styled in the Treaty of Yandaboo, Lay-gain Mengyee
Woongyee and Shwegoon Woon Atwenwoon) and Kyeewoon

[1] Bengal Secret and Political Consultations Vol. 366, The Journal,
    par. 786.
[2] *Ibid.* Vol. 363, Ava, 10 October, 1831.
[3] *Ibid.* The Ministers' Memo. 29 September, 1831.
[4] *Ibid.* Ava, 10 October, 1831
[5] *Ibid.* The Ministers' Memo.

Atwenwoon, who signed the Yandaboo Treaty, whether the following statement of what passed between them and Major-General Sir Archibald Campbell at Yandaboo is not true. After the 4th article of the Treaty had been drawn out, a question arose as to what should be the boundary of the territory which the King of Ava was to cede to the English. A map of the country was produced, and after examining it the English general said, that he would fix the Salween river as the boundary. The Kyeewoon Atwenwoon represented that by doing so he would take some of the territory belonging to the province of Martaban, and that the Salween was not the boundary of Ye. But the English General answered that the Salween river would separate the English and Burmese territories in a manner least likely to excite further dispute, and that that river should be the boundary. A sentence to this effect was then added to the fourth article. At the same time the fortune of the Burmese was bad, and if the Kyeewoon Atwenwoon had not submitted, the English General would probably have taken Martaban and one or two other towns. What is the use then of the Ministers raising question on this subject? It will be better for them to occupy themselves in improving the immense extent of territory which their King already possesses, than in endeavouring to add to it a few sandy islands in the Salween and a little jungle and waste land lying between that river and the boundary of Ye." [1]

The Ministers did by no means appreciate the manner and tone of Burney's letter. They made a most vigorous reply, seeking to repudiate every point that he had raised against them, and finally demanded an enquiry into the question. A few extracts from their letter may here be reproduced: —

> "......whether what Major Burney has replied be true or not, it is not satisfactory. The Treaty says one thing Major Burney another. If any dispute arise about boundaries, English and Burmese Commissioners shall be appointed to settle them according to ancient limits. ....The Treaty says the Sal-

[1] *Ibid.* From Burney to the Ministers, Ava, 7 October, 1831.

ween shall be the boundary, but this is not all. If any disputes arise they shall be settled according to the ancient limits by Commissioners. Major Burney does not say whether this is correct or otherwise...... Major Burney's answering in this manner will not destroy the friendship between the two countries. On considering the Letters brought by Major Burney from the English Ruler and English Woongyee, he is authorized to discuss all questions...... He says that from the time of framing the Treaty of Yandaboo he heard and knew that the English possessed it (*i.e.* the island of Kanchien) — Heresay is not suitable ground to go upon. In the Treaty the names of towns are to be seen........ When discussing the subject of boundaries, the Legain Woongyee and Kyeewoon Atwenwoon told Sir Archibald Campbell that as the Treaty mentioned only the four provinces of Ye, Tavoy, Mergui, and Tenasserim, it was not right to take a portion of that of Martaban, who replied, the boundaries can be settled afterwards; the one side should not take nor the other side lose, but the land can be properly divided, and afterwards if disputes arise they will be settled as mentioned in the 3rd article; and this was inserted in the 4th article...... He says, at the time the fortune of the Burmese was bad, and if the Kyeewoon Atwenwoon had not submitted, the English General would probably have taken Martaban and one or two other towns. Regarding fortune, when it is favourable it is so, and vice versa. It is sometimes high and sometimes low, but does not always continue so. Regarding Sir Archibald Campbell's taking one or two more towns, Major Burney has said this without due consideration........ He says, what is the use of the Ministers raising questions on this subject? It will be better for the Ministers to occupy themselves in improving the immense extent of territory which their King already possesses........ Be they few or many, it is not customary to put up with another's possessing land to which you have a claim; also supposing that we do not want the territory between the Salween and Ye, Major Burney can derive no advantage in retaining it. We only want to preserve friendship between the two countries. The English territories are very large, and it will be more advantageous to attend to the prosperity of such as really belong to you only. This is the opinion of the Woongyees and Atwenwoons." [1]

Burney now refused to discuss the question any further without fresh orders from his Government. [2] But the Minis-

---

[1] *Ibid.* From the Ministers to Burney, Ava, 9 October, 1831.
[2] *Ibid.* Vol. 366, Burney's Journal, par. 845.

ters were not willing to drop the subject. Once while the
Indemnity was under discussion, the Tshan Atwenwoon said,
" there is one point about which our hearts are very sore —
you hold our countries which we desire to get back, Moulmein, Ye, Tavoy, and Mergui." Some junior officers were in
attendance and one of them said, " Yes, and the four provinces
of Arracan."[1]

Burney left Ava for Rangoon for the first time on 10
April, 1832, for reasons of health, and it was not till March,
1833, that orders arrived from the Home authorities deciding
to retain the Tenasserim province permanently.

[1] *Ibid.* par. 825.

CHAPTER V

THE RESIDENCY AND BRITISH SUBJECTS IN BURMA; THE APPOINTMENT OF A BURMESE RESIDENT TO CALCUTTA.

Burney had been instructed, in his letter of credentials, given to him by Bentinck, to receive complaints from British subjects resident in Burma, in respect of injuries or losses sustained by them from the Government or subjects of the King, and to make representations thereon to the Burmese Government. The Resident was further authorised "to make requisitions to the British subjects, regarding complaints preferred against them by the Court and subjects of Ava to which requisitions they are already enjoined to reply, and to furnish proper explanation in every instance wherein the same may be required from them by you." [1] Commercial interests had not been neglected in his letter of instructions:—" The Governor-General also desires, that your attention should be given to the trade of Ava with a view of reporting to his Lordship-in-Council the practicability of extending and facilitating British commerce and the consumption of British manufactures." [2]

The presence of Burney in Ava proved to be a great boon to British subjects residing or trading in the country. They were now able to forward their complaints to him, and these were directly placed before the Ministers. On the whole, as will be seen, their person, property, and trade came to be better safeguarded than they ever had been before. Besides, Burney attempted to open up commercial highways between Arakan and Burma, and supported British commercial expeditions into Upper Burma and the Shan country. All these

---

[1] Bengal Secret and Political Consultations Vol. 357, Credentials of Burney, No. 33.
[2] *Ibid.* Letter of Instructions, No. 32, 31 December, 1829.

and other like efforts increased the import of British articles, especially cotton goods, into Burma.

One of Crawfurd's strongest reasons against the establishment of a permanent British residency at Ava was, according to him, the impossibility of maintaining correspondence with the Resident either from Rangoon or Moulmein or Akyab, because of Burmese suspicions. Burney's experience, however, was different. He arrived in Ava on 24 April, 1830, and on 25 May, he received letters from Rangoon and Moulmein, brought in a boat belonging to the Prince of Tharrawaddy. The box containing the letters was taken to the King, and he immediately ordered it to be delivered to Burney.[1] A week later letters again arrived for Burney, and the latter remarks in his Journal, that the Court and sub-officers showed no suspicion or jealousy, which, " Mr. Crawfurd considered as one of the strongest reasons against the permanent residence of a British Agent at this capital; not the smallest curiosity is expressed by any one to know the contents of those letters........not a word has been asked even as to the names of my correspondents." [2]

Soon it became a practice to take Burney's mails first to the Hlutdaw; sometimes they were detained there, but Burney complained, and the Ministers agreed that his letters be first taken to Maung Za, who should without delay forward them to the Resident.[3] In September, 1830, Burney succeeded in persuading the Ministers to permit his Government to establish a Dâk communication between Akyab and Ava, so that not only might he receive his letters by this route, but that a commercial overland highway might gradually be also opened up into Burma. The King also approved of the Dâk, and gave orders to the Burmese officers on the frontiers to afford a proper escort and every other facility to the dâk bearers. In April, 1831, the Government of India also sanctioned the establishment of this convenience, and approved of Burney's scheme

1 *Ibid.* Vol. 358, Burney's Journal, par. 66.
2 *Ibid.* par. 99.
3 *Ibid.* par. 286.

"that all packets should be forwarded from Calcutta to the Superintendent of Aracan at Akyab, and that the latter officer should be authorized to engage 6 suitable bearers, natives of western India, and station them at An[1] which post they might leave for Ava two at a time every 15 days or oftener according as they could return to An......"[2]

Within 13 months of his arrival at Ava, Burney received 37 packets of letters from different quarters: "The circumstance of so regular and frequent a correspondence being maintained between myself and various British officers, and of my being kept informed of everything that is doing in so many different quarters, has, I know excited much surprise and admiration at this Court."[3]

Burney induced the Ministers to agree that all British subjects, coming to or leaving the capital, should report their arrival and departure to the Resident; also, that if they had any application to make to the Burmese Government, they should do it through him.[4] This arrangement greatly improved the position of the Resident, and raised his prestige among the people in general.

On 13 October, 1830, Agha Mohamed, an Indian merchant of Moulmein, complained to Burney that Burmese subordinate officers were not allowing him to leave Ava unless he gave them presents. Burney forwarded the complaint to the Myawadi Woongyee and to Maung Yeet Atwenwoon: the merchant was immediately permitted to quit Ava on payment of the usual dues only.[5] On 4 December, 1830, Burney received a complaint from an Armenian that he had been defrauded by his Pwe-za,[6] who had passed off inferior metal as good gold. When the Pwe-za heard of Burney's interference in the matter he made good the Armenian's loss. Such cases not only encouraged

---

[1] or Aeng.
[2] Bengal Secret and Political Consultations Vol. 358, From Burney to his Government, Ava, 11 September, 1830.
[3] Ibid. Vol. 362, Burney's Journal, par. 680.
[4] Ibid. Vol. 358, pars. 162, 285.
[5] Ibid. Vol. 360, pars. 352, 354.
[6] Assayer or Shroff.

6

British subjects to trade with greater confidence in the country, but Burney also began to rise in the estimation of the people of the country.[1] His presence at the capital also proved useful to British subjects in cases of litigation: " The expense of going to law in this city (*i.e.* Ava) is very heavy. Each Woongyee has a court of justice, and depends upon the decision of cases as his principal means of subsistence. The presence of a British Resident here is the only way in which British subjects can be in some degree insured justice and protection from exhorbitant law charges." [2]

Burney interfered from time to time in the interest of British subjects in cases concerning creditors and debtors. " I must state here," he says, " that this part of my duty is of the most unpleasant nature. Many natives of British India trading in this country have accounts of long standing with Burmese subjects, or they have been induced to advance loans of money to Burmese provincial officers, or have been plundered under some false pretences." [3] Burney had several disagreeable and irritable discussions with the Woongyees in order to settle such claims, because the latter were not interested in a case if presents were not forthcoming, this being their principal source of income.[3] There were sometimes complaints from Burmese officers against British subjects. A typical case may here be reproduced in Burney's own words:—

" A subordinate Thoung-mhoo or jailor came this evening (15th March 1831) to complain against some of the Lascars of the Gunboat[4] for riotous conduct in the bazaar. The old Treasurer was with me at the time and I was amused to hear the Thoung-mhoo tell him, the men who had behaved ill in the bazaar must be some of those lately arrived, for that all those that had come up with me are now quite tamed—yeen-byee— the same term which is applied to a wild animal when broken in.

[1] Bengal Secret and Political Consultations Vol. 360, The Journal, par. 452.
[2] *Ibid.* par. 453.
[3] *Ibid.* par. 530.
[4] in Burney's service, belonging to the East India Company.

I have often heard the Burmese call us Kula-Yain, wild or savage Kulas,[1] and Kula-gyan, coarse Kulas; and as a proof that the pride and arrogance of this race are not sufficiently corrected, I may mention that all classes of the people, when they have occasion to refer to the date of the late war[2] style it, " the period when the Kulas rose, or rebelled "—" Kula tha Kula, Kala phoungan Kala." [3] ကုလား ထ ကုလား။ ကုလား ပုန်ကန့် ကုလား။

In April, 1831, a boat belonging to an old Armenian merchant was attacked by river pirates near Pagan in broad daylight. The robbers, when they boarded the boat, cried out, " You Kalas have forced us to pay plenty of money,[4] we will now retake some of it." They killed the Armenian and plundered the boat, including 15 cases belonging to Burney containing his annual supplies and stores, also books and wearing apparel which he had ordered from Calcutta and Moulmein. The Ministers immediately dispatched an officer of the Hlutdaw to enquire and effect the arrest of the robbers. Within a few weeks the culprits were arrested and sent to Ava, but it was not till one year later (on 15th March, 1832) that Burney was informed that 23 of the robbers and their families had been apprehended. At Burney's suggestion it was agreed to execute two or three of them on the very spot where the offence had been committed.[5]

On account of the presence of Burney in Ava, the number of Armenian and Indian merchants in Burma increased greatly; also the importation of British goods into the country went up considerably. Cotton goods were sold in Ava at lower prices even than at Rangoon. The returns for these importations being almost entirely in specie, there was a drastic reduction in the quantity of precious metals circulating in the

[1] Kula = Foreigner; *lit.*ကူး = cross, လာ = come, *i.e.* to come crossing the sea.
[2] The First Anglo-Burmese War, 1824-1826.
[3] Bengal Secret and Political Consultations Vol. 360, Burney's Journal, par. 594.
[4] The Indemnity of One Crore of Rupees.
[5] Bengal Secret and Political Vols. 361, 366, The Journal, pars. 649, 658, 668, 929, 947.

country as mediums of exchange. The Ministers, therefore, enacted a new regulation calling upon merchants to give a statement of articles they were taking with them from Ava to Rangoon. Care was, however, not taken to make the new regulation public. Agha Saadat, a merchant of Moulmein, while going from Ava with a large quantity of specie in his boats, was searched at Kyauk-ta-loun and detained. He applied to Burney, and the latter appealed to the Ministers that the merchant was taking the specie from one town of Burma to another in the same country, and that no trade could be carried on under the circumstances since merchants would not be able to buy Burmese products such as timber, lac, etc., in Rangoon.[1]

The Ministers replied that there was no objection to specie being taken from one town to another; but that it was exported from the country, and that they wanted traders to declare what specie they were taking with them. Burney retorted that that would be undesirable, since robbers would then easily waylay them. He demanded the release of the merchant.[1]

Burney also addressed a letter to the King explaining the situation, but the Ministers did not present it to His Majesty, so that finally he threatened to retire to Rangoon unless the merchant, who was a British subject, was released, and collections towards the payment of the Indemnity were resumed. The trader was released, but the Ministers made no promise concerning the indemnity. Burney, therefore, embarked on 14 August, 1831, but was induced to return to Ava on 16 August, under circumstances already recounted in Chapter IV pp. 120-122.

In November, 1831, the Ministers enacted a new regulation for the appointment of a few Pwezas through whom only foreign merchants were to be allowed to buy and sell in Ava. Burney protested that this would restrict the free liberty of buying and selling, and would thus be a breach of the spirit of

---

[1] *Ibid.* Vol. 362, par. 731.

the treaties between the two states. The Ministers suspended the regulation.[1]

In January, 1832, Agha Hussain a merchant complained to Burney that one Low, an Englishman, was his debtor, and had left Ava without paying him. Burney referred him to the Ministers. The Ministers consulted Burney about it, and the latter recommended to them the law of their country, and made it clear, that he had no power or desire to interfere in favour of Low if the complaint was correct. " After considerable hesitation the Ministers declined to bring Mr. Low back to Ava due to their great anxiety to avoid all unpleasant discussions with the British Government. They observed that they were afraid Mr. Low might resist their order, and some accident might occur if their officers attempted to enforce his return to Ava; and that in such event long explanations would be required of them by the British Government." [2]

It has already been noted that Burney's one great object was to open overland trade between Burma and Arakan. In pursuance of this aim he had succeded in establishing a regular dâk service along that route via An. Lane, the English merchant, however, was opposed to the opening of this new trade route because of the good profits he was making in his trade by the Rangoon route. His influence upon the King and the Ministers was so great that Burney feared very high duties would be levied upon the Arakan trade.[3]

Soon after his arrival in Ava, Burney had brought this subject to the notice of Menthagyee in the strongest manner possible, and had told him that a discouragement of the Arakan trade would be contrary to the spirit of the Commercial Treaty, and would also injure the King and the country, " as the more British goods were introduced into Ava the cheaper they would sell, the consumption would increase, and the duties or revenue of the King would increase in proportion." [4]

[1] Bengal Secret and Political Consultations Vol. 366, Burney's Journal. pars. 820, 944, 951.
[2] Ibid. par. 882.
[3] Ibid. Vol. 358, pars. 151, 279.
[4] Ibid. par. 151.

At the instigation of Lane, however, extra duties were levied on the Arakan trade. Burney remonstrated with this his countryman, recommended him to use the Arakan route for his own trade, and warned him of the displeasure of the Governor-General. Lane agreed to persuade Menthagyee to systematize the Arakan trade.[1] The question was discussed from time to time for about a month, and finally on 8 October, 1830, the Arakan duties were fixed at the Hlutdaw:—10% for the King and $\frac{1}{2}$% for the officers; molesting and delaying merchants was prohibited; traders were to be at liberty to enter Burmese territories from Arakan via An and Talak; the duties were to be levied at Maphe and Salinmyo respectively; finally, once duties were paid no additional duties were to be levied in the Burmese dominions. The export duty was also fixed:— 4 as. and 1/16th of a basket of rice per maund.[2]

Burney next endeavoured to bring about a systematization of duties levied at Ava upon exports. Hitherto these were levied upon no fixed scale. The Hlutdaw, finally, on 10 and 15 November, 1830, respectively, issued two orders fixing the same:—on rubies $5\frac{1}{2}$% plus one piece of Book muslin and one plate of sugar to each of the Atwenwoons; for each person leaving Ava in a boat 1/10th of a tical of silver and 1/16th of a basket of rice, to be paid at the Kyauk-ta-loun and Men-gwon-Kenda chokies; gold, silver, swords, spears, and muskets not to be exported from the country; each boat leaving Ava to pay from one to two ticals according to size.[3]

The systematization of the above mentioned duties was not easily conceded. Burney had several acrimonious conferences at the Hlutdaw. At one time he tried to forward a letter to the King complaining of the irregular duties levied in Ava, but the Ministers refused to comply with his request. Burney charged them with closing the door of friendship against him, and refused to hold any further intercourse with them unless they apologised. "A knowledge of the footing on which I now

---

[1] *Ibid.* par. 279.
[2] *Ibid.* par. 343.
[3] *Ibid.* Vol. 360, par. 436 and appendix. Vide Appendix II.

stood with the Ministers emboldened me to form and to express such a resolution. I should not have ventured to take such a step upon my first arrival here as at that time the Woongyees would have cared little whether I held or refused to hold intercourse with them." [1]

The Tshan Atwenwoon requested Burney to forget all and attend the Hlutdaw. But Burney refused, unless a Woondouk was sent by the Woongyees to apologise on their behalf. The Atwenwoon said that this would be contrary to all custom. The old Treasurer also came to Burney with a message from the Woongyees, " offering if I would attend the Hlutdaw, to let me have everything I had applied for, and begged of me not to insist upon the Woondouk being sent to me. I was, however, inflexible." [2]

On 21 November, 1831, finally, the Woondouk Maung Khan Ye came to explain and to apologise. Burney was satisfied, and agreed to forget what had passed and to meet the Woongyees again. The following are the reflections of Burney on the above episode:—

"........I should not have been disposed to make so much of this matter if my knowledge of the character of these people did not assure me that such a proceeding was absolutely necessary. To permit the Woongyees to treat me with slight or disrespect or to let them suppose that I could easily be prevailed upon afterwards to overlook or forget such things would soon render me a useless cypher here. I was anxious only to seize an instance like the present in which the Woongyees were clearly in the wrong and which they would not defend. In our intercourse with no people in the world is Polonius's advice more necessary to be kept in view than here — ' Beware of entrance to quarrel; but being in bear it that the opposer may beware of thee '." [3]

Burney proposed to the Ministers that the export of gold and silver be permitted on payment of a small duty, but they refused, and said, that the King would never agree to it.[4] In

[1] *Ibid.* pars. 416, 417, 420.
[2] *Ibid.* pars. 422, 424.
[3] *Ibid.* par. 425. There is a slight error in this quotation made by Burney. See *Shakespeare's Hamlet,* Act I, Scene III.
[4] *Ibid.* par. 433.

August, 1831, the King even absolutely prohibited the export of these precious metals from Ava and all other towns to Rangoon.[1] This order was issued because from Rangoon foreign merchants were able to export these metals quite easily.

Burney's presence in Ava, and the greater security enjoyed by foreign merchants in consequence thereof, acted as a stimulus to British trade in Burma. In three months, October, 1830 to January, 1831, 250,000 pieces of cotton cloth were imported through Rangoon port alone. Burney says, " The importation of British goods into this country and particularly into the capital have been vastly increased since the residence of a British officer here." [2] The King's revenue also increased, and he was so pleased that he issued fresh orders commanding protection and encouragement to be afforded everywhere to traders. The Ministers rejoiced and told Burney that they were convinced, that a state of peace was much more advantageous than war.[3] Arakan traders also appeared at the capital with large supplies of piece goods so that prices fell ruinously.[4]

Burney suggested to the authorities in Calcutta that trade with Burma in woollen goods would prove lucrative. " I have been much struck," he wrote, " by observing the great dearth of warm clothing among the inhabitants. Even the Woongyees are covered, when cold, with nothing better than a piece of common broadcloth about $2\frac{1}{2}$ yards long edged with silk. Shawls are never seen although the Myawadi Woongyee assures me that they are much admired here, and that some of the Princes possess such an article. Neither is there anything here like the common Indian *Cumlee* or blanket which I am sure would be very acceptable to the lower classes of the people who are now seen shivering with cold under their silk and cotton dresses........When the prices of Indian woollens and imitation shawls can be lowered here I am satisfied that their con-

[1] *Ibid*. Vol. 362, par. 760.
[2] *Ibid*. Vol. 360, par. 529.
[3] *Ibid*. par. 534.
[4] *Ibid*. par. 537.

sumption will be greatly extended. The taste of the people for broadcloth is increasing." [1]

Within a few weeks of Burney's arrival in Ava, the Burmese Government also expressed a desire to send an ambassador to Calcutta.[2] Burney encouraged the Ministers in this move, in hopes that the measure would ensure at Ava much correct and useful information regarding the power, resources, and character of the English.[3] Finally in August, 1830, two men were selected as senior and junior resident respectively. The Senior Resident was Mengee Maha Tsee Thoo Maung Shwe, who was at one time employed in the Palace as Twen-then-Woon or Superintendent of attendants, and had in the previous reign served as Mye Dain or Land Measurer and Myeet Ye Woon or Superintendent of a special River Police. The Junior Envoy was Mentha Nanda Gyau den Maung Byo, a Tsaredaugyee or Clerk to the Ministers. Both were looked upon by their countrymen as men of learning, and particularly conversant with Burmese history and geography.[3]

Burney did not approve of the selection for the senior appointment, and considered the junior envoy to be possessed of more intelligence. He even spoke to the Ministers about it, but was unable to secure a change.[4] Writing about the appointments he says, " These two individuals are men of no influence or consideration at Ava although the Senior holds a higher rank in the Burmese Peerage than any person who was before deputed to Bengal by a King of Ava. Among the Indo-Chinese states it is well known that Embassadors are only considered as bearers of royal letters, and no man of any real consideration in his own country is ever employed on such a service. When these Burmese Envoys were first appointed I

---

[1] *Ibid*. par. 465.
[2] *Ibid*. Vol. 358, par. 64.
[3] India Political Consultations Range 193, Vol. 79, 6 July, 1835, No. 18.
[4] Bengal Secret and Political Consultations Vol. 358, Burney's Journal, par. 304.
   The Kone-baung-set Mahayazawin in Book 2, p. 486 refers to these two Envoys:— " Mahasithu and Nanda Kyawdin (Chief Clerk) Shwetaung Nawyahta (Expenditure Clerk)."

openly expressed to the Ministers that the Principal Envoy did not possess the necessary qualifications, and recommended them to select some individual who had lived and associated with Europeans at Rangoon, which place may really be considered as the Burmese University, for all the most intelligent men you meet with in this country have resided there for some time and have had their minds and views enlarged by acquiring some knowledge of European countries, customs, and manners. The Ministers could only assure me that they would have the Envoy relieved if after a short trial in Bengal he was found unfit for the situation, but the real fact was they had nothing to do with the selection which was made within the Palace, where it is believed a handsome present had as usual been received for the appointment by the highest female in the kingdom. As one instance of the ignorance which this Envoy displayed regarding the country and people to which he was going, I recollect his coming to me one day, just before he left Ava for Bengal, to ask me whether carrying with him a supply of Chinese needles would not enable him to make acceptable presents to our public officers." [1]

Burney, as noted before, was very anxious to have the overland route from the Irrawaddy to Arakan cleared and re-established; hence he persuaded the Ministers to depute their envoys to Bengal by that route, offering at the same time to appoint his Assistant Capt. Geo. Burney [2] to escort the Mission, and promising that a steam vessel would also

---

[1] India Political Consultations Range 193, Vol. 79, 6 July, 1835, No. 18.
   " The Burmese can manufacture no good needles and import what they chiefly use from China. Perhaps this is one reason why so little of needlework is understood in this country — not one woman in fifty can sew. The Burmese wearing apparel does not require much sewing, and they have lately taken to washing their clothes in consequence of which the Mogul (*i.e.* Muhamedan) traders complain the consumption of book muslin and cottons has been sensibly diminished. Here we see every morning numbers of men employed on the banks of the river washing clothes, a sight we never observed in Siam where the profession of a washerman is wholly unknown." Bengal Secret and Political Consultations Vol. 358, Burney's Journal, par. 336.
[2] The Resident's younger brother.

be made available to convey the party from Akyab to Calcutta.[1] The Ministers accepted this offer, and on 30 September, 1830, the King granted the title "Theeri Raja Nauratha" (*i.e.* the Excellent and Noble Son) to Capt. Burney, as well as the privilege of using a gilt umbrella. In the presence of the King the letters of the title were stamped upon a thin piece of gold about 5″ x 2″, and a Than-dau-zen chanted the title and then tied it over the younger Burney's forehead.[2]

Burney also tried to persuade the Ministers to send some young Burmese nobles of the Court to visit Calcutta with the Envoys so that they might increase their knowledge of the world, and that by this means the Burmese might come to know the British better. Maung Za and Maung Yeet owned the benefits, but said, "Burmese parents are not like English parents. We cannot part with our children and let them, when young, go away to such a distance and for such a long period as you appear to do."[3]

The Ministers furnished the Envoys with official instructions in great detail, entrusting them with three main tasks:— (1) The speedy return of the Kubo Valley to the King. This was the most important task, and they were armed with every possible argument in favour of the Burmese claim. "You must accordingly repeat," say the instructions, "that when this Munipore question is settled in such a manner as the Woongyees and Atwenwoons have fully explained to Major Burney the

---

[1] India Political Consultations Range 193, Vol. 79, 6 July, 1835, No. 18. Although good needles were not manufactured in Burma, some types of fire-arms were. Burney says, "His Majesty has been pleased to order that my Assistant should be furnished with a small piece of cannon and a musket, the manufacture of this country, in order that the same may be shown to the western countries, and that it may be known there that such warlike instruments can be properly manufactured at Ava." Bengal Secret and Political Consultations, Vol. 358, Burney's Journal, par. 336. George Burney also took with him a watch belonging to the King, in order to have it repaired at Calcutta. India Political Consultations, Range 193, Vol. 79, 6 July, 1835, No. 18.

[2] Bengal Secret and Political Consultations Vol. 358, The Journal, pars. 319, 322.

[3] *Ibid.* par. 310.

person deputed to Ava, so that good may attend the future as well as the past and the Casseyers kept in peace and quiet, then the two countries will be able to increase in friendship." [1] (2) The settlement of the King's claim over that part of Martaban district which lay east of the Salween, and which was annexed by the British. (3) The abrogation of the 7th Article of the Treaty of Yandabo permitting the appointment of exchange Residents. "Whenever an opportunity for conversing pleasantly arrives," continue the instructions, "you must say that the two countries have become friends — there is no cause for either distrusting the other, and everything is right and quiet. By stationing people in the English country great expense is incurred in maintaining them, and the English Chief also cannot station people in the Burmese Country without incurring much outlay in money and necessaries. The two countries have no cause for distrusting each other, and therefore it would be better for the English and Burmese Chiefs to withdraw the men stationed by each, and to send Royal and friendly letters to each other once in five years, and in this manner keep open the communication and intercourse between the two countries and cultivate friendship." [1] This makes it clear that although Burney had been well received, and treated as never before a British envoy had been, it was the great ambition of the Burmese Government to bring diplomatic relations through the Resident to an end, such a mediatorial link being looked upon as humiliating. Finally, the Envoys were orally instructed to obtain the retrocession of the Tenasserim and Arakan provinces.[1]

The Envoys also carried with them a letter from the King to the Governor-General. Burney was anxious to have a copy of this letter, to be sure that there was nothing offensive or unbecoming in it. He, therefore, made his request to Menthagyee, but was told that it was not customary to supply a copy. Burney threatened, that unless he knew that the letter was suitable, he would not depute Capt. Burney to accompany the

[1] India Political Consultations Range 193, Vol. 79, 6 July, 1835, No. 18.

Burmese Resident. Menthagyee finally ordered a copy to be given to Burney, together with a list of presents from the King to the Governor-General consisting of rubies, sapphires, Burma silk cloths, and lacquered boxes. As to the letter, Burney says that it had no date according to custom, the pronoun was cautiously omitted, the relative rank of the two parties being not defined, and that it was not in the style of a mandate or Edict as was the letter written by the Chinese Emperor to the Prince Regent of England, but that it was as to an equal and in the same style as the letter of the Governor-General to the King.[1]

[1] Bengal Secret and Political Consultations Vol. 358, Burney's Journal, par. 332.

Burney's Journal, 29 November, 1830, par. 444: — "For some days past the Tshan Atwenwoon had seemed to me to have some misgivings about the letter which had been addressed to the Governor-General in the name of the King of Ava. He told me to recollect that his sovereign was an anointed King or "Be-theit-Khan Shen bhuren," (အဘိသိတ်ခံရှင်ဘုရင်) and begged of me whenever I have occasion to allude to the Governor-General before the King not to style him Goombhani Bhuren (*i.e.* Company Bhuren) but Angleit Men. I had taken little notice of these observations excepting to state that I have no wish to lower the dignity of his sovereign, and that I should continue to style the Governor-General by the title of "India Taing atsho thau Angleit Men — the Englishman who governs India," as had been agreed upon between the Ministers and myself in June last." At the Myawadi Woongyee's lodgings the same day "I was requested to expunge from the passage where the Burmese King is invited by His Lordship to send a resident to *Calcutta,* the word Calcutta...... I saw what the object of the Ministers was: they wished this proceeding of sending a letter and Resident to the Governor-General to be so arranged that they might hereafter be able if necessary to pretend that they were sent to the King of England, and perhaps to have the matter so recorded in their History...... I told them that they knew very well from whom I had come here and whose letter I had brought.." Burney also explained that the dignity of the King was not at all lowered, and that the Kings of Persia and Siam had also addressed the Governor-General.

The following is a translation of the letter from the King to the Governor-General. According to Burmese custom it was not dated but was forwarded on 9 October, 1830: —

"His Most Glorious Excellent Majesty who rules over Thunaparanta, Tampadipa and other great kingdoms to the Eastwards and over many umbrella wearing Chiefs. King· of the Rising Sun, Lord of the Celestial Elephant, and Proprietor of many white elephants, Lord of Life and Great Chief of Righteousness,

On 9 October, 1830, the Burmese Mission[1] consisting of the two Envoys and their families, servants and bodyguards, numbering in all 84 men and women, and accompanied by Capt. Geo. Burney and his servants, left Ava by river, and arrived at Mimbu on 18 October. From Mimbu by land marches, via Maphemyo and Nat-ye-gan, they arrived at An on 16 November, and Akyab on 21 November. Instead of 43 days they should have completed the journey in about one-half the time, but the Envoys adopted dilatory methods: "......they stopped," wrote Capt. Burney, "at every pagoda which they met with on their route down the river in order to offer up their devotions and pray for a safe return from what they considered at the time a most hazardous service on which they were going."[2] On 2 December, the Mission embarked on board

---

informs the English Chief who rules over India and other great kingdoms to the Westward.

"Inheriting from deceased great grand father and grand father, delight is taken in ruling over Thunaparanta, Tampadipa and other great kingdoms, and over many umbrella wearing Chiefs; having been duly consecrated, all the duties of a King and Chief are constantly and diligently fulfilled. The inhabitants of the country and all living animals are watched and protected with Justice; sincere in all three objects of Righteous observance, namely God, His precepts, and His attendants or Priests by diligent and constant attention, piety is exalted and praised, and the excellent religion of God is made to shine and increase.

"Major Burney has arrived at Yatnapura, the Golden City of Ava in order to cement friendship with a royal letter and presents from the English Chief who rules over the Western and other kingdoms. In the royal letter it is stated that Friendship between the two countries shall be prolonged. In the same manner as Major Burney has been deputed, the Twen Then Woon Mengyee Maha Tsee Thoo a man of sense and prudence is vested with powers and proceeds with presents. The Twen Then Woon Mengyee Maha Tsee Thoo will represent to the English Chief all matters that have been communicated to him. And he has been instructed to submit here all that the English Chief may reply in a friendly manner, that friendship between the two countries may be prolonged with sincerity admit (Sic) into the hearts (i.e. let his sentiments penetrate the heart). This is what is to be informed." Bengal Secret and Political Vol. 358.

[1] For a complete account of this Mission see The Journal of the Burma Research Society, Vol. XXVI, Part II, History of the Burmese Mission to India, 1830-1833, by W. S. Desai.
[2] India Political Consultations Range 193, Vol. 79, 6 July, 1835, No. 18. Bengal Secret and Political Vol. 360, Burney's Journal, par. 362.

the steam vessel *Irrawadi,* and arrived at Calcutta on 6 December, 1830. The Governor-General was at the time absent in Upper India. The Envoys waited for him for 10 months, and finally in October, 1831, embarked in boats to proceed up country by river to wait on him.[1]

[1] *Ibid.*

CHAPTER VI

BAGYIDAW AND THE FIRST DEPARTURE OF BURNEY
FROM AVA, 1832.

Yule in his Narrative [1] of the Mission sent by the Governor-General to the Court of Ava in 1855 gives an account of Bagyidaw and his family. " The then King of Burma, Phagyidau, or Noungdaugyi ("Royal Elder Brother") as he is now most commonly called," he says, " a man of about forty-seven or forty-eight years of age, was popular among his subjects at the capital, on account of his partiality for public amusements, the shows, boat-races, and fêtes in which they so much delight, and he had the reputation of good nature, accessibility, and unwillingness to shed blood. But he was without ability or strength of character, restless, childless,[2] arrogant, and violent. The Ministers never dared to bring an unpleasant subject before him, and he often vented his displeasure on even the chief among them by flinging his spear, Saul-like, in open court, or by inflicting on them the most degrading punishments. He felt bitterly the loss of his provinces, never could bear to confess even the equality of the British Government to his own, and viewed the presence of the Resident with jealousy and aversion, as that of a dictator and a spy. Ever since he came to the throne, and even before that, an extraordinary influence over him had been weilded by his chief Queen, a woman of low origin, and of age at least equal to his own, but who spared no pains by the most assiduous devotion to keep up that influence which her fascinations had originally acquired. In earlier years she had been commonly known among the King's relations as " the sorceress." Her power was shared by her brother, known as Menthagyi (Great Prince), once a fishmonger, a man of

---

[1] *Capt. Henry Yule*, The Court of Ava, p. 223.
[2] Should be " childish" : Bagyidaw was not childless.

considerable intelligence, and when he chose, of unusually dignified manners for a Burman, but superstitious, cowardly,
brutal, and grasping beyond all bounds.

" The Sakya-men, the King's eldest son, born by a deceased
Queen of royal blood, was a lad of about eighteen at the time
of Burney's arrival; but he was then, and continued to be
throughout his father's reign, kept completely in the background by his step mother......"

This account is substantially corroborated by documentary
evidence connected with Burney's stay in Ava. As to the
King's temper, Burney says in his Journal, " The King lost
his temper to-day at being informed of the death of one of
his female elephants which the Tsheng-Woon or Superintendent of Elephants had privately lent to some officer on the
Tsagain [1] side of the river. His Majesty sent immediately for
the Tsheng-Woon, and suspecting that the Atwenwoons had
been bribed to conceal this man's fault, he ordered three of
them," including " Maung Yeet and Maung Ba Youk, the Tshan
and Kyee Woon Atenwoons to be beaten! They were immediately seized by the head and dragged on one side by all the
petty officers and people who were on the spot, and who eagerly
strove to testify their sentiments of duty and devotion to His
Majesty by beating the Atwenwoons most severely in the
Burmese mode called, *th'oung,* that is with the elbow and fist
on the back. They were afterwards regularly flogged with a
rattan." [2] The Tsheng-Woon was one of the play fellows of the
King and a great favourite, but this did not save him: he was
confined with three pairs of irons. This occurrence was reported to Burney by an eyewitness, and was later confirmed by
Lanciago.[2]

But the King disliked bloodshed. In March, 1831, 17 men
were decapitated for highway robbery while the King was ill.
It was generally believed, that had he been well, he would not
have permitted this wholesale execution. " The King is cer-

[1] Sagaing.
[2] Bengal Secret and Political Consultations Vol. 358, par. 231, 20
   August, 1830.

tainly very popular among his subjects for his reputed character of mild temper and unwillingness to shed blood," says Burney.[1] " The Awe-Youk also communicated to me an interesting anecdote of the King, shewing that he possesses more true delicacy of feeling than we could have expected from him, and proving at all events, the perfect sanity of his mind at present. In the course of this morning,[2] while the Burmese nobles were throwing lances at a target in the presence of His Majesty, the old Kyouk Tshaung Woongyee was thrown off his horse. The moment he fell the King turned away his body and pretended not to see the accident. All the spectators were enraptured with the gracious conduct of their sovereign, and attributed it to his desire of not increasing the mortification of the poor old Woongyee."[3]

The King enjoyed a tremendous influence over the minds of his officers as well as over his subjects in general. If the King was heard to speak well of Burney, the conduct of all classes of people towards the British Residency would automatically improve: " All think only of what may please him for the moment, not a soul cares a straw for what may benefit the people......a cross look or a word from His Majesty hereafter will make all here just as ready to vie with each other in treating us with insult and disrespect."[4]

---

[1] *Ibid.* Vol. 361, par. 610.
[2] 29 January, 1832.
[3] Bengal Secret and Political Consultations Vol. 366, Burney's Journal, par. 892.

   One of the Woongyees mentioned a circumstance to Burney which accounts for a very singular impression that the King and many other Burmans had of the English character: " He alleged that all the European merchants and captains of the ships at Rangoon once gave a public entertainment to his father, and that after dinner on that occasion most of the gentlemen set to a boxing. The King (Bagyidaw), probably from having heard this story, firmly believes that after dinner, Englishmen usually have a boxing match, and shortly before the war some very respectable English traders having come to Ava, he one day made them dine before him. After the cloth was removed he appeared very restless and impatient for some time, and at last pointing to his guests he called out to Dr. Price, When are they going to fight?" Bengal Secret and Political Consultations Vol. 358, Burney's Journal, par. 111.
[4] *Ibid.* Vol. 358, par. 112.

If the King was unable to hold his usual Kadaw day durbar, the Princes, Chiefs, and others present did obeisance to the
empty throne and made offerings.[1] If the King sent a message
to the Hlutdaw, the moment the Thandau Zen entered the hall,
all the Ministers would turn towards the throne or the spot
where the King was wont to take his seat when he visited the
place; all the Woongyees, the Thandau Zen, and all other Burmans present would then perform the Shikhoe,[2] after which
the King's order would be read.[3]

Bagyidaw was a devout Buddhist, and paid much attention
to Buddha's images, pagodas, and the priesthood. He was,
however, not intolerant towards the practice of other religions
in his dominions, although he patronized only Buddhism.
There was a Roman Catholic Mission in the country the centre
of its operations being Nga-bek and five other neighbouring
villages mostly inhabited by about 1000 Christians. They were
the descendants of the Portuguese and other Christians whom
Alaungpaya had captured at Syriam and carried away to
Upper Burma in 1756. Guiseppe D'amato, a Neapolitan priest,
resided in Nga-bek and owned a chapel as well as quarters for
his use. In 1830 he was 73 years of age, had resided in Burma
for 47 years, and lived like a Burman among his followers.
During the war he was put in irons for some time and many of
his flock apostatised.[4] He paid a visit to Burney which the

---

[1] *Ibid.* Vol. 366, par. 808.
[2] The Burmese obeisance.
[3] Bengal Secret and Political Consultations Vol. 358, Burney's Journal, par. 302.
[4] *Ibid.* Vol. 360, pars. 481, 483.
  Bigandet in his History of the Catholic Burmese Mission says on
  p. 26, that D'amato " was left free and undisturbed " during the
  War of 1824-1826. This evidently is not correct. Burney says
  that he was put in irons for some time. Bigandet also says concerning this priest: — " He had made collection of plants, and
  executed drawings of the insects and reptiles of Upper Burma.
  He gave to the English Resident, Col. Burney, a part of his
  drawings and collections. The remainder must have perished
  with all the manuscripts of the mission, in the conflagration that
  destroyed the church and priests' house at Khiansarua in 1840."
  Burney says something quite different concerning these drawings
  and collections:— " He (D'amato) also informed me that knowing something of Natural History and of painting, he had made

latter returned.   In June, 1831, two more Italian priests, Antonio Ricca and Domingo Taruli, were deputed to Burma by the Pope.   They were socially well connected and were men of education.   They were also allowed to visit Burney, who, writing about them says, " Their disposition and manners are of the most lively and cheerful description; but I fear they will not continue long so in this wretched country." [1]

It seems that the Romanist Mission had been operating in the country in a quiet manner, attending only to those who were members of the Papal Church, so that it did not come into conflict with Bagyidaw and his government.   The case of Adoniram Judson was very different.   His remarkable evangelistic career, ably and most faithfully supported by his noble wife Anne, and the privations and oppressions suffered by the pair in Burma, both before and during the war, may be studied elsewhere. [2]   After the war he made Amherst the base of his operations, and pursued the spread of the Gospel of Christ with untiring zeal.   Within six months of Burney's arrival at Ava, news was received of Judson's movements in Prome. [3]   The feelings of the King and Court may best be stated here in the words of the British Resident :—

---

a collection of drawings of about 3,000 Non-descript plants and flowers and 200 animals in four folio volumes, two containing the drawings and two minute descriptions of them.....during the late war he gave them in charge of one of his flock from whose house they were taken by a Burmese soldier and delivered to Menzagyee who gave the soldier a *Patsho* for these invaluable treasures, and who the Padre says, has cut many of the paintings out of the books and pasted them up in different parts of the interior of his house."   Bengal Secret and Political Vol. 360, Consultations 18 March, 1831, Burney's Journal, par. 483.

[1] *Ibid.* Vol. 362, par. 696.
[2] *Wayland,* A Memoir of Judson, Vol. 1.
[3] Extracts from Judson's Letter, dated Prome, 15 June, 1830: —
    " The people at Mendai seemed disposed to cavil, and some of them rather treated me uncivilly.   I gave away not many tracts......The next morning the wife of the governor in these parts, having heard of me, sent to the boat for a tract; several other people also came on the same errand, until we left the place......we reached this place (Prome), about one hundred and seventy miles from Rangoon.   I landed and found Mr. M., the only European residing here; and he invited me to stay with him a few days, until I could get settled......   He immediately

" The Ministers requested my advice as to the measures
which they ought to pursue, with respect to Dr. Judson, who,
they said, is come up to Prome and is there distributing tracts
among the inhabitants and abusing the Burmese Religion much
to the annoyance of the King. I told them that Dr. Judson is
now exclusively devoted to missionary pursuits, that I possess
no power or authority over him; but that I know him to be a
very pious and good man, and one not likely to injure the Burmese King or Government in any manner. The Ministers replied
that the King is much vexed with Dr. Judson for the zeal with
which he is distributing among the people writings in which the
Burmese faith is held forth to contempt and that His Majesty
is anxious to remove him from Prome. I said that the Burmese
King and Government have always enjoyed a high reputation
among civilized nations for the toleration which they have shown
to all religious faiths; that there are thousands in Europe and
America who would be much hurt and disappointed to hear of
any change in the liberal policy hitherto observed by the King
of Ava; and that I hoped the Ministers would not think of
molesting or injuring Dr. Judson as such a proceeding would
offend and displease good men of all nations. They replied that
it was for this reason, to avoid hurting Dr. Judson that they had
consulted me, and they proposed that I should write and advise
Dr. Judson of the King's sentiment towards him. I reiterated
my assurances that Dr. Judson is in no way connected with me
or my Government, and that I can issue no orders to him, and
I begged the Ministers to let him alone; which, however, they
said they could not as His Majesty had expressed himself much

took me to the governess of the town, whose husband has lately
been summoned to Ava. In her presence I found the deputy-
governor and a number of people. I read and preached to them.
They applauded my style of reading etc., but seemed to be more
taken with the sound than the sense. The governess, however,
was evidently impressed. She begged for the tract, that she
might get it copied. I presented it to her and she received it
thankfully. Thence I proceeded to various places in search of a
house to be let, but was unsuccessful. The people are afraid to
have any connexion with a foreigner. Ever since Major Burney
passed up to Ava, the country has been full of all manner of
rumours and fears. The very face of a white man spreads general
alarm. Mr. M., has been accused of being a spy, though nothing
can be more false.....I find that the same suspicion is generally
felt towards me......
" Failing in my attempt to hire a house, I went in search of
a vacant spot to build on...... Found, in the heart of the town
an old dismantled zayat in front of a pagoda...... Went to the
deputy-governor, presented him with a tract, and warned him not

displeased with his conduct. I consented at last to write to Dr.
Judson, but I told the Ministers to recollect that I had no right
to interfere with him, who, notwithstanding any letter he might
receive from us, would act in whatever manner his own judgment and conscience might dictate. The Ministers begged of me
only to recommend Dr. Judson to return to Rangoon and confine his missionary labours within that city."[1]

Burney was often invited by the King at state functions,
animal shows, and boat races, of all which Bagyidaw was very
fond. On 30 August, he accompanied the King to Amarapura
to witness some boat races. "......no umbrellas were allowed
to be used in the presence of the King;......the Burmese officers had considerately put up at the head of our war boat a
kind of canopy which sheltered us from the sun. The King
laughed as we passed him......The races were not very
interesting. They consisted of making two boats at a time

---

to be intoxicated with worldly splendour, for life was short etc.
He read part of the tract, and said that my words were very
proper......"

Letter dated Prome, 26 June, 1830: — "July 2. A great
change has taken place in the minds of government people towards me. Satan has industriously circulated a report that I am
a spy in pay of the British. Last night the deputy-governor
sent to inquire my name and title. This morning I waited on
him, and on the lady-governess, but met with a very cold reception at both places. The deputy-governor is probably reporting
me to Ava, and what the consequences will be, I know not.
Several visitors, who began to listen with some favourable disposition, have suddenly fallen off......

"July 3. ....Feel extremely dejected this evening. Never
so willing to enter into my rest, yet willing to offer, and I do,
with some peculiar feelings, offer my poor life to the Lord Jesus
Christ, to do and to suffer whatever He shall appoint during my
few remaining days. My followers feel some courage yet; for
they have, I hope, a little faith, and they know, also, that whatever storm comes, it will beat upon their teacher first.

"July 12. ....In the morning received private information
that the deputy-governor, as I had conjectured, did actually report me to Ava.... Felt rather dejected, but endeavoured to
put my trust in God, and resolve to work while the day lasts.
The zayats being all full of worshippers, I took my seat on a
brick under the shed over the great idol, and from morning till
night, crowd succeeded crowd. Some became outrageously
angry, and some listened with delight......

[1] Bengal Secret and Political Consultations Vol. 358, Burney's Journal, par. 257.

either row or paddle a distance of about a quarter of a mile in a straight line down to the King's pinnace where the victorious boat received a paper bouquet of flowers.   There was no skill displayed in steering or directing the different boats which came down in a direct line and passed on each side of the King's pinnace.   The King, however, seemed to be much interested at the sight, and the different boat crews shouted and danced like mad men after they passed him......Mr. Lanciago admitted that almost the whole of the boatmen in the numerous war boats, which we saw this day, were either Cassayers [1] or descendants of Cassayers." [2]

"Were it not for my resolution to see the King as often as possible," continues Burney, "and to enter into the amuse-

---

"July 13. ....the crowd around me was greater than ever before. But they were not hearers of the right stamp. Most of them being adherents of government, were rude, insolent, and wicked in the extreme. A few considerate persons remained till night......
    Letter dated Below Prome, 18 September, 1830.—" Afloat on my own little boat, manned by none other than my three disciples, I take leave of Prome and her towering god Shway San-dau, at whose base I have been labouring....for the last three months and a half......
    " ....There is no period of my missionary life that I review with more satisfaction, or rather with less dissatisfaction, than my sojourn in Prome.... Thousands have heard of God, who never, nor their ancestors, heard before.... Though warned and entreated, they have wilfully, obstinately, and blasphemously refused to listen. But, blessed be God, there are some whose faces I expect to see at the right hand of the great Judge. The young man just mentioned (Moung Kywet-nee), the carpenter Moung Shway-hlah, a poor man by name Moung Oo, in addition to some others mentioned in former letters, give us reason to hope that they have received the truth in good and honest hearts ...... Farewell to thee, Prome! Willingly would I have spent my last breath in thee and for thee. But thy sons ask me not to stay; and I must preach the gospel to other cities also, for therefore am I sent. Read the five hundred tracts that I have left with thee. Pray to the God and Saviour that I have told thee of. And if hereafter thou call me, though in the lowest whisper, and it reach me in the very extremities of the empire, I will joyfully listen, and come back to thee." *Wayland*, op. cit. Vol. 1, Chapter XIII.

[1] Belonging to Manipur, called by the Burmese Kathe or Cassay.
[2] Bengal Secret and Political Consultations Vol. 358, Burney's Journal, pars. 248, 249.

ments of himself and his Court, and to accustom them to
my presence, by which line of conduct only I see that I can
obtain any intimacy or influence here, I should have declined
going to Umarapura to-day. I have seen enough of war boats
which are mere playthings, and which the late war proved are
much more formidable and imposing in appearance than in
reality." [1] The crew of one of the war boats belonging to the
Prince of Tharrawaddy purposely and disrespectfully splashed
water up against the war boat in which Burney was. When the
Prince was told about the incident he ordered the men to be
flogged, but Burney requested that they might only be admonished. " The boatmen here possess to this day the same turbulent
and insolent spirit and character which Symes noticed in this
class of people 35 years ago." [1]

On 29 September, 1830, a subordinate officer with two
common war boats came to invite Burney to another function
of royal boat races. Burney protested to the Myawadi Woongyee against this insult, and the latter assured him that they
would be careful in future. The next day the invitation was
repeated, but a gilt war boat and two other boats in charge of
the Sagaing Woon were sent for the use of the Resident. During the races the King summoned Burney to his presence, and
the latter presented him with a pair of pistols and requested
that he might be allowed to see His Majesty every eight or ten
days. The King agreed to the request. [2]

On 10 December, 1830, Burney attended the ceremony
of laying the foundation stone of a monastery. " On our
entrance the King came forward and met us and pointed out
to us where to take our seats......The King twice came forward and stood close to me as if about to address me, and twice
appeared to check himself. I have observed him do this once
or twice before. His natural inclination is to enter in familiar
intercourse and which before the war he was always doing with
English merchants here, but he now seems to think that such a
proceeding is derogatory to his rank and dignity. I must take

[1] *Ibid*. par. 252.
[2] *Ibid*. pars. 321, 323.

care not to force him into conversation, but let him take his own time." [1]   Burney had to do a lot of unslippering at this Kyaung function, and was " obliged to walk a good deal over hard mud and broken bricks barefoot." [1]

In July, 1831, Burney was invited to attend a function in connection with the removal of a large brass image of Buddha from the Palace to a new pagoda south of Ava. " Near the King's temporary shed I was met by the Woondouk Maung Khan Ye, who attempted, as usual, to play off a Burmese trick upon me. He conducted me in the first instance to the wrong door, and just as I had removed my shoes, he pretended to discover his error, and proposed to me to walk round barefoot in the presence of an immense crowd to another entrance. I stopped, however, called for my shoes, and having put them on followed the Woondouk to the other door." [2]

In September, 1831, Blundell, Deputy Commissioner of the Tenasserim provinces, arrived at Ava to relieve Burney, who for reasons of health was expecting to go on leave. On 15 December, 1831, both Burney and Blundell were invited to the Elephant Palace to see a wild elephant separated from the females. " When His Majesty had finished his breakfast we were requested to approach him, in doing which we found the walk without shoes on the top of the walls of the Elephant trap very uncomfortable, and Mr. Blundell, who had not before seen the extent to which the ceremony of uncovering the feet is exacted here before the King, owned that he felt himself degraded in submitting to it in this manner. I wished, all who questioned the propriety of my endeavouring to evade this ceremony on my first arrival here, could only come and try it in their own persons." [3]

Since the King's influence counted for everything in all affairs of government, Burney made it his policy to appear before him as often as possible in order to humour him and establish direct friendly relations with him. This was undoubt-

[1] *Ibid.* Vol. 360, par. 457.
[2] *Ibid.* Vol. 362, pars. 717, 718.
[3] *Ibid.* Vol. 366, par. 856.

edly a stupendous task, and the Resident ultimately met with failure; nevertheless, his attempt is worthy of note.

On 6 September, 1830, at an audience with the King, Burney spoke to him of the advantages of a regular dâk between Ava and Akyab via An, and that newspapers from Calcutta would come regularly, thus bringing world news to His Majesty. The King immediately gave the necessary orders permitting the establishment of the desired postal service.[1]

On 17 October, 1830, Burney was invited to meet the King at 11 a.m., but an officer came to call him at 8 a.m., and said that the Ministers wanted him at the Hlutdaw. On reaching the Hlutdaw he found there only a few petty officers, all the Ministers being in the Palace. Burney sent word to them, but they replied that he had come too early and had better wait. Burney refused to wait for three hours in the company of subordinate officers, and returned to his house. Soon after, another officer came and apologised for the stupidity of the messenger, who, he said, had been confined for his action. Burney now proceeded to the Hlutdaw, found the Woongyees assembled there, and told them that when the mistake was discovered, one of the Woongyees or Woondouks should have come to explain matters to him and not a petty officer. The Woongyees readily acknowledged their error. " I deemed it right," says Burney, " to make so much of this affair to prevent the Burmese officers holding me too cheaply which they are always inclined to do to a Kula[2] officer if he does not check it and observe self-respect." [3]

At the audience with the King, whom Burney found in very good humour, there was a chatty conversation between the two on guns, painting, books, etc., for about three hours: " he spoke more to me than he had ever done before approaching close to me, addressing me directly and not through his Ministers, and

---

[1] *Ibid.* Vol. 358, par. 261. See Chapter V, p. 144.
[2] A Kula is one who has crossed over and come: a foreigner.
[3] Bengal Secret and Political Consultations Vol. 360, The Journal, pars. 359, 360.

calling me familiarly by the Burmese corruption of my name,
Bhauranee."[1]

Three weeks later there was another conference with the
King during which the Tshan Atwenwoon asked Burney to
request His Majesty to confer upon him a Burmese title, which
the Resident refused to do.   The Ministers had often before
this spoken to Burney on this subject, and had urged him to
ask the King for a title, which, they said, all persons whom the
King wished to honour are obliged to do as a matter of form
before the title is granted.   "When the Ministers saw me still
refuse, they mentioned the matter to His Majesty who ordered
a title and gold chain or Tsalway to be prepared for me......
but I am afraid I did not receive this token of royal favour with
sufficient marks of gratitude, for His Majesty seemed to get a
little out of humour and shortly after left the Hall of audience.
The truth is I would have altogether declined His Majesty's
honours did I not know that my accepting them would flatter
and please him.   The Ministers wanted me to flatter him still
more by asking him for them."[2]

A few days later at an audience of His Majesty the Than-
dau-zen sang out Burney's title [3] "Maha Zeya Raja Nauratha"
(*i.e.* my great, victorious and noble son), "and assisted by the
Atwenwoon tied round my head the thin piece of gold on which
those words are stamped, and then put over my shoulder a gold
belt consisting of nine chains.   His Majesty smiled and looked
gratified, and I was obliged to address him and say that I was
highly sensible of the honour which he had conferred upon
me."[4] The title added much to Burney's consideration among
the Burmans, and gave him a further opportunity to associate
more familiarly with the Woongyees and other officers, so that
the dispatch of public business might be facilitated thereby.[5]

---

[1] *Ibid.* par. 361.

[2] *Ibid.* par. 412.

[3] The King had conferred upon Sir A. Campbell the title, "Maha
Thura Nauratha," *i e.* My great and brave son; upon Crawfurd.
"Maha Zeya Nauratha," *i.e.* My great and victorious son.

[4] Bengal Secret and Political Consultations Vol. 360, The Journal,
par. 440.

[5] *Ibid.* Burney's Letter, Ava, 15 December, 1830.

The Governor-General appreciated the services rendered by Burney in Burma, but only hesitatingly sanctioned his acceptance of the title from the Burmese King, and directed the discontinuance of such a practice in future. The ground taken by the Governor-General was that " in Europe no British officer can accept any mark of honour from a Foreign sovereign without the express permission of his own, and then in the sole case of his having performed some distinguished service." [1]

Burney made the following defence in his acceptance of the title :—" I omitted to make a previous reference on the subject of the titles conferred by the King of Ava because I was aware that the Supreme Government in reply to a question put by Capt. Cox, when he was coming to this country as Resident, had distinctly informed him that it ' would have no objection to his accepting of any honorary distinction from the Court of Umerapurah '; and because I knew that at the present day Major-General Sir A. Campbell, Col. W. Cotton, Capt. Campbell, Mr. Crawfurd and several other British officers as well as the whole of Mr. Crawfurd's suite when he visited this capital, had received titles from the King of Ava. I had never heard of any objection made to the Khelats [2] etc., which the King of Delhi [3] bestows upon almost every officer introduced to him, and my mind had certainly never connected " distinguished services " with Asiatic titles. I had believed also, that the permission of my own sovereign was indispensable only to the measure of making use of a foreign title, as the declining to accept one, when offered, might not sometimes be practicable without giving offence to the foreign potentate. But I shall take care in future to be guided by the orders on this subject conveyed in your despatch now acknowledged." [4]

On 17 December, 1830, Burney informed the King of the demise of George IV of England and the accession to the throne

---

[1] *Ibid*. Letter from Secretary to Governor-General Bareilly, 5 February, 1831.
[2] Robes of honour.
[3] The Moghul Emperor.
[4] Bengal Secret and Political Consultations Vol. 361, Burney's Letter, 19 May, 1831.

of William IV.   The King enquired the disease of which the
monarch had died, " and seeing a Bengal newspaper which I
had brought with me, he desired me to let him know as much of
its various contents as I could.   He was highly amused at the
different advertisements, and showed great anxiety also to learn
all the particulars regarding the present state of France, and
the difference between the King of that country and the Chamber of Deputies, showing that he was aware of some of the
events of the French Revolution.   His Majesty seeing my black
gloves and black crepe on my arm and hat, asked me as a joke,
why we did not blacken our faces[1] too — a joke which one of
the courtiers repeated, and as in duty bound the rest laughed
very heartily." [2]

Burney presented to the King and the Queen each a pair
of gaudy Hindustani slippers, " not without some expectation
that the offer might be construed into a joke or sarcasm, after
the discussions which have passed between me and the Court
regarding shoes upon my first arrival.   The shoes, however,
were very graciously received, and I saw His Majesty try on
his pair before I left the house." [3]

On 18 January, 1831, for the first time the King spoke to
Burney on topics of business, and also enquired about the
Revolution in France.[4]   " I was rather startled," says Burney,
" at His Majesty styling the Governor-General ' The Myowoon
of Bengal ' "; but not wishing to discourage him into further
talks on official concerns, the Resident connived at the royal
impertinence, only in reply he pointedly called his Governor-
General, " The Angleit Mein."   The King, however, was
pleased to grant to Burney the privilege of using a gilt umbrella.[5]
Burney spoke to the Woonyees about the King calling the

---

[1] One of the punishments in Ava was to blacken the face of a
   culprit and parade him about the town.   *Ibid.* Vol. 360, The Journal, par. 469.
[2] *Ibid.* par. 369.
[3] *Ibid.* par. 470.
[4] The Revolution of 1830.
[5] Bengal Secret and Political Consultations Vol. 360, The Journal,
   pars. 512, 513.

Governor-General by an inferior title, and advised them to correct him in a quiet manner, and consider that they would not like their monarch to be called a mere Saubwa or Raja. The Myawadi Woongyee agreed that the term "Angleit Mein" should be used, and said that he would take action in the matter.[2] It is inconceivable, however, that any of the Woongyees or Atwenwoons could have had the courage to correct the King.

The late war had really brought home to the Ministers the fact of the military weakness of the country, but there was no desire to acknowledge it. On the other hand, pride of race was very evident among officers as well as the people in general. "Maung Yeet amused me," says Burney, "by repeating for the 100th time that if the English and Burmese were only united in a sincere friendship they could conquer the whole world. This speech has been so often made to me by the other Ministers as well as by Maung Yeet, that I really think they believe the truth of it. Certainly the pride and arrogance of this race have not been sufficiently corrected, and I think some of our negotiators, by talking to them about 'the two great countries,' and treating their officers with profound respect, handing them chairs and reasoning with them, have prevented their forming correct notions of their own rank and station in civilized society."[3]

[2] *Ibid.* par. 524.
[3] *Ibid.* Vol. 358, par. 194.
    On 4 February, 1831, the Woongyees dined with Burney; there were expressions of friendship and cordiality throughout the function. "They asked me after dinner to tell them frankly what had been said of them before I visited Ava. I endeavoured to evade the question, but they pressed me, and I owned at last that most British officers considered it quite useless for an Envoy to be sent to Ava as the Burmese do not know how to negotiate with a civilized state, and the only way of treating them is with a sword in one hand and a watch in the other. This last phrase the Ministers did not immediately comprehend, but when they did, they expressed their hopes that the public business which had been transacted between them and me would prove to our officers that the Burmese are not such savages as had been believed. Of course I encouraged them in this persuasion." Bengal Secret and Political Consultations Vol. 360, Burney's Journal, par. 544.

Bagyidaw was smarting under the loss of his provinces,[1] and feared further territorial encroachments from his new victorious neighbour, so that he paid some attention to his Army, and tried, by indirect means, to impress upon Burney that he would defend himself if the need arose. In Burney's opinion, the King was preparing for an offensive war for the recovery of his provinces on an opportunity arising. A deeper study of the King and his Government, however, shows, that his warlike attitude was occasionally due to temperamental excitement: his policy really was one of peace and self-defence.

Writing to his Government on 15 December, 1830, Burney says, " Having in some of my former reports expressed an opinion that the present King of Ava will take the first favourable opportunity of engaging in another contest with us, I beg to take the present occasion of submitting a more detailed statement of the grounds upon which I have formed that opinion. The King and those about him are manifestly dissatisfied with the present state of things. Nothing shows this more decidedly than the eagerness with which they listen to any tales brought here of disasters suffered by us in India or of hostilities projected against us by Runjeet Singh [2] or any other Chief, and their ignorance of the real superiority of our power and resources is very great. Their History also teaches them that their loss and disasters in their wars with the Shans and Peguers [3] were much greater and more severe than what they experienced in their contest with us. The Shans as well as the Peguers took and destroyed the capital, the King and Royal family, and drove the people into the woods and mountains; yet the Burmese rose again and recovered their power and consequence. All here are certain that Ava will rise again from her present reduced condition......and not only the King's Court but the lower ranks of the people and even many of the inhabitants of the Tenasserim provinces firmly believe that in the last war it was our turn to conquer, but that in the next contest it will

[1] Assam, Arakan, and Tenasserim.
[2] The Indian Sikh Ruler of the Punjab, 1792-1839.
[3] The Talaings: of Pegu.

be the turn of Ava. Our native troops [1] are spoken of by all classes in this country with the most mortifying contempt, and Mr. Lane, whose intercourse with the inhabitants of the country has been much more intimate and extensive than mine, assures me that he has never heard but one Burmese confess the superiority of our European troops. This individual was an old officer who declared that in the actions which he had seen with the Shans, Siamese and Peguers their progress was always checked if a good fire was opened upon them, but that he had never before seen anything like the attack of our European troops the main body of whom, notwithstanding many were falling from the Burmese fire, kept advancing till they entered the enemies' stockades. These are the grounds upon which I have been anxious that the British Government should be prepared against any attempt on the part of Ava to recover Arakan, Munipore, and Tenasserim provinces on the very first occasion in which some Native power in India or other cause may engage our attention. I am sorry to add that there is scarce an article in the Yandaboo Treaty upon which the Court of Ava may not found a dispute; not only the question as to the boundary of Munipore and the quality of the silver in which

---

[1] On 7 June, 1830, there was a fire in the outer town of Ava not far from the Residency. " Lt. Geo. Burney and some sepoys of the Escort went and soon put a stop to the progress of the flames. They found the Burmese either looking on with apathy or plundering the houses as they caught fire, and under not the smallest control or direction of the Woongyees and Atwenwoons who were on the spot upon Elephants. The Sepoys have gained much credit by their exertions in extinguishing the fire. I ought not to omit to take this opportunity of stating how very meritoriously all the men of my escort have conducted themselves since our arrival here. The Burmese were at first inclined to treat these Bengal Sepoys with great contempt, but they are now beginning to feel a little more respect for them. The Sepoys have always been disposed to evince a manly forbearance towards the inhabitants of the country, but notwithstanding all their caution they have occasionally come into conflict with some of the more insolent Burmese who have provoked them by abuse or challenges to fight, and on these occasions the feats of strength which they have displayed and ugly falls they have given to some of the professional Burmese wrestlers, have forced the Burmese to change their tone and beware of laying their hands on Bengal Sepoys." Bengal Secret and Political Consultations Vol. 358, Burney's Journal, par. 102.

7

the money was to be paid to us but the boundaries of the Tenas-serim provinces, of Assam and even of Arakan are points which I have reason to know this Court do not consider as clearly fixed.

"I have more than once urged the Ministers and recom-mended the King to send some of the sons of Burmese nobles to their Resident at Calcutta for a short time as the most simple mode of introducing into this Court a more correct knowledge of the relative power and resources of our two nations. To impart this knowledge here is an object of my constant solici-tude, believing that such an acquisition on their part would best ensure the continuance of peaceable relations between us. Should, however, the death of the King of Ava take place in the present state of the country, the succession will most prob-ably be contested and the country split into factions, in which case we shall be less likely to be troubled." [1]

On the early morning of 27 December, 1830, "all the Burmese military force at Ava came out to the plain near our house to drill and target practice. There were more serviceable muskets than I had ever seen before. Most of the soldiers fired at the target in a sitting posture, and the recoil of the piece often threw them on their backs. Among the manoeuvres performed was one of which the Burmese have a high opinion and call it Kharoo-pat.[2] It consists in making the men march in file, and wheeling the front file until the whole forms circles within circles like the spiral lines of a shell, whence the name. The Bogyoup or Colonel or other Bos were unusually civil and polite, and answered our questions very readily. They pointed out one party dressed in black Shan jackets belonging, they said, to the *Shine* pyeegyan[3] regiment, and another party in white with red coloured handkerchiefs around the head belong-

---

[1] Bengal Secret and Political Consultations Vol. 360, Burney's Letter, Ava, 15 December, 1830.

[2] ခရုပတ်॥ - ခရု॥ = shell, ပတ် = spiral line.

[3] ရှိန်းပြီးကြံδး॥ Shein pyee gyan = An army of people made fierce through certain charms devised upon them.

ရွှေပြည်ကြံး॥ Shwe pyi gyan = The army of the Golden country.

ing to the Khyouk gyoung,[1] which consists, they said, of 6 regiments of 1000 men each. The men now being drilled, the Bo said, were a few only, the sons and grandsons of the other men of the regiment, all of whom were perfect in the exercise. The Bos seemed to think that these troops had attained all the discipline and efficiency of ours."[2]

A week later there was a grand display of troops in the King's presence. His Majesty came to the ground dressed in gold brocade and mounted on the neck of the White Elephant which he guided himself. The King, on alighting, took his seat on a gilt chair, and Burney and party were invited to sit near him. The Queen wore a comfortable Indian shawl, while the rest of the Ladies of the palace, about twenty in number, were covered with common white chudders or sheets with a narrow silk border. Her Majesty sat to the right of the King and her attendants by her; the Princes sat to the left of the King. The programme included lance throwing by Woongyees, Atwen-woons and Bos on horseback: very few were successful in reaching the target. The Queen gave to the most successful ones muslin and flowers. Another item was a Cavalry display — marching past the King two at a time, and trying to pick up oranges with their lances while on full gallop; but only two oranges were picked up including one by a Mahomedan who was once in Col. Skinner's Horse. Most of the cavalry men were Manipuris or their descendants, and were armed only with lances, and possessed no swords or carbines or pistols. They were good horsemen, but their steeds were small being no match for those used in the Indian Army.[3]

The Myawadi Woongyee gave to Burney the following account of the organization and state of the Burmese Army:—

"The Regiments are innumerable, named usually from some Pali terms, and divided chiefly into 2 battalions of 500 men, each distinguished as North and South. At the head of each 500 men

---

[1] ချောက်ကြောင်း။ or ချောက်ချောင်း။ = Six pieces of army, that is, six regiments.
[2] Bengal Secret and Political Consultations Vol 360, Burney's Journal, par. 482.
[3] *Ibid.* par. 487.

there are but one or two Bos who only can be compared to our
commissioned officers...and most of them use gilt umbrellas...;
under the Bos are officers called Thwe-thouk-gyee,[1] 10 of which
rank belong to each battalion, that is, one to each 50 men; under
these are officers called Akyat[2] one of whom is over every 10
men, there being 50 in a battalion. The Thwe-thouk-gyees and
Akyats possess no rank or consideration about the Court, and
appear in fact to be nothing more than our serjeants and corpo-
rals; the Bos are like our Lieut.-Colonels; and the Woongyees
said that the Ministers are the Colonels and Generals, the Bogyee,
Bogyoup and Tseet Thoo-gyee.

" Some of the soldiers wore red leather and tin caps, and the
muskets were in general in a very serviceable condition.... He
(the King) has just now a military mania upon him. The troops
are daily exercised and employed at target practice from day
break until 1 or 2 in the afternoon. The King's military proceedings are imitated by the Governors of most of the Towns in the
Kingdom. Drilling and target practice are the order of the day,
and I understand at Rangoon and every other part of the
country.

" The skill which the Burmese are now acquiring in the use
of the fire-lock may render the capture of their stockades more
difficult in a future war should they confine themselves within
their defences; but it is most likely that the attainment of this
skill will encourage them to quit their stockades and jungles and
meet us in the open plains, exactly as we could wish......the
whole scene gave us a better opinion of the Burmese power and
finery than anything I have yet seen."[3]

In January, 1831, a relation of the Queen was appointed
Governor of Bassein: he left Ava in great state. " In addition to the office of Myowoon, he as well as the Governors of
Prome and other places to the southward, has been appointed
a Bo or military leader. This is said to be quite a new arrangement, showing that the Court is placing everything on a war

[1] Lit., great blood drinker.
[2] Section-commander, non-commissioned officer.
[3] Bengal Secret and Political Vol. 360, The Journal, par. 487.
    The King possessed in August, 1831, 164 War-boats: Khat
Lhe or boats with oars, Tait Lhe or war-boats, and Lan Lhe or
long boats with paddles. Besides these he had 37 Lango or
State boats with high prows and sterns. Before the war the
navy was larger so that the King had ordered the construction
of some 36 more war-boats. Bengal Secret and Political Consultations Vol. 362, The Journal, par. 761.

establishment, and preparing to meet or undertake any military operations which may become necessary. These Bos have the power to call out the inhabitants of their districts to meet armed at any point and at any time they please, and this power is a source of great emolument to them, the inhabitants being released from appearing on payment of a fine, and the Bos taking good care to act like Falstaff, 'misuse the King's press damnably, press them none but good householders, yeomen's sons, and enquire them out contented bachelors......'".[1] In the interior of the country in the neighbourhood of Ava also there was much activity in military exercise and drill, some of the trainers and drillers being Marathas.[2]

The late war not only stimulated military reform, but also produced a salutary effect upon the civil administration of the country: "I may mention here, that the late war has wonderfully improved the conduct of the Burmese Government towards its own subjects, and thus proved a real benefit in the end to humanity. In former days whatever the Government required it seized without hesitation, but now pecuniary remuneration[3] is given to each man while engaged in the public service, and a regular hire is paid for boats or anything else required by the Hlutdau.... This Government now shows some deference to the feelings and opinions of the governed. An apprehension that its subjects may remove into our territories is secretly influencing it to treat the people with extraordinary mildness and indulgence; and this is the principal cause why so few Burmese have emigrated to Arakan or to the Tenasserim provinces since the conclusion of the war."[4]

The King and his Ministers were usually inclined to give credence to rumours which tended to place the British in India or in Europe in difficulties. Ranjit Singh figured very promi-

---

[1] *Ibid.* Vol. 360, par. 521. There is much inaccuracy in this quotation from *Shakespeare.* See Henry IV, Part I, Act IV, Scene 2, lines 12-15.

[2] *Ibid.* par. 533.

[3] Attendants accompanying officers to Kendat on the Manipur frontier from Ava and back, each received 25 ticals. ·

[4] Bengal Secret and Political Consultations Vol. 361, The Journal, par. 640.

nently in these rumours — the hero of a victorious war with the Company. At one time there was abroad "an absurd story of a formidable coalition having been entered into by the Turks, Persians and Ranjit Singh for the purpose of driving the English out of India."[1] Rumours of a war between England and France, and of the Governor-General having been made a prisoner by Ranjit Singh were also common.[2] It was one of the duties of the British Resident to deal with these rumours officially.[3]

The attitude of the Burmese people in general towards the Residency was hostile, not only on the claim of race superiority, all foreigners or Kulas being held in contempt, but also because the defeat in the war had become a great burden owing to the Indemnity which was being raised by forced contributions. "From my first arrival," says Burney, "I have always observed that the feelings of the common people of the country are very rancorous and sore against us, and that nothing but my being on intimate terms with the Ministers protects me and my followers from insult. We never meet with a drunken man who does not try to provoke us; and many disreputable characters among the lower orders, often take an opportunity, when they can do so with impunity, of throwing out abuse against the *Kulas*, as we pass in the streets. Kalagyu means a Kala of rank, and Kulagyan, or coarse barbarian Kula, is a common term of abuse applied to all foreigners. I have heard children even taught to cry after us, 'Kulagyu-an,' adding the final syllable '*an*' in a lowered tone of voice as we got to a distance.

"A few days ago as Mr. Lane was passing in the street a man of rank and his followers, one of the latter abused all the Kulas, and observed that he would like to have a cut at Mr. Lane with a sword. Mr. Lane had the man punished by his master. I have shut my ears as much as I could against such petty impertinence, and have often wished that I possessed no

[1] *Ibid*. Vol. 362, par. 728.
[2] *Ibid*. Vol. 360, pars. 548, 554-557.
[3] *Ibid*. Vol. 362, Burney's Letter, Ava, 4 August, 1831.

knowledge of the language. When I have complained against an individual I have found them [1] actuated by a very extraordinary feeling. They seemed most unwilling to punish the aggressor for some secret fear lest the common people should suppose that they had done so at my dictation, and that I made them do whatever I pleased, and on one occasion I was, therefore, obliged to punish a man by my own authority.

" An aggravated case occurred yesterday. The Keepers of the different gates of the Town, next to the boatmen, are notoriously the most turbulent and saucy characters in Ava. The Keeper of one of the gates abused me and my followers yesterday morning in too gross a manner for me to pretend not to understand or hear him. I had him seized by some of my followers, and sent him to the Myawadi Woongyee, who on pretence that it was the Burmese Sunday released the man without punishing him. I sent my clerk afterwards to the Woongyee, and went myself in the evening to point out to him that I could not overlook such insulting conduct on the part of the gatekeeper, and that I must insist upon his being punished. The Woongyee assured me that the man should be punished if I would attend at the Hlutdau; but upon my going this morning, I found three Woongyees there, the Kyee Woongyee, Myawadi, and the Queen's Woongyee, and they were disposed to treat the offence in a trivial manner. The Queen's Woongyee wisely observed to me that if the man had looked me in the face at the time he abused me, then indeed his offence would be a serious one. After some discussion these Woongyees requested me to wait until the other two Woongyees and Tshan Atwenwoon could be summoned, as they did not like to punish the Gate-Keeper unless all the Ministers agreed on the propriety of the measure. I declined to wait, and told the Woongyees present, that I had on this occasion complained to them and applied for redress, but that if they did not punish the offender they must not be surprised to see me hereafter take the law into my own hands, and punish myself on the spot the

[1] The Ministers.

next man who insulted me. The Ministers then begged of me
to wait and see the man punished which I refused to do, as I
found that they were endeavouring to let the headman of the
Gate, who was the real offender, escape, and to fix the penalty
on a poor subordinate and innocent individual. The Gate-
Keeper pretended that he had applied the abuse to some Burmese at the Gate and not to me and my followers; but the real
truth is he was unaware that I could understand what he said.
The circumstance of my forcing the Ministers to raise money
from the inhabitants of the country on account of the balance
due to us, is of course, not calculated to make the common people regard me and my followers with much complacency, and
it is perhaps very natural for the Ministers to enter into the
feelings of the people, and to lean as much as possible towards
them in any dispute with me." [1]

After all this ado the Ministers did not punish the Gatekeeper. Burney, therefore, drew up an address to the King
giving a full explanation of the affair, and solicited him to order
his Ministers to afford him suitable protection against insult.
" I deemed it right to add a sarcastic observation: I said that
I feared all His Majesty's subjects are perfectly correct in
asserting, that the present Woongyees are not like those of
ancient times, who would not have taken 6 days to settle such
a trivial affair, nor would they have forced me to bring it under
the particular notice of the King." [2]

To Burney's mortification, when his address was presented
to the King, His Majesty said nothing. As a last resort, Burney
called upon the Ministers to punish the Gatekeeper, and
threatened that otherwise he would mete out justice himself,
which would alarm both the King as well as his Court.[3] The
Ministers immediately climbed down: they removed the Gatekeeper and put him in stocks. Burney made sure that it was

---

[1] Bengal Secret and Political Consultations Vol. 362, The Journal,
    par. 758.
[2] *Ibid.* Vol. 366, par. 763.
[3] *Ibid.* par. 764.

the right individual that was punished, and thus ended this disagreeable tension.[1]

Reflecting upon the episode, Burney says, " Nothing could
be more simple and clear than this case, and yet, apparently to
show how wrongheaded these Ministers are, and how very difficult it is to transact any business with them, they have taken
10 days to settle so trifling an affair. Their great misfortune is,
that they are labouring under a kind of squint of the understanding: they dare not look straightforward at anything in
which I am concerned. They are in continual dread of being
considered as too friendly with me, and as favouring the *Kulas*.
No charge is more easily made, and more dreaded, or more
likely to ruin a man in a moment here than the charge of being
too partial to them." [1]

One day the Myolat Woon visited Burney. " In the course
of conversation, upon my observing that I hoped our two
nations are now better acquainted with each other, and less
likely to engage in hostilities again, he laughingly answered,
' Yes, we (meaning the Burmese) only want one more trial for
the sake of *letza-kya* '— which means revenge or taking satisfaction, and which the Burmese Yazawin or History, I remember, lays down as one proper ground for going to war with
another nation. The Treasurer also observed to me to-day, ' In
your country you are obliged to pay people to learn the use of
muskets, none but those who are paid know anything about it,
but in this country every male inhabitant is now taught the use
of the musket ' ".[2]

Reports of military preparations in Burma led the Government of India to keep a good watch so as to be prepared for
emergencies:—" In the meantime," says the Governor-General
in his Minute dated 24 June, 1831, " to intimidate the Burmese from manifesting the hostile feeling towards us, which
they are reputed to foster, and to convince them of their error
in supposing us so exhausted and embarrassed as to submit to

[1] *Ibid.* par. 765.
[2] *Ibid.* Vol. 366, par. 848.

concessions, rather than venture a fresh conflict, we must seek the best military positions on the Ava frontiers and show that we are prepared, and as determined as prepared, not only to repel but chastise aggression.

" I have undesignedly fallen into these remarks owing to my attention having been recently engaged in considering the means of maintaining tranquillity on the northern and western confines of Ava, and of avoiding the recurrence of a contest with that state, which certainly requires to be narrowly observed." [1]

Early in the year 1831 the King's health broke down. In April, his illness took a serious turn, and in the heat of the month of May, he became worse. He began to mend in June, but soon there was a relapse, and early in July he was reported to be in a serious condition. There was again some improvement in August, but it was not till December 1831, that he was able to take part in public affairs. In February, 1832, his health began to decline again, and when Burney left Ava in April, 1832, the King had not fully recovered from his prolonged ailment. [2]

There were many speculations as to the nature of the King's trouble. The Ministers tried their best to hide the seriousness of the illness from the people as well as from Burney, and told the latter that there was nothing wrong, only " his heart was not right." [3] Evidence shows that he was suffering from recurring fits of melancholia. At one time he was im-

<hr>

[1] *Ibid.* Vol. 361, The Governor-General's Minute, Simla.
[2] *Ibid.* Vols. 360, 361, 362, 366; pars. 544, 634, 657, 692, 694, 709, 781, 788, 857, 924. Burney's Journal.
[3] *Ibid.* Vol. 360, pars. 569, 577.
"I was amused to see the farce, which the Atwenwoons and Woongyees were enacting at the Hlut-dau more to deceive the common people around us than me, pretending that their discussions with me, would prevent their attending the King's levee at the appointed time, sending into the palace for one of the Nakhan-daus and begging of him to let the King know how they were employed. I have good information that the King has not appeared at the morning levee for the last week and the Nakhan-dau could scarcely keep his countenance." *Ibid.* Vol. 362, par. 703.

pressed with a notion that he was to be assassinated; and on one occasion when a Bo presented a petition to him, he started back, stared wildly at the petitioner, and ran into an inner apartment.[1]

On 28 March, Burney had an audience of the King, who " on the whole conducted himself with much propriety. He is evidently seriously unwell and is become extremely thin and pale. When he first appeared also he was a good deal agitated, but he showed no other symptoms of mental derangement than what always characterises him,— a remarkably wild and wandering eye." [2] Royal physicians, celebrated witches, and dancers, were all busy seeking to effect a cure, but without much success.[3] The expedient of public charities was also tried: a suit of clothes was given to every inhabitant of the three districts of Ava, Amarapura and Sagaing.[4] Silk Patshos [5] were given to respectable people. This proved expensive, but most of the officers came to their King's rescue and presented him with Patshos.[6] Burney's Escort, consisting of Indian soldiers, and his other followers were also given presents of clothes and carpets.[7]

In Lanciago's opinion, the King's indisposition was due entirely " from chagrin and melancholy, which reflection on the results of his war with the British Government is constantly exciting, and which the very sight of a British Resident is only calculated to aggravate. Just before the death of the late King,

---

[1] *Ibid.* Vol. 360, par. 569.
[2] *Ibid.* Vol. 361, par. 617.
[3] *Ibid.* Vols. 360, 362, pars. 569, 712.
[4] Royal officers brought a memorandum of the King's charities to the three districts. This document gives some idea of the population of these three cities: —

Those who received charities, Priests and Pupils,	7252
Brahmins and Religious Mendicants,	1294
Public Officers and Inhabitants,	117,119
Total,	125,665

(*Ibid.* Vol. 366, par. 970).

[5] A Patsho is a lungyi or loin-cloth.
[6] Bengal Secret and Political Consultations Vol. 366, The Journal, par. 917.
[7] *Ibid.* par. 925.

his present Majesty became gloomy and melancholy in the same manner from anxiety as to the proceedings of his two uncles, the Princes of Toung-ngoo[1] and Prome who were preparing to contest the throne; and His Majesty did not recover until he had established himself as King.   Mr. Lanciago also informs me that His Majesty continues very sore about the territory of Kubo, a subject upon which Mr. Lanciago still, as he has always done, expresses himself most warmly as to the injustice of our proceedings, and anxiously as to the consequences of our deciding in favour of Gambhir Singh."[2] As to the credibility of Lanciago's report, Burney says, " I place more reliance on any intelligence which I can collect from Mr. Lanciago than on that which any other persons here can furnish me, for with a peculiar shrewdness of character, I have generally found him honest and sincere."[3]

On account of the King's continued indisposition and his inability to attend to affairs of state, His Majesty in either September or October, 1831, appointed a Commission of Four to represent him.   It consisted of his brother-in-law the Menthagyee and the three Royal brothers, the Princes of Tharrawaddy, Thibau[4] and Bo Woon Men.[5]   The Ministers kept this new arrangement a secret, and when Burney questioned them they pretended that it was not a new arrangement at all, but one which existed always in the country.   Burney, however, was not deceived.   In the past when Burmese Kings appointed their sons or brothers to superintend public business, they were created regular Woongyees and sat in the Hlutdaw; while the members of the new Royal Commission met in the Palace.[6] " I understand," says Burney, " that Menzagyee has contrived

---

[1] Toungoo.
[2] Bengal Secret and Political Consultations Vol. 365, Burney's Letter, 6 February, 1832.
[3] *Ibid*. Vol. 366, The Journal, par. 903.
[4] Formerly of Yambye.
[5] The same who was styled Memiat Bo or Memiaboo when commanding at Melloon during the war. Bengal Secret and Political Consultations Vol. 363, Burney's Letter, 15 October, 1831.
[6] Bengal Secret and Political Consultations Vol. 366, The Journal, pars. 798, 799.

with the aid of the Queen, to persuade the King to make this arrangement. The influence of Tshan Atwenwoon has lately much increased, and he is said to have availed himself of the King's unwillingness to attend to anything serious, to monopo-lize much of the patronage of the country, contriving to obtain an easy acquiescence from His Majesty to any measure or appointment brought froward by him."[1]

In the month of December, 1831, there were rumours cur-rent that the King hoped to transfer the capital to Amarapura. An opinion prevailed that when Bagyidaw, early in his reign, transferred the capital from Amarapura to Ava, that is down the river, it was a mistake, and the war was lost, since in past history the Kings always changed the capital and moved up the river, e.g. from Prome to Pagan, Pinya, Ava, Amarapura. The Court Brahmans also endorsed this view, and said that the proper change up the river might restore the King to health.[2]

The inhabitants of Ava as well as the Princes and Officers were, however, not inclined to leave the old city, because of the trouble and expense it would entail. The Mekkhara Prince,[3] the most learned of the royal household, prepared the following syllogism to repeat before the King:—

> Major: — It is not right to molest and give trouble to the poor inhabitants of the country.[4]
>
> Minor: — Our removing from Ava to Amarapura will molest and give trouble to the poor inhabitants.
>
> Ergo: — It is not right for us to remove to Amarapura.

The Prince went to the palace for this purpose, but the appearance of the Royal countenance did not encourage him to try his logic.[5] Fortunately, however, in the end no active steps were taken to shift the capital.

The continued illness of the King began to tell seriously upon the administration and trade of the country. Gang rob-

---

[1] *Ibid.* Vol. 366, par. 799.
[2] *Ibid.* par. 852.
[3] The King's Uncle.
[4] This major is a principle much dwelt upon in Burmese books, so that the Prince expected all who heard it to agree to it.
[5] Bengal Secret and Political Consultations Vol. 366, The Journal, par. 853.

bery increased in all parts of the country, and at one time even the old city of Amarapura was attacked by a large party of dacoits.[1] Trade also was hampered, and its worst effects were felt in the capital itself.[2] It was also suspected that the Prince of Tharrawaddy desired to usurp the throne and was gathering a large number of followers around him.[3]

Burney began to consider seriously the developments that might take place in case of a war of succession either during the illness of the King or in the event of his death. " In the event of His Majesty's death," he wrote to his Government, " there is every reason to believe that the succession to the throne will be disputed, but whoever may be the successful candidate, I believe that much of the rancorous spirit enter- tained against the British Government, in consequence of the loss of territory, money and fame, will depart[4] with His Majesty, and that after a short time the relations between our two states will be placed on a more advantageous footing. The young prince Tsakyamen ought of course to succeed his father, but he is young: without power, resources, followers or any real consideration, having always been kept so much in the background; and the annals of this as well as of the other Indo-Chinese states afford numerous examples of a brother succeeding a brother. The King's brother, the Prince of Tharawadi, is now suspected to aim at the throne himself, and it is probable that he will succeed, unless Menzagyee the Queen's brother comes forward to support the young Prince's right — which many suppose that he will do, as he must be well aware that if the Prince of Tharawadi becomes King, his first act will be to execute Menzagyee and seize his riches. Men- zagyee has by far the most wealth, power and followers, and many confidently believe, that instigated by his sister the pres- ent Queen, who will naturally desire to save herself from fall- ing back into her original obscurity, he will try to seize the

[1] *Ibid.* Vol. 361, Burney's Letter, Ava, 8 April, 1831.
[2] *Ibid.* Vol. 362, Burney's Letter, Ava, 4 July, 1831.
[3] *Ibid.* Vol. 361, Burney's Letter, Ava, 21 May, 1831.
[4] These hopes of Burney were not realized when in 1837 Prince Tharrawaddy usurped the throne.

throne for himself.   Unfortunately the King's daughter is still
too young to be married to the Tsakyamen,[1] by which arrangement the conflicting interests of Her Majesty and of the young
Prince might be reconciled.   The battle will most probably be
fought between the Prince of Tharawadi and Menzagyee, and
I fear whichever of the two obtains the ascendency, his first act
will be to put to death the other and the young prince." [2]

Burney felt that in the probable struggle for power, strict
non-interference must be his general rule for guidance.[2]   But
Symes had been instructed in 1802, when he proceeded to the
Burmese capital on his second mission, that " such a state of
events as a Civil War and a disputed succession ' would constitute that crisis of affairs which is most desired for the purpose
of establishing the British influence and promoting the British
interests in the Burmese Empire.' " [3]   Hence Burney enquired
of his Government if he should deviate from the rule of non-
interference " if by so doing I might seize a favourable opportunity of securing, without risk, all these objects which we
desire to attain.   Were a party of the more respectable Ministers to prefer their allegiance to the Tsakyamen, the rightful
heir, it is possible that my joining them, upon certain conditions might secure his right, and put down the opposition of his
uncles.   Although the King is in no immediate danger, his state
is such as to render me very desirous of learning as soon as possible the wishes of Government.   No party here has yet sounded
me on this subject as the Burmese seldom look beyond the
present hour." [4]

The Governor-General issued the following orders on
Burney's enquiry:—" Major Burney should immediately be

---

[1] He was her half-brother.   It was a practice with Burmese Kings
   to marry their half-sisters, the idea being to preserve the blood
   royal.   See *Harvey*, op. cit. p. 324.
[2] Bengal Secret and Political Consultations Vol. 360, Burney's
   Letter, 9 March, 1831.
[3] *Ibid*. Vol. 361, Burney's Letter, 25 June, 1831.
   Burney's quotation is from an additional letter of Instructions to
   Lt.-Col. Symes, given by Mr. Secretary Edmontone, 20 April,
   1802.
[4] *Ibid*. Vol. 360, Burney's Letter, Ava, 9 March, 1831.

informed, that it is the wish of Government that he should preserve a strict neutrality and avoid taking any step that shall lead either party to look upon him as a partizan. In the event of a struggle, therefore, of the kind contemplated, Major Burney should avow his intention of remaining at the capital, and transacting business as British Envoy and representative, with any one whose power is established there. He will, of course, take all due precautions to prevent the plunder of the Residency or insult to any of its members or dependents, pending the disturbances to be expected during such a contest, and His Lordship expects that he will have the aid of the Chiefs engaged on both sides in effecting this purpose.

" His Lordship is of opinion that there can be no reason for renewing or altering any of the provisions of the Treaty of Yandaboo, and that it would be very objectionable to take the opportunity of a probably disputed succession to effect any object of that kind. If applied to on the subject of the relations of the British nation with the new sovereign, it will suffice that Major Burney should point out that the Treaty was not personal with the late sovereign, but perpetual with the Burmese nation by whomsoever governed, and that so long as the provisions are strictly observed on their side, there need be no apprehension of any aggression, interference or deviation from the articles, on ours." [1]

Burney had been keeping indifferent health from the time of his arrival in Ava. Before he had been one month at the capital, the heat of Ava began to tell upon his health, added to the anxiety over the questions under discussion. [2] After a stay of eleven months he found himself badly in need of a change, and expressed to the Woongyees his desire of retiring to Rangoon temporarily for the purpose of recouping his health. The Ministers " observed that I had been deputed by the Governor-General to reside at Ava, and that if I now left it, they would have no one with whom to concert the necessary measures for

[1] *Ibid.* Vol. 361, Letter from the Secretary to the Governor-General, Simla, 18 April, 1831.
[2] *Ibid.* Vol. 358, The Journal, par. 72.

keeping the two states in friendly relation......and the Ministers still supposed that vexation and anger had induced me to determine upon leaving them. I assured the Ministers that I will not quit them in haste or anger, and that I am willing to wait a few weeks until His Majesty and they become better reconciled to my departure. I laughingly added, that upon my first coming to Ava, many persons had said that the Ministers woul not agree to my remaining here for any time; but that now I see they will not allow me to leave them. The Ministers caught eagerly at my offer to remain or to prevent my departure: I believe, that their real motive for desiring to detain me is, that I may remain here as an hostage for the good conduct of the British Government." [1]

On 15 September, 1831, Blundell, Deputy Commissioner of the Tenasserim provinces, arrived at Ava to relieve Burney, but it was not till in April, 1832, that the latter departed for Rangoon. Burney introduced Blundell to the Ministers at the Hlutdaw, and they came to acquire an instant liking for him: " all the Ministers became in excellent humour, and Tshan Atwenwoon displayed, as he always does when he is in spirits, his knowledge of Burmese moral philosophy, quoting Pali texts and denominations and divisions into classes of virtues and moral qualities, and explaining them for my edification." [2]

On 15 December, 1831, Burney had an audience of the King who looked remarkedly well, and showed no sign of bodily or mental illness. " I told the Myawadi Woongyee and Tshan Atwenwoon that I should not forget the kindness which I had always experienced from His Majesty, and that I should always do my utmost to apprise my superiors in Bengal of His

[1] *Ibid.* Vol. 361, pars. 608, 621.
[2] *Ibid.* Vol. 366, pars. 775, 777.
   Burney delayed his departure because he had proposed to his Government a temporary withdrawal of the Residency, and so waited for an answer; but his proposal did not carry much weight in Calcutta. Burney felt that his Government would decide the Kubo question in favour of Gumbheer Singh, and being convinced that he would not be able to reconcile the King and Court to such a verdict, suggested a temporary withdrawal of the Residency, while the Governor-General made known his decision. *Ibid.* Vol. 362, Burney's Letter, 28 August, 1831.

Majesty's wishes and desires. This last promise was made a great deal of and repeated to His Majesty by the Ministers in the most effective manner." [1] Burney had his last audience of the King on 10 March, 1832, and presented His Majesty with a complimentary address in which " I expressed my thanks for the acts of kindness with which His Majesty had honoured me during my residence of nearly 2 years in Ava, and promised to continue my exertions for promoting friendly feelings and advantageous commercial intercourse between our two nations; and I assured His Majesty which I really can safely and conscientiously do, that it will be my duty to report, wherever I go, that I never heard of a more popular sovereign than the present King of Ava who is loved in a very extraordinary manner by all classes of his subjects." [2]

At this last audience Burney noticed a great change in the appearance of the King as well as of the Queen: the former looked very pale and unwell, and the latter thin and haggard. " I never saw a human being apparently so full of ennui and melancholy, so tired of life and its cares, as the poor King struck me to be. I felt more pity for him than I can describe." [3] When a Thandau-zen read out Burney's address, " the contents excited the King, made him smile repeatedly, and evidently gratified both him and the Queen very much, whilst all the Courtiers looked full of delight and approbation........ The Kyeewoon Atwenwoon urged me to address His Majesty myself, and I cried out that I should always endeavour, wherever I go, to be serviceable to His Majesty and to do honour to his character. The King nodded his head kindly, and I own I was so much excited by the whole scene, and felt so much pity for the state of the King, that I could almost have been persuaded, at the time, to promise much more than what I should ever have been able to fulfil." [3]

On 4 April, 1832, Burney paid farewell visits to all the Woongyees and Atwenwoons at their houses. They received

[1] *Ibid.* Vol. 366, par. 857.
[2] *Ibid.* par. 922.
[3] *Ibid.* par. 924.

him most kindly, asked him to correspond with them, and reminded him not to forget to press before his Government the claim of Burma to Kubo.[1] "I hope it will not be considered any weakness in me to own, that I took my leave of them all with much regret, and with the kindest feelings in their favour."[2] The next evening the Woongyees and Atwenwoons dined with Burney, and "they all displayed a great deal of cordial and kind feeling. They observed that no British officer had ever been treated with the same familiarity and kindness as I had been, that they have not disguised or concealed anything from me, but have allowed me to see and learn everything regarding their customs, manners, modes of thinking and acting, and that they hoped, therefore, when I go to other countries, I will not fail to do justice to them and to their characters. I replied that I am very sensible of the extraordinary liberality and kindness with which I have been treated, and that I shall ever entertain grateful feelings towards them, and I also assured them that I shall have great pleasure in contradicting any unfavourable reports, which may exist in other countries regarding the disposition and characters of the great men here, who will obtain, I added, great credit when it is known that they are not insensible to unfavourable opinions, but that, on the contrary, they desire to acquire fame and good name among other civilised nations."[3]

On 10 April, 1832, Burney handed over the charge of the Residency to Blundell, and at 10 a.m. quitted Ava by boat.[4] On 23 May, he reached Rangoon, "having received during my passage from Ava marked kindness and attention from the different provincial authorities."[5]

Burney was struck upon his arrival in Rangoon at the appearance of the town: "the stockade has been rebuilt, the streets newly paved and improved, and from a thousand five

---

[1] *Ibid.* par. 843.
[2] *Ibid.* par. 954.
[3] *Ibid.* par. 957.
[4] *Ibid.* par. 969.
[5] *Ibid.* Vol. 367, Burney's Letter, Rangoon, no date, Consultations 9 July, 1832, No. 11.

hundred to two thousand men may be seen under arms four times a month, with scarlet jackets and good muskets, escorting the Woongyee to the Great Pagoda. In no part of the Empire, not in the capital itself, have I observed so much military preparation on the part of the Government and so much speculation as to the probability of peace or war with the British Government, on the part of the local officers, as in this Town; and I attribute this state of things, as much to the constant disputes and jarring between Moulmein and Martaban, as to the circumstance of our maintaining a steam vessel and an European Regiment so immediately in this neighbourhood." [1]

Although Burney had, on the whole, been well treated by the Burmese Government it was not the desire of the latter to entertain the British Residency permanently at the capital. The Tshan Atwenwoon had more than once observed to Burney, "that bye and bye, when the Munnipore and Martaban frontiers are adjusted, there will be no occasion for Residents to be maintained here or in Bengal, but that the best plan will be to follow the custom which prevails between Ava and China, that is that envoys should be sent to each other with complimentary communications and gifts periodically, or as often as there is any business of importance. I took no notice of this observation, but I am satisfied, that it emanated from the Atwenwoon being well aware of the feelings and wishes of the King on this subject. From all I have been able to learn here, I plainly see, that although the Ministers are reconciled to the measure of a British Resident being permanently stationed here, and are aware of its advantage and convenience, the King is decidedly hostile to it. He considers it as a proof of our supremacy and a badge of his servility and vassalage, and I see no chance of such impressions being removed from his mind. The common people seemed to be best pleased with the presence of a British Resident, as before I came up here, I am assured that scarcely a day passed without some alarm and some false report of a British armament being about to enter or having

[1] *Ibid.*

actually entered the river. There is now no such anxiety to learn the news from every boat which arrives from Rangoon." [1]

Burney's duties in Ava during his stay of two years had been very arduous; but he possessed the knack of adapting himself to circumstances, and so he was popular with the Woongyees as well as with the Royal Family. The Governor-General, in his letter of 8 September, 1831, appreciated his services in the following words:— " The acknowledgement of His Lordship and of the British Government are due to this officer for the uncommon zeal with which he has discharged the arduous and responsible duties with which he was entrusted at the sacrifice of his health and personal comforts. His Lordship is led to believe that his conciliatory manners and disposition have made a favourable impression on the Court, and have removed much of the jealousy and prejudice which before existed against the presence of a British representative at the Burmese capital. In the success which has attended Major Burney's efforts to accomplish this object His Lordship recognizes a very high degree of merit and political skill." [2]

[1] *Ibid.* Vol. 366, The Journal, par. 920.
[2] *Ibid.* Vol. 362, Letter dated, Simla, 8 September, 1831.

CHAPTER VII

BURNEY IN RANGOON AND THE SETTLEMENT OF THE
KUBO QUESTION, 1832-1834.

While on his way down the River to Rangoon, Burney submitted to his Government his views regarding the maintenance of a permanent British Residency in Ava, and suggested that it be stationed at Rangoon:—"Although the Ministers and the inhabitants in general of Ava have been reconciled to such an arrangement (*i.e.* the Residency being at Ava)," he wrote, "yet there is every reason to believe, that it is most obnoxious to the pride and feelings of the King, who considers it as a standing proof of his subjection and servitude to the British power. His illness indeed is attributed by Mr. Lanciago and several other persons on whose information I have some reason to depend, to the chagrin and melancholy, which reflection on the result of the late war, and particularly on this result of being forced to maintain a British officer at his capital is constantly exciting. I am of opinion that some officer, after he has had an opportunity of becoming personally acquainted with the members of the Court of Ava and with their modes of thinking and acting, should be fixed as the British Agent at Rangoon which place he should make his headquarters, and that he should go up to Ava for 2 or 3 months only every year, pay his respects to the King, and transact any business which might occur. Such an arrangement would be most acceptable to the feelings of the King, and I think it might be made equally efficient with that of always maintaining a Resident at the capital. It would lead also to a very great saving of expense, by not only relieving us from the presence of the Burmese Vakeels in Bengal, but by placing the British Agent at Rangoon under the general superintendence of Mr. Maingy as his first Assistant — the allowance of such an officer need not be more than one half of those now drawn by Capt. Rawlinson and myself. The great point,

however, would be, that such an Agent, should in the first
instance, have an opportunity of becoming personally acquainted
with the Ministers of Ava, and of acquiring their goodwill and
confidence." [1]   The Indian Government, however, did not approve of this proposal, and decided to carry on with the Residency at Ava.

Burney at Rangoon continued to hold the office of the Resi-
dent, charged with all its responsibilities and privileges. This
was a wise arrangement, because the influence of the British
Mission in Burma would be better sustained at the King's
Court as well as in the country by Burney's remaining the
acknowledged British representative than if all the duties fell
into new hands. Burney, therefore, corresponded with the
Woongyees on matters of importance through Blundell in Ava.
Blundell was at Ava as Burney's Assistant in charge of the
Residency, but was permitted to correspond direct with the
Chief Secretary to the Government in Calcutta. Burney, before
his departure from Ava, gave to Blundell in writing full directions as to the problems in hand, and how he should handle
them; he was also instructed to conduct the ordinary details of
the Residency, and refrain from entering into discussions with
the Ministers upon matters of importance.[2]

Blundell as Burney's Assistant was in charge of the Residency at Ava from 10 April, 1832, up to September 1832, when
he was relieved by Capt. H. Macfarquhar. During these five
months Blundell was on the most friendly terms with the Ministers.[3] Macfarquhar did not keep good health and in August,
1833, had to go on leave.[4] Capt. McLeod took his place, and
remained in charge of the Residency until 6 November, 1833,
when Burney returned to Ava and to regular duty.[5] During

[1] Bengal Secret and Political Consultations Vol. 366, Burney's Letter, 14 April, 1832.
[2] Ibid. Burney's Letter of Instructions to Blundell, 10 April, 1832.
The Governor-General's Minute, Simla, 24 May, 1832.
[3] Ibid. Blundell's Letter, Ava, 1 May, 1832. Ibid. Vol. 368, Burney's
Letter, Rangoon, 22 August, 1832.
[4] Ibid. Vol. 377, Burney's Letters, 26 August, 1833 and 28 September, 1833.
[5] Ibid.

this period of Burney's absence from the capital no developments or occurrences of importance took place. The King continued to be in the same state of health or ill-health as during the previous two years.[1]

Burney had Rangoon for his headquarters from May, 1832, to October, 1833, but during January - March, 1833 he was in Calcutta, and at Moulmein during the months of May and June, 1833.

The complaints of the Moulmein authorities against Martaban robbers and Burmese officers had not yet ceased; the Woongyee of Rangoon, however, at this time was an intelligent and an obliging man, and paid instant attention to the complaints.[2] Burney, on his arrival at Rangoon, had repeated conferences with him, and finally it was agreed that the Burmese officer at Martaban should go over himself and communicate with the Commissioner of Tenasserim whenever any business of importance occurred.[3]

Hitherto the British Government had been largely the complaining party; now the Burmese began to bring up counter complaints. The Governor of Rangoon reported to Burney that certain messengers of the Burma Government, while on their way to the Burmese Resident in Bengal, had met with inhospitable reception from British officers at Akyab. On enquiry Burney discovered that "their complaint dwells on the unkind reception at Akyab of their messengers, contrasting this conduct very warmly with the attentions which the Burmese authorities have always shown to me......and with the kind and hospitable reception which all Burmese authorities have invariably given to messengers employed by me, as well as to officers returning from Ava or coming up there to join me on which account the Burmese Court have never hesitated to incur con-

[1] *Ibid.* Vol. 375, Burney's Letter, Moulmein, 29 May, 1833.
[2] *Ibid.* Vol. 366, Letters from the Commissioner of Tenasserim, Moulmein, 13 February, 1832 and 13 July, 1832.
[3] *Ibid.* Vol. 367, Burney's Letter, Rangoon, no date, Consultations 9 July, 1832.

siderable expense." [1]   Burney lost no time in assuring the
Woongyee, and wrote to Blundell at Ava also to assure the
Ministers, that such a complaint would never occur again.[1]

The Kubo question, so important to the King of Burma
as well as to Raja Gumbheer Singh of Manipur, had not yet
been settled, but it was during Burney's absence from Ava that
the dispute was brought to a termination.   Every indication
pointed to the decision of the Governor-General-in-Council
being finally in favour of Gumbheer Singh, the Burmese
Embassy in Bengal notwithstanding; but Burney now champ-
ioned the Burmese cause, and it was ultimately due to his
influence that the Valley was returned to Bagyidaw.   When he
first arrived at Ava he gave no hopes to the Burmese Ministers
concerning Kubo; gradually, however, he realized that it would
be the line of wisdom to grant this concession to His Burmanic
Majesty.   While on his way down the River to Rangoon, he
expressed himself to his Government in the following words:—

" Perhaps now that I have quitted Ava, Government will
allow me to express with more freedom my sentiments regarding
the disputed territory of Kubo......the inclination of my
opinion has always been in favour of the abstract right of the
Burmese, and that views of expediency only founded on an apprehension that Ava might advance some other claim, as well
as the circumstance that our officers in Munnipur consider the
Khyendwin as the most eligible boundary, made me question the
policy of acknowledging such right.   I was aware also that Government desired to establish the Khyendwin as boundary, to
accomplish which object indeed, was one of the principal points
of my instructions when first deputed; and I saw that the
Governor-General-in-Council had confirmed the proceedings of
our Commissioners in Munnipore, before any reports were
received from me in Bengal as to the state of feeling here, and
as to the precise nature of the Burmese claims.

" Such appearing to me to be the fixed determination of
Government, I have considered it to be my duty to use my best

[1] *Ibid.* Burney's Letter, Rangoon, 2 June, 1832.

exertions to discover how its wishes could be accomplished, and
to reconcile the Burmese Court to the Khyendwin being made
the boundary between Ava and Munnipore.

"I am sorry to say, however, that I have failed entirely in
this last object, and it remains for my superiors to decide,
whether the maintenance of this point and the keeping Gumbhir
Singh in possession of an unhealthy and depopulated strip of
territory, which is divided from Munnipore by a range of hills,
and with which our officers even cannot communicate without
being always attended by large parties of coolies to convey every
necessary of life for their subsistence, is worth the risk of
thoroughly disgusting the Court of Ava, and accelerating another
war. I consider our having already held this territory for so
many months contrary to the wishes of Ava will save us from
the imputation, that fear alone has induced us to restore it to
her:........the long delay which has occurred in answer to the
reference [1] of the Court of Ava, has not diminished its desire
or hopes on this point in the smallest degree. It is a remarkable property in the character of the Burmese Government that
the inference that they draw from any fact or circumstance, is
that most consolatory to their pride and flattering to their hopes
and wishes, and I am certain that there is not a man in the
capital at this moment who does not firmly believe, that the
Governor-General, if he has any regard for truth and justice,
must ultimately decide this dispute in favour of Ava." [2]

The Government of India was taken aback at the above
communication, and requested Burney to submit a clear statement of the arguments and grounds on which he had come to the
conclusion, that the Government of Ava was entitled to the
restoration of the Kubo Valley.[3] Burney made a detailed reply,
in which, first, he admitted "that the Burmese Ministers had
advanced many untruths in support of their claims to what we
call the Kubo Valley but what they style the territory of

---

[1] This refers to the Burmese Embassy in Bengal.
[2] Bengal Secret and Political Consultations Vol. 366, Burney's
    Letter, 14 April, 1832.
[3] *Ibid.* Chief Secretary's Letter, 21 May, 1832.

Thoungthwot," that "Ava has not had uninterrupted possession of Kubo for 2000 years, and lastly Capt. Grant and Gumbhir Singh did certainly expel the Burmese from the whole of the Kubo Valley before the conclusion of the Treaty of Yandaboo." [1]

Second, Burney stated, as follows, the grounds upon which the British Commissioners in Manipur supported the claims of Gumbheer Singh:—

"1st.   Col. Symes in his work on Ava states that the Khyendwin divides the country of Cassay from that of Ava.

"2nd.   In an old work in the Shan language, said to be the Royal Chronicle of the Kings of Pong (called by the Burmese Maw Shan and Mogaung) it is stated that in the year 1363 a King of Pong destroyed the city of Takaing (Tsagain) and rendered the country of Ava tributary, and that about the year 1474 a King of Pong requested a daughter in marriage from the reigning prince of Munipore who sent her in the following year; but that on her way, on the western frontier of Sumjok (the Burmese Thoungthwot) she was attacked and carried off by a Rajah of Khambat, and that in consequence of this outrage the Chiefs of Pagan and Munipore attacked and took Khambat on which occasion an increase of territory, extending far to the eastward of the Khyendwin and including apparently the whole of the Kubo Valley, was made to the dominions of the Chief of Munipore.

"3rd.   For 12 or 15 years antecedent to 1812, the period when Marjeet Singh obtained the sovereignty of Munipore with the aid of Ava, the principal towns in Kubo Valley were held by Munipore Rajah Choorjeet Singh and of his brother and father before him.

"4th.   Gumbhir Singh reconquered the whole of Kubo Valley before the conclusion of peace at Yandaboo." [2]

Lastly, Burney made an examination of the above claims and drew his conclusions as follows:—As to the first point, he said, that Symes had obtained his information from Dr. Hamilton [3]

---

[1] *Ibid.* Vol. 367, Burney's Letter, Rangoon, 5 July, 1832.
[2] *Ibid.*
[3] He was in medical charge of the First Symes Embassy to Burma, 1795; he was then known by the name, Buchanan.

who had studied the subject and published an article in the Edinburgh Philosophical Journal together with a map of Burma,[1] clearly showing that the Kubo Valley was a part of Burma; also that later he published more articles in the same journal proving the same point.[1]

As to the second point, Burney declared that he had studied the Burmese Chronicle or Mahayazawin-daugyee in 39 Vols., dealing with Burmese history down to 1821, and that it showed that Kubo had been a possession of the Burmese King since 1370 A.D., although during the eruptions of the Shans in the 15th and 16th centuries it as well as other parts of the Burmese King's territory had been repeatedly overrun; also that there were stone inscriptions to corroborate Burma's claim to the Kubo Valley.[2]

On the third point Burney had nothing to say, except that the Burmese Ministers themselves acknowledged the fact of some of the principal towns in Kubo having revolted from the authority of the King of Burma for a period of about 15 years anterior to 1175 A.D., and again previous to 1812.[2]

On the fourth point Burney submitted, that for 12 years prior to the outbreak of the late War, the Burmese had uninterrupted possession of the Valley; and that although the Manipur Raja had conquered Kubo during the War, when the Burmese negotiators at Yandabo agreed in the second article of the Treaty that Gumbheer Singh might " return to his territory and remain ruler," there were no grounds for believing that they referred to anything but what had been the Manipur territory at the time when the war broke out, and that they certainly did not mean what might have occasionally belonged to Manipur several years before the war.[2]

Finally, Burney wound up the case for Ava with the following words:—

[1] A Map of Burma (1795) by a   Burmese Slave, by *W. S. Desai* in the Journal of the Burma Research Society, Vol. XXVI, Part III, December, 1936.
[2] Bengal Secret and Political Consultations Vol. 367, Burney's Letter, 5 July, 1832.

"I hope the.Honourable The Vice-President-in-Council will observe that it is not my intention to gainsay anything which the very able and intelligent officers[1] who were our Commissioners in Munnipore reported. But my opinion is that although the statement made by the officers is perfectly correct, still the facts which I have submitted above furnish such evidence on the side of Ava as must outweigh the proofs upon which those officers founded their belief that the Valley of Kubo belongs of right to Gumbhir Singh.

"Dr. Richardson[2] by his overland journey from Ava to the frontiers of Munnipur has dissipated all idea of any British Army ever venturing to march by that route against the capital of Ava, and I humbly conceive, that British alliance and protection are a far better defence to Munnipore against Ava than any line of boundary whatever.

"There is not the smallest doubt that the Burmese Government, in the event of our now conceding Kubo, will soon advance some other claim; and this is the point on which I have always felt most difficulty and hesitation. But here is the question of policy and expediency for the consideration of my superiors whether if we are satisfied of the right of Ava to Kubo, any apprehension of the Burmese embarrassing us hereafter with some new demand, ought to be a motive with the British Government for refusing to perform an act of justice......"[3]

While Burney from Rangoon was stating the Burmese case, the Burmese Embassy in India was endeavouring to negotiate the Kubo and other questions with the Governor-General. The fortunes of the two Burmese Residents might now be followed up.

Escorted by Lieut. Geo. Burney, the two Envoys arrived at Calcutta on 6 December, 1830, with a Royal Letter to the Governor-General. But the Governor-General was absent from Calcutta, and the Vice-President-in-Council refused to enter upon

[1] Grant and Pemberton.
[2] Vide infra. p. 285.
[3] Bengal Secret and Political Consultations Vol. 367, Burney's Letter, 5 July, 1832.

any discussion until the Envoys had first delivered the Letter to the Governor-General and communicated in person with His Lordship.[1] The Envoys, therefore, waited in Calcutta for over ten months, but since the Governor-General failed to return to his capital, they decided to proceed up country to have an audience with him. Escorted again by Lieut. Burney, they, together with their followers, left Calcutta on 11 October, 1831, by river boats, hoping to meet the Governor-General in Benares. After touching Barrackpur, Murshidabad, Monghyr, Patna, and Ghazipur, they arrived at Benares on 27 December, 1831, by easy stages. They were disappointed to discover that the Governor-General had meanwhile moved further inland. They spent over seven weeks in Benares, and were finally told by Geo. Burney that they would be able to see the Governor-General at Farukhabad.[2]

On 15 February, 1832, they left Benares, and after touching Mirzapur, Allahabad, and Cawnpore, they reached Farukhabad on 31 March, 1832. Here they were told to wait for the Governor-General who was expected to come down from Simla. They made a stay of seven months in Farukhabad, and finally they were told that His Lordship would see them at Agra.

On 4 November, 1832, they left Farukhabad, and travelling by road reached Agra on 16 November. All along they were under the impression that the Governor-General was trying to avoid them, so that they were pleasantly surprised to hear that Lord Bentinck's camp was at Agra, and that he would see them on 23 November. It was now the turn of the Company's Government to reciprocate, at least in a measure, the humiliations imposed upon British envoys at the Burmese capital. The Burmese envoys were required to abide by the following form of etiquette on the day of their presentation to the Governor-General :—

---

[1] Ibid. The Secretary's Letter, 2 July, 1832.
[2] History of the Burmese Mission to India, 1830-1833, by *W. S. Desai*, The Journal of the Burma Research Society, Vol. XXVI, Part II. August 1936. India Political Consultations, Range 193, Vol. 79, 6 July, 1835.

" The Vakeels, on reaching the point where the double line of soldiers are posted, should dismount from the Elephants and walk up the avenue without umbrellas, sword bearers, armed men, betel boxes......or other utensils.

" Out of respect for the letter [1] from His Burmese Majesty, of which the Vakeels are understood to be the bearers, the Guard of Honour will present arms on the Vakeels entering the avenue.

" The Vakeels on arriving at the landing place of the great Tent, will take off their slippers and proceed to the audience tent attended by the Interpreter, Clerk and four followers.

" The Vakeels will be received at the entrance of the audience Tent either by the Secretary or Aide-de-Camp in waiting and conducted to seats.

" On the appearance of the Rt. Hon. The Governor-General, the Vakeels will rise from their seats, and remain standing until requested to seat themselves.

" On the Governor-General's retiring from the audience Hall, the Vakeels will return in the same manner as they entered the Audience Tent." [2]

The Burmese Envoys, in their letter to their Government describe the procession as well as the presentation in the following words :—

" On the night of the 22nd November Kappitan Theeri Yaza Nauratha [3] came to our tents and said, ' At 10 o'clock tomorrow you will have to go to Goombhanee Men's [4] tents: I wish to convey before hand and arrange the royal presents, deliver them to me.' We counted and delivered the whole of the presents,[5] and said that when we were admitted ourselves we would convey in a proper manner and present the royal letter of mandate. The Royal presents were then taken away.

---

[1] Inasmuch as to say that the presentation of arms would not be done out of respect for the Envoys.
[2] Bengal Secret and Political Consultations Vol. 369, Government Letter to G. Burney, Camp Agra, 19 November, 1832.
[3] This is Captain Geo. Burney. " Theeri Yaza Nauratha " was the title conferred upon him by Bagyidaw King of Burma. It means " The Excellent and Noble Son." Bengal Secret and Political Consultations Vol. 358, Burney's Journal, par. 322.
[4] Goombhanee = Company; Men = Ruler, *i.e.* The Governor-General.
[5] The list of presents from His Burmese Majesty to the Governor-General: —
>   2 Gold Rings, (said to be) set with very valuable rubies.
>   2 Gold Rings, (said to be) set with very valuable sapphires.

" On Friday morning the 23rd November, when the English hour of 10 arrived, the Ayèbain Mengee Maha Tsee Thoo[1] and Tsaregyee Mentha Nanda gyau den [2] mounted on horses with gilded bridles and saddles, and dressed in our complete Court dresses left the tent; but we placed before us on an Elephant completely caparisoned, Mengee Maha Tsee Thoo's son Nemyo Zeya Shwe doung bearing in a respectful manner the Royal letter of Mandate, 20 Burmese soldiers with muskets as well as some of our attendants with muskets and swords and lances regularly arranged on the right and left, and behind us came the more respectable men, the Writer, Interpreter, Painter, Doctor, together with 30 of the subordinate servants, the betel box and water goglet bearer. The Goombhanee had arranged 500 Tsi-payees [3] on each side. They were dressed in white jackets and pantaloons, and had cock feathers in their caps, and were standing upright holding muskets. On arriving at the beginning of the Tsipayee line those of our party who had muskets, swords and lances were stopped, and we dismounting from our Elephant and horses, and accompanied only by our betel box and water goglet carriers and the more respectable attendants, advanced. Kappitan Theeri Yaza Nauratha came and met us and told us how to proceed, and we proceeded in the manner pointed out.

" On arriving close to the Goombhanee Men's tent we were told to leave the more respectable attendants and betel box and water goglet bearer, and for us two Chiefs and the man bearing the Royal Letter only to enter. We entered as we were told, and in the inside of the tent there was a very handsome large table about 3 cubits high and upon it were placed in a suitable manner all the royal presents which we had before delivered. In the middle of the table we placed the royal letter in a spot pointed out to us. On the eastern and western sides of the table the English Ministers and Officers were seated on chairs, and on the southern side we took our seats on two chairs which were placed there. In about 30 minutes after some fine English music had sounded, the Goombhanee Men appeared from the inner apart-

---

    1000 Rubies cut and polished.
    1000 Rubies rough and unpolished.
      40 Burmese Silk cloths.
      37 Burmese Lacquered Boxes of kinds and sizes.
           (Bengal Secret and Political Consultations Vol. 369, 24, December, 1832.)

[1] He was the Senior Burmese Envoy.
[2] The Junior Burmese Envoy.
[3] Sepoys or Indian soldiers.

8

ment towards the northern end of the table having chowries[1] borne to the right and left of him, and seated himself on a chair which had been placed at that end of the table. The Goombhanee Men was not dressed in the same kind of coat as the English Ministers and officers. On the left side of the coat there was a gold mark like the figure of a lion, and his hat which was black was long before and behind and tapered to the top, and on the left side of it also there was a gold mark like the figure of a Lion, and at both ends of the hat there was a gold tassel.

"About a Burmese hour[2] after the arrival of the Goombhanee Mengyee a translation into English of the royal letter....was read out by the Kappitan Theeri Yaza Nauratha. The Goombhanee Men then said, the Royal Letter contains matters relating to the affairs of the country, and after conversing the same an answer shall be given on my arrived at Calcutta; let the Burmese Chiefs also return thither, which order having been explained to us by Kappitan Theeri Yaza Nauratha, we returned home."[3]

The Envoys were bitterly disappointed with the interview, because the Governor-General did not discuss with them any questions of state. They complained that they had come so far into the interior of the country, not merely for a formal interview, but to settle their King's business. On 26 November, 1832, therefore, they wrote to Macnaughten, Secretary to the Governor-General, explaining the claims of their King to the Kubo Valley as well as to the villages and dependencies of Martaban south of the Salween. They also requested, that in the name of friendship, the entire province of Arakan be returned to their King, and that the British Residency in Burma be recalled, and in its place a biennial or triennial embassy be substituted.[4] The Secretary assured the Envoys that their letter would be fully considered and replied to, and requested them to return to Calcutta, to which place the Governor-General would also shortly proceed.[5]

[1] Whisks of horse hair used in India to keep off flies.
[2] A Burmese Nayee or hour is equal to 22 minutes.
[3] India Political Consultations Range 193, Vol. 79, Consultations 6 July, 1835.
[4] Bengal Secret and Political Consultations Vol. 372, The Letter, 26 November, 1832.
[5] India Political Consultations 6 July, 1835, Range 193, Vol. 79.

The Envoys began the return journey on 28 November, 1832, and moving leisurely reached Calcutta on 6 March, 1833.[1] Meanwhile the Supreme Government had summoned both Major Burney and Commissioner Maingy to Calcutta, and early in 1833, the Governor-General himself also arrived at the Indian capital. After fully consulting the two above mentioned officers, the Governor-General wrote his Minute, giving his decision in respect of Kubo and other Boundary questions raised by the Government of Burma. The verdict given was in favour of the King of Burma as to the Kubo Valley, but clearly so out of expediency.

"Upon the best consideration," says the Minute, "I am not convinced that our first decision was erroneous, though I am free to admit that the question is involved in considerable doubt and confusion........I am notwithstanding of opinion that expediency is in favour of the concession to Ava."[2] The fear that the Burmese Government might look upon the concession as a surrender was also considered. "But", the Minute continues, "although this consideration......namely, the misinterpretation that the conceit of the Burmese may put upon the concession to their own prejudice and the more reasonable ground of dissatisfaction that will be given to Gumbheer Singh, might forbid any change, yet, with reference to the anxious desire for Kubboo expressed by the Government of Ava, to the humiliation of their pride, and to their reduced if not extinguished power, I think it will be both generous and expedient to grant them this gratification. It is true that we give up the best boundary line, and the admission of the Burmese into the Valley may tend to much more collision with the Munneeporees, but with our superior power a better or worse military boundary is of no consequence whatever, and these boundary disputes if arising can lead to no war......

"I beg, therefore, to propose in pursuance of the orders of the Secret Committee, that Major Burney be directed to return

[1] India Political Consultations 6 July, 1835, Range 193, Vol. 79.
[2] Bengal Secret and Political Consultations Vol. 372, The Governor-General's Minute, Calcutta, 26 February, 1833.

to Ava, and to announce to the King that the Supreme Government still adheres to the opinion that the Ningtee formed the proper boundary between Ava and Munneepore, but that in consideration of His Majesty's feelings and wishes, and in the spirit of amity and good will subsisting between the two countries, the Supreme Government consents to the restoration of the Kubboo Valley to Ava, and to the establishment of the boundary lines at the foot of the Hills — the exact line to be established by Commissioners on both sides to meet in November next when the Kubboo Valley will be given up."

As to the boundary dispute on the Salween river, the Minute says, " Major Burney will take the opportunity of settling all questions relating to the islands in the Salween River, which will belong according to universally accepted usage to the right or left bank as the course of the deep water channel may determine. If any claim should be raised to the Bilugum [1] Island at the mouth of the Salween it should receive the same instant rejection as it has done from Sir Archibald Campbell, and upon the same principle that the deep water channel runs round the north extremity of the island........"

Of the three members of the Secret and Political Committee at Calcutta, Sir C. T. Metcalfe and Mr. Ross were in agreement with the views of the Governor-General; [2] but Lieut.-General Sir Edward Barnes, the Commander-in-Chief, at first differed.[3] However, under the influence of Burney and Maingy, he too was won over, and agreed to the surrender of Kubo. " I have since conversed with Major Bruney," says the Commander-in-Chief in his second minute,[4] " and from them hear that the Kubboo Valley is an object of particular cupidity to the King of Ava, and that unless Major Burney be authorized to announce its surrender he would have but little hope of preserving an amicable connexion with the Court, though fear

[1] Bilugyun.
[2] Bengal Secret and Political Consultations Vol. 372, Minute by Metcalfe, 2 March, 1833; Minute by A. Ross, 11 March, 1833.
[3] *Ibid.* Minute by the Commander-in-Chief.
[4] *Ibid.* 11 March, 1833.

might for the present avert an open hostility......Major
Burney seems to think that his being empowered to promise the
restoration of the Kubboo Valley would so much facilitate his
negotiations in other points with the Court of Ava, and particularly in regard to the Islands at the mouth of the Martaban
River which if ceded would at once settle the point of the
Tenasserim provinces, because it would be absurd to suppose
that we should stipulate for these Islands without at the same
time contemplating the retention of the Provinces, that I now
feel disposed to coincide with the proposition of the surrender
of the Kubboo Valley, at the same time I think it will increase
our obligation to support Gumbhir Singh."

The Government of India now gave a final reply [1] to the
Burmese Envoys in Calcutta in respect of the four claims of
their government. As to Kubo they were merely told that the
boundary would be revised; but undoubtedly they received
verbal information from Burney and Maingy that the revision
would be in favour of their monarch. As to the Tenasserim
boundary dispute they were told that the Salween was the right
line of demarcation and would continue to be so. With respect
to their request that the provinces of Arakan, Ye, Tavoy, and
Mergui be restored to their King, they were informed that
these areas did not form uninterruptedly a portion of the
ancient empires of Ava and Pagan, that they had been conquered from the Kings of Arakan, Pegu, and Siam, in the same
manner as the British later conquered them from Burma, and
that therefore the British Government would not relinquish any
portion of the territory ceded to it by the treaty of Yandabo.

The fourth and the last request, which required an abrogation of the 7th Article of the Treaty of Yandabo was also
rejected. The reasons given were, " that much advantage has
already accrued from the presence of the Burmese Vakeels in
Bengal, and of Major Burney at Ava. Confidence has been
given to travellers and merchants, trade has increased, several

---

[1] *Ibid.* Chief Secretary's Letter to the Burmese Envoys, 16 March,
1833.

questions regarding the surrender of fugitives and boundary incursions have been quietly and satisfactorily adjusted, and the two nations are likely soon to understand each other's customs and manners. The Governor-General, therefore, is unwilling to depart from the custom of all great civilized countries to the Westward until such time as the Burmese and British nations become more intimately acquainted with each other." [1]

The Burmese Envoys did not embark for Rangoon till on 29 June, 1833: they were busy collecting Buddhistic relics and images for their King. They finally arrived at Ava on 19 September, 1833, highly pleased at the settlement of the Kubo problem, and for which they took all credit to themselves. They were in daily expectation of some substantial reward, but it was not till ten months later that the senior envoy was promoted to the office of the Woondouk.[2] The Envoys, among other things brought with them a black marble image of Gautama Buddha. Burney says that "no act of theirs has secured them so much credit and approbation or given such satisfaction. That idol was received here with the greatest demonstrations of reverence, the King and the Court, and indeed most of the inhabitants of the city (i.e. Ava) having proceeded down the river some way in order to meet and bring it up." [2]

When Raja Gumbheer Singh was informed of the Governor-General's decision he felt much vexed, but was persuaded to accept the new arrangement in good grace.[3] His principal objection was, "the humiliation and shame he felt in agreeing to cede to the hereditary oppressors of his country a part of the territories of his ancestors, and the anxiety, apprehension and alarm the near neighbourhood of the Burmese would be certain to create amongst the inhabitants of Munnipore." [3] The Valley was officially returned to Burma on 9 January, 1834, and

---

[1] *Ibid.*
[2] *Ibid.* Vol. 380, Burney's Letter, Ava, 25 November, 1833.
The Kone-baung-set Mahayazawin says that the Envoys brought with them "the image worshipped by Asoka and three Mahabodhi plants." Book 2, p. 487.
[3] *Ibid.* Vol. 375. Grant's Letter, Manipur, 2 June; The Raja's Letter to Grant, 30 May, 1833.

Raja Gumbheer Singh died on the same day. He was suc-
ceeded by Raja Chandra Kirtee Singh an infant son. The
Government of India, in order to compensate the Raja for the
loss of the Valley, agreed to give him a monthly stipend of
Rs. 500 from 9 January, 1834, with the proviso that if ever
Kubo reverted to Manipur the stipend would cease.[1]

---

[1] *Ibid*. Vol. 380, Pemberton's Letter, Calcutta, 19 April, 1834, Appendix No. 7.

    N.B.— According to Major-General Sir J. Johnstone, Political
Agent, Manipur, 1877-1882, Gumbheer Singh died of cholera,
but the present Government of Manipur has informed the author
that the Raja died of snake bite: —

    "When Ghumbeer Singh heard the final decision he quietly
accepted it, saying, "You gave it me and you can take it away.
I accept your decree." The proposed transfer was distasteful to
many of the inhabitants, including the Sumjok (Thoungdoot)
Tsawbwa, but they were not consulted. The Kubo Valley was
handed over to the Burmese on the 9th of January, 1834, and on
that day Ghumbeer Singh died in Manipur of cholera. Perhaps
he was happy in the hour of his death, as he felt the treatment
of our Government most severely." *J. Johnstone,* **My Experiences in Manipur and the Naga Hills,** p. 87.

    "Raja Gumbheer Singh died on the 9th January, 1834 *of
snake bite* according to the report of the Historical Research
Society of the Nikhil (All India) Hindu Manipuri Mahasabha
which is accepted by the State Durbar.

    "It is a matter of history that Gumbheer Singh felt very
deeply indeed the overriding of his rights and deprivation of his
territory (of Kubo Valley) from mere motives of expediency....

    "His acceptance of the situation was dictated entirely by
his loyalty to the British Government, who had assisted him to
recover his lost territory. But neither he nor his descendants
ever willingly acquiesced in the cession of their ancestral territory, the right of Manipur to which had been so definitely and
conclusively established by the enquiries and investigations of
the British officers on the frontier, and emphatically confirmed
by the Governor-General of India himself.

    "By virtue of the Treaty of 1834 the Manipur State is still
enjoying the compensatory stipend of 6,000 Sicca rupees (*i.e.*
Rs. 6,270 when converted into the present currency) per annum
from the Government of India." Letter from the President,
Manipur State Durbar to W. S. Desai, dated Imphal 26 June,
1937. No. 3759G/IA-22.

    The following extracts from *Johnstone's* book, on Manipur
and Burney are quite interesting: —

    "The territories of Manipur varied according to the mettle
of its rulers. Sometimes they held a considerable territory east
of the Chindwin river in subjection, at other times only the Kubo
Valley: a strip of territory, inhabited, not by Burmese, but by
Shans, and lying between Manipur proper and the Chindwin.
Again they were driven back into Manipur proper. For the

Burney's task having been completed in Calcutta he embarked for Burma, armed with 60 stands of fusils, carriages, telescopes, broadcloths, and gold and silver flowered muslins, as presents for the King, together with permission from his Government to signify to His Majesty, that the British Government would grant him the indulgence of purchasing from Indian

---

greater part of the last century (18th century) the Kubo Valley unquestionably belonged to Manipur, and it was never in any sense a Burmese province, being, when not under Manipur, a feudatory of the great Shan Kingdom of Pong." p. 81.

"He (Gumbheer Singh) was a wise and strong though severe ruler, and though he owed his throne greatly to his own efforts, he to last retained the deepest feelings of loyalty and gratitude to the British Government, promptly obeying all its orders and doing his utmost to impress the same feeling on all his officers.

"As is always the case, though we had carried all before us in the war (with Burma), we began to display great weakness afterwards. We had an agent, Colonel Burney at Ava, and the Burmese who were not disposed to be at all friendly, constantly tried to impress on him the fact that all difficulties and disputes would be at an end if we ceded the Kubo Valley to them, that territory belonged to our ally Ghumbeer Singh of Manipur. Of course the proposal ought to have been rejected with scorn, and a severe snub given to the Burmese officials. The advisers of the Government of India, however, being generally officers brought up in the Secretariat, and with little practical knowledge of Asiatics, the manly course was not followed. It was not realized that a display of self-confidence and strength is the best diplomacy with people like the Burmese, and with a view to winning their good-will we basely consented to deprive our gallant and loyal ally of part of his territories. An attempt was made to negotiate with him, but Major Grant said, "It is no use bargaining with Ghumbeer Singh," and refused to take any part in it. He was asked what compensation should be given, and he said 6,000 sicca rupees per annum." pp. 86-87.

When Upper Burma was annexed in 1885, there was an opportunity for Manipur to regain the Valley. Representations were made to the Government of India; but in the end it was decided to maintain the status quo. Says *Johnstone* on p. 272 of his work, "I regret I did not, as I might in that case have again urged the claims of Manipur to have the Kubo Valley restored to her, as she had a right to expect that it would be; substantial hopes having been on at least one occasion held out to her, and her many good services and constant loyalty entitling her to consideration.

"However, it was not to be; and in the summer of 1886 another misfortune befell her, in the death of Maharaja Chandra Kirtee Singh. Perhaps, like his father, Ghumbeer Singh, he was happy in the hour of his death, as he did not live to see the disgrace of his country, and the ingratitude of our Government to his family."

stores a supply of 1000 stands of fusils and ten to twelve thousand stands of muskets, on condition that some facilities were granted to British trade in Burma, such as a reduction in the heavy anchorage fees at Rangoon, or permission to export bullion from the country upon payment of a small export duty.[1]

On 30 April, 1833, Burney arrived at Moulmein,[2] and on 3 July, at Rangoon.[3] On 6 November, 1833, he was back in Ava. He gives the following impressions of his journey up the river—a tedious and uncomfortable passage of 36 days in Burmese boats:—

" At this season of the year the country on both banks of the Erawadi has of course a better appearance than what it had during the hot season of 1830 when I first passed it; still I had now repeated occasion to notice, that the towns and villages show increasing wealth and population; the inhabitants have returned to their former homes from the interior in which they had taken refuge during the late war, and they are constructing more substantial houses and surrounding them with little gardens. Unfortunately, however, a scarcity of rain this year and consequent high price of rice had tended to check some of these signs of improvement, and many of the younger male population had left their homes to rob and plunder, hence the river is much infested by pirates who had the boldness even to attack some of the fleet of the Burmese Vakeels when they were on their way up from Rangoon. I fear our Arracan frontier will be disturbed by these robbers, and I considered it, therefore, my first duty on my arrival here to draw the attention of the Burmese Ministers to this point to call upon them to adopt vigorous measures for preventing our territory in Arracan from being subjected to incursions from these hungry marauders, and to caution them that in the event of the Burmese Government being found unable to prevent or check such depredations, I have no doubt the Supreme Government will autho-

---

[1] *Ibid.* Vol. 372, Burney's Letter, Calcutta, 25 March, 1833; Government Letter, 26 March, 1833.
[2] *Ibid.* Vol. 375, Burney's Letter, Moulmein, 29 May, 1833.
[3] *Ibid.* Rangoon, 3 July, 1833.

rize our officers in Arracan, not only to pursue and apprehend robbers within the Burmese jurisdiction, but to take further steps there for putting an effectual stop to such violation of our territory."[1]

Burney was received at Ava by the Woongyees and other officers with much kindness, and he soon resumed his former relations of friendly and familiar intercourse with them. The King had not yet recovered from his sickness. He was at first unwilling to grant an audience to Burney, but after some persuasion agreed to do so. The Resident was presented to him on 20 November, 1833. Burney says, " His Majesty spoke little and scarcely noticed me, showing much timidity, dejection of spirits, listlessness, and all signs of hypochondriasis verging on insanity."[2] The King usually remained in his palace, appeared in public about once in three or four months, and was perfectly ignorant of and indifferent to the affairs of government. His brother-in-law the Menthagyee was the *de facto* Regent of the kingdom, the Crown Prince Tsakyamen being a mere cypher in the Court as before. [2]

Burney had brought with him a letter[3] from the Governor-General to the King containing sentiments of friendship, also a letter from the Chief Secretary to the Ministers, conveying the decision of the Governor-General to return Kubo to Burma:— " The Burmese Ministers having completed the payment of the crore of rupees, and having shown a disposition to cultivate friendly relations with the British Government by surrendering fugitive criminals, adopting measures for preventing and punishing border incursions, affording protection and encouragement to British traders, and by treating the British Resident Major Burney with kindness and confidence, the Governor-General has been induced to consider how he may yield to their earnest and repeated wishes respecting the territory of Thoungthwot. The Governor-General will propose some compensation to Gumbheer Singh to induce him to relinquish this territory to

[1] *Ibid.* Vol. 380, Burney's Letter, Ava, 25 November, 1833.
[2] *Ibid.*
[3] *Ibid.* Vol. 372, The Letter, Fort William, 16 March, 1833.

Ava; but the Governor-General trusts, that the Burmese Ministers will not make him regret having taken such a step by
bringing forward hereafter some new claim........Let the
conduct of the Governor-General on this occasion satisfy the
King of Ava and the inhabitants of Ava in general that the
British nation requires from them only peace, commerce and
friendly intercourse.

"But everything on the frontiers of Munnipore must
remain as at present until the month of November next, when
the Burmese Ministers may depute to that quarter two officers
of rank to meet two British officers who will deliver over to
the Burmese the towns of Khambat, Tummoo, Thoung-thwot,
and fix and point out the line of hills which may be selected as
the future boundary between Ava and Munnipore. The eastern
foot of the hills known in Munnipore as the Mirang (Muring)
Hills, and supposed to be the same as that called by the Burmese
Yoma Daung, will form a good line of demarcation between
the possessions of the two states; but the Burmese authorities
must on no pretence ever interfere with any of the Kheyns
(Chins) or wild tribes residing on those Hills or on any hill
lying to the westward of them......"[1]

The Ministers were highly pleased at the Kubo decision;
but they objected to the Yoma Daung being established as the
line of boundary, and claimed the eastern face of those mountains as far as the summit. They also desired to reimpose their
authority over the Chins. Burney pointed out to them the utter
hopelessness of exceeding the limit designated by the Governor-
General, and the folly and impolicy of receiving the concession
ungracefully. They finally relinquished the claims and accepted
the new arrangement.[1] They also dropped their claims concerning the Salween frontier and the restoration of Tenasserim
and Arakan.[1]

On 23 November, 1833, two Burmese Commissioners.
Woondouk Maung Khan Ye and Tsaredaugyee Nemyo Khyan
Thoo, accompanied by Lieut. McLeod, Burney's Assistant,

[1] *Ibid.*

left for the Manipur frontier to receive the Kubo Valley from the British Commissioners in the service of Gumbheer Singh. They arrived at Tammu, and on 1 January, 1834, the British Commissioners, Grant and Pemberton, joined them. The Burmese Commissioners, however, objected to the boundary being fixed at the eastern foot of the Muring hills, and claimed that the Yoma Daung range was the boundary fixed by the Governor-General, and that this range lay further to the west of the Muring hills.[1] The British Commissioners said that their Government had instructed them not to enter into any discussions on the subject, but to fix the boundary as directed; also that if the Burmese Commissioners failed to agree to the boundary mentioned, no part of the Valley would be made over to them. The Burmese Commissioners then agreed to receive the Valley, but recorded their protest, and expressed a desire to appeal to Calcutta again. The Valley was handed over on 9 January, 1834, the boundaries fixed being as follows:—The eastern boundary, the foot of the Muring hills; the western boundary, the Ningtee or the Chindwin river; the southern boundary extending from the eastern foot of the Muring hills at the point where the river Nawsawingand[2] enters the plain up to its sources, and across the hills due west down to the Kathe Khyoung or Manipur river; and the northern boundary beginning at the foot of the Muring hills at the northern extremity of the Kubo Valley running due north up to the first range of hills eastwards up to the village called Loo Hooppa by the Manipuris.[3]

The contention of the Burmese Commissioners that the Yoma Daung was not the same as the Muring hills was correct; the former lay to the west of the latter. The geography of these parts being not sufficiently known, the Governor-General had made a mistake in considering the two to be the same.[4]

[1] Kone-baung-set Mahayazawin, Book 2, p, 488.
[2] Called by the Manipuris, Numsaeelung.
[3] Bengal Secret and Political Consultations Vol. 380, Burney's Letter, Ava, 22 January, 1834; Ibid. McLeod's Report to Burney; Ibid. The agreement between the British and Burmese Commissioners, No. 5.
[4] Ibid.

Under Burney's influence, however, the Burmese Ministers dropped the dispute, and wrote two letters to the Government of India acknowledging in a most friendly manner the return of the Kubo Valley and the good treatment received by the Burmese Envoys during their sojourn in India.[1]

The long drawn out Kubo question was thus finally and fully settled. The death of Gumbheer Singh also removed all feelings of personal resentment from the minds of the King and his Court. It is most certain that the Government of India would not have returned the Valley to Ava but for the representations of Burney. It is strange, however, that immediately after Burney had rendered this great service to the King of Burma, the Ministers under His Majesty's orders proposed that the British Residency be removed from the capital. The Ministers confessed to Burney, that they themselves and the people at large viewed the Residency as a public proof of the existence of amicable relations between the two governments, but that their King was opposed to a permanent foreign residency at his capital.[2]

The Ministers even offered to grant some facilities to British commerce and shipping at Rangoon in return for the removal of the Residency from Ava. The continued illness of the King, however, put a stop to further discussions on the subject, although the Ministers often urged Burney to obtain the permission of the Governor-General to draw up in concert with the Rangoon Woongyee some plan of arrangement on the subject. Their idea was that the Residency be removed to Rangoon, and that the Rangoon Woongyee be in charge of all diplomatic relations with the British Resident. Burney did not recommend to his Government the removal of the Residency from the Capital, but he pointed out in no uncertain terms the difficulties of the Resident in Ava:—

" Judging from my own experience and from what has occurred during the last four years, I am inclined to believe,

[1] *Ibid.* 5 March, 1834.
[2] *Ibid.* Burney's Letter, Ava, 15 April, 1834.

that until some change takes place in the state of affairs and in the circumstances of the Residency at Ava, few British officers will be able to reside here uninterruptedly for more than two or three years. It is not really the hot weather, although that is bad enough at a place where it seldom rains and where the thermometer often exceeds 100°, and does not fall below 92° before 12 o'clock at night, but it is the want of wholesome vegetables, of the means of taking exercise, and of adapting the house occupied by the Residency to the climate in the same manner as houses in India are adapted. It is these last mentioned circumstances, added to another I shall submit at the close of this paragraph, which renders a residence at Ava so irksome and trying to the constitution. The roads such as they are, are impassable during the greater part of the hot weather owing to the overflowing of the Erawadi, and the spot of ground allotted to the British Residency does not admit of being enlarged although it has scarcely 10 sq. yds. of open space, covered as it is with the huts of the Escort and servants and followers. But what ought chiefly to be mentioned, when any important event or discussion arises here, the consideration that there exists no certain means of communicating with your own Government which possesses less knowledge of the real character and customs of this than of any other Indian Court, greatly enhances in such a climate and situation, near a crazy King and an ignorant and trembling set of Ministers, the mental anxiety which prays upon the health of a public servant holding a highly responsible office." [1]

The Indian Government, however, definitely refused to accede to the proposal of the Ministers, and instructed Burney not to encourage any proposition on the part of the Burmese Government which had for its object the removal of the British Residency from Ava. [2]

---

[1] *Ibid.*
[2] *Ibid.* Letter from the Chief Secretary, Fort William, 22 May, 1834.

CHAPTER VIII

BURNEY'S SECOND DEPARTURE FROM AVA AND THE BURMA-ASSAM FRONTIER, 1834-1837.

Burney had to some extent recouped his health in Rangoon and in Calcutta, but the summer of 1834 in Ava again began to tell upon him.[1] The King's malady also showed no signs of abatement. In February, 1834, he betrayed "such irritation of mind that few of his Ministers dare approach him and the Queen even is reported to be afraid of being left with him." [2] One day in March, 1834, "he chased with a spear Tshan Atwenwoon, the Interior Minister, who takes a leading part in all discussions with me. Another day he turned the whole of his Interior Ministers out of the Palace and prohibited their being again admitted. Two or three times he has shut himself up in his own apartment, refusing to hold intercourse with any one or take any kind of sustenance for two days together." [3]

Under the circumstances of his own ill-health and his inability to transact business because of the King's state of health, it became necessary for Burney to quit the capital for a while. He had intended to leave his Assistant, Lieut. McLeod, in charge of the Residency, not only because he was an able man, but also because the Burmese Ministers had a special liking for him; McLeod, however, received a summons from Moulmein requiring his attendance at Madras to give evidence in the trial of a British military officer, so that Burney had no option but to let him go. On 16 April, 1834, Burney quitted Ava and left the Residency in charge of Assistant Surgeon Bayfield. Burney has summed up the doctor's qualifications to hold such an important charge in the following words:—That he " has

---

[1] Bengal Secret and Political Consultations Vol. 380, Burney's Letter, Ava, 15 April, 1834.

[2] *Ibid.* Ava, 20 February, 1834.

[3] *Ibid.* Ava, 5 March, 1834.

resided among the Burmese for the last four years, and has during such time closely applied himself to acquiring a knowledge of the language and character of this people and our past and existing relations with this Court, and on whose discretion, firmness and temper I know that I may rely with every confidence." [1]

Burney arrived at Rangoon on 1 May, 1834 [2]; the months of February and March, 1835, he spent in Cálcutta. He returned to Rangoon in April, 1835, and finally arrived at his headquarters at the Burmese capital in July, 1835. During all this period Bayfield was in charge of the Residency. No important developments or occurrences took place at the capital, although the King continued in the same state of ill-health as before. On 28 September, 1834, Bayfield had an audience of the King on the occasion of the festival of boat races. [3]

Bayfield employed himself to writing a Historical Review of the political relations between the British Government in India and the Empire of Ava from the earliest date on record to 1834. This work was revised by Burney, and in 1835 was published by the Government of India at the Calcutta Baptist Press as a Supplement to the Report on the Eastern Frontier of British India, by Capt. R. B. Pemberton. [4] Burney was so highly pleased with Bayfield's discharge of his duties, that, in the following words, he commended him to the Supreme Government for employment in the political service:— "......it gives me great pleasure to be able to add that since this Gentleman has been serving under my orders he has applied himself very sedulously and successfully not only in acquiring a knowledge of the Burmese language, customs and manners, but

[1] *Ibid.* Ava, 15 April, 1834.
   The Supreme Government approved of Burney's arrangement of leaving the Residency in charge of Bayfield. *Ibid.* Letter of the Government, Fort William, 22 May, 1834.
[2] India Political Consultations Range 193, Vol. 55, Burney's Letter, Rangoon, 9 May, 1834.
[3] *Ibid.* Vol. 62, Burney's Letter, Rangoon, 27 October, 1834.
[4] *Ibid.* Vol. 71, Consultations 17 March, 1835, No. 30.
   This work together with the Supplement is mentioned in the Bibliography.

in availing himself of the means which I placed before him for obtaining an acquaintance with all such historical and other information as might enable him hereafter to be useful to the public service in this country. His conduct also at Ava since I left him there in charge of the Residency has given satisfaction to the Ministers of Ava as well as to myself......I consider it therefore a duty incumbent on me to bring the talents and qualifications of this Gentleman to the notice of His Excellency the Governor-General-in-Council of India. I am aware of no person more capable of holding political employment in this country." [1]

While Burney was at Rangoon, an English Schooner, the *Young Rover*, commanded by Capt. Ewers, sailed from Moulmein for the Bengal coast on 28 September, 1834, with silver worth Rs. 70,000 on board. After six days, when the boat was not far from the island of Negrais, eleven of the crew composed of Manillians and Indians mutinied, because the Captain and the Mate were in the habit of beating and ill-treating the men. The mutineers confined the officers and their sympathisers, and made an attempt to steer the vessel towards Bengal, but failed, and grounded the vessel off the coast within the jurisdiction of the King of Burma near point Negrais. Finally, the mutineers set fire to the vessel together with the Captain and the Mate, and after killing some of the passengers and crew, themselves escaped. The Myothoogyi of Dalla (opposite Rangoon) however, apprehended the eleven culprits and handed them over to the Woongyee of Rangoon.[2]

Burney requested the Woongyee to surrender the men to him, so that he might send them to Calcutta for trial. At first the Woongyee was willing to deliver them over, but some of his officers led him to doubt if he would be justified in doing so, as there was no precedent for the surrender of such criminals; also the Anglo-Burmese Treaty was silent on the subject. Burney says in his report, that if he had been satisfied, " that these men would have had a proper trial in this country, and

---

[1] *Ibid.* Burney's Letter, Rangoon, 31 December, 1834.
[2] *Ibid.* Vol. 61, Burney's Letters, Rangoon, 25 and 28 October, 1834.

that the guilty would have been duly punished, I think I should have endeavoured to persuade the Woongyi to make an example of them here, where such an example might perhaps be more beneficial than at Calcutta."[1] But the British Resident did not wish to omit this opportunity of establishing a useful precedent in Burma. He, therefore, informed the Woongyee that although there was no article of treaty stipulating for the mutual surrender of criminals, yet the general law of nations rendered the reciprocal surrender of criminals of this description incumbent as a common interest and duty. Burney also assured the Woongyee that if the crew of any vessel under Burmese colours should cut her off in the same manner as the *Young Rover* had been, and enter British territory, the criminals would be handed over to him on his application for their surrender.[2] The Woongyee immediately responded to Burney's offer: the men were handed over, and Burney shipped them to Calcutta to stand their trial before the Supreme Court.[3]

A minor case arose out of this *Young Rover* affair and may be recorded here. The spot where the vessel was grounded and burnt was not exactly known, but Capt. William Spiers, a British subject, and a Lieutenant in the Royal Navy on half pay, residing at that time in Rangoon as a merchant, volunteered to proceed by the inland route and ascertain the spot as well as the possibility of saving any portion of the property. With the consent and assistance of the Woongyee as well as of Burney, Spiers with a few followers discovered the spot where the vessel had been burnt, and found it plundered. But Staig,[4] a British merchant residing in Rangoon, and Sarkees Manook an Armenian gave out that Spiers had plundered the *Rover* of its silver, and that two boxes full of silver he had removed to his

---

[1] *Ibid.* Vol. 61, Burney's Letters, Rangoon, 25 and 28 October, 1834.
[2] *Ibid.*
[3] *Ibid.* Government Letter to Burney, 21 November, 1834.
[4] He had fled from his creditors in Calcutta and established himself as a trader in Rangoon. He had also renounced his British nationality and put himself under the protection of the Burmese Government. He was a hot tempered man and was called "Kula Zo" by the Burmans.

own house. At Burney's request the Rangoon Woongyee insti-
tuted an enquiry, and decided that the charge against Spiers was
without any foundation.[1]

Spiers now charged Staig and Manook with a conspiracy
against his honour. Burney also pointed out to the Woongyee
the reprehensible conduct of the two men; but the Governor
entirely acquitted them of the charge, and said that no censure
was necessary. Spiers felt that the Woongyee had failed to
do him justice, and presented him with a written affidavit, but
it was rejected as being irrelevant and frivolous. Burney was
unwilling to move any further in behalf of Spiers without orders
from his Government, and so submitted the whole case to the
Governor-General, enquiring if he should appeal against the
Woongyee to the Ministers of Ava, and press them to inflict
some fine or censure on Staig and Manook.[2] The Indian Government directed him to refrain from further action in the
matter.[2]

In August, 1834, the Rangoon Woongyee applied to the
Governor-General through Burney to be allowed to purchase
50 stands of Fusils and 100 stands of new muskets from the
arsenal of Fort William. The Supreme Government called
upon Burney to give his opinion on the policy of supplying the
Burmese with superior arms. Burney saw no objection to the
arms being supplied, and in his reply gave the following interesting information on the passage of foreign arms into Burma:—

"I beg leave to state that Mr. Secretary Swinton's dispatch
to Major-General Sir Archibald Campbell of the 22nd June
1827 as well as your letter to me of the 26th March 1833 had
led me to believe that the Supreme Government had already
decided that no mischievous consequences were likely to ensue
from the Burmese being supplied with fire-arms. Since June
1827 the Burmese have been abundantly provided by British
Traders, so well indeed that an Armenian vessel, the Cashmere,

[1] India Political Consultations Range 193, Vol 61, Burney's Letter,
28 October, 1834, and Vol. 85, Abstract of Burney's Letter, Rangoon, 29 June, 1835.
[2] Ibid. Vol. 85, Abstract of Burney's Letter, Rangoon, 29 June, 1835.

which touched here this month could find no sale for 800 stands of serviceable muskets which her cargo offered to the Woongyee at the rate of 13 Rs. a piece only. The application which the Woongyee made through me was on Fusils and new muskets for the purpose of equipping his own personal guard with fine shiny arms. I beg leave to submit my own opinion, however, that the British Government cannot prevent the Burmese from obtaining as many arms as they may require by means of American and other foreign traders, and that the possession of muskets will in all probability lead the Burmese in any future war to relinquish their own native system of warfare and to issue from their stockades and jungles to meet our troops in the open plains by which proceeding the Burmese force will become more tangible, and the qualities of discipline and steadiness in which our troops must always be superior to theirs, will have a better field for display, and a better chance of soon bringing the contest to a close.

" I hope, therefore, that His Excellency-in-Council will be pleased to comply with the Woongyee's application, but as he has lately received 30 Fusils through Capt. McLeod, who was allowed to purchase them at the arsenal of Fort William, 20 more Fusils only with 100 stands of new muskets will meet his wants." [1] The Government of India proved itself to be more generous than Burney's recommendation: 20 Fusils and 100 stands of new muskets were sent to the Woongyee as a present from the British Government.[2]

Another question settled by Burney was that of the expenses in respect of the Residencies at the two courts. Hitherto the practice was for each Court to pay the salaries of its own envoys and followers, but other expenses as to travel, board, and lodging, were reimbursed by the Government in whose territory the foreign envoy moved or lived. The Burmese Embassy to India (1830-1833) had cost Ava Rs. 20,160 per annum. This was a heavy expense for Burma, and the Minis-

---

[1] *Ibid.* Vol. 67, Burney's Letter, Rangoon, 30 December, 1834.
[2] *Ibid.* Letter from Secretary to Government 11 February, 1835.

ters had often complained to Burney of the charge. The Burmese Government also at first supplied to Burney and his followers food stuffs worth about two to three thousand ticals per month; later Burney had this reduced to 500 ticals per month. The Indian Government had also been put to a heavy expense for the Burmese Envoys and followers during their sojourn in India, and the Court of Directors, in their Dispatch dated 6 March, 1834, had commented upon this item of expense. Burney suggested to his Government that negotiations should speedily be opened to bring about an arrangement by which each government would become responsible to defray its own political charges.[1]

Burney immediately took the matter in hand, and on 13 February, 1835, Bayfield wrote to the Ministers placing the proposition for their consideration and acceptance. Without delay they availed themselves of the opportunity, and the new convention came into force at once.[2]

On 11 August, 1834, Burney applied to his Government for permission to repair to Calcutta in November, preparatory to applying for further leave to proceed to Europe. The permission was granted, but the letter of sanction, dated Fort William, 16 October, 1834, somehow did not reach Burney until 18 December, 1834. He left Rangoon on 15 January, 1835, and arrived at Calcutta on 3 February. He soon discovered that it was impossible for him to settle his public accounts and provide himself an outfit for Europe before the unfavourable season for making such a long voyage (round the Cape) began. Besides, he was not prepared to undertake the voyage so late in the season, as it might have proved damaging to the health of his wife and young children. He, therefore, requested the

---

[1] *Ibid.* Vol. 62, Burney's Letter, Rangoon, 18 September, 1834. Letter from Secretary to Government Ft. William, 2 December, 1834.
[2] *Ibid.* Vol. 67, Burney's Letter, 15 January, 1835; Vol. 74, Bayfield's Letter, 19 February, 1835; Bayfield's Letter to the Ministers, 13 February, 1835.

Government to cancel his leave and permit him to return to duty at Ava. His request was immediately granted.[1]

The situation as to the Anglo-Burmese relations and their prospects at this time are summed up by Burney in the following words:—" At the date of my departure from Rangoon the 15 January, public affairs in that quarter continued in a satisfactory state, and by the latest accounts from Ava no occurrence of any moment had taken place at that capital. The only object requiring to be reported is, the Woongyee apprised me of his intention to discontinue from the date of my departure the experiment which I had induced him to make from July last, of levying reduced rate of port charges for a time on British vessels visiting Rangoon." [2] Bayfield in Ava tried to induce the Ministers to return to the reduced charges as proposed by Burney, but failed in the endeavour.[3]

Burney was back in Rangoon early in April, 1835.[4] Bayfield at the same time reported to the Indian Government " the inability of the King to attend to business from which I imagine His Majesty must be worse than ordinary. The general inattention to business and the uncontrolled exactions of the Prince Menthagyee and his party have for a long time past been the cause of great complaints, but unhappily during the present reign on the influence of the present dominant party there seems to be but little prospect of a change for the better......The Woongyees have neglected the Hlutdau and no business has been transacted without the greatest difficulty. The King has not been seen by his people for several months and the celebration of the festival[5] has been put off from time to time owing to his unfitness to appear in public. A new medical pretender has just arrived from the Shan country to the north-east of Ava

---

[1] *Ibid.* Vol. 67, Burney's Letter, 1 February, 1835; Vol. 68, Burney's Letter, Calcutta, 10 February, 1835; Government Letter, 19 February, 1835.

[2] *Ibid.* Vol. 67, Burney's Letter, 1 February, 1835.

[3] *Ibid.* Vol. 74, Bayfield's Letter, 19 February, 1835.

[4] *Ibid.* Range 194, Index Vol. 2, Burney's Letter, Rangoon, 11 April, 1835. This letter is missing in Vol. 76, Range 193, where it should be.

[5] In connection with the consecration of a newly built monastery.

who has promised to cure His Majesty in a few days. The whole of the old Medical Staff are consequently in disgrace, and although the King is by report worse than his usual health, still the miraculous powers to which the Shan physician pretends will, it is expected, make a temporary impression upon the King's mind......"[1]

On 29 June, 1835, Burney left Rangoon for Ava, and on the same day wrote to his Government that on his arrival at the Burmese capital, he would direct his Assistant, Dr. Bayfield, to come down to Rangoon and take charge of British interests in that city. This he did, because by experience he had realized that Rangoon being the chief Burmese port, British commercial interests would be better conserved by the presence of a British officer there; at the same time it was necessary to have a British officer at Ava so as to have a salutary influence upon the Burmese Government at the centre. The European and Indian merchants of Rangoon were also anxious that Burney should return to Ava and procure from the Ministers better conditions of trade for British subjects.[2]

In a later dispatch from Ava, Burney explained the importance of his proposal for Rangoon as follows:—" Further acquaintance with this Court and people only confirms the opinion which I submitted to Government more than three years ago, that the substitution for this Residency of a Political Agency at Rangoon could be easily arranged, so as to secure not only an important saving to our Government, but nearly all, if not all the same political, and certainly some additional commercial advantages. Yet believing it to be the desire of the Governor-General-of-India-in-Council, that this Residency should be continued, and that the Resident himself should always remain here as much as possible, I consider it my duty to act up to the views of my superiors. In doing so, however, I hope I may be permitted to urge again, the absolute necessity of some British officer being always at Rangoon for the purpose of afford-

---

[1] India Political Consultations Range 193, Vol. 76, Bayfield's Letter, 2 April, 1835.
[2] *Ibid.* Vol: 81.

ing prompt and effectual aid and protection to the numerous European and native [1] subjects of the British Government who are led to visit that place or reside there...... I earnestly recommend that a second Assistant be attached to this Residency for the purpose of enabling me to detach an officer to take charge of Rangoon......" [2]

This new arrangement, which necessarily meant more expense, fell like a bomb-shell upon the Supreme Government. Burney was immediately informed, " that the measure you have adopted of deputing your assistant to reside at Rangoon is one of such importance that it should not have been carried into effect without a previous reference to Government for its sanction. You are now directed to state on what authority you propose to adopt this measure, and to detail the grounds on which you deem it advisable. Should it not have been carried into effect you will suspend it for further orders, and explain whether the services of your Assistant at Ava can be permanently dispensed with in his medical as well as his political capacity." [3]   In a later dispatch of 12 October, 1835, the Government plainly said, that it was not prepared to bear the expense of two Assistant Residents, one at Ava and the other at Rangoon, and that if an officer was required for Rangoon, Government would make the appointment, but Bayfield would have to return to his medical post at Ava. [4]

Fortunately, Bayfield had not yet left for Rangoon, and Burney explained, that in deciding to depute the doctor to Rangoon he was only using his discretionary powers. [5] He once again pressed his view-point, and even suggested a reduction in the salary of the Resident at Ava in order to make funds available for the expenses of an officer at Rangoon:—" But my own opinions," he wrote, " are so strong that a British officer ought always to be stationed at Rangoon, and that at that place and

[1] i.e. Indian and British Burman subjects.
[2] India Political Consultations Range 193, Vol. 85, Burney's Letter. no date, but from Ava sometime in July, 1835.
[3] Ibid. Vol. 81, Government Letter, Fort William, 3 August, 1835.
[4] Ibid. Vol. 85, Government Letter, 12 October, 1835.
[5] Ibid. Vol. 89, Burney's Letter, Ava, 12 October, 1835.

not here (*i.e.* Ava) all the public business giving trouble or requiring attention now occurs in this country, that I have no hesitation in stating that the salary of the Resident ought to be reduced to pay for the expenses of an officer at Rangoon rather than that no officer should be stationed at that port." [1] The Government, however, rejected Burney's proposal, and said, that his recommendation could only be carried into effect by putting Bayfield in his former footing as Surgeon to the Residency and appointing a separate Assistant to be stationed at Rangoon. [2]

Burney arrived at Ava on 27 July, 1835, and was received by the Ministers with the usual courtesy and kindness; some of the principal Ministers and Officers even came to his house and congratulated him on his return. He found the King in the same state of ill-health. There were reports current of a war between the Chinese and the English, and of a great naval victory gained by the former at Canton. Burney's arrival further intensified the rumour, and it was surmised that the real object of his return was to endeavour and persuade the Burmese Court to allow a British army to invade China through the northern part of the King's dominions. [3]

Burney visited the principal Ministers at their own houses, and began to attend the meetings of the Hlutdaw as before, [4] but the King did not grant him an interview till on 24 September, 1835. Burney made the following report to his Government on the function :—

"His Majesty does not appear either in mind or body to be worse than when last I saw him, but during the interview he scarcely uttered a syllable, took little notice of me and less of the public presents I delivered......

"Although the state of the King's mind was evidently the cause of his silence, I found some of the Courtiers attributing it to an intention on the part of His Majesty to display his great power and superiority in the presence of the British Resi-

[1] *Ibid.* Range 194, Vol. 6, Ava, 11 January, 1836.
[2] *Ibid.* Government Letter, 7 March, 1836.
[3] *Ibid.* Range 193, Vol. 85, Burney's Letter, Ava, 31 July, 1835.
[4] *Ibid.* Vol. 87, Burney's Letter, Ava, 3 September, 1835.

dent, and it appeared necessary, therefore, for me to protest publicly against such a mode of receiving the British representative, and prevent its being established as a precedent in this land of custom and precedent. Accordingly after the audience I addressed a letter to the Burmese Ministers remonstrating against the unfriendly manner in which the King of Ava received me, and urging the propriety of treating the representative of the British Government with more consideration and cordiality. The Ministers were ready enough to apologize verbally for the seeming rudeness of the King. But I beg to bring to the notice of the Governor-General-of-India-in-Council the fact, that ever since His Majesty was first taken unwell, he has been gradually manifesting more and more reserve and disinclination towards me and the other British officers whom he has been enabled to see. We have been received in a manner which I do not hesitate to own must lead to impair the character and influence of the British Government among those who are in attendance at the time on the King of Ava. I should be inclined to avoid troubling the King to grant me an audience again, but that I am aware, that the circumstance of His Majesty not seeing me would be likely to be very prejudicial to my official character here." [1]

On 13 August, 1835, Maung Khain, the Woongyee of Rangoon, died. Burney says, that " he was by far the most intelligent officer of rank in this country, and was always distinguished by an earnest desire of prolonging and improving the friendly relations subsisting between our two governments. His loss is the more to be regretted as I know of no Burmese officer fully qualified to succeed him." [2] Maung Khain, throughout his tenure of office at Rangoon, had endeavoured to preserve peace on the Martaban frontier and to do justice in disputes between British subjects and his own people. Burney tried to persuade the Burmese Government to appoint as his successor, an officer acquainted in some degree with European customs and manners, as well as with the history of Anglo-

[1] *Ibid.* Vol. 89, Burney's Letter, Ava, 5 October, 1835.
[2] *Ibid.* Vol. 87, Burney's Letter, Ava, 3 September, 1835.

Burmese relations on the Martaban frontier; but the Queen and her brother the Menthagyee appointed Maung Wa, the Nagarané or Queen's Woongyee, to fill the vacancy. "This man," says Burney, "although a large and remarkable looking man for a Burmese, and of mild and quiet manners is unfortunately the most ignorant and obstinate Minister here, and having scarcely ever stirred out of Ava or seen any service during the late War, he is singularly ignorant of European customs and manners, and of the power and resources of the British Government." [1]

The failure of the new Governor of Rangoon to maintain amicable relations with the British merchants of that town soon justified Burney's apprehensions of his unfitness for that high and responsible office. Traders made serious complaints of injustice, extortion, and molestation, also of additional duties levied on small trading vessels coming from Tenasserim to Rangoon.[2] One Capt. Rayne, in his complaint to Burney, said, "I hesitate not to say, that unless some properly constituted officer is appointed to protect the British interests at Rangoon some fearful consequences will arise, for no British seaman will tamely submit to be robbed at pleasure......while he has the means (let them be what they may) of preventing it."[3]

On 31 March, 1836, the Bengal Chamber of Commerce also petitioned the Government of India. A part of this letter is reproduced here to show the conditions of trade in Rangoon and the protection desired by British traders residing there:—

"I am instructed by the Chamber of Commerce most respectfully to entreat that the Right Honourable the Governor-General-in-Council will be pleased to take into consideration the propriety of appointing a Consul or Assistant Resident to protect the British commercial interests at Rangoon and its maritime dependencies.

"The intercourse of trade by no means inconsiderable (the reports of Calcutta alone to Rangoon amount in value

---

[1] *Ibid.* See Appendix II, for note on Nagarané.
[2] *Ibid.* Range 194, Vol. 15, Burney's Letter, Ava, 4 May, 1836.
[3] *Ibid.* Rayne's complaint, Rangoon, 19 March, 1836.

to 9 lacs of rupees yearly) and which may reasonably be expected to increase with a people so peculiarly situated and so little
civilized as are the Burmese, obviously stands in need of the
authority of some accredited functionary on the spot to maintain its rights, to conciliate differences so likely to arise between
the subjects of the two countries, and as far as its influence may
extend to prevent collision." [1]

The petition goes on at length to detail the powers which
the Consul should enjoy so that he might be able to protect the
persons, properties, rights and privileges of British subjects as
by treaty recognized between the two governments.

The Government of India referred the matter to Burney,
and enquired if an individual could be found among the respectable members of the mercantile community in Rangoon to take
up consular duties in that city on a remuneration of about
Rs. 100 per mensem, and whether Spiers would be prepared to
undertake the responsibility.[2] This gave Burney a fresh opportunity to press his earlier proposal that a regular officer of Government be appointed to Rangoon. His letter explaining the
unwisdom of appointing a private individual to be consul at
Rangoon is most interesting:—

" I most earnestly entreat, His Lordship-in-Council will
not adopt a measure as that of nominating a gentleman residing at Rangoon as a merchant, as a British Consul there.
He would have the utmost difficulty to avoid making his
consular powers subservient towards promoting his own commercial pursuits, and would thus seriously prejudice the character of the British Government in the eyes of the Burmese. A
merchant at Rangoon cannot trade there extensively without
smuggling specie out of the country in defiance of the established laws of the Kingdom, and a consul-merchant would
always be suspected by the Burmese authorities to be availing
himself of his public character to smuggle treasure on board
ship, and would thus produce constant discontent and disputes

[1] *Ibid*. Vol. 8, From W. Limond, Secretary, Bengal Chamber of
     Commerce to the Government, 31 March, 1836.
[2] *Ibid*. Government Letter, 11 April, 1836.

as far as the Burmese are concerned, and jealousy and bad feeling on the part of his fellow-traders. Indeed, I have already reason to know that the simple duty of taking charge of the public mails at Rangoon, which Mr. W. Spiers exercised until lately, was considered by some of the traders there as calculated to confer upon him the influence of our Government and give him an unfair advantage as a trader over themselves......A Consul at Rangoon would often be obliged to interfere in political as well as commercial affairs: the line between the two cannot be sufficiently defined in our intercourse with an un-civilized state." [1] Burney concluded his letter by saying, that in his opinion, none but a covenanted servant of the Company and an officer dependent on the Indian Government should be appointed. He again recommended Bayfield for the appoint-ment, and said, "if His Lordship-in-Council, however, sees any objection to this arrangement, I beg respectfully to state that my public pride and feelings would urge me to prefer that a portion of my salary should be taken to pay for a 2nd Assistant at Rangoon rather than that a private individual, unsuited by his pursuits and habits to co-operate with me, should be appointed British Consul there." [1]

In another letter to his Government Burney gave the fol-lowing commercial reasons emphasizing the necessity of a British Agent at Rangoon:—

" The commerce of this country has of late years been steadily improving, and I am satisfied that it is still susceptible of very great increase. If the Supreme Government will only remove an impression, which it is my duty to state now very generally prevails among the British traders here, as well as among some of the Burmese officers, that our Government cares little concerning the improvement of this trade or the wellbeing of our traders who visit or reside in this country. I am and have always been of opinion, not only that a British officer should be placed at Rangoon, but that a steam vessel or one of His Majesty's ships of war ought at least once or twice a year to

[1] *Ibid.* Vol. 15, Burney's Letter, Ava, 8 June, 1836.

visit that port and thus ensure attention and encouragement to our traders there as well as keep alive a proper feeling of respect and consideration towards our nation on the part of the Burmese officers, and strengthen the political influence of our Government with the Court of Ava. The British Resident also, whilst placed as he is at such a distance from all visible signs of our military strength and resources, would have his influence and situation much improved among this vain and ignorant people were some such notice of this country and of him taken occasionally by our Government." [1]

These two representations of Burney broke down all opposition at Calcutta, and it was agreed to appoint Bayfield to Rangoon to take charge of Consular duties there.[2] He was, however, unable immediately to take charge of his new office, because he had to proceed on a mission to the Assam frontier to confer with British officers there concerning the safety of British subjects in that region and the prospects of trade.[3] Finally when he did take charge of his duties at Rangoon on 12 October, 1837, it was not as Assistant to the Resident but as discharging the duties of the Resident, Burney having departed from Burma for good.[4] Meanwhile, complaints continued to come to Burney from British traders in Rangoon concerning the bad treatment they were receiving at the hands of Burmese officers. The most serious case was that of James Dorrett, Commander and owner of *Louisa* a schooner of 50 tons. After he had cleared the port of Rangoon on 26 May, 1836, and proceeded about five miles below the town, his boat was boarded by about 40 men under the leadership of two petty Burmese officers. They beat Dorrett most unmercifully, bound him hand and foot, and confiscated silver worth Rs. 320 that

[1] *Ibid.* Ava, 4 May, 1836.
[2] *Ibid.* Letter from Government 18 July, 1836.
    Burney's proposal concerning the periodical visit of a British man-of-war was also acceded to by Government. *Ibid.* Vol. 20, Government Letter 3 October, 1836.
[3] *Ibid.* Vol. 29, The Resident's Instructions to Bayfield, Ava, 8 December, 1836.
[4] India Secret Consultations Vol. 8, Burney's Letter, 31 October, 1837.

was in his possession.[1] Dorrett's letter of complaint somehow did not reach the Residency till five months later, in October, 1836. Burney, immediately on receipt of the news of the gross outrage, placed the facts before the Ministers, and persuaded them to send two commissioners to Rangoon to investigate into the case. The enquiry revealed the truth of the outrage, but it could not positively be discovered what loss Dorrett had suffered, since before the Commissioners arrived at Rangoon he had left the shores of Burma. Burney, however, persuaded Menthagyee to send orders to the Rangoon Woongyee to inflict corporal punishment, according to Burmese laws, on the two petty Burmese officers who commanded the party which ill-used Dorrett.[2]

Another question which came into prominence at this time was the trade between Assam and Burma across the frontier. The importance of this trade was first pointed out in November, 1834, by Capt. F. Jenkins, Agent to the Governor-General, North-Eastern Frontier; but very little was known of conditions in the two frontier provinces of Hukawng and Maing-khwan, and the degree of authority that the Burmese Government was able to maintain over the Singpho inhabitants of that area. Jenkins was willing to permit Burma traders to visit Assam, and enjoy British protection as well as exemption from all imposts, provided the same privileges were conceded to Assam traders entering Burma in that region. The Marwari traders of Assam at this time were very anxious to open commercial relations with the Shan districts and with Upper Burma in general, if they could be assured of adequate protection.[3]

In February, 1835, Burney was in Calcutta, and he supplied to his government the following information concerning the northernmost districts of the Burmese Empire:—

"......a very extraordinary degree of ignorance regarding the whole of the Shan States prevails among the Burmese Minis-

---

[1] India Political Consultations Range 194, Vol. 20, Dorrett's deposition, Rangoon, 28 May, 1836.
[2] Ibid. Vol. 23 Burney's Letter, Ava, 10 October, 1836, and Vol. 29, 15 December, 1836.
[3] Ibid. Range 193, Vol. 63, Capt. F. Jenkin's Letter, Gowahatty, 22 November, 1834.

ters, not one of whom really knows anything of the present condition of the country lying between Mogaung and Assam. All the information I was able to collect on the subject whilst residing at Ava, and I took much pains to do so, was, that the Shan States and numerous wild tribes named Bwon Kadoo, Kukyen and Thein-bun (our Simpho) occupying the territory between Mogaung and Assam are subject to the Governor of Mogaung whose title is Nemyozeyagyangoung, that the seat of the Shan Chief of the province of Hookoung (our Hookoom) is Main Kon (our Moong Koon, Moun Khoom and Muen Kon) 7 or 8 days journey beyond Mogaung, and that 20 days of very difficult journey beyond Main Kuon is the Burmese frontier Chokey called Taban Ken (our Tapan)....Mogaung, although at one time the capital of a powerful Shan Chief who conquered Ava, and although so lately as when Col. Symes visited Amarapoora in 1795 the seat of a Tsaubwa or Tributary Prince, is now governed by a Burmese Myowoon or Governor.

"The Court of Ava are extremely jealous of foreigners having any communication with the Shan states over most of which Burmese supremacy is not very secure......

"The Burmese Government exercise very little authority over the Simphos or Theinbuns and other wild tribes who occupy the country between Assam, Yunnan and Ava. Even the Chinese caravans which are numerous have sometimes been attacked by these mountaineers, and the Burmese say, that a Theinbun always prefers killing a man to cutting down a tree as the possession of a common waist cloth or tinder box only from a man they may kill is wealth to a Theinbun.

"I see no chance also of the Government of Ava giving up the 10 per cent duty levied on all imports into their country, as the amount of this duty is fixed by their oldest code of laws, and is considered as ancient as the Empire itself." [1]

Burney, therefore, recommended that no propositions should be made to the Government of Burma, and no questions mooted ; but, that if any traders in Assam desired to visit the Burmese

---

[1] *Ibid.* Vol. 69, Burney's Letter, Calcutta, 14 February, 1835.

territories for the purpose of trade, they should be furnished with the " Certified Pass " written in English, Burmese and Shan languages, provided for by the first article of Crawfurd's Commercial Treaty; and that if traders with such a permit met with obstructions or extortion, a remonstrance be made to the Government of Ava and an enquiry into the conduct of the local officers be insisted upon.[1]

While this matter was under consideration, Daffa Gaum, a Singpho Chief, residing in the Burmese district of Hukawng, with his followers crossed the frontier into Assam, and attacked another Singpho Chief called Beesa Gaum, residing in British territory (July, 1835). There had been a long standing feud between the two Chiefs: Daffa Gaum completely destroyed Beesa Gaum's village, and massacred all the inhabitants indiscriminately that fell into his hands.[2] He also began to occupy the lands belonging to his rival, claiming them to be originally his own. This was a grave outrage, and Burney was immediately informed of it, so that he might impress upon the Ministers the responsibility of the King's Government. Burney called upon the Ministers to take immediate steps to keep under control the wild frontier tribes; but they knew scarcely anything concerning Beesa Gaum or of the frontier in question. Fortunately, at that very time, a new Governor of Mogaung was appointed, and he was preparing to leave Ava for his northern headquarters. The Ministers charged him with the duty of preventing Daffa Gaum from molesting the British frontier. Burney, however, had reason to believe that the Burmese local officers possessed too little power or influence over the wild tribes to be able to keep them under control, unless a respectable force was also sent to the frontier. He, therefore, proposed to send Capt. Hannay, the Officer commanding his Escort, with the new Governor of Mogaung, to ascertain and to report to the Assam authorities the real state of affairs on the frontier. The Ministers were not willing at first to allow a British officer to obtain a first hand

---

[1] *Ibid.*
[2] *Ibid.* Vol. 81, Letter from Jenkins, the A. G. G., N. E. Frontier, Gowahatty, 30 July, 1835.

9

knowledge of Burma north of Ava, but ultimately they agreed to the proposition.[1]

On 22 November, 1835, Hannay and the new Governor of Mogaung left Ava for the north with a force of about 1200.[2] Burney did not miss the opportunity of instructing Hannay to collect information on the possibilities of trade in that region, also on the geography of the country, and to obtain as much material as possible concerning the population, races, amber mines, trade routes, etc., in that area.[3]

Meanwhile, Major White, Political Agent, Upper Assam, collected a force of about 300 men and advanced upon Daffa Gaum who had entrenched himself with about 350 of his followers in three stockades on the Meenaboom Hill. Daffa was a leader of considerable talent and had spent almost all his life fighting petty battles: he was in short an enterprising border chief. Prior to resorting to hostilities, White made every exertion to induce him to come to terms, more especially because Beesa Gaum was the original aggressor, while Daffa had only retaliated. He was persuaded to accept a settlement, and he agreed to make good the loss sustained by the merchants of Beesa and to disband the Singphos, his followers, who belonged to Burma. In return White offered him permission to return to his own lands situated in Assam. Ultimately, however, Daffa refrained from carrying out his undertaking, and White finally attacked and took two of his stockades within two hours. The main stockade held out a day longer, and when it fell Daffa retreated into Burmese territory. A party was sent to capture him, but he escaped.[4]

The Hannay Mission arrived at Mogaung on 5 January, 1836, but was unable to move forwards immediately, for want of food supplies. The Ministers in Ava, meanwhile, repented for having allowed Hannay to proceed northwards, and asked Burney

[1] *Ibid.* Vol. 1, Range 194, Burney's Letter, 2 November, 1835.
[2] *Ibid.* Vol. 5, Ava, 23 November, 1835.
[3] *Ibid.* Burney's Instructions to Hannay, Ava, 21 November, 1835.
[4] *Ibid.* Vol. 3, White's Letter, Menaboom Hill, 22 November, 1835; Letter from White to Lumley, Adjutant-General, 20 November, 1835.

to recall him, because, they said, Daffa had merely taken revenge upon Beesa, so that it was unnecessary to take notice of the affair.[1] Hannay and the new Governor arrived at Hukawng on 31 January, 1836.[2] They called upon Daffa to surrender himself to them, and on 22 March, he complied with their demand.[3] On 29 May, Hannay and the Governor brought him down to Ava. The Ministers did not propose to take any severe measures against him, but admonished him, and Burney also thought no further action was necessary. The Government of India, however, was not satisfied with this tame termination of the whole affair,[4] but Burney reported that if he had demanded the surrender of Daffa, the Ministers could not have acceeded to it without submitting the matter to the King, and this they were not prepared to do.[5] " He (the King)," wrote Burney, " has of late made some enquiries regarding public affairs but shown so much instability of temper that even his brother-in-law Menthagyee trembles in his presence and dare not look up at him. I have noticed also that every means is adopted by the Ministers to prevent the British Residency and everything connected with it from being brought to the notice of the King."[5]

Burney warned the Ministers that the Burmese Government would be held responsible for any outrages committed upon British subjects by Burmese subjects on the Assam frontier.[5] He also suggested to his Government that Daffa might be pardoned for his past offences and be invited to settle in Assam,[6] but Calcutta refused to agree to his proposal.[7]

This disturbance created by Daffa is of some value as revealing the weakness of Burmese control over the wild tribes on the northern frontier, the importance assumed by the British

---

[1] *Ibid.* Vol. 5, Burney's Letter, 8 December, 1835; *Ibid.* Vol. 7, 5 February, 1836.
[2] *Ibid.* Vol. 9, Letter from Hannay to Capt. Miller at Suddeya, Hookoom, 27 February, 1836.
[3] *Ibid.* Vol. 15, Burney's Letter, Ava, 20 April, 1836.
[4] *Ibid.* Vol. 19, Government Letter, 26 September, 1836.
[5] *Ibid.* Burney's Letter 18 July, 1836.
[6] *Ibid.* Vol. 24, 10 October, 1836.
[7] *Ibid.* Vol. 46, White's Letter, 23 July, 1836; *Ibid.* Vol. 29, Government Letter, 23 January, 1837.

Resident compelling the Woongyees to take action against those who would disturb the British frontier, and the opportunity afforded to British agents to study the possibility of trade in the region beyond Mogaung.

The fortunes and achievements of the Hannay Mission might now be followed up. Hannay left Ava for Mogaung on 22 November, 1835, accompanied by the new Governor of the Northern frontier. On 22 December, he arrived at Bannu, and reported to Burney " in very high terms of the general appearance of the country." He considered " the population, particularly on the right bank of the Erawadi to be much more numerous than what the Burmese Government itself seems to be aware of." [1] After passing through Mogaung and Maing-Khwan near the amber mines, Hannay arrived at Hukawng.[2] The Ministers, meanwhile, fearing Hannay would study the northern country, began to press Burney to recall him. There was a tug-of-war between the Resident and the Woongyees, and the latter ulti- mately gave way. " I have therefore been obliged to point out to the Ministers, much to their mortification, that the conduct of their Governor has clearly proved, that the Burmese even with a force of 1000 men are unable or afraid to proceed to the frontiers of their own kingdom, and that in any future case of aggression on our territory in Assam the Governor-General-in-Council can- not be expected to apply to the Court of Ava to take cognizance of the matter. He will order our own troops to proceed and punish the offenders, and then demand from the Court of Ava compensation for whatever loss our subjects may suffer as well as payment for all the expense which we may incur by being obliged to take upon ourselves the trouble of preventing aggres- sions committed by Burmese subjects."[3]

It was Hannay's intention to proceed from Maing-Khwan (or Mainkhon) to the Assam frontier and get into personal touch with the British officers there, but Daffa having surrendered himself without delay, the return journey to Ava had to begin.

[1] *Ibid.* Vol. 6, Burney's Letter, 12 January, 1836.
[2] *Ibid.* Vol. 10, 28 March, 1836.
[3] *Ibid.* Vol. 15, Burney's Letter, Ava, 20 April, 1836.

Hannay, however, dispatched one of his followers, Sepoy Sindur Singh, to Suddeya on 28 February, from Mainkhon. This Sepoy was taken by his Burmese guides by a very difficult route to his destination; but on the return journey he discovered and came back by a much better road, which, he reported may be made practicable for wheeled carriages. These routes between Assam and Ava having at last been explored and ascertained, Burney suggested to his Government that "it should be our endeavour to keep them open and frequented; and with this view I would recommend that some pretext should be found for sending an officer from Assam to me here" via Mainkhon and Mogaung. "After two or three such missions," continues Burney, "not only a trade between Assam and this country would be placed on a more secure footing, but I think the Court of Ava would remove the prohibition which it now interposes to our traders proceeding above Ava towards Bamau [1] and Mogaung and disturbing the monopoly which the Chinese have long enjoyed of the whole trade in that quarter." [2]

Hannay returned to Ava on 1 May, 1836. During his sojourn in the Upper country he had collected a good deal of geographical and other useful information; [3] but Burney as well as the Government of India felt it would be more useful if he took another journey towards the Assam frontier. Burney, therefore pointed out to the Ministers the possibility of Daffa Gaum again violating the British frontier, and proposed that Hannay might be sent to the Assam frontier to investigate and settle, in conjunction with the Assam British officers, the dangerous family feud between the two Singpho Chiefs. [3] The Ministers were not prepared to give in easily to Burney. Besides, they were indifferent to the development of commerce in that region. "In fact," says Burney, "I have often much trouble to make the Ministers attend to a question regarding trade or to the case of some trader aggrieved. They cry out, 'That is a business

---

[1] Bhamo.
[2] India Political Consultations Range 194, Vol. 15, Burney's Letter, 18 May, 1836.
[3] *Ibid.* Ava, 16 September, 1836.

concerning the merchants and has no relation whatever to the affairs of the country' ".[1]

In May, 1836, Burney heard that the Emperor of China had written to the King of Burma, " remonstrating with the Court of Ava for having allowed an English officer to proceed to the northward and ascertain the route into China. I (*i.e.* Burney) questioned the Burmese Ministers who admitted the fact of a letter having been received from China, but denied that its contents were anything more than a complimentary communication relative to a new title conferred by the Emperor on his mother. I am inclined however to credit the intelligence I have heard because I am aware that shortly after Capt. Hannay left Ava in December last, a deputation of Chinese merchants residing here waited on the Prince Menthagyee to remonstrate against the Mission. Their remonstrance proceeded from a natural apprehension that the monopoly which they have long held of the whole trade to the north of Ava and of the produce of the amber and serpentine mines, might be disturbed by an English officer exploring the country in that direction and communicating freely with its inhabitants." [2]

A few months later, in September, 1836, Burney was able to secure, by means of a secret agent, a Burmese version of the China letter.[3] In the concluding portion of the letter there is a reference to the British Residency in Burma, disapproving of the privilege granted to the English :—" It is not proper to allow the English after they have made War, and Peace has been settled to remain in the City. They are accustomed to act like the " Pipal " Tree (wherever this plant takes root and particularly in old temples and buildings it spreads and takes such firm hold that it is scarcely possible to be removed or eradicated[4]....). Let not Younger Brother [5] therefore allow the English to remain

---

[1] *Ibid*. Vol. 19, 18 July, 1836.
[2] *Ibid*. Vol. 15, Burney's Letter, Ava, 9 May, 1836.
[3] See Appendix No. IV for the letter.
[4] This explanatory note is by Burney.
[5] The Younger Brother is the King of Burma, the Emperor of China being the Elder Brother.

in his Country, and if anything happens, Elder Brother will attack, take, and give." [1]

Burney suspected that this particular portion of the letter had been interpolated by the Viceroy of Yunnan after he had heard of the presence of Hannay in Bhamo in December, 1835. " The letters purporting to be from the Emperor of China," says Burney, " are never brought here by individau s from Pekin but by messengers from the Viceroy of Yunan who might very easily make such an interpolation and whom indeed I had before suspected of such conduct from a perusal of some letters formerly received here from China." [2]

In October, 1836, Burney was requested by his Government to direct Capt. Hannay and Sepoy Sindur Singh to repair to Fort William by the first convenient opportunity " in order that Government may avail itself to the utmost possible extent of the information which they are in possession of;........it would seem advisable that Capt. Hannay should return to you [3] from Calcutta via Assam, and he could be accompanied on his journey back by Dr. Griffiths." [4] Hannay and the Sepoy accordingly left Ava on 20 October, for Calcutta *via* Rangoon.[5] Burney, however, did not give up the project of sending a British Mission to the Assam frontier. " My own desire is strong," he wrote to his Government, " that the route should be again traversed by a scientific surveyor or in company with Capt. Hannay." [6] With this object in view he proposed to the Ministers that Bayfield be sent to the Assam frontier with a few Burmese officers to confer with British officers in that region, so that the feud between the two Gaums might be enquired into and extinguished. He at the same time recommended to his Government

[1] India Political Consultations Range 194, Vol. 23, Translation of a Letter from the Emperor of China to the King of Ava, received at Ava in April, 1836.
[2] *Ibid.* Burney's Letter, 16 September, 1836.
[3] *i.e.* to Burney in Ava.
[4] India Political Consultations Range 194, Vol. 15, Letter from the Government of India to Burney, 18 July, 1836; Dr. Griffiths was a Natural Scientist.
[5] *Ibid.* Vol. 23, Hannay's Letter, Ketgeree, 15 November, 1836, and Vol. 24, Burney's Letter, 10 October, 1836.
[6] *Ibid.* Vol. 24, 10 October, 1836.

"that Capt. Hannay with some young officer skilled in Surveying be immediately sent to Suddeya and ordered to accompany any Mission which the Governor-General's Agent, North East Frontier, may have been authorized to send into the Burmese territories after meeting with Mr. Bayfield and the Burmese Mission........Capt. Hannay with the Surveyor and Dr. Griffiths will have no difficulty in accompanying Mr. Bayfield to Ava and completing a proper survey of the whole route."[1]

The Burmese Ministers were at first reluctant to acquiesce into Burney's proposal,[1] but finally agreed to it, and on 13 December, 1836, Bayfield left Ava to join the Governor of Mogaung who was at Tingut, also on his way to the northward.[2] Burney instructed Bayfield to "collect statistical and useful information on all subjects, but particularly on the following:— The extent and nature of the trade now carried on between China and the Burmese Dominions and between them and our territories in Assam, and the best mode of protecting, facilitating and extending the last mentioned. The numbers of Assamese estimated to be detained in captivity among the Burmese Singphos and other tribes, the spots where they are located and the Chiefs whom they are serving, and the best mode of effecting their emancipation or escape back into Assam."[3] Further, he was to learn the population, character and habits of the Singphos, and discover the best means of preventing their committing incursions into British territory; finally, he was to discuss in conjunction with Burmese officers, questions of peace and trade with British officers in Assam, and fix the amount of indemnity to be claimed from Daffa Gaum because of his late incursion into Assam.[4]

Bayfield and the Burmese Mission led by the Governor of Mogaung proceeded towards the Patkoi mountains. Meanwhile Major White, the Political Agent, Upper Assam, had been waiting for them on the same range since 25 February,

---

[1] *Ibid.* Vol. 24, 10 October, 1836.
[2] *Ibid.* Vol. 29, 14 December, 1836.
[3] *Ibid.* Burney's Instructions to Bayfield, Ava, 8 December, 1836.
[4] *Ibid.*

1837. But on 5 March he was compelled to return to Assam because of scarcity of provisions and the incursions of a Singpho party in his rear cutting him off from the points of supply. He, however, succeeded in helping Hannay and Griffiths to cross the frontier into Burma.[1] Bayfield and the Burmese Mission now arrived, and on 5 March a conference was held at Nouyang Paree in Burmese territory with Hannay and Griffiths. The Burmese Governor claimed a part of Assam across the Patkoi mountains to be Burmese territory. Hannay informed him that he had no authority to discuss the boundary question, but only to point out Patkoi to be the boundary.[2] Hannay's great object was, together with Griffiths, to accompany Bayfield to Ava so as to be able to explore the routes and learn the country, but he was unable to do so since no coolies were available to carry his kit.

Meanwhile at Ava a good deal of suspicion and irritation was manifested by the Burmese Court on the subject of Hannay's going to Calcutta and Suddeya in order to return to Ava by the northern route. A report became current among the people and the Court that the British were collecting a military force in Upper Assam with the object of taking possession of the whole country belonging to the Singphos and the Shans to the north of Mogaung. Burney tried to allay the suspicions but without success.[3] The Government of India also, in order to pour oil over the troubled waters, declared, " that our objects are only to promote a safe intercourse beneficial to both states, and to ensure efficient protection to the tribes under our authority." [4]

Bayfield returned to Ava in May, 1837, and Burney, in reporting his doings while away, summed up the doctor's achievement in the following words:—

[1] *Ibid.* Vol. 35, Letter from White to Jenkins, No. 121, 10 March, 1837.
[2] *Ibid.* Letter from Hannay to White, 10 March, 1837; Letter from Government to Burney, 10 April, 1837; *Ibid.* Vol. 36, Hannay to Jenkins, 19 March, 1837; Government Letter to Jenkins, 24 April, 1837.
[3] *Ibid.* Vol. 33, Burney's Letter, 13 February, 1837.
[4] *Ibid.* Government Letter, 20 March, 1837.

"Mr. Bayfield completely succeeded in everything that rested with himself; with indefatigable zeal and exertion, he, in less than 3 months after leaving Ava, conducted the Burmese Governor of Mogaung to the frontiers of Assam as I had always anticipated that with his knowledge of the language and character of the people he would succeed in doing, and he had the Daffa Gaum taken to within one day's march of the frontier ready to be called up before our officers in Assam the moment they desired to see or examine him. But Major White was obliged to quit the place which he had appointed as the rendez-vous a few hours only before Mr. Bayfield reached it; and Capt. Hannay came there without having previously seen the Governor-General's Agent on the North Eastern frontier or obtained any instructions from him.

"Under these circumstances Mr. Bayfield could do no more than attempt to carry into effect as far as lay in his power the suggestions which Major White on his own responsibility had communicated to him in a letter dated the 3rd March, for Major White also had received no orders or instructions respecting the Mission from Ava. Mr. Bayfield assisted Capt. Hannay to shew the Governor of Mogaung the line of boundary which Major White considers the true and proper one, fully explaining the grounds on which this line is selected, and he had the Daffa Gaum privately told the terms which Major White would offer him in the event of his tendering his submission to the British Government........" [1]

[1] *Ibid.* Vol. 42, Burney's Letter, 20 May, 1837.

CHAPTER IX

BURNEY AND THE REVOLUTION IN AVA, 1837.

While Bayfield and the Burmese Mission were on the move towards the Assam frontier, happenings of an ominous character were developing in Ava. The disturbances ultimately terminated in the deposition of King Bagyidaw and the accession of his brother the Prince of Tharrawaddy to the throne of Burma.

The King had now been suffering from ill-health for six years. Ever since the commencement of his illness in February, 1831, Menthagyee, the Queen's brother, had been gradually assuming the whole power of the Kingdom, substituting his own friends and adherents for those of the King in almost every province and office, and using the name of the King to strengthen and enrich himself so as to further his own ambitious projects. The King during this period was seldom seen or heard of, and the people generally believed that he had fallen into a state of mental imbecility.[1]

Menthagyee had shown a complete lack of diplomacy during this period of power and had been marked by a singular want of feeling and delicacy towards the King's son and brothers. Burney says that "they have never been consulted on state affairs or allowed to enjoy any of the power or patronage of the state. Yet the King's son being of age, the law and custom of the country gives him a right to the office of Ain-ye-men or Crown Prince to which is attached very extensive political powers, and the King's brother, the Prince of Tharrawaddy, having possessed when His Majesty was in health, the greatest share of his affection and confidence, had a claim to much consideration. It has been the policy however of Menthagyee and

---

[1] India Political Consultations Range 194, Vol. 35, Burney's Letter, Ava, 3 March, 1837.

his sister the Queen to keep the King's son, who is her step-son only, as much in the background as possible, and to deprive the King's brother of all influence and power; and had the Queen and her brother ever shown, that they were governed by a regard for the interest of the King and prosperity of the country, some excuse might have been found for their conduct, but their object has never been any other than that of amassing wealth for themselves and insuring a continuance of their power, and they are now in fact the only two persons of wealth in the whole country." [1]

All the Princes were highly dissatisfied with the state of affairs, but none had the courage to express their feelings except the Prince of Tharrawaddy who was one of the greatest feudal lords in the Kingdom. Even he, out of regard for his brother the King, kept his feelings under control and avoided embarrassing Menthagyee's government; only, he gradually withdrew himself from all intercourse with the Regent and the Woongyees, and seldom even visited the Palace. Being a man of foresight, however, he began to collect arms and increased the number of his retainers, perhaps not with any hostile intentions to the King or his throne, but to be prepared in the event of the King's death, to prevent Menthagyee usurping the throne and injuring the King's son and brothers. Menthagyee was keeping a good watch upon Prince Tharrawaddy and looking for an opportunity to disarm him. A pretext was soon found.[1]

The Prince's own sister, the Princess of Pagan, appointed as her Woon or Minister, Nga Yé, a well known bold and resolute character and who was charged with having been a leader of bandits. The Princess had also in her possession, since the close of the war with the British, a number of small guns and jingals. Menthagyee's government charged the Princess of having collected a quantity of fire-arms in her house and appointed a dangerous character as her Minister. An order was, therefore, issued in the name of the King to seize Nga Yé as well as the arms. Accordingly, on the night of

[1] *Ibid.*

21 February, 1837, Government troops suddenly surrounded the Princess's house. She and her Woon escaped, but the fire-arms were taken. The Princess fled to the house of her brother, the Prince of Tharrawaddy, and he advised her to return to her own house. She accepted the advice, and on arrival at her house she was questioned by some of the Government officers concerning the whereabouts of Nga Yé. She replied that he was in the house of her brother the Prince of Tharrawaddy. This was the version of Menthagyee and the Ministers, and they now acted upon it.[1]

A party of troops was sent to the Prince's house with the request that Nga Yé be surrendered. He denied all knowledge of Nga Yé's whereabouts; but Menthagyee and the Ministers summoned some of the principal officers of the Prince and put them in irons. The Prince again declared that he was totally unaware of the fugitive's hiding place, and having reason to believe that the King was kept ignorant of what was going on, and fearing that Menthagyee was plotting to usurp the throne, he gathered all his followers around him and prepared for resistance.[1]

On the afternoon of 22 February, the Prince sent a messenger to Burney to enquire what part he would be disposed to play in the event of a quarrel between himself and Menthagyee. Burney replied that he had clear orders from his Government not to interfere in any quarrel of that nature; but he offered to do everything in his power to prevent an open rupture between the two Princes as long as the King was alive.[2]

Burney sent his clerk to the Ministers to ask for some intelligence regarding their proceedings. The clerk found the whole space around the palace and the Hlutdaw full of troops, but he managed to see both the Ministers and Menthagyee who told him that they had been ordered by the King to seize Nga Yé, and so they were only endeavouring to obey those orders. A rumour was also current, and it came to the ear of

---

[1] *Ibid.* pars. 4, 5.
[2] *Ibid.* par. 5.

Menthagyee, that the British Resident had joined the Prince and was in his house.[1]

On the morning of 23 February, Burney sent his clerk to the Prince " requesting him to let me know, how he thought I could interfere so as to prevent the impending collision. He begged that I would point out to the Ministers the indignity with which they had treated his sister and were now treating him, and the harsh and unjust manner in which they were charging him with harbouring Nga Yé." [2]

Burney proceeded to the Hlutdaw himself, and first " requested Menthagyee to let me know who had told him that I had joined the Prince of Tharawadi and gone to his house, and pointed out the very mischievous object of the party who had given him such false information. He pretended that on further enquiry he found that his informant had seen some Armenians at the Prince's house and had mistaken one of them for me." [2] Burney, however, did not believe the story and felt that the tale had been invented so as to create more excitement against the Prince of Tharrawaddy, who was reputed to be partial to foreigners and in secret correspondence with the English.[2]

Burney expressed a desire to see the King, but the Ministers refused to grant his request and said that the King was fully cognizant of all that was passing, and that they were merely endeavouring to carry out his orders. Burney plainly told them that he believed they were acting without the King's knowledge. He also warned them as a friend, " that the measures which they had been adopting against the Princess of Pagan and Prince of Tharawadi the King's own sister and brother had exceedingly irritated that Prince, and were likely to produce some serious consequences." [2] Finally, he recommended that one of the principal Ministers should go to the Prince and satisfy him that the measures of the Government were the orders of the King himself, and that the whole ques-

[1] *Ibid.* par. 5.
[2] *Ibid.* par. 6.

tion would be settled as soon as Nga Yé was surrendered. The Ministers, however, under the influence of Menthagyee decided against this wholesome advice. Burney says, " they all approved of my suggestion, but pretended that it could not be adopted because there was no precedent for a Woongyee going to a Prince's house." [1]

The same day Burney informed the Prince of what had passed at the Hlutdaw, and advised him to surrender Nga Yé if he knew of his whereabouts, or to try and apprehend him. The Prince "turned to a Pagoda which was visible from his chamber and made oath that he did not know where Nga Yé was, and observed that he believed the apprehending of that man was a mere pretext, and that Menthagyee and his party would not be satisfied even if he, the Prince, could seize and surrender that man; but that if they would only give him time, he would send out his followers to search for and apprehend him." [2] The Prince also informed Burney that he himself had no selfish object in view, but that he wished to prevent the sick King from injury, and the throne, which rightly belonged to the King's son, from usurpation; and finally, " that if Menthagyee and the Ministers persisted in their injurious and insulting conduct towards him, he and his sons had made up their minds to resist, and I should see something serious occur." [2]

On the morning of 24 February, the Ministers summoned the Prince's first minister and confined him with seven pairs of irons. Burney warned them of the probable consequences of their proceedings, but they ignored him; on the other hand they decided to send a military force to search the Prince's house. Burney again warned them of the seriousness of their move, and expressed his fear that the Prince would not submit to the gross indignity of his house and the private apartments of his women being searched. He begged of them to permit him to act as a mediator and prevent a civil war. Menthagyee

[1] *Ibid*. par. 6.
[2] *Ibid*. par. 7.

and the Ministers turned a deaf ear to the entreaties of Burney
and dispatched a force to the Prince's house, firmly believing
that the Prince would be cowed into submission.[1] What their
action led to might be described in the words of Burney:—

"The guard at his gateway however told the troops that
they could not enter without the Prince's permission. The
troops tried to break open the gate when the Prince's party
from within fired four or five muskets, killed one man and
wounded two. The Government troops with the Myolatwun,
the General Officer Commanding them, fled back to the
Lhwottau (Hlutdaw) and reported what had passed. The
Menthagyee and the whole Court were thrown into the greatest
dismay and confusion, and preparations were made for receiving an attack upon the Palace, which was immediately expected
from the Prince."[2]

The Ministers had not expected the Prince to resist a
search of his house; they were wholly unprepared for the situation created, and now began to think only of their personal
safety. But the Prince, on the other hand, fearing that a
second and a more vigorous attack would be made upon his
house, immediately drew out all his family and followers,
embarked them in boats, and crossed over the Irrawaddy to
Sagaing. The Government had on the spot 3000 to 4000 troops
while the Prince had not more than 400 to 500 armed men, but
no attempt was made to intercept him whilst he was crossing
the river. "The whole city," says Burney, "became a scene
of bustle and confusion, many running away and others securing their property against fire and plunder...... All the night
of the 24th the inhabitants of the town expected it to be set on
fire and plundered."[3]

Twelve hours after the Prince had crossed the river, the
Government recovered from the paralysis by which it had been
overtaken, and not only began to make defensive preparations,
but sent a force of about 2000 men to Sagaing, and another to

[1] *Ibid.* par. 8.
[2] *Ibid.*
[3] *Ibid.* par. 9.   The Kone-baung-set Yazawin, Book 2, p. 501.

plunder the Prince's house and the houses of his followers. Several of the officers of the Prince and of his sister, the Pagan Princess, were executed and their property seized. Burney earnestly remonstrated with the Ministers against this line of conduct, and told them " that they were exasperating the Prince and provoking him to return and attack them, and that their proceedings when reported by me to other countries, would be most disgraceful to them." [1] On this occasion at least Burney's warning proved effective, and the executions ceased.[1]

On 26 February, reports became current that the Prince had been encouraged into his action under the instigation of Burney, and that soon British troops would hurry to his help. Burney, therefore, proceeded to the Hlutdaw, and pointed out to the Ministers the gross absurdity of the reports; he also gave them his assurances of neutrality in the event of a civil war. Burney personally believed that Menthagyee and his party were the authors of the false reports, so that they might excite odium against the Prince by connecting him with the British. " Menthagyee," says Burney, " has always been most inimical to the English, and has always believed that our object in maintaining a Resident at Ava was to injure and destroy the country or lead to its occupation by us." [2]

From Sagaing the Prince of Tharrawaddy proceeded northwards towards Moksobomyo,[3] " seizing the muskets of some soldiers whom he met with on the road, but giving them a regular receipt for the same and keeping his men in excellent order, preventing them from committing any depredations on the villages through which they passed and in most of which he put placards, stating that he has no design against the King or the King's son, but that the injustice and oppression of others had forced him to retire from Ava." [4]

---

[1] *Ibid.* par. 9.
[2] *Ibid.*
[3] Also called Mouttshobo and Yatna Theinga; modern name, Shwebo.
India Political Consultations Range 194, Vol. 35, Burney's Letter, Ava, 3 March, 1837, par. 10

The force of 2000 men sent to apprehend the Prince was augmented to 4000, but the Royal troops tamely followed him, being either unwilling or afraid to overtake him. "The pursuing force," wrote Burney to his Government, " was commanded by the Ken Woon, an ignorant old man, who, instead of trying at once to overtake and apprehend the Prince or persuade him to stop by offering to negotiate a reconciliation with the Government, desired only to frighten the Prince's party still more and accelerate its flight. He believed that the Prince was running out of the country towards Manipore as fast as he could, and taking good care to keep at a respectful distance in the rear, halting every night on the ground which the Prince's party had left in the morning, the Ken Woon fired his guns and jingals incessantly in the hope that the report of these arms would be sure to drive the Prince out of the Burmese territory." [1]   The Prince and his followers " retreated in the greatest trepidation, and experienced during this march severe privations subsisting themselves upon handfuls of raw rice. They reached Mouttshobo on the night of the 28th February. On the following day the Ken Woon and his force of 3 to 4000 men halted at Halen a large village 12 or 14 miles to the southward of Mouttshobo, and hearing that the Prince was going to make a stand in that city this officer determined upon waiting at Halen for reinforcement from the capital." [1]

It is possible that at the time of his departure from Ava the Prince had no intention to rebel or to aspire to the throne. On his way to the riverside " he seized one of the King's officers and attendants, the *Daway Bo* whom he happened to meet, and took him with him to a large Pagoda at Tsagain, where he took a solemn oath that he had no design to injure the King or rebel against him, but that he could no longer submit to the oppression and contumely which he had lately experienced, and he made the *Daway Bo* take as solemn an oath, that he would communicate the terms of the Prince's oath to the King, and then released him." [2]   But on reaching Sagaing the

---

[1] *Ibid.* Vol. 41, Burney's Letter, Ava, 24 May, 1837 par. 2.
[2] *Ibid.* Vol. 35, Burney's Letter, Ava, 3 March, 1837, pars. 10, 11.

THE REVOLUTION IN AVA

Prince was received by leaders of banditti who had long been infesting the country north of Ava, and they offered to help him to the throne. Chins and other malcontents began to flock to his standard, and on arriving at Moksobo he had a following of about 2000. Public opinion in Ava and in the neighbouring districts was also in favour of the Prince; soon his ambition was roused and he decided to make a bid for the throne.[1]

While the Prince was strengthening himself, Menthagyee was hoping against hope that the Royal troops would soon bring the fugitive to book. The King was given to understand that his brother had meditated an attack on the Palace in order to seize the throne, but that the Government had anticipated him and forced him to flee. The Princess of Pagan was confined in three pairs of irons, and several of the royal family, who were most intimate with her, were also jailed. The general feeling, however, in official circles, at the Court, and in the city, was one of fear and insecurity. Public opinion was increasingly swinging in favour of the Prince, and an attack upon the capital was expected by every one.[2]

Burney warned the Ministers of the fast developing danger, and suggested that the dispute could be settled by marrying the King's son to the Queen's daughter, and by conferring upon the former the office of Ain-she-men. But such an arrangement would most certainly deprive Menthagyee of all power and patronage, so that he was in no mood to adopt this course. Burney also cautioned Menthgyee's Government "that the Governor-General will hear of this civil war with very great concern, not only because it must tend to destroy the trade

---

[1] *Ibid.* Vol. 35, Burney's Letter, Ava, 3 March, 1837, pars. 10, 11.
"At the Ngadatgyi pagoda, in the presence of the Daway Bo, Tharrawaddy Min swore that if it was true that throughout his life he had never plotted against the Royal brother whom he regarded as his father, he would escape from all danger caused by his enemies. He asked the Daway Bo to relate this oath to his Royal brother. With a view to cheat the Daway Bo into the belief that he had many supporters, he arranged sham interviews with his own camp people who posed as leaders of regiments from different localities." Kone-baung-set Yazawin, Book 2, p. 501.
[2] *Ibid.*

which British subjects are carrying on with this country, but
because it will fill the whole line of our frontiers with robbers
and men who may be driven from their homes by the disturbed
state of the country and forced to seek a subsistence by plunder
and robbing." [1]

Burney offered to advise the Ministers whenever they felt
inclined to consult him, but at that particular time they were
" too blind and too full of pride or too much under the influence
of Menthagyeh to hear my suggestions; and they trust to a hope
which every one else seems to consider fallacious, that the Royal
troops will overpower the Prince of Tharawadi." [2]

There was danger of the city being set on fire. The Residency consisted chiefly of plank, bamboo, and grass, so that
Burney and his followers were in great danger. The price of
food stuffs rose enormously, and people were expected to desert
the town in case the Prince appeared before it with an army.
Under these circumstances Burney began to collect stores and
supplies to meet the emergency. [3]

On the morning of 4 March, Burney was summoned to
the Royal presence and had a private audience with Bagyidaw,
most of the Ministers being also present. The King's mind
" appeared to be in a far better state than what I had expected
to find it," reported Burney. " He told me that he was now
well again and requested me to keep foreign merchants quiet.
I referred to the present state of affairs, observed that I was
exceedingly anxious to see an end to the present disturbance
quoting a Burmese saying, " If there is heat or trouble in front
of the house there will be no comfort or happiness in the rear,"
mentioned that the matter could be better settled by amicable
discussion than by arms, and requested him to order his Ministers to consult with me and hear my suggestions. He nodded
assent, but I saw plainly that he has been made to believe that
his brother sought to injure him and that he is quite ignorant of

[1] *Ibid.* par. 13.
[2] *Ibid.* par. 13.
[3] *Ibid.* par. 15.

all the causes which led to the present disturbance. The attempt which I could make to open his eyes were of little avail. He is surrounded by men-at-arms and guns and muskets as if he were in momentary expectation of an attack from his brother, and I found him so well impressed with his brother-in-law's view of the dispute between him and the brother, that I saw I should do more harm than good by pressing on his notice immediately the points which I went prepared to press." [1]

The Government of India highly approved of the part played by Burney in the Ava affairs, and assured him that the Governor-General had the fullest confidence in him, and that British interests in Burma could not be in better hands than in his.[2]

It was most judicious and politic on the part of the Prince of Tharrawaddy to take his post at Moksobo which was the old seat and capital of the great Alaungpaya, the founder of the reigning dynasty. People from the surrounding country began to flock to his standard, but above all he was joined by many robber chiefs together with their numerous followers, and by many who disliked Menthagyee's government and desired a change, or to whom a prospect of gain and plunder was inviting. Burney reported to his Government that " parties of these men went out and forced the inhabitants of the surrounding villages to join them, setting fire to their villages where the inhabitants refused, and they struck such terror into the peaceful portion of the population that they had only to appear before Khyouk Myoung, Shain Maga and other places along the western bank of the Erawadi to secure possession of them. The Prince's Emissaries at the same time went about spreading a report that the King was dead, that Menthagyee had usurped the throne, and that the Prince of Tharawadi had retired to Mouttshobo to make a stand there where he had been joined by an immense concourse of people. This report induced the most influential of the inhabitants and local officers of many places to hasten to

[1] *Ibid.* par. 16.
[2] *Ibid.* Letter to Burney, 10 April, 1837.

the Prince at Mouttshobo, whilst at other places also where the local officers disbelieved the report or were firm in their allegiance to the existing Government, the inhabitants rose upon their officers and throwing off all restraint and authority attacked and plundered each other and all traders and travellers who happened to come near them. In fact all the country to the north of Ava and around Mouttshobo became one scene of anarchy and confusion, and the Prince, as he himself has since told me, sent his emissaries in every direction to excite commotion and disorder, or to use his own expressive Burmese phrase ' To set all the country aboiling and bubbling' ".[1]

Soon the Prince was able to assume so bold and confident an attitude, that he opened the gates of Moksobo and challenged the royal troops to come and attack him.[2] The old Ken Woon waited at Halen for reinforcements, but himself had no stomach for fight. On 8 March, a small party of the Prince's men so frightened him and his whole force, that he hastily evacuated the place, leaving behind his guns and jingals. His retreat was stopped by the Bo Mhu Woon (Meng Myat Bo, the King's brother) who was advancing with reinforcements from Ava. The Bo Mhu combined the two forces, but was unable to recover Halen. He encamped at Tharain and Letweyue, two villages six miles south of Halen, threw up some defences, and applied to Ava for further reinforcements. The Prince, meanwhile, did not remain idle. He sent out small bodies of troops which attacked Debayen, Phalangoun, Yeu, and other places which were garrisoned with royal troops and contained an abundance of guns and ammunition. " The King's troops fled," says Burney, " at the first approach of the Prince's party which took the Governor of Debayen, a near relation of the Queen, prisoner, and laid waste a great portion of a very fine district. It was also generally reported and believed that at Debayen the Prince's party had discovered and taken an immense quantity of gold and silver and jewels which had been concealed there by the Queen and Menthagyeh, and that the Prince was distribut-

---

[1] *Ibid.* Vol. 41, Burney's Letter, Ava, 24 May, 1837, par. 2.
[2] *Ibid.* Vol. 35, Burney's Letter, Ava, 3 March, 1837, par. 17.

ing this treasure very liberally among his followers." [1] This report was wholly false, but it was of the greatest service to the Prince: the number of his followers continued to swell.[1]

The rebellion now assumed most dangerous proportions. The Ministers began to summon troops from the districts to the southward up to Myede, " but although they collected and dispatched 17,000 men against the Prince, not a man seemed disposed to fight for them. Many of the troops after making their appearance at Ava either returned to their villages or were induced to desert over in large bodies to the Prince." [2] A force of nearly 4000 men under the command of the Prince of Thibau, the King's brother, proceeded along the east bank of the Irrawaddy, but was obliged to stockade itself near Singu, and was unable either to advance or retreat. Another force of 2000 men under the Let-ya-when-men went along the west bank of the river with the object of recovering Shinmoga and neighbouring posts which had fallen into the hands of the rebels, but it failed to penetrate through. Meanwhile the troops of the Bo Mhu Woon south of Halen, although raised to 10,000 men, were unable to make any impression whatever against Moksobo. On the other hand large numbers of soldiers began to desert to the Prince, and soon the royal troops were reduced to one-half.[3]

On 4 March, Burney made a definite proposal to the Ministers in writing, stating, " that as the public feeling was so decidedly in favour of the Prince of Tharawadi and against the existing Government, no time should be lost in opening a negotiation with the Prince and effecting a reconciliation; and I suggested at the same time the following terms:—That the King's son should be installed as Ain-ye-Meng or Crown Prince, and that a union between a daughter of the Menthagyeh and a son of the Prince of Tharawadi, who had before offered to marry her, should immediately take place." [4] Burney also proposed to submit an address to the King containing the same

[1] *Ibid.* Vol. 41, Burney's Letter, 24 May, 1837, par. 3.
[2] *Ibid.* par. 4.
[3] *Ibid.*
[4] *Ibid.* par. 5.

suggestion. The Ministers were highly alarmed and " entreated me not to deliver my address to the King, assuring me that its contents would only irritate him, make him suspect me to be in league with the Prince, and probably lead to the execution of those Ministers who are on terms of greatest intimacy with me. I urged them in the strongest manner to submit my proposition to the King as one emanating from themselves, and earnestly warned them to follow my advice before it was too late. And as the Prince himself had in the first instance requested my interference, I now offered to go to him and mediate a reconciliation. The Ministers, however, refused to hear me, declaring that the King would put them to death if they ventured to report my plan of reconciliation to him."[1]

On 7 March, news arrived of the fall of Kyauk-Myaung to the rebels. Burney wished to send a dispatch to Bayfield in Mogaung to inform him of the state of affairs at Ava, but the Ministers were unable to forward it. A boat belonging to the Residency, manned by Bengal lascars, which Burney had sent up to Mogaung in January, with dispatches for Bayfield, was on its return journey attacked and plundered, first by the people of Kyan Nhyat and Yetha Ya, and again near Thampayanaga by the followers of the Prince of Tharrawaddy. The lascars and Kincaid, an American missionary, who was also in the boat, were severely beaten, but they effected their escape to Ava on foot without food or clothing by a circuitous route. Burney immediately (11 March) proceeded to the Hlutdaw and declared to the Ministers, " that as they would not attend to my advice, as they were unable to protect my followers from insult and outrage, and as I foresaw their inevitable destruction approaching, I considered it high time for me to retire from Ava, and therefore demanded that they should apply to the King for permission, and furnish me with the necessary boats for proceeding to Rangoon."[2]

The Ministers strongly objected to Burney's retiring from Ava, on the ground that the measure would not only alarm the

[1] *Ibid.* par. 5.
[2] *Ibid.* par. 6.

people, but the hands of the rebel party would be strengthened thereby. They earnestly requested him to remain at the capital. Burney most probably would have moved down to Rangoon, but he was unable to hire boats, and not a single Burmese boatman was available; he was therefore obliged to relinquish his project.[1]

On 15 and 16 March, Burney had long discussions with the Ministers and asked them to permit him to see the King, so that he might submit his advice to open negotiations of peace with the Prince. The Ministers refused to comply with his request. " I then told them that as I saw they would soon be unable to protect me against the lawless and plundering troops of both parties, it was necessary for me to take measures to protect myself, and that I should, therefore, immediately begin to put the Residency in a state of defence and erect a stockade around it. The Ministers vehemently objected to such a measure, and told me, that the erection of a stockade would be contrary to all law and precedent in this country, and would be considered as an act of hostility and defiance on my part towards the Government." [2]

Burney was thus placed in a queer situation: the Ministers would not let him retire to Rangoon; they were in no position to protect the Residency; and they would not permit him to put the Residency in a state of defence. But events now began to move fast, and at last, on the evening of 21 March, Burney received a confidential communication from Menthagyee himself, stating, " that all was lost, that none of the Royal troops which had been sent against the Prince of Tharawadi would fight him, and that the English Resident was the only person to whom the King and existing Government of Ava could now look for counsel and assistance." [3]

Burney saw the King with his Ministers twice on the following day, and expressed his willingness to proceed to Moksobo and endeavour to restore peace and harmony between the

[1] *Ibid.* par. 6.
[2] *Ibid.* par. 7.
[3] *Ibid.* par. 8.

monarch and his brother. He, however, warned them that it was now too late to reason with the Prince, and the chances of reconciliation were negligible. He also requested that as credentials to the Prince, his three sisters and three other male relatives, who had been confined, should be released from irons before he left Ava.[1] This was readily complied with on 23 March in the presence of Burney.[2]

While Burney was preparing for his journey to Moksobo, news was received (on the morning of 23 March) that a party of the Prince's forces had crossed the Irrawaddy and taken possession of the Royal Chokey of Kyauk-ta-loun, and that it was advancing towards the British Residency from that direction. Burney felt uneasy about leaving the Residency which at this time contained not only his own family, but also the families of many Indian traders, also three American missionaries and their families, and a good many foreign and Indian traders who had taken refuge within the same area. Besides, both Bayfield his Assistant and McLeod the Commander of his Escort were absent on distant service, and there was no one but Shaikh Abdul Latif the Indian Subadar to place in charge of the Residency. " But I thought it my duty," says Burney, " to see if any exertion of mine could put a stop to the civil war that was raging, and I had great confidence in the Subadar which he fully realized."[2] Burney directed the Subadar to construct stockades on two sides of the Residency, the attitude of the Ministers notwithstanding.[2]

At noon, on 23 March, Burney left Ava and crossed over to Sagaing. He was accompanied by an escort of Burmese Musketeers provided by the King, two Indian soldiers belonging to the Resident's Escort, a few Indian lascars, and some of his personal servants. On the 24th morning he reached Padu

---

[1] Those released were the Princess of Pagan who had six pairs of irons on, the Princess of Mengyen, and the Princess of Shwe Keng; also Maung Thenza who had been Woongyee of Rangoon during Canning's Mission in 1812, his son, and the Prince of Mendat.

[2] India Political Consultations Range 194, Vol. 41, Burney's Letter, 24 May, 1837, par. 8.

where he heard that a detachment of 400 of the Royal troops had been driven out from the Kekkha village, and that the whole route before him was infested with robbers and plunderers. The Burmese Escort was unwilling to proceed, but depending upon the faithfulness of his sepoys, lascars, and servants, Burney determined to go on, confident that he would be able to repel any small body of plunderers. With the help of an intelligent guide he pressed on. At Aunguebouk he came across some horsemen in the Prince's service pillaging that village, but Burney's party being too strong for them they pretended to belong to the King's army. On reaching Enbe, instead of heading directly for the Bo Mhu Woon's camp at Tharain, Burney had to make a long detour westwards towards Letweyue, since large parties of rebel troops lay to the south of Tharain. On the way to Letweyue a good deal of firing was heard during the whole day. On approaching the village Burney dispatched some men to report his arrival. The Royal Commander immediately sent a party of 50 horse and 100 musketeers to meet the Resident. The King's troops were in an extraordinary state of panic: "the moment they saw my party," says Burney, "they turned round and fled, and it was with the utmost difficulty I could persuade them to approach me." [1]

From Letweyue Burney proceeded towards Tharain, and reached the camp of Prince Bo Mhu Woon at 10 p.m. of 24 March. Immediately before his arrival the rebel troops had begun a general attack upon the Royal forces. They were informed of the arrival of a mission from the King under the British Resident, but they considered the intelligence to be a mere ruse, and fired and yelled with redoubled vigour, and continued the attack until 1 a.m. "Both parties, however," writes Burney, "seemed to me to be firing at an angle of about 45 degrees and to be hurting each other very little. The state of the King's troops will scarcely be credited. With the exception of the Bo Mhu Woon and the Commander of the Letweyue position, every person whom I saw or spoke to, was

[1] *Ibid.* par. 9.

in a most pitiable state of fear and anxiety ready to run at the slightest alarm. All the officers were quiet peaceable men with families in Ava where they had always been employed in Civil duties and were not only entirely ignorant of military service but most cordially averse to it, whilst the private soldiers were poor villagers summoned at a moment's notice from their homes and sent on a most unpopular service without pay and provisions." [1]

On the morning of 25 March, Burney opened a communication with the advanced post of the Prince of Tharrawaddy about a quarter of a mile distant from the Royalist camp. He received a civil message and proceeded to that post. There he was furnished with a suitable escort to convey him to Moksobo. The state of the Prince's army was a most remarkable contrast to that of the Royal troops. " Most of the officers belonging to the Prince," says Burney, " were bold, reckless characters and notorious robbers, and the private soldiers, although miserably armed and very deficient in military appointment in comparison with the King's troops, many of them even at the advanced posts having only sticks and bludgeons, were yet full of confidence, owing to the knowledge which they had acquired from numerous deserters of the state of panic of the King's troops, and full of threats and boastings and of false tales of the Prince having been joined by hundreds of thousands and by large parties of wild Khyens (Chins) and Kakhyens (Kachins). The Prince's party also had established themselves in every direction around the posts held by the King's troops, had burnt to the ground Tharain, Enbay and other villages, and driven away the inhabitants from several more." [2]

Burney passed through the large village of Kaba and reached Moksobo at 2 p.m., 25 March. The Prince sent out a party of horse and an officer of rank to meet him, and himself received Burney with great kindness and cordiality. Hostilities between the two armies were now suspended. The conversa-

[1] *Ibid.*
[2] *Ibid.* par. 10.

tion and discussion which took place between these two men
at the first interview may best be described in Burney's own
words :—

> "I soon discovered that there was not the slightest chance
> of his listening to any proposition for reconciling him with the
> Government of Ava. Upon hearing the object of my Mission he
> observed, 'I will not act like the English and retire from any
> territory upon which I have once planted my standard.' He
> seemed pleased that I had released his relatives from irons, and
> still more so when he learnt that the families of several of his
> most attached followers had secreted themselves within the Resi-
> dency since the day he left Ava. At his request I retired and
> prepared a short note to try and effect a reconciliation with his
> Brother and the Government of Ava, that I had seen the distress
> and misery which the civil war had created in the country be-
> tween the capital and Mouttshobo, and that I desired to know
> how he thought peace might be most speedily restored. I sent
> him the note at 9 o'clock at night and he summoned me at 10
> and kept me until 1 o'clock in the morning going over a long list
> of his grievances and of instances of misgovernment and rapacity
> on the part of the Queen and her brother Menthagyeh. To the
> proposition of a union between his son and the daughter of
> Menthagyeh he observed that he himself had once demanded the
> daughter in marriage, but as she had been refused neither he nor
> his son could ever think of such a union again. To the proposi-
> tion of making the King's son Ain-ye-Meng he observed that his
> father the late Ain-ye-Meng had directed the present King to
> consider him the present Prince of Tharawadi as the successor
> to the throne before the King's son. I used my best endeavours
> to excite his fraternal feelings, reminding him how very kind and
> affectionate the King had always been to him from his youth,
> and entreating him to avoid the reproach of injuring one who
> with all his faults had been so excellent a brother to him. But
> the Prince was not to be moved, and openly expressed an opinion
> that his Brother did not deserve to reign for having raised a
> woman of low origin to the station of first queen. I hinted that
> the Ministers of Ava were still summoning troops from all quar-
> ters, and that they were expecting to be joined by all the strength
> of the Shan Tsaubwas and by a large army from the southward.
> He laughed at the intelligence and shewed that he was intimately
> acquainted with everything that had been said or done at Ava
> and with the state of affairs there, and that in fact some of the
> officers and ladies of the Palace were in secret correspondence
> with him. Learning from the Prince himself that only two days
> before he had doubts of his ultimate success and was proposing

to send a Catholic Priest Don Nicholas whom his troops had
taken prisoner near Dabayen with a communication to me requesting my mediation, I felt still more vexation at the folly and
obstinacy of the Ministers of Ava who had rejected my advice
so repeatedly." [1]

"The Prince openly avowed his intention of sacking and
destroying the city of Ava and recommended me to quit it as
soon as possible. I told him that it was impossible for me to
do so and leave the foreign merchants to the mercy of his troops,
and remonstrated earnestly against the unjustifiable cruelty of
destroying the city, hinting that if his troops injured the British
Residency or the person or property of any merchant entitled
to my protection the Governor-General would hold him responsible and most probably interfere in the present dispute. He said
that he would do all that he could to prevent coming into collision with our Government, or any injury occurring to me whom
he considered as his friend, that he would give the strictest orders
to all his troops to respect the Residency and the houses of all
foreign merchants, that he would furnish me with letters to the
Commanders of the different division advancing against Ava, and
that he wished all foreign merchants should make an inventory
of their property, put up placards on their houses and assemble
at the Residency when his troops came before Ava and stormed
it." [2]

On the morning of 26 March, Burney had another audience
with the Prince who produced a written reply to the Resident's
note. The purport of the note was that he would consent to
negotiate with the King his brother, only after the latter had
executed those who were ruining the country and disgracing
His Majesty. On Burney persuading him to insert in the paper
the names of the persons to be executed, he ordered those of
the Queen and Menthagyee to be put down. Burney remonstrated against the word "execute" and he consented to substitute for it "set aside." Burney said that he would communicate every word of the contents of his paper to the King, and
that he himself would join in trying to effect the removal from
office of Menthagyee, but that he was not prepared to have a
hand in separating a husband from his wife, meaning the King
and his Queen. The Prince observed that the Queen was the

---

[1] *Ibid.* par. 11.
[2] *Ibid.* par. 12.

root and cause of all evils, and that unless she was removed
Menthagyee might recover his power, and the people of the
country be again subjected to their rapacity.[1]

From the general attitude of the Prince, Burney felt convinced that he had made up his mind to strike for the throne,
and that he would certainly attack and sack the capital. He,
therefore, made an attempt to prevent, as far as he could,
murder and massacre, and save if possible the lives of the King
and his officers. He asked the Prince that if he persuaded the
Government of Ava to open the gates of the City at once to
him and submit to his authority, would he promise not to
destroy the caiptal or take the life of any of the officers or
inhabitants. "He replied that he had not hitherto put to death
a single person who had thrown down his arms and submitted,
and summoned the Governor of Debayen and other officers in
proof of the truth of his assertion, and then distinctly assured
me that if the Government of Ava would not resist him but
would open the gates of the City he would not injure his
Brother the King in the smallest degree, molest any of his officers, put a single soul to death or allow the city to be destroyed
and plundered. I repeatedly asked him, may I make such a
pledge in your name to the Ministers of Ava and he repeatedly
answered in the affirmative." [2] Burney had not been authorized
by the Government of Ava to agree to any proposition of surrender, so that he was unable to require the Prince to put the
pledge in writing, but he made him repeat it frequently so as to
prevent all chance of misunderstanding.[2]

The Prince's second son Thait-ten-gyeh exercised the
greatest influence over his father, and wished to recommence

[1] *Ibid.* par. 13. The Kone-baung-set Yazawin refering to Burney's
conversation with Tharrawaddy says:— " Tharrawaddy Min told
him that nothing had happened between him and his brother the
King whom he regarded as his father. Yet Salinmyosa (the
Menthagyee) and other Court officials had through backbiting
and intrigues caused all these troubles. Hence, conciliation, he
said, would be possible only when these mischief-makers were
removed. Thawrawaddy Min also said that being English they
did not understand Burmese strategem and diplomacy." Book
2, p. 518.
[2] *Ibid.* par. 14.

hostilities after waiting for three days only. When Burney pointed out to him the impossibility of returning an answer in so short a time, he said, " Very well, for the sake of the English Resident we will give the King's troops a fourth day before we attack and destroy them."[1] Thait-ten-gyeh and all the other officers around the Prince were full of threats and boasting, and most anxious to prevent peace and reconciliation, since they did not wish to be deprived of the rich harvest of plunder in the city of Ava. Burney warned the young Prince that the whole of his proceedings would be reported to foreign countries, and urged him to so act as to secure a high character for wisdom and humanity in other parts of the world. He replied, " Yes, yes, I know all will be printed in the Gazette (using the word), and I will have my statements inserted then too."[1]

Burney left Moksobo on 26 March, at 4 p.m., passed through Halen and Tharain, and reached Ava on the 27th evening at 9 o'clock. The whole of the 27th he was on horseback, and covered 40 miles under a hot sun. Early on the 28th morning he saw the King and Ministers and reported to them the particulars of his mission. He advised them not to depend upon the Bo Mhu Woon's army, and on their confessing that no other fresh troops were available, he communicated the pledge of the Prince that he would not shed blood if the King and his Government submitted to him. He at the same time advised the King not to trust his brother, but to obtain a fresh pledge from him through the Prince of Mekkhara for whom the Prince of Tharrawaddy had kindly feelings. The King and his Ministers requested Burney to go himself again to Moksobo and obtain a definite pledge, but he was physically not in a fit condition to undertake such a journey a second time, and consented to send his clerk Edwards with a letter to the Prince.[2]

Burney addressed a letter to the Prince, apprising him, that the King and Ministers had decided not to resist him, but to open the gates of the City, counting upon his pledge, that he

[1] *Ibid.* par. 15.
[2] *Ibid.* pars. 16, 17.

would not injure his Brother, or plunder the city, nor molest or put to death any of the Royal officers. Burney also advised him to come to Sagaing at once and take possession of the city of Ava. After showing this letter to the King and Ministers, he entrusted it to Edwards, who departed for Moksobo on the 28th evening. The King also sent a deputation to Moksobo consisting of the principal priests and headed by the Mekkhara Prince to obtain the promised pledge.[1]

Meanwhile, the Ministers began to fortify the city against any attempt on the part of the Prince's forces to plunder the town before his arrival, or before the return of the deputation. "The whole of the Royal troops," says Burney, "were ordered to fall back upon the City, the Gates were shut and guns placed at most of them, the ramparts were thickly manned and long heavy timbers slung along the tops of the walls by ropes which might be cut and the timbers thrown down upon any party attempting to escalade."[2]

Edwards on reaching Saye found that the Bo Mhu Woon and his whole army had evacuated their positions and were in full retreat towards Ava. The countryside was so infested with plunderers belonging to the Prince, that Edward's Burmese escort of horse deserted him; but he pressed on attended only by two Indian soldiers and a few Lascars that Burney had furnished him with, and finally reached Moksobo. He delivered the letter to the Prince, who, after perusing it said, " Yes, I have made this pledge to Col. Burney and I am a man and will keep it faithfully, but I will not go to Tsagain until I have surrounded the city of Ava with the whole of my troops."[3] His object in first surrounding the city was, as he told Edwards, to prevent Menthagyee and the Ministers from escaping and carrying away the King with them. Edwards returned safely to Ava on the evening of 31 March.[3]

[1] *Ibid.* pars. 16, 17.
[2] *Ibid.* par. 17.
[3] *Ibid.* par. 18.

10

On 29 March, Burney, in the presence of the missionary Kincaid as a witness, warned the King that the promises of his brother could not be trusted, and that as the advanced divisions of the rebel troops consisted entirely of robbers and evil characters, there was every danger of the city being plundered and His Majesty's person violated. He, therefore, advised the King to prepare his war boats and retire to Rangoon in the event of his brother not coming immediately to Sagaing. The King pondered over the suggestion and on 1 April, sent Lanciago to consult with Burney concerning the plan of his retiring from Ava, and to enquire if there was any chance of the British Government assisting him to recover his capital. Burney declared that he himself possessed powers " only to assure His Majesty protection and an asylum in any British Territory to which he might repair, but that the question as to interfering in his dispute with his brother and affording him military aid to recover his capital was one which the Governor-General of India alone was competent to answer." [1]

Lanciago also told Burney, " that the King and Queen themselves were desirous of trying to go down to Rangoon, (but) that the principal officers of the government were not prepared for such a measure; and that he (Lanciago) himself considered it to be impracticable." [1] The King after all did not try this expedient, although Burney offered him letters to the Commanders of English vessels at Rangoon to receive on board His Majesty and his Court, and convey them to Moulmein. In Burney's opinion it was quite possible for the King to have escaped from Ava; subsequent events justified the view taken by Burney for the King's safety. The King, however, followed the advice of his Ministers, and decided to remain at the capital and face his brother. [2]

On 2 April, the whole of the Royal Army, retreating before rebel forces, crossed over from Sagaing to Ava. The same evening the advanced divisions of the rebel army occupied Sagaing

---

[1] *Ibid.* pars. 17-19.
[2] *Ibid.* par. 19.

under the joint command of a son [1] and a younger brother [2] of the great Bandula. These commanders set fire to some houses in Sagaing and drew up their men directly opposite to Ava along the river side, where during the greater part of the night they shouted and yelled, and sang songs in abuse of Menthagyee and the officers of the Government. On 3 April, a large portion of the Prince's army arrived at Sagaing under his fourth son Thetten-byn. Burney immediately opened a communication with him, and ascertained from him that he had strict orders from his father to respect the Residency. He even offered to send over a party of about 250 of his men to assist in protecting the Residency from his undisciplined plunderers. On 4 April, another force commanded by Prince Thait-ten-gyeh and Maung Toung Bo, the Pagyi Woon advanced upon Ava from Kyauk-ta-loun, plundering and maltreating the villagers and laying waste the country. Burney sent a message to the commanders protesting against this vandalism, and the young Prince sent a civil reply, declaring that he was not aware of his advanced party committing atrocities upon the people, and that he had received the strictest injunctions to respect the Residency. [3] Burney also sent a message to the Prince of Tharrawaddy to repair immediately to Sagaing and put a stop to the sufferings inflicted by his troops upon the poor villagers around Ava. [4]

The struggle for the throne was soon brought to a head by the mission of priests led by the Prince of Mekkhara. This Prince left Ava on 28 March and had an interview with Tharrawaddy at Moksobo. The details of the conversation are not available, but Tharrawaddy made two demands: (1) That the Queen be removed from the presence of the King, and (2) That

---

[1] The Records do not furnish his name; but Burney says that he was a young man of only 22 years of age and of extraordinary size for a Burman.

[2] This man's name is also not given; but Burney speaks of him as being "a drunken vicious character who is said to have taken shelter in a monastery to save himself from the consequences of some crime and to have thrown off the priest's garments to join the Prince."

[3] India Political Consultations Range 194, Vol. 41, Burney's Letter, Ava, 24 May, 1837, par. 20.

[4] *Ibid.*

Menthagyee, the Bo Mhu Woon, the Myawadi Woongyee, three other Ministers, and seven of the principal military officers, who had been most faithful to the King, go over to his son Thet-ten-byn at Sagaing.   On fulfilment of these requirements, he promised to stop all hostilities, come over himself and take charge of the Hlutdaw at Ava, and not injure a single individual in person or property.   The deputation returned to Ava on 6 April, and the King and his Government decided to accept the terms.[1]

The Prince of Mekkhara seemed convinced that his nephew Tharrawaddy would faithfully keep his pledge; but he requested Burney to accompany the Ministers to Sagaing.   Burney proceeded to the Palace, and found the 13 officers ready to cross over to Sagaing, apparently confiding in the goodness of the Prince's intentions.   " But the communication," says Burney, " appeared to me so very extraordinary, demanding as it did the persons of all the Ministers and officers who composed the most efficient members of the government and garrison that I could not avoid suspecting some cruel treachery, and offered to precede the party to Thet-ten-byn, and endeavour to secure them civil treatment by my presence." [1] " At this time," continues Burney, " there were at least 7 or 8000 troops within the walls of Ava infinitely better found in arms and ammunition than the Prince's forces and with a large number of guns of every description. But these troops were not only panic struck to an incredible degree but much disaffected, so much so that one of their principal officers, the Taroup Bo, had already opened a secret correspondence with Thet-ten-byn, and offered to set the city on fire. The more respectable Ministers of the King of Ava now displayed very strong personal attachment to their sovereign, expressing their hope and belief, that as their troops could not be depended upon, the only way left for saving the Palace from attack and the King from molestation and danger would be for them to comply with the Prince of Tharawadi's requisition and go over to his son." [1]

---

[1] *Ibid.* par. 21.

Burney preceded the party to Sagaing, and the young Prince not only promised that no damage would be done to the King's officers, but gave Burney an escort to go down to the river side and receive and conduct to him the 13 Ministers and Generals. Burney describing the procession says: "On their way through the crowd assembled to see them pass I was much pleased to observe that the populace so far from shewing any violence or insult which I had apprehended, was perfectly silent and respectful. The Ministers and officers were on foot. Menthagyeh manifested the utmost alarm, and seemed to have lost the faculty both of hearing and speaking, but the whole demeanour of Prince Meng Myat Bo excited my warmest admiration. He led the party with a firm step and a bold upright carriage, grave and serious, but evidently suffering much from feelings of indignation and wounded pride. Some of the military officers also appeared justly to view the whole proceeding as an insulting degradation." [1]

The young Prince received the officers with civility, but refused to permit them to return to Ava, and told them that they must remain with him until his father's arrival. Burney returned to the Residency the same evening, "after reminding the young Prince of his father's pledge and engagement, and strongly pointing out the disgrace and infamy with which his own and his father's name would be connected in every civilized country in the world if any insult or injury were inflicted on these officers and Ministers whilst in his power." [1] Soon after this occurrence Thait-ten-gyeh took possession of Amarapura, reached the Myit-nge, the little river flowing by the eastern face of Ava, and then crossed over to Sagaing. His first act in that town was to place two pairs of irons on Menthagyee; the other Ministers and officers he placed in separate sheds under guard. [1]

The Prince of Tharrawaddy arrived at Sagaing on the evening of 8 April. He had no interview with his brother the King, but the very next day, in spite of all his pledges and promises, he took over the sovereignty of the Kingdom, and

[1] *Ibid.*

gave out that his brother had abdicated in his favour. He took the title of "Yatna Thainga Kounbaung Myo Ya Thau Meng" *i.e.* the King who has dominion over the city of Yatna Thainga Kounbaung. Bagyidaw was kept as a state prisoner in a special mat building to the south of the capital. The Queen and her daughter were removed from his presence and lodged in a distant mean building. All the military stores and other valuable property were transferred to Sagaing, and 20 to 30 of the youngest and best looking of Bagyidaw's subordinate queens were removed to the new King's establishment.[1] Burney had several interviews with Bagyidaw and "found him perfectly recovered, conversing rationally regarding everything that was going on. He appeared, however, much concerned about his queen and was repeatedly obliged to get up and withdraw for a while to recover his composure."[1] The separation from his wife caused him so much distress and annoyance, that finally she was allowed on 16 April, to return to her husband.[1]

As to the 13 Officers, Tharrawaddy had his brother the Bo Mhu Woon confined near his own house in Sagaing; he put irons on Menthagyee and the other eleven officers, and sent them to the common jail at Ava. He also apprehended and confined in irons 20 others of the Ministers and officers of the late Government, and confiscated their houses and other property. The principal Ministers were examined before Thait-ten-gyeh, and under severe punishment they were made to say that Mentha-

---

[1] *Ibid.* pars. 23, 32. The Kone-baung-set Yazawin gives the following version of Bagyidaw's deposition: — "At the request of Sayadaws, he ordered his troops to abstain from plunder and outrage. He jailed Salinmyosa and Woongyee Nga Za, deprived the Pindalai Prince of his estates and title......, and executed some of the accomplices of Salinmyosa.
"Tharrawaddy Min proposed to carry on the government for the King and asked him to permit him to attend on him (Bagyidaw) in his illness. But the King replied that he was old and wanted to retire to a residence near Maha Thetkyathiha pagoda leaving the reins of government into the hands of his royal brother Tharrawaddy Min.
"On the 12th waning of Kason the King abdicated in favour of Tharrawaddy Min and left his palace from the North Gate accompanied by his wives and sons, escorted by his successor." Bagyidaw was 54 or 55 years of age at the time of his deposition.

gyee had intended to put the Prince of Tharrawaddy and all the other members of the Royal family to death and usurp the throne. The wife and two daughters of Menthagyee and the families of some of the imprisoned officers were also seized and subjected to horrible tortures in order to induce them to reveal their supposed hidden property.[1]

On the evening (9 April) of these tragic occurrences, Tharrawaddy sent a civil message to Burney and the latter went over and waited upon him at Sagaing. " He received me kindly," says Burney, " but I soon saw that his head was turned by his extraordinary success, and that he was already a very different person from what he was two months ago." [2] Burney reminded him of his pledge, and remonstrated against the harsh and unworthy proceedings of Thait-ten-gyeh against the ex-Ministers and their families; but Tharrawaddy was in no mood now to respect his pledge repeatedly given at Moksobo. " He spoke with much rancour against his prisoners and manifested a disposition to release himself from his pledge, saying, that he had mentioned to me the names of certain of the Ministers and had therefore a right to punish any of them against whom he might now prove any crime."[2] Burney reminded him that his pledge included all the Ministers, officers, and inhabitants who would not resist him, and that since they had submitted to him because of his pledge, " he could not execute one of them without entailing on his name and character the deepest disgrace in the estimation of every good and honourable man." [2] " He pretended," continues Burney, " that he could not see how he, a King, could not put to death any man who might be proved guilty of crime."[2]

The next day, 10 April, Burney visited the jail, and a most heartrending scene fell upon his view. He found there Menthagyee and about 30 other men, who had lately been the first Ministers and Officers of Burma, confined in irons, their legs in chains, with scanty dirty clothing on them, and treated as

[1] *Ibid.* par. 23.
[2] *Ibid.* par. 24.

common felons.   They all expressed much gratitude for what Burney had hitherto tried to do for them, and begged him to continue to intercede in their favour.   According to Burmese custom, prisoners were not fed by the government, but none of the servants or friends of the unfortunate men had the courage to bring food for them.   Burney took this task upon himself and supplied them with the necessaries of life.   Menthagyee sent a confidential messenger to Burney to solicit his good offices in his behalf, and offered a present of 10,000 ticals in return.   Burney declined the present and assured him that he would do his best for him.   Menthagyee, fearing the present was considered too little, raised it to 30,000 ticals; this also Burney refused and assured him of his good offices.[1]

Burney was so overcome by the sight in Ava jail, that he feared the new King would break his pledge.   To prevent this, he wrote a strongly worded letter protesting against the treatment the ex-officers were receiving, and advised Tharrawaddy to act in the manner most becoming the name and character of a wise and great King, so that he might secure fame and honour in foreign countries and cultivate the friendship of the English. The letter was handed to the King by Edwards.   The King read it very attentively, then displayed a little vexation, and finally observed, " Col. Burney has not got my pledge in writing, and the 500 men in Parliament in England will laugh at it as no written paper can be produced." [2]   After some discussion the King told Edwards that he would not put any of the prisoners to death, but would only confiscate their property. Money was required to reward the robber chiefs who had joined Tharrawaddy for the sake of plunder: they were also displeased with Burney because his intervention had saved Ava from sack, and deprived them of the gold and ruby rings which they had desired to plunder.[2]

Tharrawaddy, however, did not keep his word.   Between 14 and 20 April, he released the old Padien or Legain Woongyi.[3]

---

[1] *Ibid*. par. 28.
[2] *Ibid*. pars. 29, 30.
[3] He was one of the negociators of the Yandabo Treaty.

the Woondouk Mahasithu,[1] the Myawadi Woongyee, and about 14 others, but their properties were confiscated. Within three weeks' time, however, most of those who were released, including the Myawadi Woongyee, were rejailed. On 24 April, the Aenda Bo and the Woondauk Maung Khan Ye were secretly put to death in the jail. Burney addressed a letter to the King protesting against the violation of his pledge. " The King after reading it," says Burney, " threw it down in anger, crying out, it is my royal prerogative to put to death any of my subjects whom I find guilty of crime. I ordered these men to be executed and I shall order one more individual, the Atwen Woon Maung Ba Youk,[2] to suffer in the same manner, on the day I take my seat on the Throne." [3] These three men were particularly obnoxious to Tharrawaddy, because they had advised Menthagyee to demand the surrender of Nga Yé in the month of February; also they were suspicious at that time of the Prince's preparations for a rebellion.[3]

On 8 May, three more prisoners were cruelly executed, one of them being the Pinzala Woon, who, says Burney, " was an officer of much energy and activity under the late government and in charge of the district lying about midway between Mogaung and Mouttshobo. He had been very successful in suppressing robberies and was a terror to some of the robber Chiefs who are in the service of the present King and to please whom he is generally said to have been put to death." [4]

Tharrawaddy was not satisfied with mere executions of officers. Menthagyee's wife and daughters were most horribly tortured. Burney protested to the King in the presence of the officer who was in charge of those unfortunate women, and although that officer promised to desist from his cruel proceedings, the King said, " Yes, these hat wearing people cannot bear to see or hear of women being beaten or maltreated." [5]

---

[1] He was the principal envoy to Calcutta, 1831-1833.
[2] He was also one of the negociators of the Yandabo Treaty in which he is styled, Shwe Zoon Woon.
[3] India Political Consultations Range 194, Vol. 41, Burney's Letter. 24 May, 1837, pars. 31, 32, 35, 36, 40, 55.
[4] Ibid. par. 52.
[5] Ibid. par. 37.

Tharrawaddy appointed Thait-ten-gyeh President of the Hlutdaw. The new Woongyees, Atwenwoons, Woondauks, etc., were largely drawn from his supporters the robber chiefs. Maung Kha and Maung See Nyo the Woongyees were "coarse ill-informed characters." Most of the other officers were of the same type, filled with pride and insolence, because of their success and sudden elevation. Thait-ten-gyeh possessed energy, but he had no experience and was overbearing in his manners. Maung Douk-gyeh, one of the new Woondauks, was intelligent, but rapacious and unprincipled. Maung Shwe Zah, one of the Atwenwoons, was a well known criminal, and had escaped from the British jail in Moulmein. He was now one of the most confidential attendants of the King and was in charge of the tortures inflicted upon the family of the ex-Menthagyee. Very few of the new King's officers were reputable or well-informed men or used to public business: one such was Woondouk Gale of the old government who had through bribery escaped the fate of his colleagues. Lanciago was appointed the Chief Customs Officer at Rangoon.[1]

The revolution and particularly the character of the new government encouraged disorders in the country. Everywhere, except in the immediate neighbourhood of the caiptal, there was general disorganization. Dacoits as well as the new King's followers began to plunder merchant boats on the river; only in Rangoon no disturbances broke out. The new government took vigorous measures to put a stop to the pillage and plunder, and executed some 25 of their own men for the offence. In spite of this action, however, all the villages between Moksobo and Ava were burnt down or otherwise destroyed, and the country from Pagan upwards was laid waste by marauders. The inhabitants of the villages between Kyauk-ta-loun and the eastern and southern walls of Ava fled, and their houses were plundered, while a great many houses in the capital itself suffered in the same manner; but not a single house occupied by a foreign trader was molested except in Amarapura, where all the

[1] *Ibid.* pars. 31, 33, 39.

Arakan traders were plundered of the whole of their property. According to Burney, soldiers slaughtered cattle and ate them in spite of their Buddhist faith.[1]

Many of those who had previously sympathised with Tharrawaddy now realized their mistake. The common people began to complain that they had gained nothing by the change, but that on the other hand trade had been brought to a standstill, and distress had increased. Even Armenian merchants began to say openly, "that the late government was infinitely superior to the present one, that it possessed some idea of property and desire of doing justice."[2] On the other hand, Burney's attempt to prevent the civil war, and later to bring about a reconciliation, gained him much influence not only with the people in general but with the new King himself and the respectable portion of his followers. It was largely due to Burney's influence that Tharrawaddy was prevented from carrying out a general massacre of the Ministers and officers of the old King, as well as the sack of Ava. Massacres or murders, at least on a small scale, were the normal accompaniments of succession to the throne or usurpation of the throne in Burma. When Bagyidaw came to the throne in 1819, about 200 people had been executed.[3]

On 30 April, proclamations were made throughout the Kingdom that Bagyidaw had resigned the throne to his younger brother. The same day the ex-King was removed from the Palace to a mat building. Crowds gathered to see him pass, and openly expressed pity and regret. His son, the Tsakyamen was not disturbed in any way; even his jagirs were confirmed to him. Thait-ten-gyeh, on the day of the Royal proclamation, was created the new Menthagyee.[4]

[1] *Ibid.* par. 34.
[2] *Ibid.* pars. 46, 60.
[3] *Ibid.* par. 66.
[4] *Ibid.* pars. 45, 46.

CHAPTER X

FROM THE ACCESSION OF THARRAWADDY TO THE FINAL DEPARTURE OF BURNEY FROM AVA; OR, THARRAWADDY AND THE PROBLEM OF THE BRITISH TREATIES.

Tharrawaddy was now the King of Burma. His character and personality have already been observed, but now that he was King a change took place in his general demeanour and outlook. This became especially evident in his relations with the British Residency. Burney enjoyed one privilege which was denied him during the previous reign, namely, that of personal and direct conversation with the King on public affairs. It is doubtful, however, if this privilege was a help. The new King was fully aware of the advantages of cultivating a friendly alliance with the British Government, and in his early days had expressed himself accordingly, but he disliked business, and was wholly unused to it.[1] He was unable, therefore, to handle public affairs in a business like manner, and ultimately decided to have nothing to do with the British Residency.

The British Government in Tenasserim had been endeavouring to develop the trade of Moulmein. With this object in view, Dr. Richardson had explored in 1829 the region from Moulmein as far as Laboung near Zimme. In 1834 and again in 1835 he had journeyed to the same place by two different routes in order to study commercial possibilities. In 1837 he visited Zimme, and thence he moved northwards through the

---

[1] India Political Consultations Range 194, Vol. 41. Burney's Letter, 24 May, 1837, par. 33. At one time Burney complained to Tharrawaddy concerning the plunder by the King's officers of a boat in which were two of the Resident's servants. " The King lost his temper and said that he had no idea of the cares of sovereignty, that he would have been happier had he been left alone to amuse himself in his garden at Ava as Prince of Tharawadi and that he wished he was dead." He promised, however, to punish those who were guilty of the offence. *Ibid.* par. 31.

Shan Sawbwaships of Mokme, Mone, and Nyaung Yuwe.[1]
On 24 April, 1837, Burney received a letter from Richardson,
dated 18 April, reporting his arrival at Nyaung Yuwe, a week's
journey from Ava, and requesting for an order from the new
Government that the Sawbwa of Nyaung Yuwe might furnish
him with an escort for his journey to Ava, the country intervening being infested with robbers.[2]

On the morning of 25 April, Burney called at the Hlutdaw
to see Thait-ten-gyeh, but he was kept waiting for an hour, and
since the Prince's followers were inclined to be insolent, he
returned without an interview. Burney next sent his interpreter
to the Prince, requesting for orders to Nyoung Yuwe that an
escort might be supplied to Dr. Richardson. The Prince offered
an apology for the rude behaviour of his attendants, but made
the following strange reply to Burney's request: " He cannot
be allowed to come here, and must go back by the way he
came." [3]

In the evening Burney waited upon the King, who told him
that Richardson had not come by an established road and that
there was no precedent for allowing an English officer to come
to Ava by that route. " To my representation," says Burney,
" that the late government had agreed to let Dr. Richardson
come on from Moneh, that that officer is in charge of several
traders from Moulmein, and that according to the first article
of Mr. Crawfurd's treaty merchants with an English pass have
a right to go to any part of the Burmese Empire, the King cried
out, Do not refer to any acts of the late government, and I have
nothing to say to any treaties which they may have entered
into." [3] Burney made a long explanation to prove that the
treaties subsisting between the two states were not personal with
the late King, but perpetual with the Burmese nation by whomsoever governed, and that the provisions of the treaties were

---

[1] *Yule,* Mission to the Court of Ava, 1855.
[2] India Political Consultations Range 194, Vol. 41. Burney's Letter,
    24 May, 1837, par. 37.
[3] *Ibid.* par. 38.

equally binding upon succeeding Governor-Generals as upon
Lord Amherst who concluded them.   The King failed to comprehend the subject, and shortly replied, " That may be the
English custom, but it is not the Burmese, and we can now
enter into a new alliance of friendship." [1]

On another occasion Burney told the King that it would
be impossible for Richardson to return to Moulmein by the
route he had come.   The King said, " I know why English officers like being sent on long journeys, because they always get
an increase of pay while so employed.   I will consult with
my Ministers and let you know bye and bye if Dr. Richardson
can be allowed to come on to Ava." [2]

On 27 April, the King informed Burney that Richardson
would be allowed to come to Ava, if the Resident made an
application to say that Richardson had trespassed, and also
asked for forgiveness, and agreed not to trespass into Burmese territory again.   Burney felt mortified at this arrogant
tone of the King, but he smothered his feelings and made one
more attempt to secure Richardson from his uncomfortable
and helpless situation at Nyoung Yuwe.   On 28 April, accordingly, he informed the King that Richardson had not travelled
on his own authority but at the orders of the Commissioner of
Tenasserim and the Governor-General of India, and in accordance with the friendly alliance subsisting between the two
nations, " and that it was impossible for me to state that
Dr. Richardson had committed a trespass or was wrong in
coming by such a route, because such a language, to say the
least, would be disrespectful to the Governor-General as well
as to Mr. Blundell.". [3]   Burney, however, offered to report to

---

[1] *Ibid.* par. 38.   Burney explains in the same place that the King
was not in good humour at the time, otherwise he would have
corrected him by pointing out that the same was the Burmese
custom, *e.g.* a treaty was made in 1769 between Burma and
China, and it was acknowledged by all the succeeding Kings of
Burma, and the treaty was referred to in every letter which
passed between the two sovereigns.   On 22 May, however,
Burney mentioned this treaty to the King.   See p. 293.

[2] *Ibid.*

[3] *Ibid.* pars. 41, 42.   Blundell was the Commissioner of Tenasserim
at this time.

Calcutta and Moulmein the King's wishes, that no mission be sent in future to the Shan country without previously obtaining the permission of the Government of Burma.   The King received this communication in the most offensive manner, charged Burney with catching at trifles, and said, " Well, if Col. Burney will not write as I require, let him go to those with whom the English made their Treaties." [1]

The next day Thait-ten-gyeh, the new Menthagyee, invited Burney to the Hlutdaw to consider the case of Richardson. Burney took full advantage of this opportunity and declared strongly his sentiments regarding the King's expressed desire of denying the validity of the treaties subsisting between the two countries, and explained to them that it was a most important question as the British Resident had no right to be at Ava except on the faith of the Treaty of Yandabo. [2]

On 2 May, the Hlutdaw informed Burney that the King had agreed to allow Richardson to come to Ava, but that in future no British officers should be sent to the Shan country. " When asked what is the King's opinion now in respect to our treaties, the Woondouk Maung Dout Gyeh begged that that question should not be mooted.   It was pointed out to him that it was the King who had mooted it and not I who never entertained a doubt on the matter.   He then begged that the subject should not further be agitated at present, and stated that the circumstance of the King having agreed to allow Richardson to come to Ava notwithstanding my refusal to write such a letter as His Majesty required, and the fact of my continuing to reside at Ava, ought to be considered by me as proofs that the treaties between the English and Burmese are acknowledged to be still in force." [3]

Burney had won the point in connection with Richardson, but he began to be oppressed with a fresh problem, namely, the new King's attitude towards the Treaties.   " Had I consulted my

[1] *Ibid*. par. 42.
[2] *Ibid*. par. 45.
[3] *Ibid*. par. 48.

private feelings," he wrote, " I own, after the above cited instances of the King's want of faith, and attempt to bully me, I should have declined all intercourse with him excepting what was indispensable, but reflecting that such a line of conduct would probably irritate him, I determined on the 3rd instant (3 May) to pay His Majesty another visit." [1]   On this occasion Burney was received with marked kindness and attention. The King himself " brought out some little presents which he requested me to give in his name to my children, asked me whether I had ever inspected the inside of the palace at Ava, and desired Maung Thein Za to take me all over it, and spoke on a variety of topics with much affability, expressing his desire to construct a canal between Kyouk Myoung and Mouttshobo and to introduce a regular coinage in Burmah etc. In the course of conversation also, he laughingly cited as an instance of the folly of the late Government, that the first thing they did when they commenced the late war with us, and before they knew if they could beat us, was to appoint different officers to be Governors of Bengal, Madras, Bombay, and other places in India."[2]

When a Prince, Tharrawaddy, in his conversations with Burney had given expression to liberal sentiments, and had condemned the law against the exportation of precious metals from the country. He had even ridiculed the conduct of the late Ministers objecting to Christian missionaries and British trade agents moving about in the country, but now he was altogether a changed man.[3] It was not easy to transact business with him, " because he is so extremely uncertain and fickle : one hour, good-humoured, affable and attentive, the next harsh, peremptory and inconsiderate. His former mode of life, and by the character of those with whom he usually associated, I fear, we shall be obliged to form rather an unfavourable opinion of his principles. He indulged in spiritous liquors and gambling, and his house was much resorted to by the dissolute

[1] *Ibid.* par. 49.
[2] *Ibid.*
[3] *Ibid.* par. 50.

and disreputable. All the foreigners also who now are or who ever were engaged in his service were notorious for bad character......; to the prominent vices of Burmah deceit, falsehood and ingratitude, he appears to me to add some of the vices of those foreigners with whom he has associated, cunning and plausibility. He is further subject to fits of ungovernable passion, particularly when heated with liquor at which times also he is cruel and sanguinary."[1]

On 15 May, Bayfield arrived from the Assam frontier accompanied by Dr. Griffith, the Calcutta naturalist. The King readily granted permission to Griffith to botanize among the Sagaing hills. Burney explained to the King that Griffith was a scientific man, and would be happy to visit the mines and make a full report of their condition, and the best mode of working them. The King's suspicions were immediately roused and he avoided the subject.[2]

Reflecting upon the newly created situation, Burney felt persuaded that it would be best to retire from Ava to Rangoon so as to avoid conflict with the King whose head was turned and who was daily proving himself to be more offensive towards the Residency. "The truth is," says Burney, "His Majesty's military advisers are not yet prepared to quarrel with us. The Treaties which we forced upon the Burmese are no doubt viewed by the present as well as the late Government with much vexation and mortification, and as the leading members of the present Government consist of military officers puffed up with their own success and ideas of their immediately thirsting for plunder and profoundly ignorant, some early attempt may be made to shake off these irksome Treaties. The King himself desires to follow the example of Alompra as much as he can, and his Court and Government resemble in many points those of his ancestor. I am privately informed that his Chiefs are offering to recover for him all the territory ceded to us by what they consider the late imbecile government, but that the

---

[1] *Ibid.* par. 50.
[2] *Ibid.* pars. 60, 62.

present Burmese year which commenced on the 13th ultimo is considered unlucky, and that the next year 1200 will according to the astrologers be a propitious one for engaging in war." [1] Tharrawaddy, however, with all his bluster, was fully alive to the danger of coming into collision with the British, and in spite of his spectacular military displays, kept himself always on the safe side of peace.

Burney also felt strongly the King's violation of his pledge not to hurt any one in Ava, and thought his presence at the capital would no longer be of any use. Besides, the country was still in a most unsettled state and trade was languishing. Under these circumstances he thought it most judicious to withdraw the Residency for a time, until the new Government settled down to order and quiet. He decided for this purpose to avail himself of the too well founded plea of indisposition. Accordingly on 12 May, Burney wrote to the King desiring permission to retire to Rangoon for a time for change of climate. The King immediately pounced upon the opportunity, sent a civil answer agreeing to the proposal, and added, " that if the two countries, however, desired to be friends they could do so without stationing officers at each other's capital, and that he well knew as I was an officer of high rank and character much would depend hereafter upon what I might report." [2]

From this time onward, Burney having committed himself at least to the temporary removal of the Residency to Rangoon, the King began publicly to express his determination not to submit, as he put it, to the humiliation of a British Resident being imposed upon him. To induce Burney to leave Ava quickly, he even desired to confer a Burmese title upon him. At the same time he requested Burney to inform the American missionaries " that they must not circulate any more religious tracts in this country, and that if they do so after this warning he will not act like the late Government, but will take care and see his order duly obeyed. He objected also to my taking

[1] *Ibid.* par. 48.
[2] *Ibid.* par. 56.

facsimiles of some ancient inscriptions at Tsagain and Ava for which a learned gentleman at Paris has applied to me, and he founded his objection on a curious reason that these inscriptions contain religious truths and doctrines which foreigners might not undersand and therefore be likely to turn into ridicule." [1]

On 16 May, the King personally advised Burney to remove the Residency to Rangoon, and to return to his capital after the country had settled down to normal conditions again. He also desired the Resident to correspond with him from Rangoon meanwhile.[2] On 17 May, the King in open Court declared, "that he had nothing to say to the Treaties which had been concluded with the English in the reign of his Brother."[3] On 22 May, Burney, while discussing the question of custom duties at Rangoon, happened to make a reference to the Treaty of Yandabo and to the Commercial Treaty; the King observed, "that he would have nothing to say to those treaties and desired no reference should ever be made to them, that they are a matter of reproach and shame to the Burmese, that the English frightened the Burmese officers into signing them, and now always referred to them when they desired to shame the Burmese into granting anything which they desired." [4]

"I begged," says Burney, "His Majesty would listen to me and take this subject into better consideration before he made up his mind upon it. I then represented that what His Majesty had just been pleased to observe, would throw a very heavy responsibility upon me who am charged with the duty of preventing any difference between the two countries, that I have an earnest desire to see a continuance of peace and harmony between the Burmese and English, and that if His Majesty does not like the treaties concluded in the reign of his brother, I would advise him to send an embassy to Bengal to express his wishes and propose to conclude a new treaty of peace and

[1] *Ibid.* par. 57.
[2] *Ibid.* par. 60.
[3] *Ibid.* par. 61.
[4] *Ibid.* par. 65.

friendship." [1] The King replied, " that he could see no occasion for any Treaty, that merchants and traders only draw up written Papers and documents, that such individuals when they differ about the meaning or construction of any point can refer to others to decide it, which states cannot do, and that as there are several articles in the Treaty of Yandaboo which if referred to, would create a difference of opinion and quarrel, he thought the best plan is to throw aside these treaties and have no written engagements." [1]

Burney " pointed out that there is nothing clearer among civilized states than that treaties are not annulled by the death or removal of the King in whose reign they have been executed, and that the Burmese themselves still acknowledge the treaty which they made with the Chinese in 1769, engaging that Envoys shall be sent by each state to the other once in ten years. The King said that the Burmese and Chinese had made a simple engagement only and had not executed a written one. I referred him to the Burmese Yazawin History which shews that a regular instrument was drawn up in the names of a certain number of Chinese and Burmese officers. He also said that treaties are made only after a war, and I told him that a treaty was made between Alompra and an English Envoy at a time when there had been no war or dispute between the two states." [1]

During the conversation the King was in excellent good humour, but he paid little attention to Burney's representations, and showed clearly that he would not recognize the treaties concluded in the reign of Bagyidaw. [2] There were rumours afloat that the King would even demand the restoration of all territory ceded by the treaty of Yandabo, and place the British Residency under restraint until the demand was complied with. [3]

On 28 May, Griffith left Ava for Rangoon, and on 29 May, Richardson arrived at the capital from Nyoung Yuwe. [4] On 2

[1] *Ibid.* par. 65.
[2] *Ibid.*
[3] India Secret Consultations Vol. 8, Burney's Letter, Rangoon, 12 July, 1837, par. 2.
[4] *Ibid.* pars. 4, 5.

June, news arrived that a British man-of-war had entered the mouth of the Rangoon River. The Governor of Rangoon in much alarm, had sent an exaggerated report to the King concerning the arrival of the warship, so Burney thought it best to send his clerk to the Royal presence to explain matters. His Majesty observed in an imperious tone, " Rangoon is a port open to vessels of all nations, and English men-of-war may of course come there. If they come as friends they shall be treated as such, but if to fight we can fight too." [1] The King also sent a message to Burney to say that he had not been conquered as the late monarch was, so that he would not submit to any dictation from the British Resident; and further " that he is a King who has none but the gods over him, that he is not responsible to any one like the King of England, and that he possesses the power to issue any orders, and to put any one to death at a moment's notice, and that for these reasons he thinks it will be best for English officers to avoid communicating directly with him in matters of business, and to address him always through the Governor of Rangoon." [1]

Perhaps overcome by a sense of his autocratic powers, Tharrawaddy gave a practical form to them by ordering on the same day (2 June) the execution of Maung Boo who was one of the most able and faithful military officers of Bagyidaw. He was executed in a most shameful and cruel manner. " This unfortunate man," says Burney, " bore a most excellent character, being highly respected in private life, and having proved himself a good soldier and servant of the late King; and he conducted himself with manliness and great fortitude during the two evenings on which his barbarous executioners were harassing his feelings and making him and his family pay them money......; his only crime was that of having been true to the oath of allegiance which he had taken to the late King of Ava......" [2]

---

[1] *Ibid.* par. 8.
[2] *Ibid.* par. 9.

At about this time also a trick was played upon the ex-Menthagyee and his fellow-prisoners. They were given to believe that the King had decided to release them, and a few prisoners were released as a feint. The relatives of the unfortunate men then collected some 3000 ticals and gave them to Woondouk Maung Doutgyeh in anticipation of the release. Maung Doutgyeh, however, not only did not release them, but on the other hand re-imprisoned those who had been released as a feint. " His Majesty laughed very heartily " when he heard of this trick played upon the prisoners.[1]

On 6 June, the Resident, Bayfield, and Richardson had an audience with the King. Burney spoke of the Assam frontier, when the King heatedly protested against the British annexation of Burmese territory, and asked, " Is it right and proper for you to set aside a long line of Kings and appropriate Assam to yourselves ? " Burney replied that the British had conquered Assam from the Burmese more than 10 years ago, and that the arrangement could not now be questioned. The King said " that the Burmese officers had been frightened into signing the treaty of Yandaboo, and that it contained everything for the English and nothing for the Burmese, that some of its articles were too hard, that the late Government had never shown him the whole of it, which he had only lately seen, and that at all events the English had not conquered him or made the treaty with him, and that he was determined to have nothing to say to it." Burney replied that it was the custom of war for the conqueror to force or frighten the conquered into signing whatever he desired; that if the King desired a modification in some of the articles of the Treaty, the proper and established course would be to send an embassy to Bengal; and finally that an engagement entered into by two parties can never be annulled at the option of one of them.[2]

The King sharply answered, " I will not send an embassy to Bengal; if I send one it shall be to the King of England. I

---

[1] *Ibid.* par. 10.
[2] *Ibid.* par. 12.

know nothing of Goombhanee[1] (Governor-General) and will not acknowledge him. He is an officer who receives pay and is not a King. Let him correspond with his equal the Governor of Rangoon. I will receive no communication from him or in his name."[2]   Burney pointed out that the King of England himself may be said to receive pay from Parliament, that the same Parliament which controls the King also empowers the Governor-General to make war and treaties of peace, powers which Burmese Governors did not enjoy, and that the Governor-General has always corresponded directly with crowned heads. The Resident feared the King would be annoyed at the explanation, and so requested him not to be angry, but the King said, "You may say whatever you like, I will not be angry with you."[2]

Burney further argued that he himself as Resident was a representative of the Governor-General, and if the Treaty of Yandabo was not acknowledged, then neither he nor any other British officer could reside in Ava. He illustrated his point by saying, "that the Governor-General was the Tree and that I was its shadow only, and that if the King would not see the Tree I could not tell how he could see the shadow." The King laughed, as did all his courtiers, and replied, "I will leave the Tree alone; but I desire to see it bear the same fruit as it did in the time of my ancestor Alompra and of my grandfather. I am determined to place the relations between the two countries on precisely the same footing as they were previous to the reign of the late King who committed a blunder in going to war with you, and all of those acts I wish to have annulled and forgotten. If I had a desire to go to war with you I would order you to quit the capital, but I will not tell Mr. Bayfield or you to go or stay, you may stay or go, just as you please. If

---

[1] A Burmese corruption of the term "Company"; it was applied to the Governor-General as well as to the British Commander-in-Chief.
[2] India Secret Consultations Vol. 8, Burney's Letter, Rangoon, 12 July, 1837, par. 12.

you stay I will make use of you, and if you want more officers I will send for them; but then you must all stay here not upon a treaty as a matter of right, but dependent upon my will in the same manner as Col. Symes and Capt. Canning came to this country in the time of my grandfather." [1]

Richardson said that the Treaties could not be annulled in the manner proposed, and His Majesty replied " that he would have nothing to say to them, that they had not been made by him, and that we had never conquered him, and asked, if any breach of the Treaties had been committed by either party who could decide between them." Burney said that a war generally decided it. The King then observed, that he would appeal to the Kings of France, Persia, Turkey, and Siam. The Resident said that if the King rejected the treaties, then his enemies would think that he was also disputing the territory ceded to the British by the treaty of Yandabo. At this the King laughed, and said, " Oh, no, I have no intention of seizing those countries from you." [1]

Tharrawaddy was extremely frank and blunt in the way he expressed himself, but at times he could assume very engaging manners. After the foregoing conversation he presented a ruby ring each to Burney, Bayfield, and Richardson, and showed them the Crown jewels of Ava taken from his brother: one sapphire was very beautiful, about the size of a duck's egg.[1] On 7 June, Burney brought to the King's notice an outrage committed by robbers upon the Residency servants while they were in a boat, and Tharrawaddy liberally gave 1000 ticals to be .distributed among the victims.[2]

It has already been mentioned how Burney had on 12 May, committed himself to quitting Ava. Later conversations with the King further convinced him that it would be wise to retire to Rangoon. His reasons for leaving Ava were based upon three causes:— First, the King and his officers were showing signs of a warlike attitude, so that it would be wise not to provoke them

---

[1] *Ibid.*
[2] *Ibid.* pars. 16, 17.

further by his presence at the capital; second, it was not much use his remaining in Ava, since there was great disorder in the country and trade was hampered; also he had not been able to prevent the King from ill-treating and executing the old Ministers; and third, the unfriendly and aggressive attitude of the King towards the Treaties as well as towards the British. Burney, however, proposed to leave behind him Bayfield and a portion of the Residency, so that touch with the new Burmese Government might not be lost. The King had decided to make Kyauk-Myaung his capital, and Bayfield was to accompany him to that place. Tharrawaddy, however, was not willing to agree to this arrangement. On 6 June, Burney told the King of the proposed change, and hoped that Bayfield and party would be given suitable accommodation at Kyauk-Myaung. The King made no reply.[1]

On 7 June, the King held a full Court, which Edwards the Clerk attended. "The King took the opportunity of expressing himself in the most offensive manner regarding the Governor-General of India. He ridiculed the idea of His Lordship possessing any real power or authority, and said, he knew nothing of the Governor-General or of any office or appointments conferred by him; that the Burmese Governor of Bhamo had also Tsaubwas under him and was just as great a man as the Governor-General, and that he would acknowledge no titles or official designations but such as were conferred by the King of England; that he knew nothing of the titles of Residents and Assistants to the Resident, but that he knew I was Colonel and my Assistant a doctor, and he would only call us by such titles and by no others." [2] Edwards delivered a message to the King from Burney, requesting to know if Bayfield and his escort of sepoys could accompany His Majesty to Kyauk-Myaung, and if they would be provided with suitable accommodation. The King immediately broke out, " What, are you going to assume over me with sepoys? I told Mr. Bayfield only

[1] *Ibid.* par. 13.
[2] *Ibid.* par. 17.

to accompany me and not any of the sepoys or their officer. Why do they not go down to Rangoon?".[1]

On 9 June, it being the eve of Tharrawaddy's departure for Kyauk-Myaung, Burney and company waited upon His Majesty to take leave of him. The Resident showed regret that the King should have spoken so disparagingly of the Governor-General in open Court, and explained that the latter enjoyed Kingly powers. Tharrawaddy replied, " Yes, the Woongyee of Rangoon is a greater man, he is responsible to me only — to one man, but your Governor-General is responsible to 500 men, to your Parliament in England, and the Woongyee also when he goes out in state is preceded and followed by bodies of Troops which none of the Princes even at Ava but the King only can have." Burney requested the King to refer to the chronicles of his ancestor Alaungpaya, and he would see that the monarch wrote in his own name to the Governor of Bengal, and also received letters from him. The King replied, " True, you know these things better than Burmese officers, and I will not object to the Governor-General writing to me in the same manner as Alompra was written to."[2] The Governors of Madras and Bengal did write to Alaungpaya, but before the letters were read to the King they were converted into abject petitions by Burmese translators, so that Tharrawaddy's desire was, that, the Governor-General should not address him on terms of equality, but as a petitioner.[2]

Burney submitted to the King that he had been striving to maintain friendship between the two states for the past seven years, and that he would be very sorry if a rupture took place after his departure. He also declared that in Calcutta he would tell the Governor-General of the nature of the King's speeches and sentiments on the relations with the British. His Majesty replied, " My brother's reign was a bad one, and I only desire to remove all the evils thus produced, and to replace everything in the excellent condition in which it was in the reigns of my grandfather and ancestor Alompra."[2]

[1] *Ibid.* par. 17.
[2] *Ibid.* par. 20.

As to Bayfield and his escort, the King said, "*If the sepoys are not to stay here on the strength of the Treaty* I have no objection to their remaining or to your having 3 or 400 more of them, and Mr. Bayfield may remain here too, but not in virtue of the Treaty of which I will not hear another word. However as it will not be right to separate him from the sepoys let them all stay at Ava for the present, and bye and bye when I have marked out a site for the foreign merchants at Kyouk Myoung, Mr. Bayfield may come up and live with them there." The King also made it clear that he would not acknowledge Bayfield as a public officer under the Treaty. " I will have nothing to say to the treaties," he said, " I will not acknowledge or grant anything to which you may found your right upon them, but in everything else you shall be treated much better than you ever were before." [1] Thus Tharrawaddy made up his mind to shake himself free of the treaties and at the same time endeavour to maintain peace with the British. He stuck fast to this policy throughout his reign.

Burney had also some talk with the King about the dispute concerning the Assam-Burma boundary. The King said that he did not wish to take a single inch of British territory, and he would not allow the English to take a single inch of his territory, and that the Yazawin would show the correct boundary. But when Burney declared that the ancient history of Assam agreed with the present boundary fixed by the British, the King changed his ground, and said, that histories being human compilations were unreliable, and that interpolations were often made to please reigning sovereigns. The King then proceeded to expound a theory of his own by which the boundary between two countries can be discovered: He said "that the limits of every country are marked by certain natural appearances, and that the boundaries of Burma in every direction are well known by the trees on the frontier line growing in a very peculiar manner, those within Burmah growing with an inclination towards Burmah, and those within their neighbours' territory

[1] *Ibid.* par. 21.

bending towards that territory."[1]   Burney and his companions might simply have smiled at the King's new discovery. It is doubtful, however, if the King was really serious about his theory.

On parting, the King was very kind and gracious; he particularly requested Burney to procure him some gardeners and fire engines from Calcutta.[2]

Burney had been contemplating the removal of the Residency to Rangoon ever since the outbreak of the revolution in Ava. When the Indian Government received full information of the developments in Ava, the Governor-General-in-Council highly approved of Burney's conduct, and praised him in no uncertain terms for his energy, judgment, and humanity; but in two things his action was disapproved of. First, that the Resident took the attitude of the new King towards the treaties too seriously, and unnecessarily discussed the question with him; and that the King because of his success against his brother had become so intoxicated with his power that he was incapable of serious discussion. Second, that the Resident's decision to remove the Residency was particularly regretted. The Government recognized the difficulties because of the King's cruelties in violation of his solemn pledge, the unsettled state of the country, and the breakdown of trade; but argued, and rightly so, " that though all these evils might be mitigated by your presence they could hardly fail of being aggravated by your retirement. It is at the present juncture of the highest consequence that accurate information should reach the Governor-General-in-Council of everything that occurs in Ava, of the value indeed to us of that provision of the treaty which authorizes our keeping a Resident at the Burmese Court.......
if the protection of the Residency should be removed during times of so much trouble there is every reason to fear that the interests of the English and others settled in Ava will materially suffer."[3]

---

[1] *Ibid.* par. 23.
[2] *Ibid.* par. 25.
[3] India Political Consultations Range 194, Vol. 41, Letter, dated 1 July, 1837, Consultations 3 July, 1837.

Finally, the Government instructed Burney to attach himself to the King's Court wherever that might be, and that if his health did not permit him to do so, another officer would be appointed to take his place. Meanwhile Bayfield was to be directed by Burney to remain with the King, or to return to the King should he have actually set out on his way to Rangoon.[1]

The above instructions from Calcutta were penned on 1 July, 1837, and did not reach Burney till at the end of the month. Meanwhile, in keeping with his resolve, Burney and the whole Residency had already quitted Ava on 17 June, accompanied by three American missionaries, Kincaid, Simons, and Webb, together with their families. On the way down the river the Resident met with extraordinary want of civility by all provincial officers. There was a general impression around that the Residency had been dismissed by the new King who would soon go to war with the British, so that even the common people were afraid to give assistance to the Resident. But on his arrival in Rangoon, Burney was received with respect by Maung Phi who was in temporary charge of the government at Rangoon. The new Governor, Maung Shwe Meng, arrived from Bilin on 10 July. He was an old acquaintance of Burney and had some knowledge of the power and resources of the British. He received Burney in a very friendly manner.[2]

---

[1] India Political Consultations Range 194, Vol. 41, Letter, dated 1 July, 1837, Consultations 3 July, 1837.
[2] India Secret Consultations Vol. 8, Burney's Letter, Rangoon, 12 July, 1837, pars. 38, 39.

CHAPTER XI

THE AVA REVOLUTION AND THE GOVERNMENT OF INDIA.

The instructions of the Indian Government to its Resident in Burma were to maintain strict neutrality in the event of a civil war in the country. Burney had faithfully carried out the desires of the Governor-General-in-Council. The Governor-General, Lord Auckland, under instructions from the Home Government, was at this time planning to interfere in the affairs of Afghanistan, and this was one reason why he did not wish to be embroiled in any Burmese trouble or war. He, however, wanted to maintain the Residency in Burma and recognize any new government that night establish itself in that country. In the instructions to Burney, dated, 1 July, 1837, the Resident was informed, " that His Lordship can contemplate no event with greater uneasiness than that of a rupture with Ava. The idea of another contest (to say nothing of the calamities of war) must in a financial point of view prove ruinously embarassing, and he expects therefore that every officer entrusted with the conduct of our relations in that quarter will use his utmost exertions to preserve unimpaired the friendly feelings which have subsisted between the two states since the former war, so far as the same can be preserved consistently with the maintenance of our national dignity and honour." [1]

The Governor-General was very anxious to maintain the Residency at the Burmese capital, but as has been noticed, Burney, acting upon his own judgment withdrew with all his suite to Rangoon. From his new headquarters he forwarded to his Government the following observations for consideration of the Governor-General-in-Council:—

[1] India Political Consultations Range 194, Vol. 41, No. 35.

"From the moment the King disappointed the expectations
of his best friends, and shewed that the possession of power had
turned his head, I became satisfied that it would be a judicious
course for me to withdraw the Residency from Ava until he
had settled his Government and appointed some intelligent
Ministers with whom I might transact public business.   I
waited, however, for a month after I had received permission
to retire,[1] and during this time I saw His Majesty daily more
and more intoxicated with his extraordinary success, and as he
had not a single respectable or moderate man near him, I lived
in constant uneasiness that his faithless and savage proceedings
towards the Ministers and Officers of the late King, the
ignorance and insolence of his followers, and the extravagant
and arrogant style of conversation, which he habitually indulged
in, would inevitably force me into a personal collision and
dispute with him, and into leaving Ava with a public quarrel.
There was one principle which I especially endeavoured to lay
down for my guidance during the last two months and it was
this, carefully to avoid saying or doing anything likely to commit my Government for which I had received no communication of a later date than January, and to keep His Lordship-in-
Council at full liberty to settle whatever line of policy or course
of measure he might consider most advisable to adopt after
having full accounts of the altered state of affairs at Ava.
Even after I had resolved to withdraw the Residency, fearing
that His Lordship-in-Council might have deemed the measure
premature, I was willing to take advantage of the want of
boats and leave my Assistant with a portion of the establishment at Ava until such time as I could ascertain the sentiments
of Government.   But the increasing arrogance and pretentions
of the King, his continued determination to consider the treaties
with us annulled, his refusal to acknowledge the rank and power
of the Governor-General, and his declining to consider Mr.
Bayfield as an official agent, who was to reside near him in
virtue of a treaty, and these declarations of his determination

[1] That is, permission from the King of Burma.

and opinions were not made once or twice, or to me only, but repeatedly, publicly, and to every one who approached him, left me no alternative but to try and remove the whole of the Residency at once without waiting for a reply to my dispatch of the 25th May. The manner also in which the King left Ava in charge of a notorious set of robbers, made me feel very doubtful as to the safety from outrage of any portion of the Residency which might remain at the deserted capital. In my numerous discussions with him, I could not, nor indeed would I have been allowed to express myself in such forcible terms as I was often obliged to do to the Ministers of the late King, and as I might have done to his Ministers and Officers if the discussion had taken place with them. Had I assumed a high tone with His Majesty or attempted the language of threat or intimidation, I am certain I should soon have pushed matters to extremities between us. Besides having none but violent unprincipled characters near him, ready to encourage him to break with us, he himself is just now so drunk with success and so confident in his fate and good fortune that he is wholly inaccessible to reason, and has no fear of consequences. I was told by many, and I believe it, that nothing but his personal respect for me, and his belief that I had done him some service during the late disturbances, restrained him from breaking all terms with me at once. Some of his disreputable followers, who could see the Residency from Tsagain, were often attracting his attention to it in the most mischievous manner, and it was remarkable the distinction which he secured always to draw between my personal and my public character, being always kind, attentive, and affable, excepting when public matters were concerned, and then he was imperious, arrogant, and ready to take fire. The numerous reports also which were current throughout the country of my having had a violent quarrel with the King and of his having confined the whole of the Residency and put me in irons, may be fairly taken as proofs of a general impression on the part of the inhabitants that it would be impossible for me to continue on terms with the present King, and that he was not a man to hesitate committing any violence or outrage upon the British Resident. I earnestly hope then,

11

that the Governor-General-of-India-in-Council will approve of my having avoided of what if required, I could most easily have produced, an immediate rupture with the King of Ava, and of my having withdrawn the Residency on a fair and reasonable pretext with the full consent of the King without breaking with him or allowing him to suppose that I was departing with hostile intentions, and particularly without imposing upon our Government the necessity of adopting any measures against His Majesty excepting at whatever time and in whatever manner His Lordship-in-Council may consider most advisable. It can hardly be necessary for me to add here, that I saw no use or advantage to be gained by refuting or replying to any remark which the King made in his flighty and extravagant manner at my different interviews with him. Many of his subjects believe that the sudden acquisition of power has developed the disposition to insanity which has affected several members of his family."[1]

After thus explaining his reasons for retiring from Ava, Burney placed before his Government the following two alternatives as to the line of action to be taken in the relations with Tharrawaddy:—" One is to leave him alone for a time, and see if he will recover his reason and good sense, and if after he has settled his government and appointed intelligent and respectable Ministers, he will hear and follow better counsels, recognize the existing treaties, and allow the British Residency to return and remain with him on the same footing as it was during his Brother's reign..........The other plan is, to decide at once to declare hostilities against His Majesty and frighten or beat him into reason." [2]

In connection with the second alternative, Burney gives the following interesting information concerning the desire of the Burmese Government and of the Burmese people in general to recover their lost reputation in the late war:—

---

[1] India Secret Consultations Vol. 8, Burney's Letter, Rangoon, 12 July, 1837, par. 40.
[2] *Ibid*. pars. 41, 42.

"It is well known that nothing but dire necessity forced the late Government of Ava to agree to the Treaty of Yandaboo, and that it always intended to take the first opportunity of releasing itself from the engagements it had so unwillingly entered into. During my residence at Ava also, all the good which I could do, by cultivating the personal regard and good-will of the Ministers, encouraging increased friendly and commercial intercourse, and shewing the advantages to be derived therefrom, was much more than counterbalanced in the estimation of many of the Burmese by the irritation and sense of degradation produced by my frequent disputes with the Court regarding frontier incursions and demands for the surrender of criminal refugees, and punishment or removal of frontier officers. I was considered not only as a spy but as a dictator set over them......I fear in spite of a kindly feeling being entertained towards me personally, the Residency was as unpopular as the Treaty. One of the charges brought by the new King and his friends against the late Government is that of having yielded too many points to me, and I saw them jealously seek for opportunities to shew that they would not allow me to exercise any influence over them. Most of the present generation of Burmese have either forgotten or never learned the lessons which their last War with us gave their armies. They have all a strong belief in fate, and the fortune of the present King is considered by his followers as extraordinary and invincible. He himself observed one day that the Burmese in the last War with the English would not fight zealously because of the unpopularity of Menthagyeh and the Queen. This is believed by all his followers, who further impute the defeats of the last War to the bad fortune and imbecility of the late King and his government, and confidently look forward to different results in another war under a King possessing the vigorous talents and great good fortune of the present monarch. One universal impression therefore exists not only at Ava, but throughout the country, that the present King has determined to declare war against us for the purpose of recovering the Territories ceded by the Treaty of Yandaboo and restoring the empire of Ava to its former extent of power and dominion." [1] It was also Burney's opinion that Tharrawaddy would not immediately declare war: only he refused to acknowledge the Treaties, and "pretended not to dismiss us, and told us to stay or go, just as we pleased." [2]

Undoubtedly, if Burney himself, or if his health did not permit him, Bayfield had continued to reside in Ava or had accompanied the King to Kyauk-Myaung, the Indian Government would have been kept in touch with important happenings in Burma. It is also possible that if the Resident had hung on to the King, the latter might have ignored him or placed difficulties in the matter of food supplies, residence, mails, etc., and the Governor-General would have had finally to withdraw the Residency. Burney seems to have foreseen these difficulties which later befell his successor Col. Benson, and honourably withdrew to Rangoon. Burney's action was supported by Blundell, Richardson, Bayfield, Adoniram Judson, and Sarkies Manook. [3] But, as has been already noticed, the Governor-General-in-Council disapproved of the proposed retirement of the Resident and instructed him to send Bayfield up north so that he might attach himself to the King's Court.

In order to carry out the wishes of his Government, Burney wrote several letters to the King informing him of the proposed arrangement, that Bayfield should reside near him. [3] He even proposed that Blundell, the Commissioner of Tenasserim, would pay a friendly visit to the King if the latter was willing. His Majesty took no notice whatever of the proposition concerning Bayfield, and with respect to Blundell, he said, " I shall not ask Mr. Blundell to come to me, nor stop him nor tell him not to come. He may come if he likes. He or any other English officer may come in the same manner as they used to do in the time of my grandfather." [4] Under the circumstances, therefore, fearing that Bayfield would not be treated in a suitable manner and would not be allowed to be of any public use, Burney did not send him to Kyauk-Myaung. [4]

[1] *Ibid.* par. 43.
[2] *Ibid.* par. 44.
[3] *Ibid.* Burney's Letter, Rangoon, 1 August, 1837.
[4] *Ibid.* 25, August, 1837.

Tharrawaddy meanwhile was not sitting still: he was importing arms and ammunition, strengthening his frontier garrisons, and recruiting new troops on a large scale in different parts of the country. Burney did not think that there was any prospect of an immediate declaration of war, but felt convinced, that the disgrace and loss imposed by the Treaty of Yandabo upon the country in 1826, had roused intense national hostility against the British, and that as soon as the King would find himself prepared he would make a bid for the recovery of his lost territories. Burney, therefore, on 30 September, 1837, made definite proposals to his Government, suggesting that it was a desirable and opportune moment immediately to attack the new King, and establish British influence in the country on a more extensive scale, and that if the opportunity were missed, when the Government and the country were still in a disorganised condition, it would later be ten times more difficult and expensive to reduce his power. "We should proceed," he wrote, "if forced by the King's obstinacy even as far as to threaten to invade his country, and that we should not neglect the present opportunity of establishing a more extensive influence and control over the Court of Ava, and of placing our relations with this country on a more solid and secure footing......No English officer should be sent to the King until after he has been distinctly made to acknowledge the subsistence of the Treaty, the authority of the Governor-General, and our right to have a Resident stationed permanently near him; and if the King will not do so without our making an extensive military demonstration against him, I think we should not hesitate to adopt such a step. To intimidate him and his Court into terms just now would be most easy when compared with what it will be when the King has reconciled his subjects and increased his means, and when he may take advantage of any occupation which some other power may give our armies in Hindosthan."[1]

In the same letter Burney also told his Government that a war with Burma at that particular time would not be as trouble-

[1] *Ibid.* Burney's Letter. By Hindusthan is meant here Northern India.

some and expensive as the first one had been, that it would most surely secure the British from all future molestation, and not only repay all cost, but relieve Government of the heavy expenses which must otherwise be incurred to maintain the earlier conquests. Finally, Burney gave his opinion from personal experience, that a British officer at the capital would not be able to do much good, if he was there merely on sufferance, and that no officer should be sent at this time, because, if the King were to realize that there was no immediate danger of a British attack, he would become more insolent.[1]

Burney's health was in a failing condition. On 12 October, 1837, he left Rangoon for Moulmein, and on 22 October, he left Moulmein for Calcutta. The British Residency was thus withdrawn from Burma by Burney without orders from the Indian Government. He, however, left Bayfield at Rangoon in charge of British interests in that city, and with definite instructions that he was to be under the authority and direction of the Commissioner of Tenasserim to whom also he was to make all reports.[2]

Burney arrived at Calcutta on 1 November, 1837, and reiterated his opinion that the King of Burma will not accept the Treaties without a show of force, but that if necessary Richardson and McLeod might be sent to Kyauk-Myaung to conciliate him.[3]

While Burney was still at Ava, towards the end of the month of May (1837), the ex-King Bagyidaw sent a messenger to him soliciting the interference of the British Government in his favour; but Burney considered it right and prudent not to encourage such communications. Soon after Burney's arrival at Calcutta, he received a second message of the same nature from Bagyidaw through Maung Shwe Dwot, a Burmese Mahomedan, who had escaped from Kyauk-Myaung to Moul-

[1] *Ibid.*
[2] *Ibid.* Burney's Letter, Ship Mermaid, off Kedgree, 31 October, 1837; Burney's Instructions to Bayfield, Rangoon, 12 October, 1837.
[3] *Ibid.* 15 November, 1837, Burney's Letter, Calcutta, 12 November, 1837.

mein, and whom Tharrawaddy wanted to execute. In his letter
to Burney he professed to have been commissioned by Bagyidaw to induce the British Resident to lay before the Governor-
General his grievances, and to solicit the Government of India
to rescue him from the hands of his faithless brother. Shwe
Dwot was an intelligent man. At one time he was the Shahbunder of Arakan, and in 1813 was commissioned by Bodawpaya to visit Delhi and certain Indian Princes' states for the
purpose, it was supposed, of uniting the principal Indian rulers
in a confederacy against the British. After the war with the
British, he was appointed Collector of Customs, but fell into
disfavour and was dismissed. He was, however, a friend of
Menthagyee and helped him in his commercial speculations.[1]
His letter to Burney, because of its importance and interest is
reproduced below almost in full :—

"..........on seeing me His Majesty (the ex-King)
called me to his presence, and told me that his younger brother
the Prince of Tharrawaddy has not kept to his engagement, but
has taken the throne and kingdom, seized the property, wives
and daughters of the Ministers, executed some of them, and
imprisoned and ill treated others; and that he has not attended
to the agreement entered into with Lt. Col. Burney. His
Majesty, therefore, desired me to wait upon you, and to request
that you will represent the unjustifiable conduct of his brother
to the British Government. If the British Government will
attack him and reinstate His late Majesty on the throne, His
Majesty assures you that he will attend to whatever the British
Government may dictate. If this be delayed, His Majesty fears
poison will be administered to him to cause his death. He
therefore hopes that the Resident Lt. Col. Burney will assist
him and save his life...... I have correctly stated in this letter
whatever His late Majesty desired me to communicate to you." [2]
Burney gave no encouragement to Shwe Dwot, but forwarded

---

[1] *Ibid.* Vol. 10, Consultations 29 November, 1837, Burney's Letter,
Calcutta, 27 November, 1837.

[2] *Ibid*: Shwe Dwot's Letter to Burney, received at Calcutta on 26
November, 1837.

his letter to the Governor-General who approved of Burney's attitude.[1]

It now remains to consider the attitude of the Governor-General-in-Council towards the new King, and towards Burney's proposals as well as his action in withdrawing the Residency not only from Ava but also from Rangoon. When the Government became aware of the attitude of Tharrawaddy towards the Treaties, there was much alarm and excitement at first. It was, however, definitely agreed that war should by all means be avoided. Auckland in his Minute, dated 29 August, 1837, wrote, " To the immediate declaration of War I am directly and unequivocably opposed. Hostile operations of the most decisive character should follow close upon a declaration of War. For these we are not ready, the very seasons would indeed not admit of it even were there not upon other grounds the strongest reasons against such a course (and among these the obvious one that Col. Burney has withdrawn the Residency from Ava by his own voluntary act, and has parted with the King on friendly terms) every consideration of prudence would oppose itself to our thus hastily and violently committing ourselves."[2]

The three members of the Governor-General's Council, Ross, Morrison and Shakespear, entirely agreed with Auckland in his view. Morrison said, " I deprecate War with that state as one of the greatest evils, from which, whatever it might cost, and however successful it might prove, we can derive no ultimate advantages."[3] In the opinion of Shakespear, " No event is more to be deprecated than a war with the Burmese; neither honour nor advantage would be gained by it, while the disasters of the late war, the loss of Troops by the unhealthiness of the climate and the ruinous expenses attending it from which we are only now beginning to recover are still fresh in our recollection."[4]

---

[1] *Ibid.* Consultations 24 January, 1838, Letter from Secretary to Governor-General, Futehpur, 15 December, 1837.
[2] *Ibid.* 8 September, 1837, Vol. 8.
[3] *Ibid.* Col. Morrison's Minute, 1 September, 1837.
[4] *Ibid.* Shakespear's Minute, 1 September, 1837.

Auckland's Government felt strengthened in this decision, because Burney's dispatches impressed them with the fact that Tharrawaddy " was not anxious at least immediately to provoke a rupture with the British Government. His primary object seems to be to set aside the Treaty of Yandaboo without a positive breach of it." [1] Any way the Governor-General was not prepared to take any risks. Tharrawaddy was strengthening his army and defences, and could not be trusted. It was agreed, therefore, to strengthen the troops in Sylhet, Manipur, Suddeya, Bishnath, Dacca, Kyaukpyu, and Moulmein, and to keep them ready for the purpose both of defence as well as of offence.[2] " He is a savage," wrote Auckland, ".... surrounded by the worst of his own subjects and advised by the bad of other countries ......I greatly fear that a rupture may ultimately be forced upon us, and while it must be our anxious care to avert this result, we are also bound at once to consider what should immediately be done for the further guard and securities of the territories which are open to Burmese encroachment." Shakespear concurred with the Governor-General that to a certain extent there should be preparations made for war, but added, " that we should put up with anything short of actual aggression or national insult rather than press matters to a rupture with Ava. The King is ignorant and arrogant, but we are no more called upon to notice the folly and impertinence of a rude uneducated Prince, than a gentleman would be, to require, what is called satisfaction from any low persons who might choose to abuse him. Of our power to chastise the insolence of the King there can be no doubt, but it is questionable whether it would be worth while to dissipate our resources for so unprofitable, so unworthy an object as asserting our superiority over a people who can do us very little harm, and whom we can always keep and check at a very small expense, compared with that of an open war......"

After thus laying down the military policy of the Government, the Governor-General decided to watch further develop-

---

[1] *Ibid.* Government Letter to Burney, 4 September, 1837.
[2] *Ibid.* Governor-General's Memorandum, 8 September, 1837, No. 9.

ments, and act as the situation required. The Government also considered at length the part played by Burney in his relations with the new King and the withdrawal of the Residency from Burma.

The Governor-General was satisfied that Burney's position in Ava after the revolution was one of extreme difficulty, being in daily danger of personal insults, collision, and even open quarrel.[1] But blame was laid upon Burney for raising with the King unpleasant topics when the latter was in an excited state of mind. This action of Burney, it was inferred by Government, was to some extent responsible for the King's provocative and undignified speeches directed towards the Governor-General and his government. The Government did not feel disposed at attach too much weight to the unguarded expressions of the King who at the time was intoxicated with success. Burney, in the opinion of Government, should have shown an attitude of greater reserve, discretion, and quiet firmness, upon all occasions. Besides, Government felt, that in some cases the reports received by Burney, concerning the strong language used by the King, were second hand (e.g. the reports made by Edwards), and so were not quite reliable; and that it was not a desirable practice to send such a subordinate as his clerk to confer with the King.[2]

Second, the Government unequivocally and decidedly rejected Burney's suggestion of war, and instructed him to " take special care to act so as to cause no unnecessary excitements. You will maintain a friendly but dignified tone with the Burmese officers, and without raising the question yourself, you will, when it is raised by others, hold the most decided language as to the integrity of our frontiers. You will avoid of all direct controversy where it is not forced upon you, and you will regulate your communications with the King in such a manner as may be least likely to provoke collision, but at the same time to convey the distinct impression that whilst desirous to main-

[1] *Ibid.* Auckland's Minute, 29 August, 1837.
[2] *Ibid.* Government Dispatch to Burney, 4 September, 1837.

tain peace the British Government is yet resolved to uphold all its rights and possessions, and prepared to resist acts of aggression in any quarter. His Lordship-in-Council trusts to your discretion for stating all this in language unaccompanied with offensive menace, and he is not without hope, that it may be put in such form, as without imposing upon the King the necessity of retracting offensive expressions or of appearing too abruptly to descend from the height of his pride, may lead to something more of moderation in his words and in his actions."[1]

Meanwhile, Burney had withdrawn from Rangoon to Moulmein, and on 1 November, he arrived at Calcutta. He had received permission to return to Calcutta[2], but Government had also instructed him to send Bayfield to Kyauk-Myaung to act there as Resident. Burney, however, considered it unsafe for Bayfield to go up north, and placed him in charge of British interests in Rangoon, but under the orders of the Commissioner of Tenasserim. Thus legally the Residency was withdrawn from Burma. The Governor-General-in-Council disapproved of Burney's action in "transferring the Residency to Moulmein" as Government put it, "and placing Dr. Bayfield your assistant in direct subordination to Mr. Blundell an officer holding a separate responsible charge beyond the frontiers of Ava."[3] In the opinion of Government, Bayfield should have been left in charge of the Residency at Rangoon and under the direct control of the Governor-General. Burney's arrangement was summarily cancelled: Bayfield was to be at Rangoon not in subordination to Blundell, but as Acting Resident, and to hold communications directly with the Government of India.[3] Thus the Residency was re-established in Burma.

Burney, upon his arrival in Calcutta, again recommended that the Burmese King should be intimidated and brought to his senses by means of military force. Government refused to

[1] *Ibid.* Government Dispatch to Burney, 4 September, 1837.
[2] *Ibid.*
[3] *Ibid.* Government dispatch to Burney, 6 December, 1837.

adopt this policy.[1] The Governor-General did not hold that Tharrawaddy had dismissed the Resident from Ava, but that Burney had retired voluntarily. "He (the King) may have marked out his own line of policy" wrote Auckland, "and it is not surprising that he should at first have adopted a notion which was for a long period prevelant even in Europe, that Treaties may be regarded as personal with the sovereign and not permanent with the state. It would not be wise, the Treaty being observed, to risk the sacrifice of blood and treasure for the sake of extorting a present admission in terms that it is also acknowledged and respected, nor is it likely that such an admission, extorted by menace and war, would be binding beyond the moment at which the King might find his convenience in denying it."[2]

Although Auckland's attitude was intensely pacific and conciliatory, there was no thought of allowing the King to set aside the Treaties at his own will. "But on the other hand," continues the Governor-General, "the British Government can make no sacrifice of principle on a point so vital. Its determination should be fixed to hold unimpaired every right which is founded upon the Treaty and not for an instant to admit that the Treaty itself can be set aside. Opportunities may be taken probably without risk of immediate collision of making this determination known. With this exception, it may be well to combat the absurd pretentions of the King by the exhibition of a calm and steady resolution on our part, rather than by a ready sensitiveness of resentment or an instant appeal to arms."[3]

The government was strengthened in this attitude of peace because of reports received from private merchants in Burma, who affirmed that the King was anxious to avoid war: for instance, when he heard of the arrival of a British warship near Rangoon, he was reported to have exclaimed, "What cause

[1] *Ibid.* Government dispatch to Burney, 6 December, 1837.
[2] *Ibid.* Governor-General's Letter, 25 November, 1837.
[3] *Ibid.*

of war have I with the English? What have I done? I did
not send the Residency away."[1]

In keeping with these sentiments, namely, peace, readiness
for war if attacked, maintenance of the Treaties, and continuance of the Residency in Burma, Auckland's Government
decided to appoint a new Resident in place of Burney. Burney
was not only not willing to go again to Burma, but Government also considered it wise not to reappoint him, because
his opinions were more actively warlike than the Governor-
General was willing to agree to. In the meantime Bayfield was
instructed to keep charge of the Residency at Rangoon, and to
notify his appointment to the Ministers and the Rangoon
Governor. In all his dealings with the Burmese officers, written or oral, he was advised to show "prudent and courteous
firmness that the British Government will of course maintain
all its rights although it seeks to be on cordial terms of peace
and friendship."[2]

Thus the policy and doings of Burney in his relations with
Tharrawaddy, were, on the whole, severely censured by
Auckland and his Counsellors, and especially so his action of
withdrawing the Residency. In August 1837, when Auckland
wrote his Minute on the Burma situation, he was cautious
enough to refrain from definitely blaming Burney: "Whilst I
remain," he wrote, "on the whole, unsatisfied upon the discretion of his conduct in his communications with the Court, and
yet regret that the Residency should have been wholly removed
from Ava, still in his firm and active endeavours to check
violence and to save life I see much to praise, and (especially
upon first and uncertain impressions) I own that I am never
disposed to exact a severe responsibility from officers fairly
acting (as I must presume Col. Burney to have been) in strange
and hazarding dilemmas to the best of their judgment, because
my judgment of what was feasible does not entirely coincide
with theirs. I would not, therefore, upon our present informa-

---

[1] *Ibid.* Extract of a confidential letter from Rangoon, 27 October,
    1837.
[2] *Ibid.* Governor-General's Letter, 25 November, 1837.

tion, although pointing out the instances in which his proceedings seem to have been obviously injudicious, repeat the strong censure which was conveyed in our former dispatch, as applicable to the removal of the Residency by Col. Burney in the state of things which is in these papers, reported to have there existed."[1]   Later, on 27 November, 1837, the Governor-General definitely declared that the affairs of the British Residency in Burma had been mismanaged by Burney. He also totally disapproved of the warlike attitude of the Resident.[2]

Burney felt very keenly the censure heaped upon him. He had been discharging for some years a most arduous duty at the expense of his own health; during the revolution in Ava, he had risked his life in the cause of peace; and now he was not only censured, but was pronounced unsuitable for further employment as Resident. He put up a strong defence of his own actions and policy which may best be presented largely in his own words.

In reply to the Government view that the King made irritable remarks because of Burney's indiscretion, the latter wrote, " I certainly had no idea that His Lordship-in-Council would have been better pleased if I had refrained from noticing the offensive and disrespectful remarks which the King was uttering every day before hundreds of people, and which they were sure were all duly reported to me. My knowledge of the Burmese character taught me that silence and forbearance under such circumstances would have rendered my Government and me the object of contempt and derision with all classes of the people of Ava." [3]

A few weeks after his arrival in Calcutta, Burney wrote a long letter direct to Auckland in which he answered the charge of " the King's provocation " in the following words:—
" Your Lordship seems inclined to decide that I provoked and irritated the King of Ava and that I repeatedly mooted questions of a most unnecessary and impolitic character. I can

[1] *Ibid.* Minute of the Governor-General, 29 August, 1837.
[2] *Ibid.* The Governor-General's Dispatch, 27 November, 1837.
[3] *Ibid.* Burney's Letter, Rangoon, 24 September, 1837.

produce witnesses of the most unimpeachable testimony to assure your Lordship that I never once provoked or irritated His Majesty, that I bore with the insolence of his followers and with his own remarks insulting to our Government and nation more than most British officers would or could have done, and that in every conversation I had with him, he never displayed anger or personal insult but was good humoured and even kind although most firm and determined. On one occasion only, on the 25th April, he was a little warm from the effects, I believe, of liquor, but even then there was no disposition on his part to be angry with me or to treat me with personal disrespect. I heard for several days that the present King after his return to Tsagain was daily holding forth in open durbar before hundreds of persons — abusing our Government and nation, avowing his determination to repudiate our treaties, and to have no British Resident near him. Several of his hearers were encouraging him in these opinions, and none, dared even hint an objection. I was the only person who could do so. I was requested by his own uncle, the Prince of Mekkhara, to wait as often as I could on the King as the best mode of preventing the success of mischievous counsels, and I considered myself bound to seek for opportunities of teaching him and his Ministers what no one else dared to do — of pointing out to them the impolicy of his language and the irrevocable nature of our treaties, and I did so with prudence and discretion, never, as I said before, provoking or irritating the King, but keeping him always good humoured and willing to hear all I had to say. Lord William Bentinck on one occasion observed to me that I must go to Ava and act as "Schoolmaster" to the King and Ministers. Surrounded as the King was by a set of violent, reckless and ignorant characters, I was, always fearful that from words he might be very easily led into action, and I must submit that there could not have been a more judicious and politic course of preventing this than that which I adopted." [1]

[1] *Ibid.* Vol. 10, Burney's Letter to Auckland, Calcutta, 21 November, 1837, No. 4.

The charge in connection with his clerk Edwards, Burney answered by saying, that it was the usual practice to send messages through subordinates of that status; that in 1812 Canning had done the same; and that the commonest individuals were used by the Burmese Government for the same purpose. Edwards was a native of Madras; his salary was Rs. 300 per month; he was very intelligent and a great favourite with the King. In Burney's eyes he was of higher status than the messengers sent by the Ministers to him. Burney was afraid that since Edwards was in favour with the King, some young English merchants had been jealous of him, and it was possible that they had made unfavourable reports to the Government of India against him. Burney was satisfied that Edwards was a man of honesty and character. " But when I say," wrote Burney, " that they imagined that because Mr. Edward's colour was dark, my deputing him to the King was ' of itself sufficient to cause much irritation,' I think I need say no more regarding their competency to form an opinion on the subject." [1]

With regard to the removal of the Residency to Rangoon, Burney drew the attention of the Government to the Instructions given to him, dated, 31 December, 1829, Par. 13, where he was authorized to quit the capital if the Burmese Government showed an invincible repugnance towards the Residency.[2] Burney had acted exactly in keeping with these instructions, and had retired from Ava without committing his Government to anything, and on terms of friendliness towards the King.

In his letter to Auckland, Burney says that it was useless for him to remain in Ava, and the King would not allow him to accompany him to Kyauk-Myaung the new capital. He did not leave Bayfield behind him at Ava or at Kyauk-Myaung, because he was disliked by the King, and the people called him *Tshethema* or compounder of drugs; besides, Bayfield was inclined to be proud towards the Burmese, and if he had been left behind there was danger of an outrage being committed

[1] *Ibid.* Vol. 8, Burney's Letter, 24 September, 1837.
[2] Vide Supra. p. 61.

upon him.[1] " Those who directed that the British Residency
should remain at Ava during the progress of a revolution there,
little know, I fear, anything of the history of these Indo-
Chinese states. What do these races know or care about the
sanctity of an ambassador's character? The Burmese have in
their time massacred the whole of a Chinese Embassy.[2] In
their last war with Pegue they attacked and destroyed the French
factory at Syriam and all the Catholic Missions, and carried
away such of the foreigners as survived to a location near Ava.[3]
In their last invasion of Siam they destroyed the Dutch factory
at Ligor and at Yathea (Ayuthia) and all Catholic churches.
In the last revolution in Siam, the Siamese attacked and over-
threw the French Embassy and all their posts. I was aware of
all these historical facts."[4] Burney's fears were not unjustified.
During the difficult days of the revolution, when Ava was
expected to be sacked by Tharrawaddy, a number of Indian
and foreign traders, American missionaries and their families,
and even some Burmese Princes had taken refuge in the Residency grounds. Also the cash belonging to all the foreign
merchants had been lodged within the Residency.[5] " The lawless plunderers of both armies," reported Burney, " had heard
of the large quantity of treasure deposited in the Residency,
and the troops of the Prince of Tharawadi's advanced division
under Bundoolah's son and Brother, who were posted directly
opposite to us at Tsagain, loudly called to each other that they
must attack the Residency and get possession of the gold and
silver collected there. Many of the King's troops who were
posted on the walls of Ava came down them at night and
pillaged close around us, and parties of Maung Taung Bo's
force also repeatedly approached us, and inspite of the Prince
of Tharawadi's orders entered the houses of the poor villagers

---

[1] India Secret Consultations Vol. 10, 21 November, 1837.
[2] This happened in 1273 A.D. in the reign of Narathihapte (1254 —
    1287) the last Pagan King.
[3] This was the work of Alaungpaya (1752 — 1760) in 1756.
[4] India Secret Consultations Vol. 10, Burney's Letter to Auckland,
    21 November, 1837.
[5] India Political Secret Consultations Range 194, Vol. 41, Burney's
    Letter, 24 May, 1837, par. 8.

plundering and destroying everything. Several respectable Burmese householders near us were so certain that we should be attacked that they thought it prudent to withdraw from our neighbourhood, and it will scarcely be credited that on the evening of the 7th April the Ministers in charge of Ava turned out of the city the whole of the Taroup Bo's division, 1500 armed men who were known to be disaffected, and to have offered to set the town on fire, and who came and took post for the night, without a single officer, close to the Residency. In addition to stockades on two sides, I had thrown up some breastworks in front and rear of the Residency, and the King of Ava had lent me two small guns. These preparations probably kept intruders from us, but I always hoped that I should not have much difficulty in beating off any party of plunderers with my escort of 25 sepoys, Gunboat Lascars, and servants. My chief care and vigilance were required to prevent the suspicious and bad characters who approached us from setting fire to our neighbourhood, for although I had removed the roofs of all our out officers' and servants' houses it would have been scarcely possible to prevent our being burnt out in the event of any of the houses adjoining the Residency catching fire during the present period of dry weather and high winds. I had also early adopted the precaution of collecting some boats on which I embarked the public records and a portion of our property, and intended to have embarked the whole of the Residency with such foreign merchants as come to me for protection, and pushed off to a landbank on the Tsagain side of the Erawadi, had the Residency premises caught fire, or had the new King continued to decline coming to Tsagain and allowed his troops to storm the City and thus place us between two fires." [1] This gives some idea of the difficulties the Residency had to face and the reasons which induced Burney to withdraw to Rangoon. The action, however, of Burney in withdrawing the Residency to Moulmein and placing Bayfield at Rangoon under the orders of Blundell, was unauthorized and

[1] *Ibid.* par. 67.

unwise. He should have maintained the Residency and placed Bayfield in full charge of it. His idea, however, was that it was useless to maintain a resident who could not defend British rights in Burma, and it is also possible that he expected his Government to take stern measures against the new King.

As to Burney's recommendation that the King should be coerced into a right attitude, it is clear, that he did not hurriedly come into this frame of mind. In his letter, 24 September, 1837, to his Government, he explained that when he mentioned the plan of declaring war, he had no idea of recommending its adoption unless the King persisted in ignoring the Treaties.[1] Later, Burney was satisfied that the King was resolved not to acknowledge the Treaties nor the authority of the Governor-General, nor British right to maintain a Resident near him.[2] It was for this reason, therefore, that Burney suggested the use of intimidation and force. On his arrival in Calcutta he wrote to Auckland, that, " the present King of Ava is a restless intriguing character without any proper principle. He occasionally exceeds in liquor, and he is surrounded by a set of reckless and ignorant soldiers of fortune who are offering to recover Assam, Munnipore, Arracan and Tenasserim for him. If in a moment of exhilaration he consents to the proposition of one of these military chiefs, the first we shall hear of it will be the intelligence of an inroad into our territory and the destruction of the lives of a good many of our subjects. The presence of an officer on our part near the King would not prevent such a catastrophe or give us timely notice to prevent it........We cannot for an hour be certain of peace with the present King and Court of Ava." [3] Burney's suspicions of the King's motives were perhaps justified, but later events showed that Tharrawaddy did not really wish to fight: he simply desired to do away with the British Residency, and was prepared to defend himself if attacked. In another letter to his Government, Burney defended his war policy in the fol-

---

[1] India Secret Consultations Vol. 8.
[2] *Ibid.* Burney's Letter, Rangoon, 25 August, 1837.
[3] *Ibid.* Vol. 10, Burney's Letter, Calcutta, 21 November, 1837.

lowing words:—"I believed and still believe that the present King of Ava is incapable of long remaining quiet or proving a safe neighbour, and that no time ought to be lost in letting him see our determination not to submit to his tone of defiance and insult. I believe and still believe, that the late events at Ava offered a most safe and justifiable opportunity for our establishing a more permanent and secure influence over the government and people of Ava, and that, in fact, they came within the very description laid down by the Supreme Government to one of my predecessors......(6th paragraph of Mr. Secretary Edmonton's letter to Lt. Col. Symes dated 26th April, 1802). "Such a state of events would precisely constitute that crisis of affairs which is most to be desired for the purpose of establishing the British influence and of promoting the British interests in the Burmese Empire."[1] Burney finally warned his Government, that British interests and influence had not been sufficiently secured in Burma, and he feared that the country having passed to an ambitious and self-sufficient monarch, whose Ministers were inexperienced and ignorant, but who had acquired the knowledge of the Indian Government's overwhelming anxiety to keep on terms of peace with them, the British would possess no security for the continuance of friendly relations, and the office of the Resident at the Burmese capital would not be an enviable and useful one. As to the new King, Burney claimed to have studied him, and gave his opinion, that although in private capacity he was a very pleasant companion, "as regards his public character I know him to be one who entertains opinions and harbours designs that may one day render him a very formidable and troublesome neighbour to us."[1]

In spite of Burney's unanswerable arguments, Auckland and his Government stuck to their view, namely, that the Residency should not have been removed readily from Ava, and that irritating topics with the King should have been avoided. Government, however, recognized the difficult situation of

[1] *Ibid*. Burney's Letter, Calcutta, 16 January, 1838.

Burney, and in every other way gave him credit for his doings in Burma.[1] The Home Government also agreed with the Governor-General-in-Council in thinking that Burney had erred in his judgment in his measure of removing the Residency from Ava to Rangoon.[2]

Burney's connection with Burma now ended, not only because he desired it to be so, but also because the Government thought in unwise to re-employ him in the capacity of Resident. To prevent the Burmese Government from misunderstanding the situation, Government asked Burney to inform the Ministers that he himself would not be able to resume his duties at the Royal Court for reasons of health, but Bayfield would be in charge of the Residency till a successor was appointed; and that if the Burmese Government showed a friendly disposition the Governor-General would respond to it, but that the British Government would never depart from the Treaties.[3]

Burney remained on leave as Resident from 6 December, 1837, to 8 March, 1838. On 8 March, 1838, he relinquished charge of his office, and the same day departed from Bengal on board the *Barque Cornwall* having been granted a furlough to Europe.[4] He returned to Calcutta on 9 April, 1842, and was posted as General Officer to the 28th Native Infantry. On 23 March, 1843, he was transferred to the 5th Native Infantry as General Officer. But his health failed him and he again took furlough; while on his way to England on board the *Maidstone* he died at sea on 4 March, 1845, being only 53 years of age.[5]

[1] *Ibid.* The Governor-General to Burney, 15 December, 1837.
[2] Bengal Service Military List, Vol. 2, Military Records Room No. 204; Range No. 6; Shelf No. 27.
[3] India Secret Consultations Vol. 8, Consultations 6 December, 1837, Government to Burney, 6 December, 1837.
[4] India Political Consultations Range 194, Vol. 58, Burney's Letter, Calcutta, 16 January, 1838; Government to Burney, 24 January, 1838; Vol. 60, Government to Burney, 14 February, 1838; Vol. 61, Burney's Letter, 8 March, 1838.
[5] Bengal Service Military List, Vol. 2, Military Records; Room No. 204, Range No. 6, Shelf No. 27.
    Burney's son, H. B. Burney, was the chaplain of General Godwin's army in 1852 — 1853, at Prome and Rangoon. When Mindat Min, the Crown Prince (1855) was told by Phayre concerning this chaplain, the former exclaimed, "Oh, a Poongyi! Burney's son a Poongyi!" *Yule*, op. cit. p. 123.

CHAPTER XII

KING THARRAWADDY AND THE BRITISH RESIDENCY
UP TO THE APPOINTMENT OF COL. BENSON,
1837 — 1838.

It has already been noticed that after the surrender of thirteen of the greatest officers of Bagyidaw, the Prince of Tharrawaddy arrived at Sagaing on 8 April, 1837. The very next day he deposed his brother the King, and himself took over the sovereignty of the Kingdom. His measures against the old King and Ministers have also been recounted; but it was not till on 15 May, 1837, that the new King came in great state with his Queen to take his seat on the throne at the Hlutdaw and secure possession of the Palace. Burney was invited, but did not attend the function on the excuse of indisposition. The King received the homage and congratulations of all his officers; but he would not enter the Palace. He only visited the Hlutdaw, and without taking his seat on the throne did obeisance to some gilded images representing his ancestors,[1] and then returned to Sagaing before noon. According to custom, at this time he should have also assumed the white umbrella, but he went away without this symbol of Royalty as well, and satisfied himself with his gilded umbrellas only, on which he had some strips of white muslin tied. People were surprised at his attitude, and said, that his oaths, that he would not injure his brother, were troubling his conscience.[2]

On assuming the reins of government, the first important decision the new King made was to destroy Ava and establish a new capital city. His first thought was to make Moksobo his

---

[1] For note on ancestor worship in Burma and elsewhere, see *Harvey*, op. cit. p. 327; also p. 46 concerning Alaungsithu bowing to the golden images of his ancestors.
[2] India Political Consultations 3 July, 1837, Range 194, Vol. 41, Burney's Letter, Ava, 24 May, 1837, par. 58.

capital, it being at one time the city of his renowned ancestor Alaungpaya. He told Burney that Ava " had proved a very unlucky city, the sovereigns residing in which had always been getting into quarrels and misfortunes."[1] The King's most confidential officers made urgent and repeated representations to him against the measure of removing from Ava, but Tharrawaddy was adamant: he had set his heart upon making Ava a heap of ruins. The common people and traders were also in great alarm, fearing that on the departure of the King to establish a new capital, Ava would not only be destroyed but molested by robbers as well. Burney felt convinced that Tharrawaddy was bent upon destroying Ava, and to prevent this awful catastrophe he reasoned with the King. " I submitted," he wrote, " the many disadvantages attending the site of Mouttshobo, that it was 14 miles distant from the River side and surrounded by sand and salt springs, that the water of the place was brackish and unhealthy, and that it would take many years before so many inhabitants, houses and gardens could be established there as Ava contained. I mentioned also the hardship of making the poor inhabitants of Ava, who had already suffered so much by the late revolution, remove to Mouttshobo, and pointed out how difficult it would be for the foreign traders to give up their houses and establishments at Ava, and convey their merchandise to Mouttshobo which contained no houses or accommodation for them."[2] Tharrawaddy was, however, not to be moved. He was too full of his own project of removing the capital to listen to the difficulties and inconveniences that would attend such a measure.[2]

---

[1] *Ibid.* pars. 25, 58, 61.
[2] *Ibid.* par. 25.

Moving the capital was a frequent practice with the Kings of Burma, the underlying idea being the superstitious belief that the old capital had served its purpose and might prove unlucky, while the new one, fixed on astrological calculations, would bring prosperity and success. Hsinbyushin, Bodawpaya, Bagyidaw, Tharrawaddy and Mindon, six of the ten kings of the Konbaung dynasty shifted their capitals. The process, however, was a great burden to the people of the old capital who were required also to move to the new royal choice. Vide, *Harvey,* op. cit. pp. 139, 265, 356.

On a second thought Tharrawaddy decided to make Kyauk-Myaung his capital. On 8 June, the ex-Menthagyee, his wife and two daughters, also the ex-Myawadi Woongyee Maung Za, and other state prisoners were embarked in a common boat and taken to Sagaing. The two daughters of the ex-Menthagyee were first sent about the town to beg for money to pay the boat expenses. On 9 June, the prisoners were produced before the King in Sagaing, dressed in dirty robes, and each with a large whitened ladle in his hand. This was intended as a joke, to show that these men had been active in stirring up and plaguing the country.[1]

The poor old King also embarked on 9 June, on a common boat for Sagaing. "Some of his brother's attendants," wrote Burney, "came to fasten a white umbrella in front of his boat. The old King objected to the measure, and told the man to take the umbrella away to his Brother; but they fastened it and went away without taking any notice of him. Bagyidaw had recovered perfectly from his old malady and was in full possession of all his faculties. On arriving in Sagaing, when Thait-ten-gyeh told him that the King's orders were that he would have to proceed to Kyauk-Myaung with the Royal party, Bagyidaw observed, ' My brother thinks me mad, but he is showing that he is more mad than I by removing the capital in the manner he is doing, and annoying and distressing the poor inhabitants of the country much more than ever I did' ".[2]

On the morning of 10 June, the King embarked from Sagaing for Kyauk-Myaung, accompanied by almost every man of rank and by about 2000 boats. A large portion of the inhabitants of Ava also quitted the city by river, bound for the new capital. Ava was left in charge of the Mindat Woongyee, an imbecile old man, and a military commander, Maung Thoung Bo, a notorious robber, with about 350 armed men. They were to remain there till all stores and guns were removed to Kyauk-Myaung, after which they were under orders to join the King.

[1] India Secret Consultations 4 September, 1837, Vol. 8, Burney's Letter, 12 July, 1837, No. 1, par. 26.
Ibid. par. 27.

Tharrawaddy had expressed a definite desire to turn Ava into a heap of ruins, and that if the inhabitants did not quit the city he would set fire to it.[1]

"Nothing can better shew," says Burney, "the self-will of the King, his selfishness and utter disregard of the wishes and comfort of his people than this measure of removing the capital in so sudden a manner and at this stormy season. He has persisted in it contrary to the earnest advice and entreaty of every person near him, and even of his Queen and sons." [2] The people were terror struck at the numerous executions, yet, "all classes openly complain of the distress and loss which the gratification of a mere whim on the part of the King will occasion." [2] Kyauk-Myaung was an unhealthy site, and it is no wonder that soon it had to be given up in favour of Amarapura.

The King was unpopular with all the lower classes as well as with the more respectable people, who looked upon him as a cruel, faithless and a heartless man. According to Burney, "the body of the people are much attached to the person of the late King and to his son Tsakyamen......and if any bold and talented leader only would appear, I am sure the present King would soon be deprived of the power which he has seized in so unjust and unexpected a manner; but I see no one likely to oppose him excepting his own sons who are all very averse to this removal of the capital, and some of whom are quite unprincipled enough to destroy their father and seize the throne if they could only be sure of retaining it." [3]

Burney and the whole Residency embarked for Rangoon on 17 June. During the seven days that the Resident was in Ava, after the departure of the King, none of the Burmese officers there took the slightest notice of the Residency.[4]

Tharrawaddy remained in Kyauk-Myaung for only six months. He soon discovered that it was not the place for a capital, so that he abandoned his whim, and on 12 December,

[1] *Ibid.* pars. 1, 28.
[2] *Ibid.* par. 29
[3] *Ibid.*
[4] *Ibid.* par. 1.

1837, arrived at Amarapura which he finally established as his new capital.[1] During this period he defined his policy towards the British Government in India. It might be summed up in a few words:— Neither to denounce nor to recognize the Treaties officially; neither to refuse to entertain a British Resident nor to agree to the appointment of one; to try and restore the Burmese Empire to its ancient glories as in the days of his great ancestor Alaungpaya, but at the same time to take no offensive measures against the British, and to maintain peace on all the frontiers. In his Durbar speeches, in the presence of foreigners, he plainly and boldly announced that he had nothing to say concerning the Treaties concluded by his deposed brother, but that he wanted to be let alone, and desired his Kingdom to be what it was before the days of Bagyidaw.[2]

It is clear that Tharrawaddy did not wish to entertain another British Resident, but he also did not desire at this time to come into conflict with the Indian Government, since he had a good appreciation of the British power, and understood the danger of running so great a risk. For fear of being attacked by the British, he began to increase his army, imported ammunition and guns in great abundance, and began to place the points of strategic importance in his dominions in a state of defence. In September, 1837, the Governor of Rangoon said to Burney, "You are all wrong in supposing that the King is going to attack you immediately. He has plenty to do just now in settling his Kingdom; but in two or three years hence, when we are better prepared, we shall either ask you to sell us the Tenasserim provinces back, or fight you like men and try and recover them."[3]

The Governor-General summed up the situation in the following words:—"I am of opinion that the King of Ava is not

[1] *Ibid.* Vol. 10, Consultations 31 January, 1838, Letter from Thomas Spiers to Rev. T. Simons at Rangoon, dated Amarapura, 15 December, 1837.

[2] *Ibid.* Vol. 8, Minute by the Governor-General, Consultations 4 September, 1837, dated 29 August, 1837, No. 6.

[3] *Ibid.* Consultations 8 November, 1837, Burney's Letter, 30 September, 1837.

anxious to provoke an immediate rupture with the British Government. He will not admit himself bound by the Treaty, but he will break none of its conditions. He speaks offensively and insolently. His head is turned with success and with personal vanity, yet he seems to have sufficient acuteness to take in some respects a just measure of his position and so know that this at least is not the moment at which he could prudently provoke a quarrel with us.

"There is much cunning in his proceedings. His primary object is to set aside the Treaty of Yandaboo without its breach......and he takes special care not to dismiss the Residency. He advises a removal for a time to Rangoon, 'and he will see the gentlemen again by and bye'......he disavows all intention of territorial aggression......and he has more than once disclaimed all intention of seizing the countries ceded to us......

"All this pride and vanity and folly might be borne in the confidence that as the real difficulties of his situation should press upon him, as his Government should become more nearly settled and the intoxication of triumph shall wear off, there might be a return of good sense and of reason in his proceedings, but whilst his variable demeanour is consistent to his object of not at once provoking a quarrel, yet......the attitude which he is assuming is one injurious at once to the dignity and power of the British Empire. He has taken for his prototype Alompra the conqueror of Munnipore, Assam and Aracan. He disavows all that was done in his brother's reign which was a "bad one" and would replace everything in the excellent condition in which it was in the reign of his great ancestor. He would, he says, commit no aggression, but the pretenders to the thrones of Assam and Munnipore are received with favour at his Court. It is reported that the Duffa Gaum and other such turbulent characters have been sent for, that pains are taken to collect arms, and that Toungngoo (Toungoo) to the north west of our Tenasserim provinces is immediately to be fortified......" [1]

[1] *Ibid.* Consultations 4 September, 1837, The Minute, 29 August, 1837.

The Governor-General felt that Tharrawaddy's pacific avowals could not be depended upon, and that it would be best to be prepared for any and every emergency. " Nor can it be denied," continues the Minute, " that the tone of defiance and of disregard to all engagements and to all friendly relations, and the assumption of bygone dominion and power, must, if it continue unchecked, have their influence upon whatever there is of turbulence and pretension upon the whole of our Eastern frontier. Under all these circumstances I cannot but feel that there is undoubted hazard of our being at no distant period involved in War with Ava, and it is at least incumbent upon us at once to apply ourselves to the considerations of the measures by which either an event so much to be deprecated may be averted, or by which if it should be forced upon us, we may be found in the best state of preparation."

The troops on the Assam, Arakan, and Tenasserim frontiers had already been augmented; now they were further reinforced, and the officers in those areas were cautioned to be on their guard.[1] Tharrawaddy heard exaggerated reports of British reinforcements on the frontiers, and naturally feared an attack. His measures for self-defence became more active: he was, however, in no position to engage in a war with the British, and he was well aware of his limitations. On 25 August, 1837, the Governor of Rangoon addressed a letter to Burney (in Rangoon), undoubtedly inspired by the King, expressing sentiments of mutual goodwill and friendship. " I have repeatedly submitted to His Majesty," wrote the Governor, " what the Resident Col. Burney told me, that the troops which have arrived at Moulmein are intended for the defence of that place, and that he will do everything in his power to prevent war between the two countries. The King not having been a party to the making of the Treaty for that reason only says, that he did not make the Treaty but my brother; at the same time does not desire to be the first to molest the English country. I will continue to do everything as it was done in the time of the

---

[1] *Ibid.* Memorandum by the Governor-General, No. 9.

Woongyee Maung Khain and will attend to whatever the Resident says. But I am positively informed that many armed men have arrived at Moulmein. We are on terms of friendship and confidence. Do not let me fall into an error, but write a letter and let me know the truth."[1] In September 1837, Burney received letters from Princes Thait-ten-gyeh and Mekkhara, two principal Ministers of the King, expressing a desire for peace and friendship.[2] The King at the same time, in order to avoid all appearance of hostility, withdrew his force stationed at Toungoo.[3]

During his stay in Kyauk-Myaung, Tharrawaddy continued to rule in the same old revengeful manner. He tried to construct a road from his new capital to Moksobo, and forced the ex-Menthagyee and the old Ministers, his prisoners, to work like common felons in cutting the jungle.[4] In December 1837, Burney, then at Calcutta, heard from an intelligent Ava trader well known to him, and who had resided in Kyauk-Myaung for nearly three months, " that the whole of the inhabitants of the country are much dissatisfied with the present monarch, and anxiously looking for our (i.e. British) interference, and that he is positive if we only sent one steam vessel and 200 Europeans the whole country would join us and aid in overturning the present government."[5]

Having got tired of Kyauk-Myaung, Tharrawaddy again thought of transferring his affections to Moksobo, but ultimately decided in favour of Amarapura. He arrived at the last mentioned place on 12 December, 1837, and proceeded to rebuild this old city. The country generally was quiet by now, and people had got used to the new King and his methods. The ex-Menthagyee was not relieved of his irons and was still kept

[1] *Ibid.* Consultations 8 November, 1837, Letter from Woondouk Mg. Shwe Meng the Governor of Rangoon, 25 August, 1837, No. 105.
[2] *Ibid.* Letters Nos. 8 and 9.
[3] *Ibid.* Consultations 6 December, 1837, Extract from a confidential letter from Rangoon, 27 October, 1837, No. 2.
[4] *Ibid.* Consultations 4 September, 1837, Burney's Letter, 31 July, 1837, No. 3.
[5] *Ibid.* Consultations 27 December, 1837, Burney's Letter, 8 December, 1837.

in close confinement. The old Ministers were still in jail, but not worked on the roads as formerly.[1] On the deposition of Bagyidaw, Tharrawaddy had taken charge of the Tsakyamen; he treated him kindly and made him one of his attendants; he even confirmed to him his landed estates.[2] As ex-Crown Prince, however, he continued to be a source of anxiety and apprehension to the King, although there was no likelihood of a Prince with so timid a disposition asserting his rights. Tharrawaddy's two illegitimate sons, Tait-ten-gyee and Tait-ten-phyoo, were particularly jealous of him, and finally they brought against him a false charge of treason. The King did not fail to miss this opportunity and had him executed in April 1838. Six other unfortunate persons, alleged to have been implicated in his treason, suffered the same fate, including three females — the Prince's wife, his nurse, and the King's half sister.[3] Bayfield in his Journal says, " The Prince certainly possessed neither superiority of intellect nor amiability of disposition to command the respect or love of the nation, but from his position in the state he has for several years past been looked up to as its future sovereign, and until the Revolution his succession to the throne was almost universally desired as a means of liberating the country from the irksome and oppressive rule of the late Queen and her Brother Menthagyee. The Revolution, although it weakened, did not entirely destroy the hope of his ultimate succession, whilst the national sympathy has been strangely excited by his misfortunes, so that his execution has occasioned no other feelings than those of regret and indignation." [4]

It has already been mentioned that in December 1837, Bayfield was appointed Acting Resident at Rangoon with

---

[1] *Ibid.* Vol. 10, Consultations 14 February, 1838, Bayfield's Journal, 8 January, 1838, No. 2.

[2] *Ibid.* Vol. 8, Consultations 4 September, 1837, Burney's Letter, 12 July, 1837, No. 1, par. 27; India Political Consultations Range 194, Vol. 41, Consultations 3 July, 1837, Burney's Letter, Ava, 24 May, 1837, par. 46.

[3] India Secret Consultations Vol. 10, Consultations 30 May, 1838, Bayfield's Journal, pars. 196-198; Bayfield's Letter, Rangoon, 30 April, 1838.

[4] *Ibid.* Bayfield's Journal, par. 198.

powers to communicate directly with the Government of India. He resided in Rangoon to the end of March 1839: up to 16 July, 1838, as Acting Resident, and from 16 July, 1838 to his departure for India as Agent to the new Resident, Col. Benson.

In January 1838, Bayfield informed the Amarapura Government of his appointment as Acting Resident, but no direct reply was received to this communication. The Governor of Rangoon, however, was friendly, and it appears, he had orders from the Hlutdaw to transact business with Bayfield.[1] The Ministers resolved not to hold direct intercourse with him: "they seem determined," wrote Bayfield, "by every evasive means to prevent if possible the necessity of receiving a Resident at Court."[2] The general report among the traders was that the King would not reject a Resident at the expense of war, but that he would not receive one if he could avoid it, nor would he make an open acknowledgement of the Treaties unless compelled to do so. Bayfield, however, advised his Government that the sooner a Resident was sent to Court, the greater would be the prospects of a favourable reception.[2]

In order to avoid what he considered to be a humiliation, namely, the presence of a British Resident at his capital, Tharrawaddy appointed an Ayébain[3] or Burmese Resident as Governor of Rangoon, so that he might transact all business with the British Resident in the same town. The King was bold enough to take this step, since he felt relieved from the fear of immediate war being declared against him by the British. In Bayfield's opinion, the King had "availed himself of this

---

[1] *Ibid.* Consultations 31 January, 1838, Bayfield's Letter, 5 January, 1838.
[2] *Ibid.* Consultations 28 March, 1838, Bayfield's Letter, 10 March, 1838.
[3] The British Resident was also known in Burma by the same term. This new Ayebain-Governor was a Woondouk not a Woongyee. Tharrawaddy's object was to confine the British Resident to Rangoon, where he could negotiate with a King's officer of equal rank with himself. The Resident was to be accorded the status of a Woondouk (not of a Woongyee as enjoyed by Burney). With this object in view now a Woondouk was appointed as Governor of Rangoon, so that he might handle any questions or problems raised by the British Resident.

subterfuge by which he probably hopes to avoid the necessity of receiving a British Resident at his Court, although he appears to have no objection to an officer in that character being recognized at Rangoon."[1] Notwithstanding this evident evasion of the Treaty by the Government at the centre, the local authorities at Rangoon continued to speak of it as being in force, and evinced a pacific and friendly disposition. British subjects also, both Indian and European, felt no apprehension of danger either to person or property.[2]

The Ayébain-Governor arrived in Rangoon on 6 March, 1838. Bayfield called upon him the next day and again on 9 March, and was received politely and with kindness. The Ayébain explained to Bayfield that he had been appointed to grant full satisfaction to British complaints and to maintain friendship.[3]

The Burmese Government thus created a new situation for Auckland to tackle. The Governor-General, dwelling upon the subject in his Minute, says, "The impression which I have taken from reading the dispatches lately received from Mr. Bayfield is that there exists a strong wish on the part of the Government of Ava for the maintenance of peace, but these papers mark also a continued disposition on the part of the King to avert if possible the reception of a British Resident at his Court and yet so to act as neither to break the letter of the Treaty nor in terms to deny or to admit its obligations."[4] It will soon be seen how the Government of India handled the problem.

Bayfield's duties at Rangoon consisted of settling petty cases such as, assaults, debts, etc., in which British subjects were involved.[5] The following are extracts from Bayfield's Journal

[1] India Secret Consultations Vol. 10, Consultations 28 March, 1838, Bayfield to Capt. Hobson of H. M. S. *Rattlesnake,* Rangoon, 26 February, 1838.
[2] *Ibid.*
[3] *Ibid.* Bayfield's Journal, pars. 110, 111, 118; Consultations 18 April. 1838, par. 159.
[4] *Ibid.* Consultations 30 May, 1838, The Minute, Simla, 30 April, 1838.
[5] *Ibid.* Consultations 28 February, 1838, Bayfield's Journal, pars. 22-30.

12

to show the nature of the miscellaneous type of business transacted by him in Rangoon as Resident:—

"A Tavoyer named Nga Nyo the chief of a small trading boat complained that the Raywoon had demanded an extra fee of two bundles of wax candles, value 2½ Rupees, on granting port clearance, and that some extra charges amounting to 2 Rs. had been demanded by the chokeydars (or watchmen) down the River. Represented the case to the Raywoon and pointed out its illegality — demand relinquished and pass granted."[1]

"Sent my Interpreter with Mr. Snowball of the Schooner Louisa who had been summoned to the Myowoon's Court to answer a charge of assault against one of the Government Ghaut coolies. Assault (a severe one) proved, and Mr. Snowball fined Rs. 60 and costs, with a reduction of ten rupees in the amount of fine, the coolie having abused Mr. Snowball. After my interpreter left the Court, Mr. Snowball refused to pay the costs, and in default of giving security was locked up. In the evening I received a letter from him informing me of his situation and soliciting my interference in consequence of the danger to which his vessel, now ready to sea and riding at single anchor, was exposed during his absence. Stated these circumstances to the Myowoon who released Mr. Snowball, my Interpreter being responsible for his appearance toworrow."[2]

The next day Bayfield saw the Myowoon and

"brought to his notice Mr. Snowball's case, and asked him as a favour to Mr. Snowball to make some reduction in the Law charges on the ground of the Plaintiff having abused Mr. Snowball on two separate occasions. I took care to explain that I was satisfied with the justice of his decision, and asked this as a favour in consideration of Mr. Snowball being a poor man, and having received provocation. The Myowoon said he had fined Mr. Snowball but a small sum because he was a British subject, that had he been a Burman he would have made the fine heavier, but that he would on my account remit one half of the Law charges which he did. I thanked him for his kindness. Mr. Snowball was then released."[3]

"A native of Mergui named Shwe Bo applied for a certificate of his being a British subject, he being about to proceed into the

[1] *Ibid.* par. 60, 14 February, 1838.
[2] *Ibid.* par. 78, 19 February.
[3] *Ibid.* par. 80, 20 February.

interior on a mercantile speculation. Proof being given certificate granted." [1]

" A Moulmein subject named Ma Mentha applied for my
assistance under the following circumstances: — Twenty years
ago she had been sold as a slave by her mother whose name is
Ma Ai to a person named Shwe Ao (for the sum of 60 tickals of
80 per cent silver, equal to about Rs. 12) with whom she lived
until the breaking out of the War in 1824. When the English
army evacuated Rangoon in 1826, she and her mother accompanied it to Moulmein where they have ever since resided.
Complainant is now married, and with her husband came over to
Rangoon on a pilgrimage to the great Pagoda." [2]

Shwe Ao recognized her, had her arrested, and claimed her
as his slave. Bayfield applied to the Governor, who

" at once ordered the woman to be liberated, disallowed the
claim, and summoning the officer who had arrested her gave him
a sharp reprimand, and threatened to punish him if he ever did
such a thing again." [2]

Bayfield's duties were of far too multifarious a nature to
be dealt with here in any detail. He had often to interfere in
the settlement of disputes, as to port charges, between the Burmese authorities and British shipowners. One illustration in
this respect will suffice.

Shortly after Tharrawaddy came to the throne he revised
the Rangoon Port regulations, and abolished or reduced duties
that were considered to press heavily on foreign traders. The
duty of 10 per cent upon the labour of ship-carpenters, caulkers,
and coolies was also abolished. The Government also tried to
control the employment of skilled and unskilled labourers at
the Port. English and certain other merchants resident in
Rangoon were in the habit of keeping private ship coolies, who
were not under the control of the Burmese Government, and
who claimed exemption from all Government assessments on
the ground of their being in the private employ of the merchants. The King, therefore, directed that merchants should
not keep private carpenters, caulkers or coolies; and to prevent

[1] *Ibid*. par. 88, 21 February.
[2] *Ibid*. Consultations 18 April, 1838, pars. 156, 157, 29 March.

a violation of this order, all such labourers were placed under the superintendence of the Shahbunder.[1]

The merchants, however, ignored the Royal order, and continued to employ their own workers as before. As a result, difficulties arose with Burmese officers who were already smarting under the reduction of duties which had seriously affected their emoluments. To prevent disputes and to maintain a check upon the conduct of labourers, the Governor issued orders reiterating that merchants should not keep private labourers; that when coolies were required the Shahbunder would furnish them in any numbers; that coolie gangs should be employed in rotation as ships required them, without favour or selection; and finally, that coolies should not demand higher wages than the usual. The European merchants protested against this arrangement; " and as it appears to me," wrote Bayfield, " with more vehemence than justice, and refuse to receive or employ any coolies appointed by the Government. They insist upon a continuance of the old rules allowing only that part of the King's order to take effect that abolishes the 10 per cent duty." [2]

Bayfield now intervened, and objected to that part of the Governor's order which deprived the merchants of control over the coolies, and of the choice of persons whom they might consider the best qualified to perform the duties required of them. He placed before the Governor the justice of preserving to the merchants the right of hiring freely in the bazaar whatever labourers they liked, and at whatever rate that may be agreed upon mutually without the interference of Government. The Governor agreed to Bayfield's suggestion, and the deadlock came to an end.[3]

Although the Burmese Government had changed hands under circumstances of much commotion in and around Ava, the whole of the Burmese frontier from Upper Assam to Cape Negrais maintained a pacific complexion. But the Tenasserim

[1] *Ibid.* Consultations 20 June, 1838, par. 213, 9 May. Shahbunder: *lit.* Prince of the Port; Chief Customs Officer.
[2] *Ibid.* par. 214.
[3] *Ibid.*

frontier, on the two banks of the Salween at Martaban and at Moulmein, continued to be one sore spot in Anglo-Burmese relations.[1] During the year 1837 a number of serious gang robberies and murders had been committed in British territory by dacoits belonging to the Martaban region, while the new year opened with fresh attacks in which British subjects suffered serious losses. Blundell and Bayfield both lodged their complaints to the Governors of Bilin and Rangoon respectively.[2] In January 1838, Blundell also deputed Richardson to Bilin, to enquire if the Burmese frontier officers were at the bottom of the robberies. Richardson reported that the outrages were not authorised by the Burmese Government, and that the Governor of Rangoon was sincerely desirous of putting an end to the robberies, but that he was unable to do so since he had no jurisdiction over the Governor of Bilin, and so could only make reports to the Central Government at Amarapura.[3] Former Governors of Rangoon, who were also Woongyees, did possess this jurisdiction, but the then incumbent was only a Woondauk and did not possess those powers.

Blundell, however, had his doubts concerning the pacific desires of the King, and believed that the gang robberies had been officially planned in order to frighten British subjects to cross over to the Burmese side. He, therefore, threatened on the first recurrence of a gang robbery, " to take immediate possession of Martaban, sending out parties to apprehend these gangs of robbers, to acquaint the Rangoon authorities without delay of this step, in order to the report of it being transmitted to Court to apprise them that no harm will be done to Martaban or its people, and that it will be held until our Government is satisfied of the pacific intentions of the Court, that the robbers if apprehended will be returned in custody to be tried by a Burmese Commissioner from Court, that though most reluc-

---

[1] *Ibid.* Consultations 21 February, 1838. The Governor-General's Minute on the Tenasserim frontier, 8 February, 1838.

[2] *Ibid.* Consultations 31 January, 1838, Bayfield's Letter, 5 January, 1838; *Ibid.* Consultations 14 February, 1838, Bayfield's Journal, pars. 3, 14. Blundell's Letter 15 January, 1838.

[3] *Ibid.* Blundell's Letter, Moulmein, 15 January, 1838.

tantly obliged to take this step for our own safety, yet we trust the Court of Ava will consider it as unavoidable and as not contemplating farther hostilities in evidence of which they may be assured that unless provoked to do so by wanton attacks on them, the British troops will not proceed beyond Martaban, that we trust shortly to see the usual quiet and friendly intercourse on this frontier restored." [1] " It may be," continues Blundell, " that His Majesty's pride will be roused by an open hostile step of this kind, but I trust His Honour-in-Council will bear me out in it if obliged to have recourse to it, as the only means of protecting our people from murder and plunder whether sanctioned by the Court of Ava or the effect of folly and disobedience on the part of a subordinate frontier officer."

Blundell's warlike policy produced a feeling of mistrust and irritation on both sides of the Salween, and relations between the British Commissioner of Tenasserim and the Governor of Bilin became strained. Auckland and his Government commended Blundell for his intelligence and ability, his good intentions and the excellence of his administration, but disapproved of his aggressive policy, and decided that the episode of 1829, when Martaban was destroyed,[2] shall not be repeated.[3] Blundell was warned " of the danger of too local and partial a view of subjects of public and general importance, of the circumstance that his apprehensions of the designs of the Burmese Court connected with his frontier are wholly unsupported by the proceedings of the Burmese officers in any other quarter, of the right of the Government to judge and decide upon its own policy, and of the danger which may arise in nice questions of peace and war by the rash movements of any of its agents " [3] Blundell was also cautioned to be temperate as well as firm in demanding redress, and even in cases of extreme provocation to avoid direct hostility without the orders of his Government.[3]

---

[1] *Ibid.*
[2] Vide Supra. pp. 37, 38.
[3] India Secret Consultations Vol. 10, Consultations 21 February, 1838, Auckland's Minute on the Tenasserim frontier, 8 February, 1838.

British India was at this time on the eve of the First War with Afghanistan, so that it would have been totally unwise to get embroiled into another war with Burma. The force at Moulmein was sufficient for defence, and Blundell had previously been authorized to raise a small local corps; but to instil confidence it was decided by Government to send a fresh European Regiment to Moulmein.[1]

Murders and gang robberies on the Martaban frontier did not cease, and British subjects continued to suffer severely. Trouble also broke out on the Assam frontier where some of the Burmese Singphos pursued their Assamese slaves into British territory and recaptured and killed them.[2] Bayfield represented matters to the Rangoon Governor, the newly appointed Woondouk-Ayébain, who said that he had orders from the King's Ministers to give full satisfaction to British complaints. He was very sympathetic and promised to do his best.[3] " What you have said is true," he told Bayfield, " I am surrounded with difficulties. What will satisfy you? The Singphos are savages and we have no control over them beyond the town of Mogaung; this outrage is not our fault. What can we do? The Governor of Martaban is a foolish old man, but if he is the cause of disturbing the peace he shall be executed......There are bad men hoping to profit by war, but what will either nation gain by going to war?".[4] Meanwhile two British warships arrived on the Burmese coast, H. M. S. *Rattlesnake* to Moulmein and H. M. S. *Larne* to Rangoon. This created alarm in Burmese circles; but Bayfield informed the Ayébain that the Government of India had sent the ships in order to ascertain the state of

---

[1] *Ibid.*
   Ibid. Government dispatch to Bayfield, 21 February, 1838.
   Ibid. Consultations 28 February, 1838, Government to Blundell, 28 February, 1838.
[2] *Ibid.* Consultations 7 March, 1838, Government dispatch to Bayfield, 7 March, 1838.
[3] *Ibid.* Consultations 28 March, 1838, Bayfield's Journal, par. 118.
   Ibid. Consultations 18 April, 1838, Bayfield's Letter, 9 April, 1838.
[4] *Ibid.* Consultations 18 April, 1838, Bayfield's Journal, par. 159, 4 April.

affairs and the measures the Burmese were taking in the Moulmein murders.[1]

In April, 1838, the Ayébain sent two Commissioners to Martaban to enquire into the murders committed in British territory. These two officers carried out the duties entrusted to them with great dispatch. Within less than a month's time they had five of the culprits arrested, and called upon the British authorities at Moulmein to produce evidence so that the accused might be tried. Blundell, however, refused to produce evidence, and demanded that all the robbers, some ten in number, must first be arrested. The Commissioners then themselves went to Moulmein and informed Blundell that they would take the five accused to Rangoon and hand them over to the Ayébain for trial. This they did, arriving in Rangoon on 8 May, 1838.[2] The Ayébain informed Bayfield that even if the plaintiffs did not produce prosecuting evidence he would investigate into the complaints and settle the affair within 40 days. He at the same time gave strict orders to the Myowoon of Martaban to allow the same friendly and free commercial intercourse that existed between Moulmein and Martaban during the reign of the late King, and " to prevent the appearance of robbers and bad men."[3]

Blundell was dissatisfied with the work of the Burmese Commissioners, and said, that it was not necessary to produce evidence against the accused, since every one knew that they were the culprits.[4] The Governor-General, however, thoroughly disapproved of Blundell's attitude and observed with much regret, " that Mr. Blundell continues to be influenced in all cases by one idea, that namely, of the ultimate certainty of hostilities, and the propriety under this contingency of treating every peaceful overture with contempt and distrust. It is but fair and commendable that Mr. Blundell should frankly express his own

---

[1] *Ibid.* par. 111.
[2] *Ibid.* Bayfield's Letter, 9 April, 1838.
   Ibid. Consultations 20 June, 1838, Bayfield's Letter, 9 May, 1838;
   Letter from the Woondouk to Bayfield, 15 May, 1838.
[3] *Ibid.* Woondouk to Bayfield, 15 May, 1838.
[4] *Ibid.* Letter, Bayfield to the Woondouk, No. 12, no date.

opinions to the Government, and the Governor-General would not by too severe reprehension check the freedom of his communications, but whatever may be the bent of his own conviction, he is bound to look to the declared views and policy of his own Government and to act with temper and forbearance, and to endeavour to avert the evils of war until it shall be declared by the authority which it is his duty to obey that the time for forbearance has past, and that these evils are inevitable." [1]

The Governor-General approved of Bayfield's action in procuring the appointment of the Burmese Commission to Martaban, and remarked, " that the British Government have no right to demand redress until after it shall have tendered proof of any alleged grievances, and nothing could be more calculated to defeat the success of such an amicable attempt to adjust differences than the reluctant and unconciliatory spirit in which Mr. Blundell has from the first viewed the proceeding ....Mr. Blundell acted most erroneously in not permitting evidence to be produced of the guilt of the five persons who had been apprehended by the Burmese Commissioners." [1]

It follows from what has gone before, that although the King of Burma did not desire a British Resident at his Court, he certainly did not wish to fight, and was at least willing for a Resident or Agent to reside in Rangoon and negotiate with his Ayébain. The Indian Government did not consider this latter arrangement to be suitable. There were three alternatives before Auckland at this time:—(1) To follow a " wait and see " policy, and to act if cause were given for fresh remonstrance; (2) to appoint a Resident on the strength of the Treaty of Yandabo, and send him direct to Amarapura as a matter of course; (3) to instruct Bayfield to hold communcations with the Ministers by correspondence, and inform them that a Resident would soon be appointed. After much consideration it was finally decided to appoint a successor to Burney without

---

[1] *Ibid.* Consultations 4 July, 1838. The Governor-General's dispatch to Calcutta, Simla, 18 June, 1838, No. 1.

raising a discussion with the Burmese Government over the step.[1]

In the selection of an officer for this important position, it was necessary to choose a man of rank, character, and experience; also one knowing the Burmese language, and acquainted with Burmese usages and feelings. Blundell possessed all these qualifications; but Auckland rightly thought it unwise to appoint him, since he was connected with the Martaban frontier trouble and had his own views on what the policy towards Burma should be. Pemberton was another good candidate, but he was absent on a mission to Bhutan. The choice fell upon Major Benson, late Military Secretary to Lord Bentinck. He had no local knowledge of Burma, but was qualified in every other way, and in the words of Auckland, was "a gentleman whose tried ability, judgment and conversancy with public affairs I need not speak."[2] Benson was made a Colonel, and Capt. McLeod, who had before seen service at Ava and was well acquainted with the Burmese language, was appointed as the Resident's special Assistant to accompany him to the Burmese capital.[2] Bayfield was confirmed in his appointment at Rangoon as a separate charge, but under the orders of the Resident at the Royal capital.[3]

On 22 June, 1838, Bayfield visited the Ayébain and acquainted him with the appointment of Benson and McLeod to the Royal capital, and of himself to Rangoon. The Governor made no particular remarks over the news, but was taken by surprise, and did not seem pleased. Bayfield also wrote to the Ministers announcing the new appointments.[4]

The Ministers at Amarapura had all along been hoping that no new Resident would be appointed to be near the King; now they were disillusioned. It was hopeless to go to war: on the contrary their great desire was to prevent war, knowing very well what the result would be. They, therefore, now took

---

[1] *Ibid.* Consultations 30 May, 1838, The Governor-General's Minute, Simla, 30 April, 1838, No. 16.
[2] *Ibid.*
[3] *Ibid.* No. 31.
[4] *Ibid.* Consultations 18 July, 1838, Bayfield's Journal, pars. 269, 272.

refuge in the letter of the Treaty of Yandabo, and said that in it there was provision for only one British Resident. Writing to Bayfield they said, " Having spoken according to the tenor of the Treaty you have not borne the Treaty in mind. By appointing three Residents a new measure is advanced........ In all affairs connected with the British in India, if they are mentioned to the Rangoon Woondouk they will be settled. There are no others besides the (Rangoon) — Woondouk, Yenangyaung Myotsa, Mengyee Maha Mentha Gyoden, who possesses authority to speak in those affairs. According to our desire to make firm and augment the friendship between the two countries, if there are any affairs regarding the countries to be discussed, if a Resident like the Burmese Resident discusses them the friendship will increase and last firm for ever." [1]

The drift of this evasive answer, in the opinion of Benson, was, " if not an attempt to form, on grounds of which the assumed validity cannot well be denied, a loophole of retreat from the presence of a Resident at Umarapoora, at all events an endeavour to obtain a respite by pointing out a course in which the British Government might seem to have already acquiesced.".[2] It was in reality the game of the weaker party.

The Government of India, however, did not wish to insist upon Bayfield's appointment to Rangoon if the Burmese Government was definitely against the arrangement. There was a precedent for such an appointment, since Capt. Rawlinson was for some time at Rangoon, and performed political duties in that city while there was a separate Resident at the Court of Ava.[3] Benson was the only Resident; he had the authority to transact all business with the Burmese Government: Bayfield was to be just a subordinate officer under the control of the Resident, appointed to Rangoon to settle the quarrels of English merchants in that town.[4] But the weaker party, which

---

[1] *Ibid.* Vol. 11, Consultations 22 August, 1838, Trans. of a letter from the Ministers to Bayfield, No. 54.
[2] *Ibid.* Benson's Letter, Rangoon, 28 July, 1838, No. 52.
[3] *Ibid.* Government dispatch to Benson, 20 August, 1838, No. 57.
[4] *Ibid.* Letter from the Government of India to the Rangoon Woondouk, 20 August, 1838, No. 58.

was afraid to repudiate the Treaty officially, now began to split hairs over the legal aspects of the Resident's appointment. This attitude ultimately went so far into emphasising the "letter" merely of the Treaty, that the Resident found it impossible to discharge the duties assigned to him by his Government. The whole establishment had, therefore, finally to be withdrawn.

CHAPTER XIII

THE RESIDENCY AT AMARAPURA UNDER BENSON, 5 OCTOBER, 1838, TO 14 MARCH, 1839.

Major Richard Benson, of the 11th Native Infantry, Bengal Army, was created Colonel (local rank) and appointed Resident at Amarapura with effect from 30 May, 1838.[1] He was furnished with the following papers:—(1) His Credentials as Resident, dated 20 June, 1838, signed by the Hon. Alex. Ross, President of the Council of India at Calcutta, and by two members of the same Council, the Hon. Col. William Morrison and the Hon. William Wilberforce Bird; (2) a letter to the King of Burma from the same three high placed gentlemen; (3) a letter of the Secretary to the Government of India to the Ministers and Generals of the King of Burma; and (4) a letter from the Governor-General to the King of Burma, dated 18 June, 1838.

The letter from the President and Council to the King was a new feature in Anglo-Burmese relations. His Burmanic Majesty considered it beneath his dignity to receive letters from the Governor-General; a letter, therefore, from his ministers would be construed as a direct insult. Besides, there was a reference made to the treaty of Yandabo in this letter; this would have annoyed Tharrawaddy, so that it was good that after his arrival in Burma, Benson decided not to present the letter to the King. "Col. Benson is directed to proceed," says the letter, "to your August Presence with all particular expedition, and is charged to convey the assurances of our adherence to solemn engagements, of our scrupulous observance of that good faith which is the well known characteristic of the British

---

[1] India Secret Consultations Vol. 10, Consultations 30 May, 1838, No. 31; Minute of the Governor-General, 30 April, 1838, No. 16.

Government, and of our favourable disposition towards Your Majesty."[1]

The letter from the Secretary to the Ministers definitely made mention of the Treaty: " Lt. Col. Burney having proceeded to Europe, the Rt. Hon. the Governor-General, George Lord Auckland has been pleased in accordance with the Article of the Treaty of Yandaboo, to appoint Col. Richard Benson to be British Resident at the Court of Ava."[2] The letter from the Governor-General to the King expressed the sincere desire of the British Government to maintain peace, explained the benefits accruing from the presence of Residents at the two Courts, and commended Benson and McLeod to His Majesty.[3]

Benson left Calcutta by H. M. S. *Rattlesnake* on the morning of 26 June. On 5 July, he arrived at Amherst. On 7 July, he repaired to Moulmein where he had his credentials and letters translated into Burmese. He also acquainted himself with the frontier troubles and collected opinions on the attitude of Amarapura and of the Rangoon Woondouk-Ayébain towards the new Resident. After the translations were made by Edwards, Clerk and Interpreter, and corrected by Blundell, Benson took them to Dr. A. Judson who revised them. Blundell earnestly disuaded Benson from presenting to the King the letter from the Government of India, which, he said, being unusual, might be looked upon by the King as an indignity put upon him. Judson was definite that the letter would offend His Majesty, and wished that even the Secretary's letter to the Ministers had not made a formal mention of the Treaty of Yandabo.[4] Under the shelter of these opinions Benson decided to withhold the letter to the King. Calcutta agreed with him and left the matter entirely to his judgment.[5]

Blundell, Richardson, and Judson were all inclined to believe that the presence of an official agent at Rangoon, in

---

[1] *Ibid.* Consultations 20 June, 1838, No. 15. Vide Appendices V — VII.
[2] *Ibid.* No. 16.
[3] *Ibid.* Consultations 4 July, 1838, No. 3.
[4] *Ibid.* Vol. 11, Consultations 22 August, 1838, Benson's Letter, 18 July, 1838.
[5] *Ibid.* Government dispatch to Benson, 20 August, 1838, No. 57.

addition to the Resident at the capital, would decidedly be objected to by the King. Judson even told Benson, " that the Resident will be sullenly received at Amarapoora, will be neglected, kept under surveillance, and long amused with excuses for adjourning an audience of the King. He does not apprehend that the Governor-General's letter to the King will be treated with disrespect or remain unanswered, but thinks the vexatious topic will prove to be the Yandaboo Treaty." [1] These words proved ultimately to be too true throughout Benson's stay in Amarapura. As to Judson, Benson wrote to his Government, " This gentleman avows himself predisposed for war, as the best, if not the only means of eventually introducing the humanising influences of the Christian religion." [1] Benson, of course, did not agree with Judson in this view, and for safety's sake decided, under the then circumstances, to discourage missionaries from proceeding to the interior under the countenance of the British Resident. [2]

Benson sailed from Amherst on the *Rattlesnake* on the evening of 13 July, and arrived on the 16th noon at Rangoon. All musketry practice on board the warship was suspended to avoid any sinister interpretation. McLeod immediately landed and informed the Woondouk of Benson's arrival. The Woondouk not only received McLeod politely, but made a spontaneous proposal, that if the Burmese flag were saluted by the British warship, he would recognize the compliment by a corresponding number of discharges. Benson was surprised at this friendly attitude. Thirteen guns were accordingly fired on board, and repeated on shore. [3] The Yewoon, the second authority in Rangoon, then boarded the *Rattlesnake* at the head of a deputation and congratulated the Resident. The next morning at 9 o'clock the Resident disembarked at the principal wharf under salutation of 13 guns from the *Rattlesnake,* 13 from the *George Swinton,* and 13 from the Burmese battery. The

[1] *Ibid.* Consultations 22 August, 1838, Benson's Letter, 18 July, 1838.
[2] *Ibid.* No. 51.
[3] *Ibid.* 28 July, 1838, No. 52.
   Ibid. Consultations 26 September, 1838, Benson's Journal, pars. 1, 2, 5.

Yewoon received him ashore and conducted him in procession through streets, lined with soldiers and spectators, to Bayfield's house. So far the reception was quite satisfactory, and there was no complaint whatever nor any disappointment.[1]

The next day Benson visited the Woondouk and there was a friendly conversation. The Woondouk hinted that the Resident should remain in Rangoon, and when Benson spoke of his impending journey to the capital as a matter of course, the Woondouk talked of the unwholesome water of Amarapura. " I withdrew from the interview," wrote Benson, " with a favourable impression of the Woondouk's understanding and decision of character. He is a kind of person not unfrequently met with about Indian Government, and belongs to a class of men who from force of mind and physical bearing have an imposing presence, and who, in all conditions of society, are frequently the instruments of much good or much ill as circumstances may happen to have set the bent of their powers."[2]

On 20 July, the Woondouk summoned McLeod and Bayfield and had a long conversation with them. The Governor gave expression to sentiments, which undoubtedly were the real views of the King and his Ministers regarding the newly constituted Residency and the relations between the two countries. The views, summed up in a few words, were, that friendship should be maintained between the two powers; that Burney had interfered unnecessarily into the affairs of the Burmese Government and created misunderstanding; that Bagyidaw's government had erred in submitting to these interferences; and finally, that, if the British Resident made Rangoon his headquarters, and transacted all business with the Ayébain, friendship would be strengthened and all would go well.[3]

It was, therefore, to persuade the British Government to agree to this arrangement that Benson had been received with

[1] *Ibid.* 28 July, 1838, No. 52.
   Ibid. Consultations 26 September, 1838, Benson's Journal, pars. 1, 2, 5.
[2] *Ibid.* Benson's Journal, pars. 8-12.
[3] *Ibid.* par. 18.

marks of honour. Benson, however, had been sent to reside at the Royal Capital, and when the Governor realized that he was bent upon proceeding to Amarapura, he allowed him to do so; but, in the meanwhile, the King and his Ministers had decided to transact no business with him at the capital. For fear of war they did not prevent him proceeding northwards, but created difficulties for him. This was again the game of the weaker party which looked upon the presence of the British Resident near the King as an indignity. The Burmese Government wished to maintain peace, but did not desire to be checked by a Resident, and in order to prevent interference, had resort to passive opposition.

In his conversation with McLeod and Bayfield, the Woondouk complained that in the past the British Resident instead of confining himself to his duty, had interfered in matters which were not his concern; " that the late King felt so ashamed at the result of the war that he did not attend to the affairs of the country......The present King, however, even then watched the acts of our Resident with jealousy and displeasure, but after his accession to the throne, the Treaty of Yandaboo had been frequently alluded to in a taunting manner. The King being of a hasty temper became annoyed and said, he would have nothing to do with the treaties, though he had no intention or wish to disturb the existing good understanding between the two countries, nor did he wish the Resident to quit the country......His Majesty had often speaking of Arracan, Tenasserim etc., said he had no desire to regain them as they had been given by his brother (though he did not relish being constantly reminded they had been wrested from them), but everything should remain as during his brother's reign." [1]

The Woondouk also wrote to the Secretary to Government in Calcutta. This letter too contained the views of the Burmese Government on the question of Burney's and Benson's appointments :—

[1] *Ibid.*

"For a long time friendship existed between the two countries of India and Burmah, and the gold and silver road (of commerce) was open, but during the reign of the Elder Brother (the late King) insufficient causes, owing to the mismanagement of the frontier officers, produced a great War. After the Treaty of peace was made, Major Burney having arrived and remained at the Court, the Elder Brother being indisposed, delivered over the Government to the former Tsaleng Myo-tsa (the Salin Myosa; Menthagyee) and officers. Major Burney did not confine himself to the duties of a Resident according to the instructions given him by the Governor-General, but exceeded the provisions of the Treaty, opposed the King's wishes and authority, interfered in affairs concerning merchants smuggling money on board ships......and meddled in disputes between merchants regarding money matters......His Majesty when Prince disapproved of such proceedings, and on attaining the throne, in order not to create alarm amongst the people of the country and Priesthood, remained at Tsagain. While His Majesty was taking possession of the Kingdom according to Law and Justice, Major Burney brought forward improper subjects......and unnecessarily persisted in introducing the subject (of the treaty) which was not denied and was settled for upwards of 10 years. But in consequence of its occurring to us to represent to the Governor-General all Major Burney's proceedings he departed of his own accord, and knowing that he acted improperly, did not remain quiet, but wishing to justify his own conduct made reports so as to cause misunderstanding and disagreement between the English and Burmese nations. While ships and boats were being sent to ascertain the views of the Burmese, the Burmese nature also being doubtful (as to the intentions of the English), Col. Richard Benson arrived in Burmah, and having spoken with a view of cementing the friendship between the two countries, everything now is right and proper......I possessing the confidence of the King am the only person who has been appointed by His Majesty to take charge of all the Southern Provinces, and from the period of my having done so, no disputes have arisen on the frontiers;

and those that took place previous to my arrival I have settled justly that there may be peace and friendship.

" With reference to Col. Benson, what affairs of the English Government is he to take cognizance of?......it is proper that the two Residents (Burmese and English) only should discuss together on various subjects connected with the British Government etc., etc., according to custom......After Col. Richard Benson has had an audience of His Majesty, and a friendly interview with the Ministers, and taking into consideration the contents of your letter, that at the principal port of Rangoon there are many subjects to be discussed regarding the affairs connected with the British Government etc., etc., it is proper if you advise it that the Resident Col. Benson only should remain here." [1]

This letter contains in brief not only Tharrawaddy's version of his usurpation of the throne, but also his attitude towards the British and the Residency. The King wanted the Resident to remain in Rangoon and have dealings with the Burmese Ayébain who was also the Governor of Rangoon; but it was the settled policy of the Governor-General to station the Resident at the Royal Capital. The Government of India informed both the Woondouk and Benson that the Resident was not to live in Rangoon but at the capital.[2] Auckland, writing to Sir Henry Fane, the Commander-in-Chief in India, said :—

" The language of the Burmese authorities has of late been generally pacific, and there is strong ground for hoping that hostilities with that country may not be forced upon us, though on the other hand the tone of the Court is at least repulsive, its domestic administration is one of barbarous violence, and its external policy is yet unsettled and is open to the adverse speculations of all who wish us evil, and without absolutely threatening war it makes peace precarious.

[1] *Ibid.* Consultations 22 August, 1838, Letter without date, No. 55.
[2] *Ibid.* Letter from Secretary Prinsep to the Woondouk, 20 August, 1838, No. 58; Letter from same to Benson No. 57.

" The Government has determined under these circumstances upon tendering a Resident to the Court of Ava......
and upon the manner of his acceptance or rejection the course of the measures to be presently adopted must depend. But though I have every hope and every desire for the preservation of peace, I would not overlook the chance of War, and it behoves us at least to be so far prepared as to have the means of waging it......" [1]

Auckland also had plans prepared for the invasion of Burma, if such a course became necessary. The prospects of an invasion from the north were considered, but an advance from Rangoon up the Irrawaddy was again thought to be the best course. " In the prospect, however, of a rupture being actually forced upon us," continues Auckland, " it may perhaps be well...... that I advert to the objects with which a war may be carried on against a country possessing a loose though unwarlike population, and having at present scarcely any well constituted army or even a capital against which military operations could be directed. I am led to believe that the population of ancient Pegue would upon a declaration of permanent protection at once reject its allegiance to the Court of Ava, and though without further information I might hesitate to authorize such a declaration, I should think in the event of this speculation being strengthened that our efforts should first be directed to the occupation of this province by a sufficient force, and that pains should then at once be taken for the organization of an auxiliary force within it for assistance to us and for its own subsequent maintenance." [2]

During his stay in Rangoon, Benson took up the question of the Martaban culprits. Eleven men had been tried by the Woondouk: five were condemned to death, and the other six convicted of receiving stolen property. The Resident desired that the sentences be carried out, but the Woondouk said that July, August, and September, being Burmese Lent months, ac-

[1] *Ibid.* Consultations 29 August, 1838, No. 2.
[2] *Ibid.*

cording to ancient custom, the executions must be postponed.[1]
While Benson felt that the Woondouk was anxious to keep the
frontier quiet, and prevent violence and injustice in the future,
he also thought that there was diplomacy behind the delay in
carrying out the executions. " I suspect notwithstanding the
pride and ignorance of the Court," wrote the Resident, " that
there are connected with the Government men gifted with
sagacity and possessed of cunning, who pretend to have discovered that acknowledgements, explanations, and compensations
are accepted as satisfactory by a Government such as they conceive that of India to be, which would be rejected as unsatis-
factory if offered to a state which they deem of like consideration with their own." [2]

Benson was carrying on business with the Woondouk
through messengers, since the latter had not yet paid him a
return visit. On 6 August, McLeod and Bayfield waited on
the Woondouk and informed him that the Resident had been
surprised and hurt that his visit had not been returned. The
Woondouk plainly told them that he wished to visit the Resident, but feared the displeasure of the King; that Benson's rank
according to the Treaty was merely that of " an officer with
50 men "; and that he hoped the Resident would not claim at
the capital as precedents what had been done by Burney, since
the King disapproved of it all.[3] Thus it was now the policy of
the Government of Burma not to accord to Benson the honours
enjoyed before by Burney as Resident. Since the British insisted upon the maintenance of the terms of the Treaty, the King
would agree to a British officer residing at the capital " with
50 men ": the Treaty did not prescribe any transaction of business, but that friendship might be maintained. Later, the
Woondouk also informed Benson that he was unable to pay the
return visit unless his Government permitted him.[4]

[1] *Ibid.* Consultations 26 September, 1838, Benson's Journal, pars. 42,
43, 46, 49, 66-76, 85.
[2] *Ibid.* Vol. 12, Consultations 3 October, 1838, Benson's Letter, 28
August, 1838, No. 127.
[3] *Ibid.* Vol. 11, Consultations 26 September, 1838, Benson's Journal,
pars. 79-81.
[4] *Ibid.* par. 82.

This was the first rebuff met with by Benson, but others were soon to follow. On 17 August, the Woondouk received orders from the Ministers to permit Benson to proceed to the capital. " His Majesty has considered it proper to order them to come up," they wrote; " we bearing the Royal Order on the crown of our heads acquaint you of the same...... In order not to destroy the existing friendship with the English Resident, we should receive them according to the due rites of hospitality; but they shall not be allowed to transgress the stipulations of the Treaty." [1] A messenger from Amarapura, when questioned by the Woondouk, said, " that His Majesty has said that should the Resident on his arrival allude to any business he will refer him to the Woondouk of Rangoon to whom all matters connected with the English are delegated, and that should the Woondouk not be able to satisfy him, then His Majesty would pass his decision. But should the Resident merely say he had no business then he would let him remain quietly." [2]

Benson now decided to leave for the capital, and to station Bayfield at Rangoon as his Assistant to settle with the Woondouk commercial and other questions within the competence of the local Burmese functionaries to adjust. But obstacles were placed in his way. The Woondouk informed him that " he could not, knowing the sentiments of the King and Court, acknowledge any other officers as capable of transacting public business with him during *Col. Benson's absence from Rangoon;* also that Dr. Bayfield will not be allowed to remain in the house now occupied by him after Col. Benson's departure." [3] The Woondouk Gale of Amarapura also warned Benson through the Ayébain, " that he will use his best endeavours to promote Col. Benson's views towards cementing the friendship between the English and Burmese Governments, that he hopes Col. Benson will not interfere in matters not connected with his duties as Resident, and that no reference is made to what had taken place

---

[1] *Ibid.* Vol. 12, Consultations 3 October, 1838, pars. 123, 125.
[2] *Ibid.* pars. 129, 133.
[3] *Ibid.* par. 157.

during the late reign. That the appointment of Dr. Bayfield is disapproved of both by the King and Ministers."[1] On 23 August, the Woondouk also received a letter from the Ministers condemning Bayfield's appointment. " This is contrary to the Treaty," they wrote, "......we do not think it proper that Mr. Bayfield should remain in charge of affairs at Rangoon." [2] In keeping with the Amarapura orders, the Woondouk informed Benson that he would not recognize Bayfield. Benson explained that Bayfield's appointment was actuated by friendly feelings, the sole aim of the Governor-General being to expedite the transaction of business, and thus to relieve the Woondouk and the Ministers from references and correspondence. He admitted that there was no provision in the Treaty for such an appointment, and that if the King was against the measure, the officer would be withdrawn. The Woondouk declared that the Treaty provided for only one Resident in the country so that the stipulations should not be transgressed.[3]

The Government of India had already informed Benson that Bayfield's appointment was not to be insisted upon, if the Burmese authorities strongly objected to it. Benson, however, requested the Woondouk to allow Bayfield to continue to live in the house provided for him by the Burmese Government. But the Woondouk said that he had orders from the Ministers not to permit Bayfield to do so after the Resident's departure from Rangoon.[4] Benson protested against this unceremonious treatment of Bayfield, and said, that the courtesy and usage of enlightened and great nations had not been observed by the Burmese Government, in requiring Bayfield to vacate the house immediately on the departure of the Resident from Rangoon.[4]

In spite of the refusal of the Woondouk to transact business with Bayfield, Benson, on departing for the capital, instructed his Rangoon Assistant that should the Ayébain himself in a becoming manner offer to have dealings with him, he should

[1] *Ibid.* pars. 155, 156.
[2] *Ibid.* pars. 179-188.
[3] *Ibid.* pars. 194-261.
[4] *Ibid.* pars. 256-261, 265-269.

take advantage of every opportunity so to do; but that if the Woondouk's conduct were to oblige him to quit Rangoon, he should retire to Moulmein or Amherst.[1]

Before Benson left Rangoon he was made to experience a fresh rebuff. On 29 August, at about 10 a.m. he informed the Woondouk that he would embark that morning, and that the Hon. Company's armed steamer would fire a salute. At 10-15 a.m. Benson went on board his boat and the salute was fired. The Woondouk immediately wrote to him disapproving of the firing, and that it was contrary to Burmese custom to fire guns when a dignitary left the place, except in the case of the King. Benson replied that he had done nothing contrary to custom, because Burney had always been saluted in the same way while he was Resident. The Woondouk wrote again to say, " that in places where the Woongyees and Woondouks are stationed it is the Royal Order and custom of the Burmese to consult the authorities of the place if a salute was necessary, and after a satisfactory explanation it is allowed to be fired. But now it is the Royal Order and custom of the Burmese not to allow even muskets to be fired; if application is made to fire (muskets) permission is granted to do so at a place where the report will not be heard......It is the custom among men of rank to consult with each other on all matters, and after rendering satisfactory explanations either to allow or disallow an affair to be accomplished...... His Majesty and Ministers will be displeased......When the Royal Elder Brother was indisposed Col. Burney and the Ministers acted as they thought proper contrary to custom......If on Col. Benson's arrival at the capital references are made to what Col. Burney had done as precedents, they are contrary to friendship and the Treaty. The Woondouk could patiently put up with acts against himself, but as this is contrary to the orders of His Majesty, the Woondouk cannot say that Col. Benson's letter is satisfactory."[2]

The Government of India thought that Benson had just causes of complaint against the Woondouk, but advised him to

---

[1] *Ibid.* Benson to Bayfield, 29 August, 1838, No. 120.
[2] *Ibid.* Benson's Journal, pars. 279, 280, 283-289, 293-297, 314-325.

use his discretion in ventilating them before the Ministers. The occurrences in Rangoon concerning Bayfield's appointment and the firing of salutes, said the Government letter, " afford reasons for apprehending that you may be compelled to bring matters to an issue, and you will understand that the Government is quite prepared, in perfect reliance on your judgment and discretion to support you if the perverse conduct of the Court should leave you no other resource consistently with the honour of the nation and the character of your Mission." [1]

As noticed earlier, Benson embarked at about 10-15 a.m. on 29 August, to proceed to the capital. Since Ava was no longer the capital, his designation was changed from " Resident at Ava " to " Resident at Amerapoora."[2] His followers consisted of 10 officers, 42 Sepoys, 2 Drummers, 40 Servants, and 40 Lascars. His boats were of three kinds: 2 gunboats, 3 accommodation boats, and 10 baggage boats.[3] Maung Lauk, the Yewoon of Rangoon, was appointed the Mehmandar (i.e. one in charge of the guests). He accompanied the party, and was responsible to conduct it to the capital and see to their needs and comforts during the journey.

On 4 September, the Resident reached Prome. Men were sent to buy stores, but the shopkeepers were unwilling to sell. The Headman also performed no civilities. It was discovered later that the Woondouk of Rangoon through the Mehmandar had forbidden the shopmen to sell poultry, but through fear they refused to sell other articles as well.[4] On 18 September, Myede was reached. Again poultry could not be bought. Benson was so exasperated that he charged the Mehmandar with inhospitality and interference, but the latter tried to fix the responsibility on the Town officers, who in turn denied the charge. Finally, with difficulty three very indifferent fowls were pro-

[1] Ibid. Government Dispatch, 26 September, 1838, No. 133.
[2] Ibid. Vol. 11, Consultations 22 August, 1838, Nos. 62, 64.
[3] Ibid. Vol. 12, Consultations 3 October, 1838, Benson's Journal, pars. 218-221.
[4] Ibid. Vol. 13, Consultations 28 November, 1838, The Journal, pars. 351, 352, 355.

cured for Rs. 4.[1] After touching Yenangyaung and Sale, the party reached Pagan on 26 September. Benson desired to see the ancient ruins of this city, and sent his clerk Edwards to get some ponies from the Myowoon. The Myowoon, thinking Edwards was a follower of some one about the Royal Court, immeditely ordered out the ponies, but when he discovered that he belonged to the Resident's party, he refused to let him have the animals. Benson, however, visited the ruins on foot. Before leaving Pagan, the Mehmandar instructed the helmsmen not to permit the rowers to sing on their approach to a town as he feared, " all the country was much alarmed at the report which had got abroad that the Resident was accompanied by 500 men and 500 more were following."[2]

On 27 September, Benson wrote to the Ministers informing them of his approach towards the capital, and assuring them and the King of his desire to maintain and to augment friendship and cordiality between the two countries. Edwards took the letter by a fast boat and delivered it to the Woondouk Gale. The Ministers neither granted him audience nor gave a written reply, but the Woondouk Gale delivered merely a verbal message, that Benson would be welcomed to the capital. Edwards met Sarkies Manook in Amarapura and learnt from him that the King had disapproved of the appointment of two officers, one at Rangoon and the other at the capital. " The English Government desires," the King was reported to have said, " that I should abide by the Treaty, but it does not itself attend to its stipulations."[3]

On 29 September, Benson touched Yandabo and on 2 October, the Kyauk-ta-loun Chokey was passed. Under orders from the Mehmandar all the flags and poles of the boats were secretly removed, and the helmsmen said that they could not re-hoist them for fear of the Mehmandar; some said that it was not the custom to hoist flags so near the capital. The idea, it appears, was, to prevent the Resident from being considered

[1] *Ibid.* pars. 359, 362.
[2] *Ibid.* par. 372.
[3] *Ibid.* pars. 376-381, 399-404.

to be a man of rank. Benson, however, had the flags and poles re-hoisted by his own men.[1]

The same day, 2 October, the Mehmandar received an order from the Hlutdaw to stop the party at Kyauk-ta-loun, and not to proceed further without orders; a halt was, therefore, made at a village north of Kyauk-ta-loun. The next day Benson called upon the Mehmandar to make a move towards the capital, but he refused. Benson threatened to move on with as many gun and row boats as his own men could manage, and leave the Mehmandar behind. This settled the difficulty, and the Mehmandar gave way and proceeded.[2] Before the party had gone very far, it was met by a merchant deputation consisting of Sarkies Manook and Carrapiet, both Armenians, and Low an English merchant. They told Benson that they had been sent by the King to accompany the British Resident to Amarapura. None of them held any office under the Crown, and they brought with them neither a message nor a letter from the King or his Ministers. Benson was surprised at this move of the Burmese Government, and made the following reply to the deputation:—"As you are Merchants only and not any of you holds an official situation, I consider your present visit as merely paid to a British officer, and I decline to recognize you as a deputation from the Government to me in my capacity of representative of the Governor-General to the Court of Amarapoora." [3]

By about noon of 4 October, the Resident passed Amarapura and arrived at Thaya-goun where quarters had been erected for him. A Tsare-dau-gyee came aboard and informed Benson that the Woondouk Myosa of Nga-Zoon was waiting ashore to welcome him. Crawfurd and Burney had been met by Woondouks a day's journey down the capital, and the Woongyees themselves had welcomed Burney ashore. Benson drew the attention of the Tsare-dau-gyee to this change of attitude, but at the same time said that he would be satisfied if the

---

[1] *Ibid.* pars. 395, 396.
[2] *Ibid.* pars. 395, 406, 408.
[3] *Ibid.* pars. 409-414.

Woondouk came aboard to welcome him. The Woondouk complied with Benson's wishes and invited him to land immediately,
but the Resident refused to be hurried. Benson accompanied
the Woondouk to the houses erected for the Resident and party,
suggested changes necessary to make them more comfortable,
and offered to pay for the workmen. The Woondouk agreed
to represent the matter to the Ministers and left with all his
followers; Benson also retired to his boat for the night.[1]

The next day, 5 October, Benson landed with all his followers, and took possession of his quarters. " They consist of
four small bungalows," he wrote, " a commodious shed for the
Escort and one cook-room. The buildings are raised on posts
as are all similar structures in the country, and are composed of
coarse bamboo mats, bamboo flooring and thatched roofing.
They are not however bad of their kind, but are very slight and
ill calculated as a defence against heat, cold or driving rain;
they are huddled together in an area extending 200 feet in one
direction by 160 feet in the other, and are closed by a bamboo
fence, having two openings for ingress and egress. Certain
essential conveniences have never been thought of; another
cook-room is required for Mr. Good (the Residency Surgeon) and
Mr. Edwards, also some accommodation for the establishments
and followers, and a shed where the sepoys and others may
dress their victuals. The space in which we are put down is
shaded by a few very fine trees, but the ground is now soaked
with wet and we are likely to be sadly hampered from the want
of a near or convenient bazaar and of wholesome water." [2]

The Residency was located " north of Amarapoora, about a
mile from the nearest part of it......on an island or tongue of
land, back water from the flooded river now lying close to our
fence on two sides, the grove of which we occupy, — one
extremity extends south towards the termination of the solid
ground and is interspersed with huts said to be owned by fisher-
men and washermen. On the north and north east are rice

[1] *Ibid.* pars. 309-404, 420, 422-425, 427.
[2] *Ibid.* par. 428.

grounds, and at a little distance groves on what may formerly
have been the bank of some channel of the Irrawaddy.

" If the attention be restricted to the place itself and the
ground in the vicinity, the site will not be an objectionable one
when the river entirely subsides, but this spot is said to have
flooded when the river attains its brightest elevation, and there is
danger that the air may be corrupted by the surrounding swamps
when the back water drains off " [1] Good, the Residency Sub-
Assistant Surgeon, made the following report on the site:—

" It being situated on a comparatively lower piece of
ground than the surrounding country, and not only subject to
annual inundations for some months, but also will continue
damp and wet for a certain period after the recession of the
rains, it being almost surrounded by extensive rice cultivation
and swamp, the consequent decomposition of vegetable and
other matter will necessarily fill the air with noxious exhalation
or malaria. These with the diurnal changes of temperature
common in this country in the beginning of the cold season or
immediately after the rains, will, I think, prove efficient cause
to render the site of the Residency unhealthy at certain seasons,
by producing intermittant fevers, ague, etc." [2]

The King of Burma did not want a British Resident in his
country. He looked upon his presence as humiliating to his
majesty; but if the British Government insisted upon sending
one, he was prepared to receive him provided he stayed in
Rangoon, and was satisfied with a rank equivalent to that of a
Woondouk, and negotiated directly with the Ayébain-Woondouk of Rangoon. The British Government, however, insisted
upon sending the Resident to the capital: this was a bitter pill
to Tharrawaddy, but he was not prepared to go to war; hence
he and his Government decided to humiliate the Resident and
place all manner of obstructions, difficulties, and inconveniences
in his way, professing most vociferously at the same time firm
friendship, so that in mere disgust the Residency might be

[1] *Ibid.* pars. 428-430.
[2] *Ibid.* pars. 570-574.

withdrawn. In order to appreciate the difficulties of Tharrawaddy, it should be remembered, that the government of Burma was still of a primitive and crude character: the presence of a British officer of the Woongyee rank, therefore, would lead to endless interferences and corrections from the Resident in the internal and frontier concerns of the country. This would undoubtedly be humiliating to an independent ruler, and it was this exactly what Tharrawaddy was trying to escape by all and every means except a declaration of war.

In order to carry out the policy mentioned above, the Residency was deliberately located in an unhealthy area beyond the city. There was no bazaar in the neighbourhood and this was a great inconvenience. Benson remained in Amarapura for nearly six months, from 5 October, 1838 to 14 March, 1839, but no real notice was taken of him by the Burmese Government. He was not invited to meet the Ministers at the Hlutdaw, and the King never granted him audience. The Ministers were not prepared to concede to him any higher rank than that of the Woondouk, and were not willing to transact any business with him. They plainly said that in keeping with Article 7 of the Treaty they would recognize him as a resident officer "with 50 men," that's all.

The Resident's party consisted of some 150 men including the lascars, but no bazaaring facilities had been provided for them. Between the Residency and the City there was a broad sheet of water. No Government officer or person of any description was stationed at or near the Residency to render aid and advice, although the authorities knew full well that the visitors were strangers, and would be at loss how to proceed. To add to the difficulties, no Burmese boatman was willing to take over any of Benson's people across the swamp, since they had been prohibited by the Government officers from doing so, under pain of dire consequences.[1] Benson complained to the Ministers concerning this inconvenience, and requested that a few vendors of the necessaries of life might be established in

[1] *Ibid.* pars. 431, 436, 522, 523, 540-546.

the vicinity of the Residency [1] For some time the Ministers took no notice of his request, although they replied to him in writing.   On 13 October, however, they permitted two Burmese boatmen to ply their canoes on hire to the members of the Residency; [2] but not till 15 December, were people and vendors allowed to visit the Residency: [3] before this, several people who had ventured to come were imprisoned under the King's orders. [4] On 7 November, a man and a woman, who happened to sit under a tree near the Residency, were seized, bound and imprisoned, and only released when it was known that they had come from a distant village and could have had no business with the Residency. [5]

Benson took up with the Ministers the question of the neglect he, as Resident, was suffering at the hands of the Burmese Government.   In his letter to the Ministers dated 11 October, Benson contrasted his reception and treatment with that accorded to Crawfurd and Burney:—

" The object of the Resident is by a very few selected facts, to call the attention of the Ministers to the unsuitable manner of his reception as compared with that of his predecessors, and thereby to evince the neglect he deems himself to have experienced: —

" 1st.   The Envoy Mr. Crawfurd was met at Kyouk-ta-loun by a Tsare-dau-gyee from the capital and at Pauk-tau by a deputation consisting of a Woondouk and three Tsare-dau-gyees.   On his arrival at the Capital an Atwenwoon instantly boarded his vessel to compliment him and led him to his assigned residence where a Woongyee was ready to receive him.   At the front gate of the enclosure of the residence Mr. Crawfurd was met by the Woongyee who handed him to the house destined for his accommodation.   Public officers forthwith remained in attendance upon Mr. Crawfurd to see that all the wants of the Mission were supplied.   On the third day after his arrival an Atwenwoon with other officers waited upon him.

" 2nd.   The Resident Lt. Col. Burney was met at Pauk-tau by a Tsare-dau-gyee from the capital, and at Let-tshoung-zoo by

[1] *Ibid.* pars. 442-449: Benson to the Ministers, 8 October, 1838.
[2] *Ibid.* pars. 488-490, 513.
[3] *Ibid.* Vol. 15, Benson's Journal, par. 1179.
[4] *Ibid.* pars. 431, 436, 522, 523, 540-546.
[5] *Ibid.* par. 682.

a deputation consisting of a Woondouk and inferior officers. On his arrival he was handed from his boat by a Woondouk and was received at his habitation by a Woongyee and two Atwenwoons. On the third day a Tsare-dau-gyee waited upon him on behalf of the Government to make complimentary enquiries; on the second day after that a Woondouk performed a like polite office, and on the day following, a Woongyee, two Atwenwoons and a Woondouk paid him a formal visit at his own house.

"3rd. On 27 September, the Resident Col. Benson reported to the Ministers his approach to the capital in a letter containing assurances of the friendly feeling of his own Government towards that of this country. On the day before he reached the capital, the Resident Col. Benson was met by 3 ordinary merchants not one of whom held any office under the King, nor had they any message or letter to deliver. On the day of his arrival opposite the City of Amarapoora, not a soul presented himself to point out where the Resident was to be located. The consequence was that his fleet mistook the channels of the River and lost much time in seeking the place assigned for his dwelling. On reaching the place a Tsare-dau-gyee boarded his boat, who after some time announced that a Woondouk waited at the house to receive him. When the Resident represented the apparent neglect he had experienced and explained his expectation that a Woondouk could conduct him from his boat to the house,"

the Woondouk did come aboard, but he also soon

"left him unattended by any, even the lowest Burmese officer. From that hour now 10 days ago, up to this moment the Resident Col. Benson has remained wholly unnoticed by the Government and its functionaries."[1]

On 20 October, Benson again wrote to the Ministers "that during a residence of 18 days near the Capital he has not been personally noticed by any officer of the Government. Undoubtedly the Governor-General anticipated that on arrival of the Resident at Amarapoora, he would be welcomed with that courtesy and consideration which are due to his high office of representative of the British Government of India, and with that regard and respect which best become the dignity of both the great nations."[2]

In reply to the above complaints, the Ministers wrote, that "in accordance to His Majesty's views to cement friendship

[1] Ibid. Vol. 13, Consultations 28 November, 1838, Benson's Journal, par. 501.
[2] Ibid. pars. 559 et. seq.

and promote peace between the Great Countries, the Royal permission was granted, and in conformity to the duties of friendship houses were prepared for the Resident's reception." [1]
They made no attempt to answer the points raised by Benson,
but hinted that perhaps he did not enjoy the rank of the former
Residents.[1] Benson found the situation very exasperating; but
to add to the insult, on 22 October, a junior Tsare-dau-gyee
called at the Residency, delivered no message, but after sitting
for some time, enquired politely respecting Benson's health
and age.[2]

As Envoy and Resident, Benson should have been not only
suitably welcomed, but arrangements should also have been made
to receive him officially at the Youndaw and to present him to
His Majesty the King. On 9 October, Benson for the first
time enquired when and where the assembled Ministers would
meet him and receive and read the letters from his Government.[3] The Ministers replied to say that since it was raining
and the roads were muddy, they were unable to grant him a
meeting. This excuse of rain and roads was reiterated in
several letters,[4] but Benson continued to press the point, and
finally, on 22 October, he received the following communcation
from them:—

> "........In accordance with the desire of the two great
> nations, that the friendship between the Burmese and the English
> states may always continue firm, there is nothing particular to
> discuss besides the cementing of friendship and peace between
> the two great countries........With respect to your wish for an
> early meeting, as you are an ambassador that has arrived from a
> Great Country, we have been waiting to invite you until the roads
> become good and there is no mire and water. But if you cannot
> wait until (the roads) become dry, and desire to come we have
> to inform you that you will be allowed to do so." [5]

Benson made a dignified protest to the Ministers against
the wording of their letter as being " certainly unsuitable to

[1] *Ibid.* pars. 517 et. seq.
[2] *Ibid.* par. 575.
[3] *Ibid.* pars. 469-472.
[4] *Ibid.* pars. 488-490, 517 et. seq.
[5] *Ibid.* pars. 581 et. seq.

13

the grave and important situations of the respective parties." [1] This produced an immediate effect: the very same day the Ministers fixed 8 November, for a meeting, not at the Youndaw, however, but at the house of the Kyee Woongyee. They also offered to send an elephant, horses, and boats, belonging to the same Woongyee, to receive Benson and his party. Benson was taken aback at this proposal of a meeting at the house of one of the Woongyees and not at the Youndaw. [2] After carefully considering the question, he felt, that if he responded to it, his official character as " Representative at the Royal Court," would be destroyed. He, therefore, rejected the offer. " It would not only be a breach of rule," he wrote to the Ministers, " but would be derogatory to the King of Ava to visit any Minister at his private dwelling house until the Resident's public function shall have been officially recognized at a formal meeting of the Assembled Ministers in a public edifice, and until he shall have had the honour of an audience of His Majesty." [3]

The Ministers pretended to be hurt at Benson's refusal to go to the Kyee Woongyee's house, and said, that according to Burmese etiquette it was extremely uncivil to turn down the invitation. They repeated their proposal, [4] and said that "in conformity to the rites of friendship we have apprised you that you might come to the Kyee Woongyee's house where you would meet officers of high rank, a Woongyee and Woondouk together who will confer with you. In the 7th article of the Treaty it is merely stated that the friendship now settled between the two great countries may be permanent, let one Government person appointed by the British Government with 50 attendants and arms complete reside in the Royal City of Burmah. Besides the Treaty there is nothing to discuss, the manner of meeting or of reception is not in the treaty." [5] Thus the Ministers now threw off the mask, and practically gave Benson to understand that they would only allow him to live

---

[1] *Ibid.* Vol. 15, Consultations 9 January, 1839, pars. 633-640.
[2] *Ibid.* pars. 656-660.
[3] *Ibid.* pars. 662-667.
[4] *Ibid.* pars. 701-706.
[5] *Ibid.* pars. 717-723.

at the capital with his attendants, and that since the Treaty did not speak of diplomatic relations, they also would not have any dealings with him, besides the exchange of sentiments of friendship.

Benson made a vigorous reply on 11 November, maintaining that the manner of his reception as Resident had already been established by precedent which could not be departed from, that the Government of Burma had neglected him for over five weeks, and that he was entitled to be received either at the Hlutdaw or at the Youndaw, and finally, that he would not discuss high matters of business in any private house, since it would be opposed to all precedent and approved usage. " Under the integrity of the treaty of Yandaboo", wrote Benson, " the Resident is now at the capital and prefers an undeniable claim to be received by the Ministers and by their sovereign with the respect and formalities due to his character as representing the rights, interests and dignity of the Governor-General of India." [1]

On 13 November, he wrote to them again:— "......the Resident Col. R. Benson is deeply concerned to find that from the tenor of the Ministers' letter...... he must draw the inference that his pretentions to be received as the permanent diplomatic Resident of the Governor-General of India are disallowed.   He gathers from the Ministers' letters that he can only be recognized by the King of Ava and by his Ministers in the capacity of an officer with 50 men attached.   Such recognition the Resident will not condescend to accept.   In that subordinate capacity to which this Government would confine him, can he be entitled to an honourable and dignified audience of the King?   Thus stripped of his representative powers can he be deemed qualified to meet His Majesty's assembled Ministers on an equality, and to deliberate with them on weighty or any national business?   Can he confer with them on affairs requiring explanations or concessions on the part of either Government?   Can he in fine discuss with them on a corres-

[1] *Ibid.* pars. 707 et. seq.

ponding footing affairs connected with territorial boundaries, with frontier aggressive attacks, with outrages committed on the confines of the two nations, with the care of the interests and grievances of British subjects residing in His Majesty's dominions and engaged in mercantile and other peaceable and laudable pursuits? In the representative character with which he is invested by the Governor-General of India he has a title to treat on all such matters at this Court."[1] Regarding the meaning of Article 7 of the Treaty, Benson said, "that in his opinion it could not have been the intention of the framers of it, sedate, high, confidential and enlightened functionaries, cautiously to deliberate on a solemn occasion concerning so unimportant a measure as that of placing near the person of the ruler of each powerful country a mere officer without occupation accompanied by 50 men."[2]

The Ministers now gave in, but most ungraciously, and agreed to receive the Resident at the Youndaw: "if he wishes to come to the Youndau," they wrote, "and will lay aside what is considered uncivil according to Burmese custom, he will be permitted to come."[3] Benson accepted the offer, and 30 November, was fixed for him to be received by the Woongyees.[4]

Benson received authentic information from Armenian, Indian and European merchants, who were in the habit of attending the King's levees, that the attitude of the Ministers towards the British Resident was the express policy of Tharrawaddy himself. The ex-King was still living, and Tharrawaddy feared the British might take up cudgels for the dethroned monarch. Had he been wise, he would have followed a friendly policy and won over the British to his cause; but he had too high a sense of his sovereignty to submit to the interferences of a foreign agent in the affairs of his own country. He did not pay sufficient attention to the fact, however, that the frontiers and foreign trade were subjects in which the interests of

---

[1] *Ibid.* pars. 726 et. seq.
[2] *Ibid.*
[3] *Ibid.* pars. 842 et. seq.
[4] *Ibid.* pars. 878 et. seq.

the British were at stake. According to information received by Benson, the ex-King resided "in an angle of the area of the Prince of Prome's Palace; people may have access to him, but the names of all visitors are noted; of course he sees few. The reigning monarch usually furnishes him with dishes from his own table before he partakes of any portion of the meal before him."[1] The old Ministers and other officers, adherents of Bagyidaw, were still in irons, but not subjected to labour. They were allowed a few attendants to minister to them, and out of their secreted effects they were able to secure comfortable food.[2]

Although Tharrawaddy had been a little merciful to the state prisoners, his attitude towards the British Residency remained unchanged. Benson heard from "a very reliable authority," that the King had uttered the following words, not in a fit of passion or under irritation, but most coolly: "The Treaty is a disgraceful one, and rather than have made it, I would have suffered myself and whole family to be cut to pieces. I will not have a Resident at the Capital. I will keep at Rangoon an officer of equal rank with the Governor-General, and business may go on there. I am a King, next to God, supreme in this country, and every man's life is in my power."[3] Undoubtedly the King was strengthened in this attitude, because he was informed by some of his hired European agents and spies in Amarapura, Rangoon and Calcutta, that the British Government was not prepared to go to war in order to force the King to receive a Resident. In Calcutta the King's agent and spy was one Mackay, in Rangoon, Staig, and in Amarapura, Low.[4] Benson did not know anything of Mackay, but he speaks of Staig and Low as being disreputable and despicable British subjects.[4] The information given by these men to the King was correct. The Governor-General, having committed himself to a war with Dost Mahomed of Afghanistan,[5] was not willing to

---

[1] *Ibid.* Vol. 13, Benson's Journal, par. 465. The idea was to prevent the adherents of Bagyidaw from poisoning Tharrawaddy.
[2] *Ibid.* Vol. 15, par. 612.
[3] *Ibid.* Vol. 13, pars. 535, 536.
[4] *Ibid.* Vol. 15, par. 767.
[5] The First Afghan War, 1838-1841.

embroil himself at the same time into another war with Burma.
Tharrawaddy was kept fully informed of the political situation
in India by his agents, and exaggerated accounts of what was
passing on the North-Western frontier of India were in circulation in Amarapura.[1]

While Benson was experiencing neglect at the capital,
Bayfield was passing through a testing time at the hands of the
Rangoon Ayébain-Woondouk.   The Woondouk refused to do
business with him, and insisted upon his vacating the house
which had been provided for him by the Burmese Government.
On 30 August, therefore, he removed to a house on the bank
of the river, placed at his disposal by one Capt. Roy who had
rented it from an Armenian, Gabriel Elijah the owner.   The
Woondouk immediately began to press Gabriel to eject Bayfield from the house, and threatened to confiscate it if his
orders were not complied with.   Gabriel was unwilling to act
as ordered, but he explained to Bayfield his own situation and
requested him to vacate the house.   Bayfield refused to vacate
it on the ground that he was tenant to Roy and not to Gabriel.
The Woondouk now called upon Roy to compel Bayfield to
vacate the house.   Roy replied that he could not do that since
Bayfield was an officer of his own Government.[2]   The Woondouk then dropped the question of the house, but began to
place fresh difficulties in the way of Bayfield.   According to
Bayfield, the Woondouk showed this aggressive and ungracious
attitude under the advice of Staig.   "I conceive it my duty to
inform you," he wrote to Benson on 7 September, "that Mr.
Staig, whose character is not unknown to you, and whose
interest it is to prevent the continuance of a British officer at
Rangoon, is the mainspring of the difficulties in the affair of
the salute[3] as well as the subsequent incivilities offered by the
Woondouk to the British Government through the persons of
its officers.   He is the Woondouk's adviser on all occasions
connected with the British Government, and openly identifies

[1] India Secret Consultations Vol. 13, Benson's Journal, par. 515.
[2] *Ibid.* Consultations 21 November, 1838, Bayfield's Journal, pars.
    9-39.
[3] Vide Supra p. 360.

himself with the interests and views of the Burmese Government to the prejudice of his own......; his influence seems just now all powerful." [1]

On 26 September, Bayfield wanted to dispatch to the Residency two boxes of military stores. The Woondouk asked Bayfield to give an account of the contents of the boxes and to receive a pass for the same. Bayfield objected, as the boxes were the property of the British Government, and the Woondouk's demand was opposed to custom, and contrary to the usage of civilized countries. The Woondouk, however, maintained that unless the contents of the boxes were declared, the Burmese Government would not be responsible for their safety. Bayfield, fearing that the attitude of the Woondouk was tantamount to a license to the dacoits to attack the boat, did not send the boxes. [2]

In October 1838, the Shahbunder of Rangoon, under the direction of the Woondouk, issued orders to the Commanders of boats, that Post Office Packets shall not in future be delivered to Bayfield, but shall be taken to the Custom House to be examined before delivery. On 17 October, the vessel *Mary* brought packets from Penang for Bayfield. Bayfield's men went to the boat to get the packets, but the Shahbunder turned them back twice. Bayfield then addressed the Commander of the boat officially, and he delivered the packet. The Woondouk now took action: the very next day he confined in jail Cowasjee the owner of the vessel, and refused to release him on bail. Bayfield wrote to the Woondouk pointing out the illegality of the order and the injustice of confining Cowasjee who was a respectable man. The Woondouk treated Bayfield's messenger very rudely, refused to receive any letter or message from him, and said that Bayfield was not a Resident and so had no right to address a letter to him. He, however, released Cowasjee on bail on 19 October. [3]

---

[1] *Ibid.* Consultations 21 November, 1838, Bayfield's Journal, pars. 9-39.
[2] India Secret Consultations Vol. 13, Bayfield to Benson, 26 and 27 September, 1838.
[3] *Ibid.* No. 135.

Bayfield represented the question of the Packets both to the Government of India as well as to Benson, and said, that Government Dispatches "if once within the Burmese power, will be opened on the most frivolous and unfounded charges of suspicion of their containing contraband articles etc." [1] This he feared would be very damaging to the prestige of the Indian Government, and suggested that orders might be issued to the Commanders to deliver Government packets to him and to no other person.[1]

The Woondouk, however, meanwhile began to enforce his orders, and did not deliver letters and packets to Bayfield before he had previously examined them at the Custom House. Benson now intervened, and on 17 November, issued two notices from Amarapura, one for Burmese officers in Rangoon and the other for Commanders of ships flying the British flag, to say that packets should be given to Bayfield, or in his absence to one J. Brown who had before acted as agent of the British Government.[2] On the same day, Benson received a letter from the the Rangoon Woondouk, through the Ministers, complaining against the attempts of Bayfield to have packets delivered to him direct and not through the Burmese authorities. He also threatened that if Bayfield continued to act contrary to established usages, " I shall order the Shahbunder (who has the right) to punish him and to adopt strong measures to prevent his doing the like in future." [3] Benson was surprised that the Ministers, after reading such a letter, should have forwarded it to him, and fearing that Bayfield and the Indian Government would be insulted by the Woondouk, he immediately addressed a letter to the Woongyees, pointing out the highly improper attitude of the Woondouk towards the officer of a friendly power. He requested them to consider how the Burmese King and Ministers would feel if the British Resident were to issue such a threat against a Burmese officer, and finally called upon them to disavow their approba-

[1] *Ibid.* No. 135.
[2] *Ibid.* Vol. 15, Consultations 9 January, 1839, Benson's Journal, par. 789.
[3] *Ibid.* pars. 808-812.

tion to the Woondouk of his policy.[1] The Ministers delayed replying, and when pressed, wrote on 25 November, but paid no proper attention to his complaint. On the other hand they said that the Resident should have only complained, and not illustrated his complaint with a " counter threat." [2]

While correspondence was going on upon the subject, the day arrived (30 November) which had been fixed for receiving the Resident at the Youndaw. " According to arrangement," says Benson, " Elephants most shabbily equipped, as compared to what my eye has been accustomed to in India, arrived at 8-30 a.m. They were accompanied by a Tsaredaugyee and a few attendants." [3] Benson set out at 9 a.m. accompanied by McLeod his Assistant, Glascott the Captain of the Escort, Edwards the Clerk and Interpreter, Good the Surgeon, 30 men of the Escort, the non-Commissioned officers, Drummers, the office establishments, some Lascars, and a few private servants.[3] The progress and experiences of the party en route may be described in Benson's words:—

After crossing the stream " we recommenced our land progress which was along as wretched a road, as dirty a bazaar, and as thinly inhabited and poverty stricken streets as it has been my lot anywhere to see. Along the street there are holes several feet deep, and here and there we met with pieces of timber, broken carts, and cart wheels......

" When we reached the end of a street one side of which is bounded at the distance of perhaps 20 paces from it by a brick wall, said to enclose the palace buildings, and from whence we could just descry the Youndau, the Tsaredaugyee stopped the procession, and desired we would alight and walk the intervening space. On being remonstrated with he advanced about halfway, and made another pause. He now left us and went for orders to the Youndau. On returning he took us on again to within 20 yards of the corner of a mill street on the other side of which stood the Youndau. There was here an interchange of

[1] *Ibid.* pars. 819-825.
[2] *Ibid.* par. 870.
[3] *Ibid.* par. 902.

messages through the Tsaredaugyee and Mr. Sarkies........
the Elephants were allowed to advance to the corner of the
street, and the Escort and myself in Tonjon allowed to pass
up to the steps of the Youndau where I unslippered, walked in,
and sat down on my hams. The other gentlemen did the same."[1]

From the Residency to the Youndaw it took 1½ hours.
Only two Woongyees and two Woondouks were present to
receive Benson and discuss questions with him. The Woongyees offered to shake hands with Benson, but he refused, since
their attitude so far had not been friendly. When he entered
the Youndaw an attempt was made to place him among the
Woondouks, but Benson by skilful manœuvring managed
to place himself near the Woongyees. All the Burmese
officers, even the Tsaredaugyees, were provided with mats to
sit on, but not Benson and suite. The Resident asked for a
waistcloth from one of his followers when Sarkies went and
brought a mat for him.[2]

Benson's Journal contains the following record of the conversation that took place.[3] The Burmese Government had evidently made up its mind not to accord to Benson the position
enjoyed by Burney as Resident; his presence at the capital was
to be only just tolerated because of the treaty:—

> " Resident: — Are you the assembled Ministers of the King of
> Ava?
>
> Ministers: — We are.
>
> R. Are you prepared to recognize me as the representative of
> the Governor-General of India?
>
> M. We do not know how you have been deputed.
>
> R. Will you receive me as the representative of the Governor-
> General of India?
>
> M. We have received you in a proper manner; we have built
> houses for you.

[1] *Ibid.* pars. 908, 909.
[2] *Ibid.* pars. 1053, 1054.
[3] *Ibid.* pars. 928-1046.

R. I do not allow that you have received me in a proper manner. But I ask, will you receive me as the representative of the Governor-General?

M. We will answer the question when we see your credentials.

R. Have you the power to recognize me on seeing my credentials?

M. We have, and will do so when we are satisfied in a proper manner.

R. Here are my credentials.

M. Stop, we have had no friendly conversation.

R. I have been long enough at the capital to have enabled you to hold friendly intercourse. At present there are matters of imperative importance before us. After they are gone through I will have much pleasure in holding friendly intercourse with you."

The Ministers then read the credentials, and the following further conversation took place:—

" M. Have you any letter for the Ministers?

R. I have, but now that you have inspected my credentials, I wish to know whether you receive me in a capacity corresponding with that on which Col. Burney was received?

M. We are satisfied that you have been appointed Resident here.

R. Then I have a claim to be received and treated exactly as Col. Burney was received and treated.

M. We will treat with you in a friendly way, but now there is a new King and there are new Woongyees and new Woondouks, and everything has been altered.

R. Do you admit my claim to be received exactly as Col. Burney was received, and do you admit that I possess the same powers?

M. There are some things good and some things bad. What is good we will do.

R. Do you admit that I have the power to discuss matters connected with concessions and explanations on both sides, British and Burmese?

M. We have admitted your credentials; all that is for the cementing of friendship we will do.

R. Do you admit that I am a diplomatic representative of the Governor-General?

M. What is the office of the Resident?

R. The Interpreter is desired to read the Burmese Translation of a letter written some days ago to the Ministers in which it is pointed out my right to discuss matters appertaining to concessions, explanations, frontier outrages, protection of British subjects etc.

M. When the King gives power to a Woongyee, a Woondouk, or a Tsaredaugyee, he can discuss and settle these things finally himself.

R. Do you admit that I have a right to do business in the same manner that Col. Burney did?

M. There is no use in referring to Col. Burney, he did what was not right.

R. I am Col. Burney's successor and must be recognized, and must be allowed to transact business as he did.

M. We recognize you having the same rank, but he did what was not right, and until now we are not satisfied with him.

R. I know nothing of Col. Burney's acts with which you find fault. If you have complaints against him state them to the Governor-General.

M. We have received you in a friendly manner.

R. In my opinion you have not done so.

M. You only think so.

R. Since the day I was about to quit Rangoon I have experienced no friendly attention, on the contrary all has been neglect.

M. On what points, in what way?

R. Whom did you send to meet me on my approach to the capital etc., etc. Why have you interdicted the subjects of His Majesty from intercourse with me?

M. We have not forbidden people to go to you.

R. I have satisfactory proof of the fact, but I will not adduce it, because sure punishment would be the fate of the witnesses. (The Interpreter now reads my 2nd and 4th letters to the Ministers). [1]

---

[1] In these letters Benson had complained of the neglect and incivilities experienced by him in Burma.

With such reception as you have given me my Government cannot be satisfied. I allude not to myself personally, but to my situation as representative of the Governor-General.

M. We have received you well.

R. I do not admit that, and that every civilized government will be against you. (sic). But to end this discussion, will you recognize me in the same light as Col. Burney was recognized under the treaty?

M. We are all new, the Government is new, and you are new.

R. I must be recognized as Col. Burney was. The Government of this country is the same. If you are all new functionaries you can refer to the records of the Government to learn what ought to be done.

M. We have received you in a friendly manner and there is nothing more to say.

R. Words are nothing, I have given you facts.

M. These are trifling matters; but did we not send men to work for you?

R. You see I have a right to interpose in behalf of British subjects.

M. It is in the credentials.

R. Then you allow the hitherto received interpretation of the 7th article of the Treaty of Yandaboo?

M. The object of it is to maintain friendship and to allow an officer and 50 men to remain at the capital of each other.

R. I have written to you that I will not condescend to be recognized in the capacity of an officer commanding 50 men, and if you adhere to such interpretation I must close the conference.

M. Yes, but an officer can discuss on matters of business.

R. You know I have avowals to demand from you.

M. What are they?

R. There are other matters to settle, but I decline to enter upon the point yet.

M. Have you come to make friends with us?

R. Certainly, and you know perfectly well that I have anxiously desired to meet every reasonable wish of the King and to cultivate your friendly regard. But I expect you will meet me halfway; you must to the full extent perform your part.

M. As you would not shake hands with us you do not wish to be on terms of preceding friendship.

R. You have given me no proof of a wish to be on friendly terms. I do not conceal what my feelings are.

M. We do not either, we wish to be friends.

R. You profess to do so, but you have given me no proof of it as the representative of the Governor-General.

M. In the Treaty there is nothing about reception, only to maintain friendship.

R. I appeal on this head to former custom here, and to the customs of all civilized countries.

M. What is bad is bad, and what is good is good in some countries and not others. We have received you properly and you would not shake hands with us.

R. I have been here two months and have not been visited by a Woongyee or a Woondouk as all persons similarly circumstanced are used to be.

M. Then because Woongyees and Woondouks have not visited you, you do not shake hands.

R. Not that alone, but the whole treatment and neglect I have experienced since I was about to leave Rangoon.

M. Are you not satisfied now with your reception today?

R. If it had taken place 6 or 7 days after my arrival I might have been satisfied, or if I had been then assured that the feelings of this Government were friendly towards mine, or when I asked in a letter written very long ago that a reciprocation of friendly sentiments on the part of the King should be given to me, that reciprocation, you know, was withheld and never has been given.

M. Is this the reason then that you would not shake hands with us?

R. Not this alone, all the reasons combined.

M. You ought not to have refused to shake hands with us. We are not satisfied.

R. Then if you will not enter into any other subject I will retire.

M. How can we say anything if you are not friendly to us?

R. It is I that have not been satisfied. I am anxious to be friendly with you and will shake hands when you have satisfied me on some points.

M. What further proof can we give you?

R. I wish to be considered as to powers and situation exactly as Col. Burney was considered. I make no allusion to anything but his official situation.

M. We recognize you as to rank.

R. Do you admit that I have power to discuss respecting concessions, explanations, etc,, etc.

M. You can discuss, but what are they? What is in your credentials?

R. Here is an English and Burmese copy of them for record.

M. Can you settle matters finally without reference to the Governor-General? What does the word "hereafter" mean?

R. Supposing changes took place on the frontiers of Assam which required recommunications with this Court such as might be called instructions which I am to receive hereafter; my powers are pointed out in my credentials."

Considerable further conversation took place, and Benson tried to induce the Ministers to agree to transact business with him at the Hlutdaw, exactly as it used to be done with Burney. The Ministers, however, cleverly evaded the issue, and constantly harped upon Benson's refusal to shake hands with them: they twitted him for this his attitude. They certainly did score one point against him in this connection. Burney always shook hands with the old Ministers; but of course Burney was not neglected as Benson was. The question of an audience with the King was also considered, and after some haggling the Ministers said, "Of course you will have an audience."

Benson next referred to the Rangoon Woondouk's threat, and put two questions to the Ministers:— "Are you, prepared to avow your disapprobation of the threat against Dr. Bayfield conveyed to me in a letter by the Woondouk of Rangoon?" "Have you warned the Woondouk against putting his threat into execution?" The Ministers refused to answer these questions on the spot, and said that they would write to him and satisfy him:—

"Resident: — Unless you satisfy me on this point I fear I cannot consider your Government to be friendly.

Ministers: — We cannot help it; but we do not now say whether we are displeased or not; we will write to you in three or four days.

R.   Be assured my Government will not allow such language to be used with respect to any of its officers. Unless your displeasure of that language be clearly expressed serious notice will be taken of it."

At these words of Benson, one of the Ministers said in an undertone, and ironically, "What a terrible thing that will be for the Burmese." When the conference came to an end, one of the Ministers said, "We will satisfy you when we write, and therefore when we part now we hope we shall part as friends." To this Benson replied, "I do not consider you as sincere friends, but as a proof of my desire that you may become so, I will shake hands with you now that I am about to retire. But remember what is due by you respecting the Woondouk's conduct. Until that matter is settled we cannot be cordial friends."

After the conference had ended, Lt. Glascott drew up the Escort to salute the Resident as Burney used to be. When the Ministers observed that the drum would be beaten, they strongly objected to it, and said that the King would be angry. Benson dispensed with the beating of the drum, but said, that he did not relinquish his right. He then shook hands with the Ministers and retired.

The conference had lasted for $4\frac{1}{2}$ hours.[1] Benson's own feelings over the conference he sums up as follows:—" It is impossible to convey by description to any one not an actor in such a scene a just sense of the vexations, slights, annoyances and insolence experienced on this occasion, as it is to convey to the blind an idea of colours. In few words the treatment was felt by me to be such as no English gentleman or more extensively no British subject ought to be exposed to."[2]

Benson looked upon the Rangoon Woondouk's threat to Bayfield to be a major issue, and waited for a reply from the

[1] India Secret Consultations Vol. 15, Benson's Journal, par. 1047.
[2] *Ibid.* par. 1051.

Ministers. Finally on 4 December, a communication arrived. The Ministers agreed that the Woondouk had used words wrongfully and in excess, but they added, they were not prepared to take any action, because, as they put it, " the Resident had repeated it " in the fact that he had enquired how the King and the Ministers would feel if Benson were to threaten a Burmese officer in those words. Benson was amazed that what he had merely said as a matter of illustration was looked upon by the Ministers to be as culpable as the threat of the Woondouk.[1] He threatened to retire immediately to Rangoon, and asked for boats and men. This was exactly what the King's Government desired: boats and men were immediately provided. Benson, however, on a second thought decided not to retire, since the instructions of his Government were, as far as possible, to maintain his ground at the capital.[2]

Tharrawaddy was keeping himself in full touch with the developments. His mind was in a wretched state since he neither wanted the Resident nor a war. At times he issued rash orders which did not mean much more than words. Soon after the conference at the Youndaw, the King was told that the Resident might demand the removal of the Rangoon Woondouk: he flared up immediately and ordered his two sons, the military commanders, to make preparations for war, and declared, " I shall not be dictated to in my capital by an English Bo." [3] When he heard of Benson's threat to retire to Rangoon, he at once ordered the Ministers to furnish the required boats and men; but according to Sarkies, the King's mind was in a wretched state, and he feared that the British would immediately occupy Rangoon. His English advisers, Low, McCalder, Staig, Donalds, and others, however, assured him that he had nothing to fear, and that his interpretation of Article 7 of the Treaty of Yandabo was correct.[4]

[1] *Ibid.* pars. 1079-1081.
[2] *Ibid.* pars. 1083, 1103, 1147-1149.
  Ibid. Consultations 9 January, 1839, Benson's Letter, 11 December, 1838.
[3] *Ibid.* Benson's Journal, pars. 1061-1064.
[4] *Ibid.* pars. 1103, 1109, 1141.

On 9 December, Benson, in a letter to the Ministers, put them three straight questions: " Will the Ministers avow their disapprobation of the threat used by the Woondouk of Rangoon regarding Dr. Bayfield? Will they instruct the Woondouk of Rangoon to execute the convicted criminals concerned in the Martaban outrages?......Will they admit the heretofore interpretation of the 7th article of the Treaty of Yandaboo, recognize the Resident, Col. R .Benson, not merely as an officer with 50 men, but as the diplomatic representative of the Governor-General of India, and treat him and transact business with him as the successor of Col. Burney in the manner pointed out at the late Conference with the Ministers at the Youndau?."[1]   On the first two questions the Ministers practically refused to satisfy Benson.   The third question was also not answered to the satisfaction of the Resident, but there was a vague admission of his being a diplomatic representative of the Governor-General.   " As regards the admission of the heretofore received interpretation of the 7th article of the Treaty......," they wrote, " they have received Col. Benson in a proper and kind manner and have allowed him to remain at the caiptal.   They have granted the Resident, Col. R. Benson, a reception at the Youndau as the diplomatic Representative of the Governor-General of India, but during the conference it was stated by Col. Benson that they should treat and transact business with him as the successor of Col. Burney and not merely as an officer with 50 men.   They object as to the same manner in which Col. Burney did, but aggreeably to your declaration of having been appointed an officer of rank by the Governor-General, they have to inform him that he can state whatever will promote the cementing of peace and friendship between the two countries."[2]   As to the Martaban criminals, the Ministers demanded in return for their execution the surrender of one Nga Khan, who, they said, had committed crimes in their country and was at the time an inmate of the Moulmein jail.[2]

---

[1] *Ibid.* pars. 1137-1139.
[2] *Ibid.* pars. 1153-1156.

Although Benson failed to obtain any satisfaction from the Ministers over the question of the Woondouk's threat to Bayfield, there was at least one happy outcome of his representations: the Woondouk ceased to interfere with Bayfield's post office department, and allowed the packets to be delivered to him as before.[1] On 17 December, however, Benson made a solemn protest in writing to the Ministers against the attitude of the Woondouk towards Bayfield, his threat, and the refusal of the Ministers to avow their disapprobation of his conduct, also against the refusal of the Ministers to execute the Martaban criminals.[2] When the letter of protest was delivered to the Woondouk Gale, he said to Edwards, " What is the use of a Resident remaining here whom we consider more as a watch set over us than an officer appointed to transact business? "[3]

The Government of India sympathised with Benson in the treatment experienced by him in Burma. Morrison, a member of the Council, suggested a blockade of Rangoon to bring the King to his senses. Ultimately, however, Benson was authorized to retire from the capital, if the attitude of the Ministers did not improve.[4] The British Government would most probably have taken stern measures, but for the North-Western complications. This is evident from the Government instructions to Benson and Blundell in November, 1838.[4]

Blundell, who was in favour of war with Burma, arrived at Calcutta in November, 1838, to receive instructions from his Government personally. He was given the following directions:— " Keeping in view the possibility of an unfavourable issue to the Mission of Col. Benson, you will make it your particular study to cultivate friendly relations with the Siamese and other bordering nations and tribes...... to cultivate existing

[1] *Ibid.* Vol. 15, Consultations 23 January, 1839, Bayfield to Benson, Rangoon, 8 December, 1838, No. 16.
[2] *Ibid.* Benson's Journal, pars. 1183-1222.
[3] *Ibid.* pars. 1223-1229.
[4] *Ibid.* Vol. 13, Consultations 28 November, 1838, Minute by Col. W. Morrison, 17 November, 1838; Government dispatch to Benson, 20 November, 1838.

relations of friendship (with Siam).........to secure the good-will of the Government and officers of Siam so that the resources of that country in supplies, in carriage, cattle and elephants may be available to you in case of the necessity arising of moving the Force in your quarter........" [1]

Benson gave up all hopes of being allowed to transact business at the Hlutdaw, but he was not in favour of war, for he wrote to his Government on 28 November, 1838, " No political, territorial, or commercial advantages to be gained in this quarter can to any satisfactory degree counterbalance the evils of diverting our attention and resources from the proper field of our duty — the Great Empire of India." [2]

All the Indian military units on the Burma frontiers had by this time been strengthened. The Burma authorities were well aware of these arrangements, and though the English advisers of the King had informed him that there was no likelihood of the British attacking him at that time, Tharrawaddy wished to be on the safe side and began to prepare for defence. The Prince of Prome was appointed to protect Rangoon, the Prince of Pagan to Maphe on the Arakan frontier, the Prince of Toungdwingyoung to the Assam frontier, and Prince Shwe Doung to the Martaban frontier. [3] According to reports, the King had 200,000 men under arms. [4] This was perhaps an exaggeration, but artillery practice certainly did become the order of the day. [5] On 24 December, 1838, Benson made the following record in his Journal:—" We hear of nothing but preparations for a campaign going on both here and in India. The alarm of the inhabitants of Pegu is said to be great, and their adherence to the Government of Ava is doubted. There is no appearance of any aversion to another conflict among the people about the capital." [6] On 31 December, he wrote again, " The constant artillery practice we hear is carried on under the

[1] *Ibid.* No. 37.
[2] *Ibid.* Vol. 15, Consultations 9 February, 1838.
[3] *Ibid.* Consultations 6 February, 1838, Benson's Journal, 1223-1229.
[4] *Ibid.* par. 1241.
[5] *Ibid.* pars. 1245, 1246, 1304.
[6] *Ibid.* par. 1266.

superintendence and instruction chiefly of natives of India both from Madras and Bengal and some native Portuguese."[1] On the same day Benson wrote, warning his Government against the King's warlike preparations in the following words:—

"That the King is placing large bodies of men in what he deems suitable positions, and that he has made, and continues to make every available preparation for war, are facts which I admit on grounds of general notoriety and of inference from the coincidence of numerous particulars which come daily to our knowledge. What change of policy, the conviction that the whole disposable Army of India is at our command for the invasion of the territories of Ava, may produce upon the King's mind, I will not venture to predict, because there are no means of judging correctly what may be the extent of his infatuation. But if his eyes could be opened to the prospect of an overpowering army ready to enter his Kingdom, he would not I think dare, by perverse obstinacy, to provoke hostilities; though should he. be goaded on by others or flattered into persuasion to which he is daily exposed, that the Government of India is at all embarrassed in its foreign or domestic relations, he would, I have no doubt, seize the opportunity for turning upon us, and for using his utmost efforts towards our undoing. At all events, in case our military resources should be extensively engaged in any other direction, the intentions of the Sovereign of Ava must be regarded by the Government of India with great and uneasy mistrust." [2]

Benson held also definite views on the advisability or otherwise of retaining the Residency in Burma. "In my opinion," he wrote, "a Resident can neither be useful to his own Government nor respectable and honourable in this country until that ground (i.e. that occupied by Burney previously) is occupied. The plan of the Court on the other hand is to keep the Resident in the humblest posture to which he can be restrained without insulting him." [3] He wrote again on 30 January, 1839, in the following unmistakable terms:—

[1] Ibid. par. 1304.
[2] Ibid. Benson's Letter, No. 46.
[3] Ibid.

" I feel no reserve in stating that my opinion has all along been that the most eligible course would be to withdraw the Residency; and had it been left to my discretion I should certainly have retired the moment I had ascertained it to be sufficiently probable that the Court was determined to treat the Governor-General's representative as he has been and continues to be treated. But as the Government may think differently, I am bound to believe the safest policy has been pursued. However, the opportunity of the Resident's departure might have been taken to invite the King of Ava to delegate Commissioners to the Presidency or to Moulmein, and his failure to do so might have been justly considered an indication of his being what I fear he is, and long has been, an enemy. No one can more seriously deprecate a war with this country than I do, but I greatly apprehend the ordinary rights of the Government of India cannot be secured without an appeal to arms. If recourse be had to this ultima ratio, no one can doubt that a properly organised force would in a season's campaign reach this capital." [1]

The Government of India disagreed with Benson in his diagnosis of the situation, and although it was accepted that there should be a preparation for every emergency, it was deemed proper to continue the Residency at the Burmese capital. The Burmese attitude was not considered to be as hostile as it appeared: the Ministers had at least recognized the Resident, however ungraciously and unwillingly this had been done. " I am thoroughly sensible," wrote Auckland in his Minute, " of all the difficulties of our position in respect to a government such as that which now exists in Ava. We are bound on the one hand to make allowances for the prejudices and the headstrong pride of a new dynasty clinging in its intercourse with foreign nations to the distasteful usages of former times and vaunting its resolution to revert to them, and we must feel that the last issue of a war must only be resorted to on the clear ground of justice and policy........I do not gather

---

[1] *Ibid.* Vol. 16, Consultations 13 March, 1839, Benson's Letter, 30 January, 1839, No. 71.

from the papers now before me any absolute impossibility of our continuing, for some time at least, to keep an accredited agent at Amarapoora, and it would in my opinion be of doubtful equity and prudence, if upon the difficulties which have been experienced by Col. Benson, we should proceed to instantly, as seems to be contemplated, to the threat and preparation of actual hostilities.

" The great point of an admission of the Treaty of Yandaboo has been settled by the direct official acknowledgement of the Ministers of the Court of Ava, and the reproach of a departure from that Treaty in the appointment of Dr. Bayfield as Assistant Resident at Rangoon is turned upon us. We may assume therefore the recognition of the Treaty, and it is open to us to endeavour by the exercise of temper and of judgment to avoid extreme collision upon our points of difference.

"........My supposition on the whole is, that as the Treaty and the office of Resident have been acknowledged and there are no evidences of a wish to bring on a hostile rupture, Col. Benson will in the end have been able to establish himself on some footing of official intercourse with the Court or the Government, but that that footing will be far from such as we may regard as honourable and satisfactory.

"......It is......by no means clear to me that we have any right to contemplate a resort to hostilities with the view only of procuring the higher honour and respect which we desire for our Resident. There would be a cause of War if though a Resident were nominally received, omissions and indignities foreign to the natural usages were practised in regard to him by the King, but we have not the right to declare war, only because the King chooses to adhere as nearly as he can, consistently with the stipulations of the Treaty, to the old and known policy of his country which towards foreign agents has ever been of a repulsive character." [1]

In the same Minute, the Governor-General discusses the question of gain and loss by a war with Burma. " I know,"

[1] *Ibid.* Vol. 15, 13 and 15 January, 1839, No. 11.

he says, " that such a war is very generally looked upon as one in which much is to be hazarded and much of life and money to be expended, and nothing to be gained but an unprofitable territory, requiring expensive armaments for its protection, and giving us a new frontier upon which we shall only have new difficulties and new enemies to contend with. I am not of this opinion, and I think that if we should be forced into a war of conquest, the possession of Lower Ava (*i.e.* Lower Burma), of a seaport admirably situated, of a productive country and fine navigable river, would be far from disadvantageous, and might in a very few years do much more than give compensation for the expense of its acquisition and maintenance. But I have no ambition to try this experiment. It would be attended with an expenditure of money not lightly to be incurred, it would occupy troops which can but ill be spared; in its progress it would keep alive that inflamatory spirit of restlessness which amongst our neighbours and even within our frontiers is but too ready to break forth, and any good result is, I am well aware, at least, but speculative. I am ready therefore to lay it down as a settled maxim of Indian policy that a war with Ava is to be avoided if possibly it may be avoided without dishonour or the sacrificing of undoubted and essential rights, and in support of such maxim I need scarcely dwell upon the degree to which the strength and resources of the state are likely to be elsewhere employed. It is by what has been threatened, and is passing on our Western and North Western frontier, that all Indian attention has for some time been arrested. It is to the establishment of security and to the gathering of strength in this direction that I have thought it wise to concentrate every exertion, and I should be sorry indeed for any event by which a division from this main object should be created. It might indeed promote this great object if all were first secured in Ava and in Nepal,[1] yet security to the West will be security also in regard to these states, and I need not advert to the effect which the discomfiture of the Persians before Herat has had upon the

---

[1] Relations had been a little strained at this time between Calcutta and Khatmandu.

policy of those who seemed to be gathering their strength for hostile demonstrations against us. None, however, can look to the North West to a possible change in the Government of the Punjab, to the condition of Sinde, to the distant and complicated affairs of Afghanistan, and to the time which may elapse in their settlement, and be of opinion that we have a particle of military strength which we can readily spare for other quarters."

In keeping with the policy laid down in the above quoted Minute, Benson was instructed by his Government to endeavour and maintain his position at the capital, and claim for himself the rank of a " Court Woongyee," but that if " the behaviour of the Burmese Court towards him is not such as he can with propriety assent to, to quit the capital for the avowed object of personal communication with his Government, leaving, provided the state of things will admit of his doing so, his Assistant in charge, who will consider it his duty to remain at Amarapoora until the receipt of further orders." [1] As to the Martaban criminals, Benson was instructed, that " if the surrender of Nga Khan be attempted to be made a condition of the execution of the sentences, you must insist on the surrender of all the parties concerned for trial according to the forms and by the authorities of the territory in which the crimes were committed." [2] Finally, as to the Woondouk's threat to Bayfield, the Government observed to Benson that the Ministers' defence was a mere pretence, and that " it is evident that they regret and are ashamed of the circumstance," so that it might be allowed to drop. [2] " It would be sufficient however," directed Auckland, " to dispose of this subject by a plain instruction to the Ministers that if any Burmese officer should be so violent and ill advised as to attempt to execute such threats, as have been expressed in regard to Mr. Bayfield, the British Government would take the remedy into its own hands by the

---

[1] India Secret Consultations Vol. 15, Auckland's Minute, 13 and 15 January, 1839, No. 11.
[2] Ibid. Consultations 6 February, 1839, Government dispatch to Benson No. 48.

immediate exercise of its powers in a manner which would make a memorable example of those who had so dared to injure it......" [1]

The Governor-General-in-Council fully sympathised with Benson in his difficult situation, praised him for his tact, temper, and judgment, and encouraged him to continue his endeavours and maintain the Residency if possible at the capital.[1]

Benson remained in Amarapura up to 14 March, 1839. He had no audience of the King at all, not because the Ministers or the King were opposed to it, but because Benson was not willing to be presented unless the Ministers agreed to read the Governor-General's letter at the audience, and also promised to make a suitable reply in the name of the King. The Ministers, on the other hand, were anxious to humiliate Benson and present him to the King as a bearer of tribute.[2]

The Resident and the Residency continued to be neglected by the Burmese Government. " The Government can be at no loss to conceive," wrote Benson, " how irksome our present situation is, unnoticed by any one, badly located, unsuitably housed, hope deferred, and surrounded with followers whose spirits are depressed by the circumstances in which they see our party placed."[3] The Residency grounds got flooded to the depth of over three feet, and to add to the gloom, Benson's health began to fail. The heat was rapidly on the increase, and by the end of February, the thermometer ranged, during the day, in the Residency huts, from 90° to 94°.[4]

On 2 March, Benson was surprised to have a visit from a Woondouk and a Tsaredaugyee, sent by the Ministers to enquire about his health. The King also desired the Woongyees " to apprise the Colonel that he could go to visit one of the Royal Gardens which is cool and pleasant, and that Elephants and horses will be furnished him for his use."[5] Benson was unable

---

[1] *Ibid.* Auckland's Minute, 13 and 15 January, 1839, No. 11.
[2] *Ibid.* Benson's Letter, 31 December, 1838, No. 46.
[3] *Ibid.* Vol. 16, Benson's Letter, 30 January, 1839, No. 71.
[4] *Ibid.* Vol. 17, Consultations 10 April, 1839, Benson's Journal, pars. 1485, 1504.
[5] *Ibid.* pars. 1504, 1518; Benson's Letter, No. 39.

positively to discover the motive behind these spontaneous civilities. "It is probable," he says, "that the recent revolt in the Province of Pegu may have shaken His Majesty's confidence in his resources for a war, and that he consequently wishes to temporize."[1]

Benson's health continued to decline. Finally, on medical advice, he decided to depart, and leave his Assistant, McLeod, in charge of the Residency. On 12 March, he wrote to the Ministers informing them of his decision for reasons of health, and commended McLeod to their consideration and attention. He took this opportunity, while thanking them for their enquiries concerning his health and the King's offer to visit a Royal garden, to induce them to acknowledge the letter of the Government of India in a friendly manner. "The Resident does not presume to suppose," he wrote, "that these civilities were paid to himself personally, but to him in his capacity of the Representative of the Governor-General of India. Under this impression Col. Benson seizes the occasion to mention how highly gratifying it would prove to him to be entrusted with a friendly message or a confidential communication from the Government of Ava to that of British India, or even to be the bearer of an answer to the letter addressed by Mr. Secretary Prinsep to the Ministers. But still more gratifying would it be to hear of an officer of rank being delegated to Calcutta to make known to the Governor-General His Majesty's own sentiments touching the relations between the two great states."[2]

On 13 March, Benson handed over charge to McLeod,[3] and the next day at about 8 a.m. quitted Amarapura. No Burmese officer came to see him off, although the Ministers readily supplied men and boats for the journey. On his way down, Benson saw no obvious signs of intended or expected hostilities. On 25 March, he arrived at Rangoon, and a British warship in the River fired a salute. A few hours after his arrival the Yewoon waited on him with an invitation from the Woondouk-Ayébain

[1] *Ibid.*
[2] *Ibid.* No. 42.
[3] *Ibid.* No. 43.

to occupy the house in which the Resident had previously resided; he also made obliging enquiries concerning his health; but the Woondouk later protested against the firing of the salute without permission.[1] Two British warships, the *Conway* and the *Favourite,* were at Rangoon at this time. Benson told the Commanders of these ships that no political purpose would be served by their presence in Rangoon; on 31 March, they withdrew to Amherst. From Rangoon, Benson proceeded to Moulmein; on 1 April, he returned to the Rangoon River; on 2 April he withdrew Bayfield from Rangoon, and both arrived at Calcutta on 9 April.[2] In place of Bayfield, Benson appointed Brown, an English merchant, as British Agent, and placed him in charge of all British property, boats, post office, etc.[3]

In spite of Benson's request, the Ministers did not reply to Secretary Prinsep's letter, but they sent a sealed case containing a letter. The case was opened at Moulmein and was found to contain a letter from the Ministers to the Governor-General, the address being, " To the Ruler and Commander of the Forces of India." Benson felt certain that the irregularity of the address was not due to oversight or want of familiarity with correct forms of correspondence on the part of the Ministers, but " to the determination of the sovereign of Ava to persevere in that system of proceeding which he has deliberately adopted, as in his opinion, suited to the relative position of the Government of India." [4] The letter was returned unopened to the Ministers from Calcutta by Benson at the orders of the Government, with the intimation that they had made a mistake.[5]

The Government entirely approved of Benson's action in quitting Amarapura, his placing McLeod in charge of the Residency, and his withdrawal of Bayfield from Rangoon.[6] The Resident was granted leave of absence for four months under

---

[1] *Ibid.* Nos. 47, 48; *Ibid.* Vol. 20, Benson's Journal, par. 1591.
[2] *Ibid.* Vol. 17, Consultations 10 April, 1839, No. 47.
[3] *Ibid.* No. 48.
[4] *Ibid.* No. 47.
[5] *Ibid.* Vol. 20, Consultations 22 May, 1839, Nos. 18, 19.
[6] *Ibid.* Vol. 19, Consultations 1 May, 1839, No. 172.

medical certificate.[1] The Governor-General thanked him profusely for the way he had conducted himself in Burma, and for his tact in his relations with the Government of that country: " I am directed to express," wrote the Secretary to the Governor-General, " the high sense which the Governor-General has, of the whole of Col. Benson's conduct during his residence at Amarapoora where he displayed a firmness in asserting the proper dignity of his situation as a representative of the Supreme Government of British India, combined with sagacity in counteracting the manœuvres of the Burmese Ministry to degrade his office, and the most patient endurance of the cold and contumacious style of his reception and of all the personal inconveniences of the situation in which he was placed, that in His Lordship's opinion entitle him to the cordial approbation and thanks of the British Government." [2]

On the expiry of his period of leave, Benson was granted an extention for six months on medical certificate. He was recognized as Resident up to 1 May, 1840, when he sailed for Europe on the advice of the Medical Department.[3]

---

[1] *Ibid.* Vol. 17, Calcutta Gazette Notificatioin, 10 April, 1839, No. 49.
[2] *Ibid.* Vol. 20, Consultations 15 May, 1839, dated 25 April, 1839, No. 1.
[3] *Ibid.* Vol. 23, Consultations 21 August, 1839, Government Letter to Benson, 15 August, 1839, No. 9.
Ibid. Vol. 27, Consultations 13 November, 1839, Nos. 99, 100.

CHAPTER XIV

THE RESIDENCY AT AMARAPURA UNDER McLEOD, 14 MARCH, 1839 TO 22 JULY, 1839.

Capt. William McLeod officiated as Resident in Burma from 14 March, 1839 to 7 January, 1840. Up to 22 July, 1839, he was in Amarapura, and for the rest of the period from 31 July, in Rangoon. During his stay at the capital he did not meet with any better treatment from the Government of Burma than that experienced by his chief, although he had an audience of the King, and was able also to transact some business with the Ministers.

The King and his Woongyees were well aware of the Company's war with Afghanistan. Some of the King's sons, legitimate and illegitimate, but more particularly the Prince of Pagan, the eldest legitimate son, were very warlike in their attitude, and wanted to recover the territory lost by Bagyidaw. The Ministers were thoroughly pacific, and understood full well the implications and dangers of a war with the British. Their situation was most unpleasant, for, in order to please the King and his sons, they had to systematically pursue a policy leading to the humiliation of the British Resident, and at the same time they were duty bound to keep those very Royal personages from madly plunging into a war which they knew would end most disastrously for the dynasty and the country. The people in general were pacific though anti-British in their feelings. The King's attitude at times was enigmatic. He was so greatly at the mercy of the humour of the hour, that a well grounded inference of his being pacific or hostile could not easily be drawn by those near him. It seems certain, however, that he was indulging in mere empty threats.

In January, 1839, a revolt broke out in Pegu under the leadership of one Maung Tsetkya, said to have been the grandson of a former Prince of Pagan who was a brother of

400 THE BRITISH RESIDENCY IN BURMA

Menderagyee. He pretended to be the late heir-apparent, the Tsakyamen, and the very name enabled him to collect followers. The revolters occupied the hills on both sides of the Irrawaddy. Large bodies of troops had to be sent against them, and it was with difficulty that the revolt was crushed and the pretender captured. On 29 March, 1839, he was executed at Amarapura.[1] It is possible that the difficulty experienced in crushing this rebellion further damped the warlike exterior of Tharrawaddy.

On 11 January, Edwards met the Myook of Pangwa, who said that he had in his possession orders from the King to the Rangoon Woondouk, " to have everything in readiness for war, and that His Majesty is vexed at the English Government sending steamers and ships of war to Rangoon. That if His Majesty was sure that the English would invade his country, he would destory all the foreigners in it, including the Mission (the Residency), with the exception of Staig, Sarkies and Antony." [2] At another time, when the King heard of British military reinforcements in Tenasserim, he declared, " I do not depend upon the people of Lower Provinces; an army collected from above Paghan would be sufficient to repel the English forces." [3] After the King had thus expressed himself, the Prince of Pakhan said, " I could destroy the English army with the assistance of the Nats alone." [3] " His Majesty," wrote Benson, " is said to call our sending men-of-war and steamers to Rangoon a piece of insolence which he will not long put up with. The King is no doubt capable, if exasperated, of committing any outrage, and being reckless there is no saying what he may do. He hesitates however at times as to the propriety of going to war, notwithstanding he is urged to this step by his sons and military followers. The Prince of Pakhan is said to be most confident as to the result of a war, and to be the most strenuous advocate for maltreating the Mission." [4]

---

[1] India Secret Consultations Vol. 17, Benson's Journal, pars. 1430, 1432, 1437; Vol. 20, pars. 1677, 1678.
[2] *Ibid.* Vol. 17, par. 1355.
[3] *Ibid.* par. 1358.   Nats are spirits.
[4] *Ibid.* par. 1361.

On account of the rumours of war, the trade of Rangoon declined, and British and Indian merchants began to remove their merchandise to Moulmein: Royal revenues consequently fell. "His Majesty was much exasperated at this intelligence and spoke very bitterly of the English, as did his sons at the same time. The King, after the excitement abated, was much depressed in spirits and became very thoughtful. Not long ago he asked Mr. McCalder how many men, he thought, the English would bring into the field. He was told, perhaps 30,000. He observed, I can bring forward five times that number, and it is improbable can be all beaten."[1] "The Court," continues Benson's Journal, "place great reliance upon the artillery now training, for which branch of the service 700 men of various countries have been enrolled."[1]

Early in March, 1839, when Benson announced his desire to leave for Calcutta, the Prince of Pakhan and his war party seriously advised the detention of the Resident, but the King said, "Let them go, I do not care about them."[2] As Benson's departure drew near, the King fell into a very pugnacious mood. "He declares he will not be a log like his brother the ex-King to be ridden on by the English whom he will teach to know that the Burmese are men and determined to settle disputes by an appeal to arms."[3] It seems, his fear was that Benson's departure might be the prelude to a British invasion of his country, since the Resident had not been treated as in the reign of Bagyidaw.

"His Majesty," records Benson in his Journal, "is represented as restless and wavering as to his plans. He has an inveterate aversion to the English, but feels whenever reflection comes to his aid that with a turbulent population in Pegu his resources are not equal to coping with us in the field. When calm, therefore, he inclines to peace, but when roused by the boastings of his sons, their followers, and the military officers around him, he breathes nothing but war. He talks too of the

[1] *Ibid.* par. 1371.
[2] *Ibid.* par. 1501.
[3] *Ibid.* par. 1502.

14

Governor-General and the Treaty sometimes in a strain of disdain, sometimes of respect, just as. the humour of the moment impels him."[1]

The Prince of Pakhan had more than once urged war, and his advice was to commence it by cutting off the Residency; but "the King," says Benson, "has the credit of spurning the idea, and the Ministers of producing their great historical work to prove that where they had twice before committed similar acts towards Chinese Envoys their country was overrun and laid waste, and their capital fell into the hands of the enemy. To injure an Envoy or any person attached to him, the Ministers represent to be dishonourable and adverse to Burmese Laws."[2]

At times, Tharrawaddy, speaking of his military prepara-tions, would say that they were merely meant for purposes of defence: "that the English have many ships which they send backwards and forwards thinking to frighten him, but that he too well knows that they do not dare to invade his country, and more than ever convinced that a little determination on his part is all that is necessary to carry his point in everything and place the Residency precisely on the footing he wishes. At other times (and that frequently too) his confidence in his resources appears much shaken, and he is much inclined to change the footing of his relationship with us."[3]

In October, 1838, Auckland had declared war upon Dost Muhammad of Afghanistan; in 1840 Dost Muhammad sur-rendered. It was not till in November, 1841, that a rising occurred in Kabul which by January, 1842, terminated in the capitulation of General Elphinstone and the destruction of the British army. In Burma, however, and particularly at the capital, rumours of British disasters in Afghanistan began to be spread by Mahomedans as early as April, 1839, when the British armies were meeting with nothing but suc-cess everywhere. These false reports were dinned into the

---

[1] *Ibid.* par. 1515.
[2] *Ibid.* par. 1522.
[3] *Ibid.* Vol. 20, Consultations 29 May, 1839, Benson's Journal, par. 1526.

King's ears. Added to these rumours, actually 20 British soldiers deserted from Tenasserim into Burmese territory by June, 1839. The King was delighted at the idea of these men coming over, and gave orders to encourage such desertions. Every deserter, who arrived at the capital, was paid 15 to 20 ticals per day quite regularly.[1] These desertions seemed to confirm the rumours of the alleged British disasters in Afghanistan, and encouraged the King and his sons to further neglect and humiliate the Resident.

Aga Hassan, the King's Indian doctor, and certain others "were pouring into the King's ears accounts of our disasters in every direction. His Majesty observed, the numerous desertions from Moulmein was a proof of our troubles and they were wise men for coming away in time, but that he would always afford the English protection if they needed it. The Doctor observed, His Majesty was too generous, that the English did not deserve any such consideration at his hands, when His Majesty declared that he would even extend his royal protection to the Governor-General if he asked for it."[2]

One Ally Khan informed (April 1839) the King, and the report was solemnly confirmed by a Burmese Mahomedan named Babi, that 100 Europeans, with their ears removed, had been sent away by the Afghans, that Calcutta was deserted, and all officers, with the exception of one clerk, had proceeded towards the north to assist in the defence of the country. His Majesty enquired what the number of British troops stationed on the Burma frontiers was, and on Babi telling him that it was no more than 6400, His Majesty remarked, "Well, that is not many at any rate." Babi added that the British had not another man to spare to send against Burma.[3]

A fakir at one time informed the Prince of Prome that the English had been routed and cut to pieces by the people of

[1] *Ibid.* Vol. 23, McLeod's Journal, pars. 313, 314.
[2] *Ibid.* Vol. 21, McLeod's Journal, par. 1846.
[3] *Ibid.* par. 1851.

"Room ";[1] the mendicant was immediately admitted into the palace and questioned in the presence of the King. After this he was sent to the Hlutdaw for further examination; but the Woongyees had a hearty laugh and did not believe him, because he did not know that Turks and Russians were two different people.[2]

In May, 1839, news was received from Sha Ban, a Burma-Bengali agent of the King in Bengal, "that the English were getting well licked, that 500 officers and 3000 men had been killed, and those who were taken had their noses and ears cut off and sent back."[3]   In June, 1839, the King was highly pleased when he was informed that 5000 Persian horsemen had reached Calcutta, that their weapons came down to the ankles, and that the British had in addition lost two men-of-war. Sarkies reasoned with the King at times concerning the absurdity of these stories and sometimes succeeded in quieting him.[4]

"His Majesty," wrote McLeod to Benson on 30 June, 1839, "continues to receive with satisfaction all reports prejudicial to the British, and looks with eagerness to our meeting with reverses in whatever quarter it may be. It will be seen how irresolute and changeable he is: one day breathing nothing but war, the next becoming quiet, and occasionally even peaceably inclined, and then breaking out again in his usual hostile strain."[5] On 13 June, one of the King's pages reported that His Majesty had been peaceably inclined and not talking of fighting the English, but no one placed the slightest dependence upon his continuing quiet.[6]   A few weeks later he was again in his usual boastful humour, and declared, "that had Bundoolah followed his advice, which was to take to the jungles and carry on a guerilla warfare instead of meeting in force, the result of the war would have been very different.   Let the English come

[1] A corruption of Rome; applied to Constantinople by the people of Western Asia.
[2] India Secret Consultations Vol. 22, McLeod's Journal, par. 14.
[3] Ibid. par. 156.
[4] Ibid. pars. 250-252, 266.
[5] Ibid. Vol. 23, Consultations 28 August, 1839, No. 4.
[6] Ibid. McLeod's Journal, par. 216.

now, the King says, and he would show them what the Burmans
are, for there is not a braver nation in the world, and with good
officers at their head, would overcome any enemy."[1]

Tharrwaddy's life was not all brag, boast, and blood. A
little information on the lighter side of his character is also
available. He was fond of billiards, and sometimes remained
engaged in this pastime for hours together. McLeod's Journal
furnishes the following information for 22 March, 1839:
" His Majesty was yesterday from 12 to 5 playing at Billiards.
He afterwards regaled his friends with a dinner in the Billiard
Room. A chest of beer was ordered to be produced, but the
Royal Steward reported that the Princes had drained His
Majesty's cellar. The Ministers are sometimes vexed at His
Majesty's frivolous amusements and his disinclination to attend
more closely to business." [2] Tharrawaddy was also fond of kite
flying. At a Royal levee, a Chinaman brought a very large kite
for the King, " who immediately left the assembly and ran out
to amuse himself in flying it." [3]

The King kept his state prisoners well guarded, for there
were often rumours that the British would espouse the cause of
the unfortunate Bagyidaw. On 6 March, 1839, all such
prisoners were taken out of irons and paraded through
the town; then taken to the Pagoda where they were fed by
one of the Queens, who also conferred a Burmese cloth, a head
dress, and a piece of silver on each; finally they were marched
back to their old quarters and again placed in irons.[4] On 6
April, Maung Za the old scholarly ex-Myawadi Woongyee
was released.[5]

Like his brother Bagyidaw, Tharrawaddy too was subject
at times to uncontrollable fits of anger, and gave hasty orders.
In June, 1839, he gave orders to place the household troops
under the Shwe Daik Woon, but the Tshan Atwenwoon did not

[1] *Ibid.* par. 390.
[2] *Ibid.* Vol. 20, McLeod's Journal, par. 1614.
[3] *Ibid.* Vol. 22, par. 201.
[4] *Ibid.* Vol. 20, Benson's Journal, par. 1531.
[5] *Ibid.* Vol. 21, McLeod's Journal, par. 1747.

carry out the orders on the ground that it was against custom. When questioned, he boldly defended himself; the King was angry and called for evidence to support the Atwenwoon's views. Out of fear no one spoke in his favour, and the King ordered that he be dragged out of the palace to the execution ground and his tongue cut out. The Princes and Ministers in a body, however, implored the King's pardon, and the Minister escaped; but his jagir was confiscated and he ceased to be an officer of the Government.[1]

McLeod, during the period he was in charge of the Resident's office, had no easy task in the attempt to maintain diplomatic relations with Tharrawaddy's Government. The Ministers had wanted Benson to have an audience of the King, but on their own terms, to which the Resident would not agree, since he did not wish to be classed as a tribute bearer. Now that McLeod was Resident, the Ministers made another attempt to present the British Envoy to the King on their own terms, and this time met with success. On 21 March, that is just a week after Benson's departure, a Tsaredaugyee came to the Residency to enquire after McLeod's health, and hesitatingly asked if he would like to see the interior of the Palace. McLeod immediately seized the opportunity of letting the Ministers know that he was most desirous of paying his respects to His Majesty the King. The Ministers lost no time in fixing the day, and decided upon 25 March.[2] On 23 March, at 1-30 a.m. there were two terrible shocks of earthquake, followed by numerous concussions, but even this was not allowed to interfere with the programme. " In the morning," says McLeod, " not a pagoda was to be seen standing whole; every brick building in the town had either been thrown down, burying in their ruins numbers of people, or so rent and damaged as to render their being taken down necessary. The Pagoda crowning the heights of Tsagain shared the fate of those at Amarapoora. In the neighbourhood of the Residency exten-

[1] *Ibid.* Vol. 23, pars. 218, 219.
[2] *Ibid.* Vol. 20, pars. 1611, 1622.

sive and deep fissures had opened out from which large quantities of water had been discharged, and the earth in many places rose up with water springing from the centre. The wells are all choked up and dry." [1]

McLeod had a little discussion with the authorities concerning the etiquette to be observed at the audience with the King, and he was pretty well satisfied with the arrangements agreed on; but it is clear from his own account of the whole affair that the Ministers were in complete control of the situation, and presented the British Resident to their King as the Envoy of a subject state.

In his letter to Benson, McLeod describes the audience in the following words:— " I went the proper road with Elephants and up to the Youn where a Bondaugyee [2] received me. I accompanied him into the Palkee, was met by the Woongyees and Woondouks near the Lhwottau, and accompanied them to the temporary palace pulling off my shoes at the steps, though they at one time intended I should have unslippered at the gate. This, of course, I would not have done on any consideration. The King came out immediately after my arrival, none of the Princes were present. He chatted with all of us about the earthquake, asked when you (Benson) expected to be in Rangoon, that he feared you must have felt the earthquake; spoke of Mr. Harapet's affairs (who was killed by the fall of his house); told me to ride about and see all that was to be seen; to visit his gardens; that I should find the one nearest the lake the coolest place here; that he considers it and the Residency the two coolest places.

"Of course nothing political was touched upon. The Ministers appeared well pleased at the visit being over." [3]

McLeod gave presents to the King. Queen, and Princes, amounting in all to nearly Rs. 1000: [3] these were read out as

---

[1] *Ibid*. par. 1626.
[2] A respectful term for a Buddhist monk.
[3] India Secret Consultations Vol 20, Consultations 8 May, 1839, No. 29.

being "presents of submission."[1]   The King's return presents
to McLeod and companions amounted to Rs. 2,199-5.[2] "The
arrangements in the temporary hall," says McLeod in his
Journal, "were much like those in the great hall of audience
at Ava. The Woongyees were seated on one side before me
between the middle line of pillars, the Atwenwoons came next,
two on each side, leaving a clear space between them for His
Majesty to see us. The Woondouk Gale was seated behind the
Atwenwoons on my left........The Atwenwoons sat with
their backs towards me, the soles of their feet partially turned
in my face particularly when they prostrated themselves before
His Majesty. Though I consider their position objectionable,
yet as the space between the pillars was narrow and they were
not seated immediately before me, I do not think any indignity
was intended......His Majesty did not keep us waiting, for
hardly were we seated when he made his appearance and took
his seat on a carpet on the floor......He had merely a silk
putsho round his waist and a fillet of muslin round his head
but no jacket. A handsome pair of gold earrings with a fine
large ruby in each adorned his ears and a cigar in his mouth
completed his toilet."[3]

On 27 March, McLeod attended the Hlutdaw and was
given a seat amorig the Woondouks. The Woongyees sat near
him; but both at the audience as well as at the Hlutdaw, the
Ministers carried their point in refusing to grant to the British
Resident the official rank enjoyed before by Burney.[4]

Now that McLeod had been presented to the King, the
Ministers arranged for him to see the Princes. On 1 April, he
visited the Mekkhara Prince who received him very kindly and
spoke of the Burmese Dictionary in the compilation of which
he had played so great a part. McLeod gave him presents
worth Rs. 400 and the Prince made a return present worth
Rs. 138.[5] He also visited the Princes of Prome and Pakhan.

[1] *Ibid.* Consultations 29 May, 1839, McLeod's Journal, par. 1647.
[2] *Ibid.* pars. 1649-1652.
[3] *Ibid.* pars. 1637-1645.
[4] *Ibid.* par. 1657.
[5] *Ibid.* pars. 1686-1690.

The total value of presents given by McLeod to the King and the Princes was Rs. 2313-8; the total value of presents received by him was Rs. 3279-4-3, thus leaving a balance of Rs. 965-12-3 in favour of the British Government.[1]

The presents received by McLeod and his companions were in gold and silver leaf, which according to custom were given to subject rulers and their agents, while articles of the country's manufacture or produce were made to others. "The personal demeanour of His Majesty and Princes," wrote McLeod to Benson on 4 April, 1839, "was on the whole unobjectionable, nay, with the exception of the Prince of Pakhan, even courteous. I do not, however, think that an officer from China or any of the neighbouring independent states would have been received and accommodated as I was, on his introductory visit; nor is it, I believe, customary, for the Princes at least, to make presents of gold or silver on such occasions, the usual ones being some article either the produce or manufacture of the country. But in the absence of positive evidence that offence was intended, any remonstrance on my part would have been, in my opinion, unattended with any advantage; indeed my declining to accept the presents from the two Princes would have been considered much more insulting on my part than on theirs in offering them. I therefore considered it more prudent to allow these circumstances to pass unnoticed."[2]

McLeod now desired to see the Woongyees in their homes, and it was agreed that he need not unshoe at the bottom of the stairs, but before entering the room. McLeod wanted to ride through the gate up to the stairs, but to this they would not agree, and said that Burney had done it in the past, but now it would not be allowed as it was contrary to Burmese custom. On 8 April, officers came to take the Resident to the Woongyees, and from the plan of the route McLeod soon discovered that it was arranged that he should enter their houses by the back gates, so that he might not ride past the gates of the

[1] *Ibid.* pars. 1696-1698, 1700, 1707, 1708, 1711-1714.
[2] *Ibid.* par. 100.

Youndaw and the Palace. The Resident was surprised at the attitude of the Ministers, because he himself had ridden past those gates many times, Edwards used to do it almost everyday, and the general public did the same. McLeod refused to submit to the indignity and his guides gave way.[1]

Maung Shwe Tha, the senior Woongyee, was the first to be visited. McLeod dismounted at the gate, left his shoes on the spot agreed on, and before he had waited a minute the Woongyee appeared and received him cordially. Maung Shwe Tha had served as the Woongyee of Rangoon several times [2] and so understood foreigners, and was inclined to be favourable to them. But he was deaf, and there was not much conversation between him and McLeod. " The Woongyee's daughter," says McLeod, " filled up all the breaks in her father's conversation, the chief topic being about herself, wishing to impress me with a high estimation of her rank, influence etc., though all said in an innocent manner, and on the whole succeeded in making herself agreeable enough." [3]

By 23 April, McLeod finished visiting all the Woongyees including the King's favourite and father-in-law the Kyee Woongyee, 70 years of age and feeble; as a member of the Government he was totally inefficient. He gave presents to McLeod worth Rs. 154 while the Resident presented articles to him worth Rs. 409.[4]

McLeod now expected that his friendly visits would be returned, but the Ministers failed to pay him this compliment. Edwards was sent to the senior Woongyee to sound him in this connection, and Maung Shwe Tha replied that they would consider the question, but in the end no notice was taken of McLeod's messages on the point, and his attempts to establish

---

[1] *Ibid.* Vol. 21, pars. 1754-1758.
[2] *e.g.* at the time of Canning's Mission to Burma, 1811.
[3] India Secret Consultations Vol. 21, McLeod's Journal, pars. 1759-1762.
[4] *Ibid.* pars. 1829-1831.

a friendly and becoming intercourse with the Ministers proved abortive.[1]

Although the Ministers refused to recognize McLeod on the footing enjoyed by Burney under Bagyidaw's government, the acting Resident did not fail to bring to the notice of the Woongyees the complaints of British subjects in Burma and of British frontier officers. He often proceeded to the Hlutdaw and discussed such complaints with the Ministers, but never succeeded in obtaining satisfaction: promises to settle all questions as friends, were, however, profusely made to him. The Government of India was fully aware of the character of Tharrawaddy's government, still there was a great anxiety on the part of the Governor-General to maintain the Residency at the capital. "The Governor-General thinks," wrote the Secretary to Auckland, on 2 May, 1839, "that as long as Capt. McLeod is subject to no greater inconvenience and privation than what were endured by Col. Benson, he should maintain his ground at Amarapoora. In the event, highly improbable, it is hoped, of any outrage or personal indignity being offered to him in his official character, it is evident that it must in a great measure be left to his own discretion........But from the description of the buildings set apart for the Residency, and the liability of the position where they are situated to being overflowed during the rainy season, it may be impossible for Capt. McLeod to remain there, and he may be compelled in consequence to apply for accommodation elsewhere. If the Court continues in the same humour that it has so long exhibited, an application to this effect might probably meet with no attention, though the buildings should be clearly uninhabitable, and in that case Capt. McLeod should, in His Lordship's opinion, be instructed to demand boats to convey him and his suite to Rangoon."[2]

[1] *Ibid.* pars. 1835, 1837.
  Ibid. Vol. 22, Consultations 10 July, 1839, McLeod to Benson, 15 May, 1839, No. 85.
[2] *Ibid.* Vol. 20, Consultations 22 May, 1839, No. 18.

If the Residency could not be maintained at the Royal Capital, then it was not the desire of Auckland to establish it anywhere else in the country. " Under such circumstances," continues the letter, " the Governor-General would not propose to admit of the Mission remaining at Rangoon, as he is clearly of opinion that it ought to be withdrawn altogether from the dominions of Ava." Fearing that the Burmese Government might object to the total withdrawal of the Residency, McLeod was instructed, if at all he had to withdraw, to apply to the Ministers for assistance to enable him to retire to Rangoon. Such a proposal, it was thought, would certainly be favourably received, " as a supposed step to the accomplishment of the Court's desire to confine the Residency to Rangoon." [1] But, continue the instructions, " If Capt. McLeod, under either of these contingencies is compelled to quit the capital of Ava, the Hon. President-in-Council will no doubt take measures for the removal of the Mission from Rangoon with as little delay as possible, after which, in the absence of all cause of additional provocation from the Burmese, and in case of their abstaining from acts of hostility, we should fall into that condition of declared non-intercourse between the two countries, which was alluded to in the Governor-General's Minute of the 15th January last." This became the settled policy of Auckland, and it finally came to be definitely adopted by succeeding Governor-Generals until 1852 when Dalhousie fought the Second Burmese War.

While McLeod was making attempts to establish friendly diplomatic relations with the Burmese Government, and the Indian Government was laying down the policy to be pursued towards Burma, the King and his sons were very busy strengthening the Army. During the month of April 1839, there was talk both in the inner circles of the Government as well as among the people in general, that three of the Princes would be placed in charge of important Army commands in Lower Burma. On 27 April, the appointments were announced, and on 18 May, publicly proclaimed: the Prince of Pakhan

[1] *Ibid.* Vol. 20, Consultations 22 May, 1839, No. 18.

in charge of Rangoon, the Prince of Prome to Bassein, and the Prince of Toungdwengyoung to Toungoo, each with a large force. It became common talk that the object of this new arrangement was to attack the British in Arakan and Tenasserim, and recover those lost provinces.[1] The King and especially the Prince of Pakhan often spoke boastfully of what they could achieve in case of war. " The Prince of Pakhan talks of outdoing the Maha Bandoola who failed to keep his promise of bringing to the capital some European captives, but he engages to have long strings of them led up for his father ere long." [2] On 25 May, 1839, wrote McLeod to Benson, " No change has taken place in the opinion of the public as to passing events. His Majesty's mind continues in a state of high excitement and he talks of being prepared to meet us and the Siamese together in the field, and that we shall find the Burmese better prepared than before to cope with us." [3] Giving his own view of Burmese preparedness, McLeod says, " Of this I think there can be no doubt, for he has been energetic in calling forth the Military resources of the country, arming the people, exercising his soldiers, teaching them to fire with precision, and practicing his artillery in various ways (the sound of cannon and musketry is to be heard all day long) and collecting large stores of warlike munitions. He has now become so excited with all these warlike arrangements and has such a large body of men in arms, most of them anxious for pillage, that he must find employment for them and some vent for the full exercise of his own military ardour." [3]

McLeod received definite instructions from his Government concerning the appointment of the three Princes. " If therefore the Princes have left the capital," says the Government letter of instructions, 3 June, 1839, " to proceed to their respective command with views generally understood to be

---

[1] *Ibid.* Vol. 21, Consultations 29 May, 1839, McLeod to Benson, 30 April, 1839; *Ibid.* Consultations 5 June, 1839, McLeod's Journal, pars. 1839, 1847, 1850.
Ibid. Vol. 22, par. 97.
[2] *Ibid.* Vol. 22, par. 104.
[3] *Ibid.* No. 89.

hostile to the British Government, it will clearly be no longer proper for you to remain at the Court of Ava, and if you have not already left Amarapoora, when this letter reaches you, it must be your study to effect the return of the Residency as safely and conveniently as possible. Whether you shall avail yourself of the plea of ill-health or ask your passports on any other ground is a question which the Government leaves to your own discretion." [1]

On 2 June, McLeod questioned the Ministers concerning the new Army appointments. They acknowledged that the King had appointed the Princes to the three important charges, but they urged that the arrangement was meant for civil purposes only, and that there was no hostile intention towards the British.[2] On 5 June, McLeod had an audience of the King. His Majesty was very affable, and addressed almost the whole conversation to the Resident. He offered him an English boat to sail about in, and showed him one of Maha Bandula's sons, 23 years of age.[3]

Burney, Benson, and McLeod, each during his term of office, had tried to impress upon the Burmese authorities the importance and necessity of maintaining the treaties between the two countries inviolate. They had lodged a number of complaints both in behalf of the British Government as well as of British subjects residing in Burma. It was not possible for the Government of Burma to give complete satisfaction in respect of these complaints, not only because their administration was of a crude, rough and ready type, but also because the King did not enjoy much of a control over the frontier tribes nor even over the Government officers stationed in those areas. The King naturally came to look upon the representations and demands of the Resident as an inroad upon his independence and sovereignty. Soon after his accession to the throne, Tharrawaddy had threatened to denounce the Treaties claiming that they had not been contracted by him but by his brother,

[1] *Ibid.* Vol. 21, Consultations 5 June, 1839, No. 113.
[2] *Ibid.* Vol. 22, McLeod's Journal, pars. 167, 170.
[3] *Ibid.* par. 186.

but he never officially did reject them. It seems almost certain, that he himself did not wish to be the aggressor in a war with the British, but he wanted to be ready for every emergency in case he was attacked. He feared an attack because of his new interpretation of the Treaty, by which the Resident was just to " reside " at the capital " with 50 men." He also hit upon an expedient to meet British complaints. Why should not his Government also bring up complaints and require satis-faction over British violations of the Treaty? A few such com-plaints were soon got together; not all were officially ventilated, but they were dwelt upon by the King and his officers on state occasions.

On 31 January, 1839, when the King heard that the British had sent more troops into Assam, he said, " One point I have to object against the English is their occupation of Assam and their keeping officers in Assam. The English talk about the treaty which gives them no right to Assam or Munipore, and I would not allow them to continue on their present footing in those countries." [1] Again, about the end of April 1839, the King said to his Atwenwoons, in the presence of Sarkies, " The English talk about the treaties, what right have they to the island of Pullogywon [2] and Kautsaing. You must see and call upon them for some explanation, and not allow matters to remain as at present. They have taken a village too on the Aracan side to which they have no right. Nor does the treaty sanction them holding possession of Assam and Kachar, or interfering with Manipore. They are not to do as they like now as they used to with Nga O. [3] They must be made to attend to the Treaty." [4] Early in July, the Prince of Prome even claimed that the King had a right to Moulmein, and that a demand for its return would have to be made upon the British. [5]

---

[1] *Ibid.* Vol. 17, par. 1403.
[2] Bilu-gyun, at the mouth of the Salween.
[3] The ex-Menthagyee, brother-in-law of Bagyidaw. Nga is a term of disgrace.
[4] India Secret Consultations Vol. 21, McLeod's Journal, par. 1860.
[5] *Ibid.* Vol. 23, par. 319.

On 9 June, 1839, " the Woondouk Gale asked Mr. Edwards how it was that vessels sailing under the Burmese flag paid more port duties than vessels sailing under the English flag, in Calcutta. Mr. Edwards said it was not the Burmese alone, but all foreign vessels were subjected to the same, and added there was no use speaking on the subject when they had not a single vessel; it would be time enough to moot the point when the Burmese had some 50 or 60 vessels." [1]

The Burmese complaint which assumed the most threatening character was in respect of an affair with which the British Government was in no way concerned, but the responsibility for which was sought to be placed upon the Indian Government by a most curious piece of argument. On 8 May, a Woondouk and a Tsaredaugee visited McLeod, and informed him, that news had been received that a party of Siamese Shans from Zimme and Laboung had made an irruption into Burmese Shan territory, and seized and carried away the inhabitants of three towns. The argument of the Burmese authorities now was, that since by Article 10 of the Treaty of Yandabo, the Siamese were associated with the British Government, it was the responsibility of the British to insist upon the Siamese, their allies, to give satisfaction to His Burmese Majesty. In any case, McLeod was told, that the British were responsible for the conduct of the Siamese. McLeod explained that the Siamese were only included in the Treaty because they had taken part in the war, and that the British were not responsible for what had happened on the Burma-Siamese frontier.[2] The following is McLeod's report of the conversation that took place between him and the Burmese officers:—

" Bur. Does not the 10th article of the Treaty of Yandaboo say, the King of Siam, the ally of the British Government, having taken part with the British in the war, shall be considered as included in the present treaty?

[1] *Ibid.* Vol. 22, par. 205.
[2] *Ibid.* Vol. 21, Consultations 12 June, 1839, McLeod to Benson, 9 May, 1839.
    Later it was discovered that this affair had been highly exaggerated, and the Siamese Government had nothing to do with the incursion.

Mcd. Yes.

Bur. The Tsaubwas of Zimme and Laboung have sent a force
under Chaw Kyaw and carried away the inhabitants from
the Burmese Shan towns, *viz.*, Maingpoo, Maing Thwon
and Maing Shap. How will you decide the matter?

Mcd. It is the custom amongst civilized nations when such incursions take place for the frontier officers to demand reparation, and failing to obtain it the ruler of the country
sustaining the injury takes the matter up.

Bur. How are we to do this?

Mcd. Through the Tsaubwa of the state to which the towns
belong or the Tseetke-dau of Mone; and should the rulers
of Zimme and Laboung refuse to give satisfaction, His
Majesty must consider what ulterior measures ought to be
adopted.

Bur. We will not have anything to say to the Siamese. It is
in consequence of the Treaty we allow the subjects of Siam
to enter our territories and trade with us. We have always
been enemies and now only restrain ourselves in consideration of the Treaty which we do not wish to infringe. We
look upon the Treaty as made with the English who included the Siamese with themselves, so we wish you to
write to the Government of Bengal on the subject of the
aggression.

Mcd. The English have nothing to say to the matter, but I will
write as you wish to the Government of India, however I
cannot answer for the course it may take.....Siam is an
independent kingdom ruled by its own monarchs, and the
utmost the English Government can do is to advise in a
friendly way, but it will be optional for the Siamese to
follow such advice or not.

Bur. Should the Siamese not attend to your injunctions will
they not thereby make themselves your enemies, and by
our not obtaining satisfaction would the treaty between
us not be annulled?

Mcd. In my opinion certainly not; we would not, I think, view
the matter in that light on either points. We have no
control over the Siamese whatever. With reference to the
Treaty, nothing that the Siamese can do can make it void
between us. All connexion as far as the Treaty and the
Siamese are concerned in my opinion ceased when the
peace was concluded I have pointed out the usual way

for you to obtain satisfaction; but it is only at your urgent desire that I have promised to write to my Government your sentiments.

Bur. You are united together by the treaty, and we consider if we do not obtain satisfaction that you do not act according to the treaty.

Mcd. The treaty is not to be interpreted by one party as it wishes, but a fair construction must be put upon it by both parties. It is not my province now to decide on such a momentous subject, but in my opinion, I do not consider the Treaty binding us in any way for the conduct of the Siamese. I cannot indeed say whether my Government in its desire to preserve peace between all the neighbouring powers will undertake to mediate between you and the Siamese or whether it will not decline interfering in the dispute.

Bur. In that case what are we to do?

Mcd. It will, I suppose, rest with His Majesty to take such measures as he may consider proper, for the case as stated is one of wanton insult and aggression for which the most ample atonement ought to be made.

Bur. Suppose on this the Burmese take strong measures what will the English do?

Mcd. I cannot presume to say in what light the English Government might view any hostile invasion of Siam, but if it declines interfering in the matter I should myself be inclined to consider it as tantamount to a declaration that His Majesty may act towards the Siamese as he pleases.

Bur. When will you receive a reply to your letter. We wish you to fix a time.

Mcd. I suppose an answer will reach me in two or three months, but I cannot fix a time as so much depends upon the winds etc., and whether there are vessels sailing to and fro." [1]

The enquiry of the Woondouk as to what the attitude of the British would be, in case the Burmese took strong measures against the Siamese, was sound and wise, but the great object of the King was to try and make this incident a handle for the rejection of the whole Treaty. When Tharrawaddy heard of McLeod's view on the question, he became very angry, and all

---

[1] India Secret Consultations Vol. 21, 12 June, 1839, McLeod to Benson, 9 May, 1839, No. 134.

his Court supported him in his interpretation of the Treaty. "He said," wrote McLeod to Benson, "it was a good joke we (the British) should select the articles we wished, and reject those we found inconvenient. That the question now was not as I supposed of receiving satisfaction from the Siamese who were his subjects, slaves, and whom he could crush whenever he pleased, but of breach of Treaty......He said he had placed the Siamese on an equality with him and ourselves by joining them with us in the Treaty. The Treaty was made with us not with the Siamese, what had he therefore to do with them? Their King or Minister was not present at Yandaboo, but the English by the step they took guaranteed their good conduct. He exemplified the subject by asking that if a friend recommended a stranger for service he would be taken, but if he misbehaved and ran away who would be looked to for reparation."[1] Ultimately, however, the King became calm, and said, he desired McLeod to write to his Government and ascertain if the British would accept the responsibility for the outrage or not.[2]

On 21 June, the King again spoke of the Zimme affair to Sarkies, and said that he would not wait a day over the three months "fixed by McLeod," and that if within three months no satisfaction was forthcoming he would punish the Siamese and consider the Treaty to be void. On Sarkies urging, that the Resident had merely said that a reply would be expected within three months, also that if the matter was referred to the Governor-General it would take four or five months, the King said, "Well, I do not care, I will then demand the island of Pulogywon and Kautshaing, and if they are not given up I will take them; what business had the English with them and other places not mentioned in the Treaty as being made over to them."[3] At another time the King told Sarkies, that he did not look to the Siamese for reparation, but to the Government of India according to the 10th Article of the Treaty, and that

[1] *Ibid.* McLeod to Benson, Demi-official Letter, 9 May, 1839, No. 135.
[2] *Ibid.* Vol. 22, McLeod's Journal, par. 78.
[3] *Ibid.* Vol. 23, par. 266.

if the British did not satisfy him he would consider it a violation of this article, and that if one article was void the whole treaty must be considered to be so also.[1]

Had the Government of India not been involved at this time in the Afghan War, there is no doubt, an attempt would have been made to protect the Treaty of Yandabo by force of arms. "You cannot but be aware," wrote the Government to McLeod, "of the reasons that exist for desiring to postpone the period of hostilities in this quarter. Your proceedings should be conducted therefore on this understanding, and tho' firm and consistent in resisting the present and similar pretentions of the Burmese, it is desirable you should avoid all irritating communications or controversy......"[2] McLeod was instructed to take the earliest opportunity to retire from Amarapura. "You will consider the previous instructions in respect to your retirement from Ava to be still in force, and will seize any occasion that may offer of coming away as of your own wish, and you will understand it to be the desire of Government to avoid bringing matters to such an issue upon this or upon any other question as that you should be directed by the Court of Ava to leave the capital consequently upon a refusal to accede to its demands or to admit its interpretation of the treaties in force......"[2]

The Government of India authorized McLeod to make the following reply in respect of the demand of the King concerning the Siamese affair:— "The Government of India cannot admit the 10th article of the Treaty of Yandaboo to bear the construction which the Court of Ava seems desirous of putting upon it. The article in question was inserted for the benefit of the Siamese and not of the Burmese Monarch. The British Government, when withdrawing from the contest, could not of course desert its ally, and therefore, inserted that article to bind the King of Ava not to molest the King of Siam on account

---

[1] *Ibid.* Vol. 21, Consultations 12 June, 1839, Post Script to Letter from McLeod to Benson, 9 May, 1839, No. 134.
[2] *Ibid.* Vol. 22, Consultations 24 July, 1839, dated 24 July, 1839, No. 22.

of the little aid which the latter had rendered towards the prosecution of the war.

" That this is the correct view of the question must become evident to the Court of Ava when it reflects that the article in question was not inserted at its instance, but was imposed by the British Government for the protection of its ally. But although in no way bound to take upon himself such a task, the Rt. Hon. the Governor-General-in-Council will be ready to interpose his good offices towards effecting an adjustment of the difference that has unfortunately arisen between the Courts of Ava and Siam, if the former power will in the first instance afford just and satisfactory redress for the outrages on our frontier committed by its own subjects." [1]

The Indian Government was at this time fully prepared to resist any aggression on the part of Tharrawaddy; every attempt was, however, to be made to keep the Burmese monarch quiet, because of the war with Afghanistan.[1] The gravity of the Burmese situation, as viewed by the Government of India, its influence upon Indian politics, and the measures to be adopted in connection with it, may best be studied in the Minute of the Governor-General, dated, Simla, 13 July, 1839:—

" The threatening intelligence from Ava communicated in the recent dispatches from Capt. McLeod to the 9th May, has led me very seriously to consider as well the questions to which those dispatches immediately relate, as the general state of our probable military exigencies and available resources, and the measures proper to be taken with a view to the possible contingency of our being involved at no very distant date in a Second Burmese War. I propose in this paper to refer to all these subjects in the order in which I have now stated them.

" ......War with the Burmese is to be altogether avoided if it be possible, and if unavoidable, it is to be postponed by every means consistent with national honour, until the time at which it may be most convenient for ourselves to enter upon it.

[1] *Ibid.*

But while I avow, and would anxiously follow up their views, I am not the less sensible of the difficulties of our position and of the disposition of the Government of Ava to violate its engagements, and to try the issue of renewed hostilities with us on the instant at which it finds an opportunity which appears favourable........The intended appointment of the three Princes with considerable armies to the command of the Frontier provinces, is a step which according to all the usages of the country and in the universal belief, is connected only with hostile motives and objects.   The pretentions put forward on the meaning of the article of the Treaty of Yandaboo relative to Siam must be felt by the Court itself to be wholly untenable, and it is difficult to believe that the purpose in advancing them has been other than that of raising a plea on which rupture with us may, at a suitable time, be founded.   On feelings thus estranged and adverse, there are many circumstances in the present state of affairs which may be reasonably supposed to act to our disadvantage......We ought now, I cannot but be satisfied, at once to prepare ourselves against the utmost efforts of their mingled presumption and hatred.

" While, however, I admit and would enforce the necessity for preparation, it is equally my decided conviction, not only on the general ground of policy to which I have referred, but also looking particularly to the emergencies which at present press on the Government of India, that we should employ every effort to escape the occasion for a resort to hostilities with Ava in the coming season........On the reasons which induce me to deprecate such war at this time, I need not enlarge in much detail.   It will be sufficient to say that our measures for the increase of our military strength are yet immature, and that all our attention and care are still required for the affairs of our North Western Frontier.   The Maharajah Runjeet Singh just expired, and the stability of the power which he has bequeathed to his successor uncertain; the Belooche Tribes on the great line of our communication with Candahar remaining to be reclaimed and settled; our bitter enemy Mehrab Khan of Kilat unpunished; our relation with the Amirs of Sinde yet unadjusted; our prospects in Afghanistan, though of fair promise, liable to unavoidable hazards and doubt........It is not amid such distractions, that, if we can help it, we should enter on a Second Burmese War. Such a war, guide it, as we may, will require great efforts, and many carefully settled combinations, and if it must be forced on us, we must seek to undertake it, and to carry it to its completion with no other task of difficulty in our hands.

"........It is not less important that we should be in ready and collected strength on the Frontier. And we must always hold a considerable force disposable as a check on the unsteadiness and perfidy of the Government of Nepaul; we must calculate that if we should engage in a war with the Burmese, the Rajah of Nepaul will be greatly tempted to hazard the rupture which he has long unquestionably meditated, and to throw his weight into the scale against us." [1]

Officers on the frontiers were apprised of the situation, so that all might work harmoniously, if war should become necessary. The first aim and object of Auckland and his Government, however, was to avoid or at least to postpone such a war. Preparations of war on the frontiers were also meant to so impress Burmese counsels as to disuade them from playing the part of the aggressor.[1]

While these questions were being discussed in India, and plans, offensive and defensive formulated, McLeod on 22 July, 1839, quitted Amarapura for Rangoon, and withdrew the Residency altogether from the Royal capital. The circumstances which led him to this step may now be discussed.

Soon after quitting the capital, McLeod wrote to his Government giving his reasons for doing so. " The continued inimical disposition of the Court, the fixed determination on the part of His Majesty to believe in our disasters as reported to him, the prospect in consequence of his committing himself, the absence of all likely benefit by my continued sojourn at the

---

[1] *Ibid.* Vol. 25, Consultations 18 September, 1839, No. 2.

capital, and the increasing difficulties of our relations, would I humbly opine have warranted me in acting on the authority conveyed in the 6th para of your letter of the 3rd June; but additional causes have not been wanting in determining me in taking the step......"[1]

In his Journal and letters McLeod explains at length the difficulties of his situation, and the circumstances which ultimately led him to withdraw from Amarapura. In the first place, the Residency had ceased to be of any utilitarian value: it was totally neglected since the Zimme question had come up, and it was practically reduced to a pitiable and humiliating position. On 15 May, wrote McLeod to Benson, "though the greatest difficulty is experienced in obtaining intelligence from the Burmese themselves, watched as we are and cut off from communicating with the people, yet when we have occasionally succeeded in getting any, it has been corroborative of what we have heard from Mr. Sarkies and others........I must point out the revolution which has taken place in the opinion of the people generally, respecting our resources and power as well as the increasing faith of the strength of their country, and the rising fortunes of this present Majesty unpopular as he still is with a certain portion of his subjects, that we are fast falling in the estimation of the public........Not only is my situation most embarrassing with matters of importance, but I am even at a loss how to conduct myself towards the Ministers and Court."[2]

A Burmese Government writer once observed to McLeod, "Matters are now much altered in your connexion with this country; formerly nothing of this sort could be done without explanations and your permission, but now the King has his own way in everything and you dare not say a word."[3] A private letter from McLeod to Benson says, "The Ministers have shewn no inclination to be on friendly terms with me, and as to the King, to see the way he goes on, one would really

---

[1] *Ibid.* Vol. 23, Consultations 28 August, 1839, No. 7.
[2] *Ibid.* Vol. 22, Consultations 10 July, 1839, No. 85.
[3] *Ibid.* McLeod's Journal, par. 8.

think he is mad. Nobody appears to have the slightest control over him, nor will he attend to business except by fits and starts or when he is irritated........The Spiers, who are in the way of picking up news, and have good opportunities of drawing conclusions from what they hear and observe, have very gloomy forbodings of what is to be our fate, and speak in a very downcast spirit. All that I can say is that Tharawadee is not to be depended on for one instant, life or death is quite a matter of indifference with him, he will certainly not remain quiet now that he is convinced he can fight us, and that we are afraid of him, but he can do as he pleases having carried every point yet.

"........I must candidly confess to you, I feel deep anxiety for all about me, more especially my servants who are all Burmese; they would fare worse than any of us, should His Majesty be inclined to make a show of us. I am thinking of sending them away at any rate. I am not apprehensive of anything occurring immediately, but it is melancholy to think of the number of people here at the mercy of a fickle and cruel tyrant."[1]

Another increasingly serious difficulty, which McLeod had to face, was the flooding of the Residency grounds; it became a grave menace to health. In December 1838, when Benson was at Amarapura, the grounds had got flooded to a depth of 3 feet or more for about three weeks.[2] In June 1839, the floods came again consequent on the rising of the river. " We found ourselves on the 20th instant," wrote McLeod to Benson on 30 June, 1839, " confined to our houses, the whole of our compound being flooded. The water rose to the height of 3 feet ....I need not, I am sure, detail to you the inconveniences experienced by the Sepoys of the Escort and followers. They cannot avoid amongst themselves making comparisons between our position and that of the inhabitants of the Capital who are enabled to move about on dry ground."[3] All the out-houses

---

[1] *Ibid.* Letter without date, No. 100.
[2] *Ibid.* Vol. 15, Consultations 6 February, 1839, Benson's Letter, 31 December, 1838, No. 46.
[3] *Ibid.* Vol. 23, Consultations 28 August, 1839, No. 4.

and cook-rooms got submerged as a result of the flood. McLeod represented matters to the Ministers, and on 22 June, workmen arrived to erect new structures. The common people said that this great rise of water had not occurred since 1824: they called it *Kala Ye* (foreign water), and feared the Kalas would again visit the country in 1839.[1] The workmen constructed new out-houses and bridges from house to house; but the Resident had to pay Rs. 277-8-4 for the work executed.[2]

On 10 July, the water rose abnormally, and came to within one foot of the Barrack floor; the fence round the compound was more or less carried away, and many of the inmates of the Residency began to suffer from rheumatism. Assistant Surgeon Good of the Residency recommended removal from the unhealthy site; McLeod, therefore, wrote to the Ministers drawing their attention to the unhealthy condition of the buildings, and requested for some other accommodation temporarily, till another spot, free from the annual floods, could be selected for the permanent location of the Residency. The Ministers made no reply. Meanwhile, on 11 July, there was further rise of water, and the Sepoys' new cook-room went under. McLeod wrote again to the Ministers, urgently drawing their attention to the state of the buildings, and asked for a fit and becoming accommodation in keeping with the friendship between the two countries. The Ministers again made no reply. On 13 July, the floods became more serious, the water at the highest part of the compound being 5 feet in depth. McLeod wrote for the third time to the Ministers, and asked for means of conveyance for himself and suite so that he might proceed to Rangoon, but received no reply.[3]

Finally, on 14 July, McLeod appeared at the Hlutdaw and recounted to the Ministers the dangers and difficulties, the unfriendliness and unhealthiness which had become the lot of the Resident and his followers. He asked for an answer to his letter requesting them to supply boats to take him to Rangoon.

[1] *Ibid.* McLeod's Journal, pars. 259, 268.
[2] *Ibid.* par. 318.
[3] *Ibid.* pars. 342, 344, 358, 359, 366, 369, 374-376.

He was stupified at their answer. They said that he could not leave Amarapura unless his Government recalled him, and that " the Ministers did not acknowledge my right to quit the Capital without a letter being addressed to them by Mr. Prinsep as my appointment had been announced to them by letter." [1] There was much discussion, the Ministers' view, in short, being that McLeod must not move unless he was officially recalled. McLeod refused to admit their claim, and said that he was responsible to his own Government for his acts, and that they might complain to his Government if they liked.[1]

The Ministers further argued, that according to the Treaty the Officer must reside at the Capital not at Rangoon. McLeod replied that there were reasons for his quitting the caiptal and referred to precedents. They said that they had nothing to do with precedents, and enquired if the Residency would be permanently located at Rangoon, which, they added was also a Myodaw (or Royal City), the term used in the Treaty for the capital. McLeod told them that he was not competent to discuss the subject. " They urged that as Col. Benson had left me here, I was the Resident, and could not leave thus; on my correcting them as to my situation in relation to Col. Benson and of my not being Resident or possessing the powers of one, the Woondouk Gale remarked in a very impertinent manner, Why, what was Col. Benson after all; nothing more than a Bearer of letters and messages, for here is Mr. Prinsep's letter saying so. I indignantly denied the construction put on the expression used in Mr. Prinsep's letter, that though it was his duty to convey the wishes of our Government to the other, they had overlooked the great powers vested in him, and which I did not possess." [2]

The Ministers refused to budge from their position and told McLeod that he should not quit the capital because the Zimme question had not been settled. As to the floods, they did not pay much attention to what McLeod had to say, but

[1] *Ibid.* pars. 395-402.
[2] *Ibid.*

offered him a dry site with no houses.[1] " The tone and manner," says McLeod, " observed by the Woondouk, who was, as 'he always is, the spokesman, was imperative, haughty, and far from friendly or conciliatory, and no offer was made further than I have stated, to give the Residency other accommodation." [2]

When Tharrawaddy was informed of McLeod's desire to depart, " His Majesty at once said, I should not go; he would not have any such trifling excuses for my departure; that Mr. Prinsep should address the Ministers recalling me or allowing me to quit, or if I had such permission I should produce the letter for his satisfaction." [3]   It became the common talk of the town that the Resident would not be allowed to leave the capital; some, like Sarkies, feared, the Resident and suite would be detained as hostages for the conduct of the British in respect of the Zimme affair.[4] McLeod, meanwhile, embarked a good part of his baggage on boats belonging to the Residency, and made every preparation to depart, but the Ministers sent him neither men nor boats. Perceiving that they would hamper him, McLeod determined to pretend to look on their offer of a location as well intended, and thinking it to be " the only means of bringing the question to an issue........I wrote the following letter couched in friendly terms:—

" Capt. McLeod in charge of the Residency at Ava, informs the Ministers of State. Capt. McLeod having consulted his medical adviser more particularly after he wrote the letter to the Ministers on the 13th, has been urged to quit this without delay on account of his health which has been very bad for months and his constitution much impaired. His conference yesterday with the Ministers was as to when they would supply him with boats. He, however, feels obliged to the Ministers for the arrangement proposed to be made for the location of the Residency........and assure them, that peace and friend-

---

[1] *Ibid.* pars. 406, 407.
[2] *Ibid.* par. 403.
[3] *Ibid.* par. 405.
[4] *Ibid.* pars. 404, 417.

ship should exist between the Burmese and English nations, and he does not hesitate to add that such is the desire of the English Government.

"Capt. McLeod has to inform the Ministers that he has already embarked the greater portion of his baggage on board such boats as he has at his command; he, therefore, trusts, the Ministers will, consistent with the friendship between the two nations, afford him the assistance he has already applied for himself and suite. During Capt. McLeod's sojourn at Rangoon he will communicate with the Ministers at Amarapoora or with the Woondouk of Rangoon as the case may require."[1]

The Ministers made no reply. The same day the Barrack floor went under water, and all the newly constructed bridges of communication were washed away. The Sepoys had to remove to the Resident's quarters, but even there, when there was high wind, the spray beat through the floor. On 16 July, there was a further rise of water: the position was every hour becoming more desperate. McLeod sent Edwards to the Hlutdaw to point out " to the Ministers in strong terms the neglected and unbecoming state we had been in for so long a time, and now with the water in our very house, that we had been before obliged to put as much of our baggage as we could in our boats and were ready to move, and to request, therefore, they would furnish me with a pass if they would not assist me with boats, and if they declined to accede to my present application, I had no alternative left but to go without it."[2]

The Woondouk Gale gave the following answer to Edwards: "Oh, only wait one day for an answer, it will make no difference." He also added in an authoritative and insolent manner, "You can of course do what you please with your own boats, but it is our wish you should not go." One of the Woondouks said that they could not help the turn matters were taking, while

[1] *Ibid.* par. 409.
[2] *Ibid.* pars. 416, 421.

Maung Loo Nyo, one of the Woongyees, observed, " It cannot be helped, it is their fate." [1]

McLeod was now determined to quit the capital. Tharrawaddy, it seems, meanwhile, was deep in thought as to what he should do. If he forcibly detained McLeod it might mean war, which would most probably end in his deposition; if he allowed him to go, it might mean that the Resident was driven out through ill-treatment: this might also result in war. The third alternative was to give way and treat the Resident in a suitable manner: but this was distasteful to him since it was a settled principle with him that the presence of the Resident was humiliating to his position as King. It was generally believed by people that McLeod would not be allowed to depart. One of the clerks of Woongyee Loo Nyo secretly informed McLeod that an order had been issued to station at Kyauk-ta-loun, on both sides of the river, a strong party of armed men to intercept McLeod and his followers if they attempted to move. Sarkies looked most gloomily at the developments, and told the Woongyees, Maung Shwe Tha and Maung Loo Nyo, that it would be against the law of nations to detain the Resident. They said that they could do nothing when His Majesty gave the order. [2]

Tharrawaddy finally made his decision. On 17 July, McLeod received the welcome intelligence that the King was again in good humour and had ordered the Woongyees to settle the question, which they, of course, did immediately in favour of McLeod. They furnished him with the boats he required, and said that so long they had objected to his departure because they were anxious to have him near them! On 19 July, 3 boats and 72 men were furnished, and on 22 July, McLeod with all his followers quitted the capital at 7 a.m. His departure and the treatment he had experienced at the hands of Tharrawaddy's Government left a suspicion of fear in the King's mind, that the British might take strong measures to enforce the Treaty. In the presence of Sarkies he said, " So he is going, is he, he may

---

[1] *Ibid.* par. 421.
[2] *Ibid.* pars. 419, 420, 422.

go, but let a Resident come up again. I am now ready to give him a proper reception." [1]

In his letter to his Government, dated 22 July, 1839, McLeod states, that he believed, that the King had meditated laying violent hands upon the Residency, and that he ultimately desisted from this course either due to a change in his mind or because of the representations of the Princes, Ministers, and Sarkies. McLeod further severely criticizes in the same letter the King's attitude, his ambitious designs, his hatred of the British, his want of sound judgment, his credulity in listening to absurd stories against the English, his refusal to listen to the truth about things, his violation of the fundamental law of nations and even of the customs of his own country as to the treatment of foreign representatives. In McLeod's opinion, Tharrawaddy was not without shrewdness, but " circumstances have so worked on and puffed him up that his better senses have become clogged, and it is the opinion of everybody that he is bent on committing some folly." [2]

When McLeod quitted Amarapura, he was to have been escorted by the Awe-Youk (Marshal of the Court), but the latter failed to join the party at the time appointed, and said, that he would meet them below the town. McLeod, however, went without him, and before 9 a.m., (22 July) reached the Kyauk-ta-loun Chokey. An officer belonging to the Chokey boarded McLeod's boat and demanded his passport. McLeod said that the Awe-Youk was in the rear and would satisfy him on all points. The officer apologized, but said that he was in duty bound to detain the whole party till the Awe-Youk arrived, since he had strict orders not to let any one pass without a passport from the Hlutdaw. " I told him," says McLeod, " the helmsman of my boat had an order respecting his duty on the joining, which, together with the fact of the boat and boatmen having been furnished me by the Burmese Government, ought to remove all doubt from his mind as to my right to proceed, and further it

[1] *Ibid.* pars. 427, 429-436, 440, 457.
[2] *Ibid.* No. 7, pars. 17-20.

was not customary for any officer thus to board or attempt to stop the boat of an officer belonging to another Government. I, therefore, would not agree to his proposition of stopping. He admitted the truth of all I advanced, but insisted on my putting to, and on my further refusing, directed the boatmen to do so which they did some distance below the Chokey."[1] Soon, however, the Awe-Youk arrived, and the Chokey officers blamed him for the delay.[1] The voyage was uneventful, and on 31 July, the party reached Rangoon.[2]

Auckland and his Government fully approved of McLeod's doings in Amarapura and his withdrawal from that city. He received high praise for his judicious conduct in withdrawing the Residency to a place of safety.[3]

---

[1] *Ibid.* Vol. 23, McLeod's Journal, par. 459.
[2] *Ibid.* par. 486.
[3] *Ibid.* Government to McLeod, 22 August, 1839, No. 14.
   Ibid. Vol. 25, Consultations 18 September, 1839, No. 3.

CHAPTER XV

THE RESIDENCY AT RANGOON UP TO ITS FINAL WITHDRAWAL, 31 JULY, 1839, TO 7 JANUARY, 1840.

McLeod arrived in Rangoon at 12 noon on 31 July, 1839. All the European and Indian merchants visited him except Staig. There was a general state of alarm among British subjects in the city and there were rumours of war;[1] also they felt that the withdrawal of the Residency would remove an institution, which had proved itself to be not only a protection, but a convenient medium of protest against any highhanded action of Burmese officers to the prejudice of British subjects.

Both the Woondouk as well as the Yewoon showed a friendly attitude; the latter welcomed McLeod in the name of the Governor, and escorted him to the house which Benson had occupied during his stay in Rangoon. The Woondouk also sent a civil message of welcome.[2]

The Government of India approved of McLeod's action in removing the Residency to Rangoon; but now a new question had to be faced. Burmese officers and people generally believed, and rightly so, that the Residency had been thoroughly neglected by their King, and so had been transferred to Rangoon. Under these circumstances would it be wise to station the Residency at Rangoon, since the respect for it had certainly greatly decreased, or would it be the line of wisdom to withdraw it altogether from the country. This was no easy problem to solve. Burmese territory touched British possessions on three frontiers, there was the factor of British trade with Burma, and there were a great many British subjects, European and Indian, living in Burma engaged in peaceful professions.

---

[1] India Secret Consultations Vol. 23, McLeod's Journal, pars. 486-494.

[2] *Ibid.* pars. 486-515.

As has been noticed, it was the opinion of Auckland that, under the circumstances, it would be unwise to station the Residency at Rangoon permanently. The Government of India, however, did not hastily decide the question, but it is clear that it was no longer anxious to retain the Residency in Burma. On 22 August, 1839, McLeod was advised, that " the question whether you should continue for the present at Rangoon and exercise there your official functions is one that His Honour-in-Council leaves to your own discretion, and you will decide to stay or to proceed to Moulmein accordingly as you may deem either step calculated to promote the known wish of the Government to avoid if possible the necessity of War." [1]

Auckland had expressed himself before against the retention of the Residency in any other place except at the capital; [2] now he laid down the policy as to the same in the following words:— " ......it appears altogether inexpedient that a British representative or an officer acting in his place, can after the treatment which the Mission has received at Amarapoora, be permitted to return to that capital without an invitation from the Court, accompanied with such security for a suitable reception as would satisfy the British Government that it would not again be subject to the annoyance to which the late Mission has been unremittingly exposed.

" When the possibility of such an event as has now occurred, of the Mission being compelled to retire from Amarapoora in consequence of the intolerable nature of its position there, was before under consideration, it was the Governor-General's opinion that in that case the officer in charge might appear like a surrender to the Burmese Government of the right which we claim, under the treaty, of keeping a Resident at the capital, but that he should withdraw at once from the Burmese territories. There are, however, circumstances in Capt. McLeod's present position which lead His Lordship to think that benefit may accrue from his continuing for a time at Rangoon. A short time will in all

---

[1] *Ibid.* Government dispatch to McLeod, No. 14.
[2] Vide Supra. p. 412.

probability suffice to show whether Capt. McLeod's communications to the Court, since his arrival at Rangoon, will excite merely the transient displeasure of the King, or will lead to any more decisive exhibition of hostility against us, and it will be well that the British Government should have authentic means of ascertaining the effect of those communications, which Capt. McLeod's residence at Rangoon and his established sources of intelligence will best afford. Again supposing a short time longer to pass by without the commission of any overt act of hostility on the part of the Burmese, the Governor-General conceives that, however unwilling Tharrawaddy may be to place faith in any intelligence except such as is unfavourable to the English, the news of the perfect success of our arms in Afghanistan and the consequent augmentation of our disposable forces from that quarter will ere long spread and obtain credit among the Burmese, and will reach the ears of their sovereign, or even if it should be disbelieved by him, may have such an effect on his principal officers and his subjects generally, as to make it difficult, if not impossible for him to carry into effect any actively warlike measures against the British power, as long as there is no indication of an intention on our part to commence hostilities. It will no doubt be of advantage that Capt. McLeod should remain at hand to watch and report the effect that may be produced by the late news [1] on the minds of the Court and the people of Ava. And for these reasons His Lordship would suggest the expediency of not immediately recalling the Mission........On the other hand it is possible that Capt. McLeod may see in the insane caprice of the Burmese Government danger even at Rangoon of personal outrage to himself and to British subjects residing in Ava, and in such case he will of course feel himself authorized to give due warning to others and to withdraw the whole Mission to Moulmein." [2]

---

[1] Of British success in Afghanistan; it was not till November, 1841, that British arms began to suffer reverses in that country.
[2] India Secret Consultations Vol. 25, 18 September, 1839, No. 3.

16

This policy laid down by Auckland was faithfully carried out by McLeod in Rangoon. The officiating Resident was personally of opinion that his sojourn in Rangoon would be of no real benefit; but he also feared that if he withdrew, Tharrawaddy would immediately assemble a force in Rangoon, and the presence of such a rabble army might lead to frontier outrages and even war.[1] McLeod was also fully alive to the danger of his remaining in Rangoon. " On the other hand," he says, " by continuing here, the King may conceive he had succeeded in getting rid of the Resident from the capital, and might for a short time remain contented with his success, but our very submission might eventually lead him to be more arrogant and drive us to take up arms in defence of our rights." [2] McLeod was certainly in a dilemma, but he decided to stay on in Rangoon and await developments.

There was one redeeming feature in McLeod's situation at Rangoon: the Woondouk of the city was very well disposed towards him. This intelligent officer of Tharrawaddy thoroughly disapproved of the Burmese policy towards the British; he deplored the King's attitude of faith in the many false rumours spread by Mahomedans of British disasters in Afghanistan; and it was his earnest desire that the two countries might be maintained in friendship and peace.[3] The Woondouk's one great wish was that McLeod should not retire from Rangoon, since he feared that in that case the King would expect an attack from the British, and anticipate them by doing something rash.[4] McLeod had several friendly conferences with him; the following is a report of the conversation between the two on 4 August:—

" Woondouk. Why have you come down, everything is going wrong in the country......I hope the Ministers have in no way denied the Treaty........

McLeod. I have come down principally on account of my health, but I must confess the Ministers showed

---

[1] *Ibid.* Consultations 25 September, 1839, No. 68.
[2] *Ibid.*
[3] *Ibid.* Vol. 23, McLeod's Journal, pars. 495-515.
[4] *Ibid.* Vol. 25, pars. 526-528.

a great want of friendly feeling towards the Residency though they admitted the binding nature of the Treaty itself, yet they have not acted up to the spirit of it.

Woondouk. I hope it is not your intention to quit this for Calcutta, if you do so everything will go wrong. I beg of you to remain here. Depend upon it I will be honest and candid with you on all points, as I sincerely wish for a continuance of peace. Be so with me also and everything you require shall be done...... The Ministers have been in every way wanting in their duty towards the King and country. The King is passionate and changeable, and every order he gives, whether it is feasible or not, right or not, they thoughtlessly answer, " It shall be done." What is the consequence? The whole country is in a state of ferment and agitation; I wish to give up, — I cannot remain here, and I will expose their proceedings. The Woondouk Gale is at the bottom of everything. However, if I had been listened to at first, matters would not have come to this. I urged that no new resident should be appointed for some time knowing the King's capricious and vain disposition. He was a new King and had obtained the throne easily, and it was natural he should be somewhat elated with his success. Had the Residency not gone up as I advised for a year or two, allowing His Majesty time to get his palace ready and the country settled, I should have accompanied it and all would have been right. Be the consequences what they may I will do my duty, and rest assured everything shall be right and I will give you every satisfaction on all points." [1]

The Woondouk was relieved to hear that McLeod would not leave Rangoon immediately. On 8 September, speaking to McLeod concerning the treatment of the Residency at the capital, the Woondouk said, that allowances should be made for the King's pride, " that Missions from China and other states were different from ours, they were only temporary visits

---

[1] *Ibid.* pars. 533-550.

during which vanity caused each state to vie with the other in politeness etc., but ours was a permanent Residency, and the other two countries were known to each other and there was no necessity for such a conduct."[1]

On 10 September, McLeod raised the question of the Martaban criminals still in jail at Rangoon, and suggested that they be handed over to the Moulmein authorities to be tried for murder. Petty offences against British subjects were still taking place on the Martaban side, and these too McLeod from time to time brought to the notice of the Woondouk. Under the loose standard of administration that prevailed in Burma at that time, it was impossible for the Woondouk to put a stop to all such outrages. Burmese officers at the frontiers received no fixed salaries, and to obtain a livelihood they some-times made contracts with dacoits and became partners in their profits. It is not surprising that the Woondouk, smarting under McLeod's demands in this connection, said rather sharply, " You wish to go on as Col. Burney did, which we cannot sub-mit to........the King never refused to see the Resident or recognize him, but he looks upon the Residency as spies placed over his proceedings, that we (the British) persevered in keep-ing up the Residency because we placed no faith in the Bur-mese, whereas they having reliance on us dispensed with their right of keeping a Resident at the capital, but a British officer was required at Rangoon to keep matters quiet."[2]

There was no prospect of the Burmese Government yield-ing to the British in this affair of the Martaban criminals.[3] McLeod was relieved, therefore, when in October, 1839, he received directions from Calcutta instructing him to refrain from demanding reparations for past outrages, and to let the various cases stand as they were under the Resident's protest.[4]

After the retirement of McLeod from the capital, the state of feeling between the two governments was one of mutual fear

---

[1] *Ibid.* Vol. 26, Consultations 23 October, 1839, par. 778.
[2] *Ibid.* pars. 791-794.
[3] *Ibid.* Vol. 25, Consultations 18 September, 1839, McLeod's Letter, 13 August, 1839.
[4] *Ibid.* Government dispatch to McLeod, 18 September, 1839.

and suspicion. Neither party wished to attack the other, but each continued to take measures for defence. The strengthening of troops on the frontiers increased the distrust, and the atmosphere became surcharged with rumours of war. The British had no intention of taking extreme measures, because, not only did they look upon the policy of conquest in Burma to be economically unsound, but also because their hands at this time were tied in Afghanistan. Tharrawaddy, with all his boastings, understood full well the military superiority of the British. He did not wish to play the part of the aggressor: his object was untrammelled independence, peace, and defence with honour.

Under such unsettled conditions, the Indian Government thought it wise for warships to visit Rangoon and Amherst in order to protect the Residency and British subjects in Rangoon in case of trouble. The visits of these men-of-war were looked upon by the Burmese to be the true signs of an impending attack upon their country. [1] On 18 September, McLeod reported to his Government, that the prospect of an invasion of Burma caused much alarm in the Woondouk, his assistants, and the people of the Lower Provinces: " indeed," says McLeod, " the idea of such an event operated stronger on his (the Woondouk's) mind than I had conceived it possible." [2]

Mirza Mahomed Ali, a Moghul, told the Woondouk that the British were meeting with disasters in Afghanistan, that the Indian Princes were preparing to rebel; so that it was positively the intention of the Governor-General to invade Burma, reinstate Bagyidaw to the throne, and obtain a footing in the country, just as they had attempted to control Afghanistan by helping Shah Shuja. [3] Crisp, a British merchant in Rangoon, was also in the habit of talking to Burmese merchants and others that it was the intention of the British to dethrone Tharrawaddy, and take Bagyidaw under their protection. McLeod warned Crisp, and pointed out to him the impropriety

[1] *Ibid.* Vol. 33, McLeod's Journal, par. 993.
[2] *Ibid.* Vol. 26, Consultations 23 October, 1839, No. 75.
[3] *Ibid.* McLeod's Journal, par. 876.

1 7

and danger of his proceedings, but without effect.[1] Merchants from Calcutta also brought rumours of an impending British intervention in the behalf of Bagyidaw. On 28 September, McLeod wrote to his Government concerning these rumours:—
" I regret to bring it to the notice of His Honour-in-Council the reports in circulation respecting the intention of the Government of India to proclaim the old King. Though Mr. Crisp has been too often in the habit of speaking on this subject both to Moguls and Burmese, yet I believe the present report coming from Calcutta has caused much alarm here in the officers of Government. This in addition to the preparations said to be making on our side for war, gives the story a semblance of truth with them, and the Moguls have not lost the opportunity of propagating a story of it being the intention of the Government of India to invade the country with the view of carrying the point into effect after the rains." [2]

McLeod did his best to contradict the rumours, but they did not cease. Many feared that the old King with all his family would be executed.[3] The Ministers also wrote to McLeod professing friendship: " The two great nations English and Burmese, being at peace and on a good understanding, if the representations of those who speak false is attended to, friendship cannot continue long. By taking into consideration all the bearings of the case which are evident, friendship will be established." [4]

McLeod's enquiries and observations confirmed him in the opinion " that there is very great disinclination for war on the part of the wiser portion of the officers of Government, but the people generally hope war will take place to remove them from

---

[1] Ibid. pars. 782, 789.
[2] Ibid. McLeod's Letter, 28 September, 1839.
[3] Ibid. Vol. 33, McLeod's Journal, par. 1142.
According to Gouger (op. cit. p. 336) the ex-Menthagyee and his sister the ex-Queen Mai Nu were executed by Tharrawaddy; but Bagyidaw died a natural death. This is borne out by Yule (op. cit. p. 226), who adds that the ex-Queen and her brother " were put to death with a number of their followers, under circumstances of horrid barbarity."
[4] Ibid. Vol. 26, pars. 912-924.

the oppressive misrule of His Majesty. The Woondouk feels sore and speaks with less caution than he was wont to do, but so much truth has been found in what he had said, that I think he has not uttered anything with a view of misguiding me. It appears to be his opinion that the Burmese will not be the aggressors and invade our territories, that in fact they are not in a state to do so."[1]

In September 1839, certain Indian traders including Yowa Ali, a respectable merchant, arrived from Amarapura, and reported to McLeod that the King was very unfriendly towards the British. The King himself told Yowa Ali that Calcutta had fallen into the hands of the Moghuls, that the British troops in Kandahar had been surrounded by Dost Mahomed and the Persians, and that he (the Burmese monarch) was strong enough not only to conquer Tenasserim, but even to make a dash for Calcutta through Arakan.[2] On 2 November a British deserter from Her Majesty's 62nd Regiment informed McLeod that " the King is very anxious to get as many deserters as possible, and expects soon to be joined by half the Europeans at Moulmein; that there are 14 at the capital (some of them artillerymen), but all attached to the artillery and in teaching the Burmese the use of guns; that these men have charge of all the artillery at the Capital."[3]

Sarkies, who was in Amarapura, wrote to McLeod, " that the King is exactly in the same state of mind as before, determined to have his own way. He says he will receive and treat kindly any Englishman who voluntarily goes to the Capital, but he will not receive any person holding any official appointment under the Government of India in a becoming manner."[4] Gregory, an Armenian merchant, informed McLeod that although the King delighted to hear rumours concerning British disasters, he would not annoy them, and that he was certainly

[1] Ibid. Vol. 25, Consultations 18 September, 1839, McLeod's Letter, 13 August, 1839.
[2] Ibid. Vol. 26, Consultations 23 October, 1839, McLeod's Letter, 8 September, 1839.
[3] Ibid. Vol. 33, McLeod's Journal, par. 1053.
[4] Ibid. par. 1095.

THE BRITISH RESIDENCY IN BURMA

afraid of a British invasion of Burma.[1] When the King heard of the arrival of H. M. S. *Conway* at Rangoon, he observed, " he was glad she had come on a friendly visit, and that matters were quiet, that there was no use going to war, for he had no desire to disturb the English in any way."[2]

Tharrawaddy, however, did not want to take any risks. He continued to collect arms and ammunition, and placed troops at places of strategic importance. On 13 August, 1839, McLeod made the following report:— " In the town and neighbourhood of Rangoon as far as Panlang there are said to be about 7000 fighting men stationed. These have come down from the Capital. The fortification round the great pagoda (the Shwe Dagon) is at a stand still for want of bricks, which, however, are being collected from the ruins of pagodas etc. When completed it will be a somewhat formidable position, but it will occupy the inhabitants of the place for some months to finish.

" There certainly does not exist the same excitement here as at the Capital, but it is well known no dependence is placed by the King on the inhabitants of the Lower Provinces who are undoubtedly in hopes of our soon releasing them from the yoke of their present rulers, but they are armed, and the whole country is in a state of preparation for war. This even the Woondouk admits, but attributes it to the excited state of the King's mind. There is little doubt that His Majesty is daily becoming more unpopular with his officers and the people; though the ignorant look upon him as gifted with unusual good fortune and determination of character."[3]

On 26 August, McLeod reported: " Muskets and ammunition continue to be imported here by English vessels from English Ports and ready sale is found for them, all being eagerly purchased up by the Woondouk and other officers of Government."[4] On 11 September, he wrote in his Journal: " The

[1] *Ibid.* par. 1102.
[2] *Ibid.* par. 1143.
[3] *Ibid.* Vol. 25, Consultations 18 September, 1839.
[4] *Ibid.* No. 6.

Woondouk has issued orders to the heads of Towns etc., to have the Militia all ready with their arms, ammunition, etc., to move at a moment's notice. There is a good deal of bustle in the Town and men passing and repassing." [1]

Besides preparedness for war, Tharrawaddy also tried to get into touch with the French at Chandernagore and Pondicherry. Even before he became King he was interested in the French. Once, for example, he asked a Roman Catholic priest, Monsieur Barbe, to persuade Frenchmen to settle in Burma. [2]

After McLeod had quitted Amarapura, a French party consisting of a leader, who called himself Comte de Brove de la Maison Forte, and two companions, M. Rocke and M. Chivelle, arrived at the capital on 22 July, 1839 [3] There were rumours that the French Government had sent this mission to contract an alliance with Burma; but actually, the three Frenchmen were private individuals, and had come to do business in the exportation of rice, and at the same time sell fire-arms to the King. [4] They soon came into high favour with Tharrawaddy, and it was commonly talked that they would manufacture mines, and lay them at the mouth of the Irrawaddy, so as to prevent British warships from entering the river. [5] M. Chivelle offered to make thirty gunboats for the King, and began constructing three or four of them. [5] The adventurers also desired to establish a communication between the King and the government of Chandernagore [6] with the object, probably, of importing arms, ammunition, and French military trainers into the country.

These French adventurers remained in great esteem at the capital till November, 1839, when they fell into disfavour, the

---

[1] *Ibid.* Vol. 26, McLeod's Journal, par. 802.
[2] *Ibid.* Vol. 33, Consultations 12 February, 1840, McLeod's Letter, 5 December, 1839
[3] *Ibid.* Vol. 23, McLeod's Journal, pars. 461, 464.
[4] *Ibid.* Vol. 25, Consultations. 25 September, 1839, McLeod to Benson, 7 September, 1839, No. 67.
[5] *Ibid.* Vol. 26, McLeod's Journal, pars. 766-768.
[6] *Ibid.* par. 816; McLeod's Letter, 8 October, 1839.

King's mind having been poisoned against them by Staig.[1] They
were summarily ordered to leave the capital, and they arrived
in Rangoon on 10 December.[2] The "Comte" had an interview with McLeod and warned him that the King would certainly attack the English and massacre the British residents in
Burma; he also strongly advised McLeod to quit Rangoon.[2]

During his stay in Rangoon, McLeod had some correspondence with the Ministers at Amarapura. They desired friendship to continue, but were definite in their attitude that the
British Resident would not be allowed to act as Burney had
done. It will be recalled that the Ministers had handed a letter
to Benson for the Governor-General, the envelope of which was
addressed, "To the Ruler and Commander of the Forces of
India." This letter was returned unopened to them through
McLeod in July 1839, at the orders of the Government of India,
on the ground that it was not a proper for the Ministers of one
state to address the ruler of another state direct. The Ministers
were offended at this action. On 25 August, they informed
McLeod that they had addressed the letter in accordance with
custom and the friendship subsisting between the two countries,
"but as its reception has been declined, there will be no occasion to forward any letter hereafter." [3] McLeod sought to
calm their angry feelings, but failed in the attempt. They took
the earliest opportunity to humble him in revenge. On 4 October, 1839, a letter was received from them questioning the
validity of McLeod's appointment; they also returned one of
his letters on the ground that it was not worded according to
custom. "Being desirous always to establish friendship," they
wrote, "we have during the stay of Col. R. Benson the Resident,
at the Royal City, written to say, that we cannot agree to whatever Col. Burney had said or discussed. The letter which we
had forwarded was addressed in accordance to the form and
custom of civilized countries as in the reigns of the Royal great

[1] *Ibid.* Vol. 33, Consultations 12 February, 1840, McLeod's Letter,
14 December, 1839, No. 104.
[2] *Ibid.* McLeod's Journal, pars. 1246, 1256, 1265, 1266.
[3] *Ibid.* Vol. 25, pars. 674-677.

grandfather, grandfather, and succeeding (sovereigns), and which form should be considered as the correct one.

" The Ministers of the English Ruler have established Col. R. Benson as the Representative, but Col. R. Benson has again placed Capt. McLeod, stating, that he is to be the officer in charge of the Residency, which, however, is not in accordance with Burmese customs.

" Whenever the representative of the Minister Col. R. Benson wrote, the address was "to inform" with the (euphonic) affix "pa," but amongst the three letters now forwarded by Capt. McLeod, the one which alludes to " his arrival at Rangoon " and " of his health being somewhat improved," not having been addressed in the usual manner, we have delivered it to the Na-khan of Henthawaddy, Ye Kyaw The-ha, for the purpose of being returned back to Capt. McLeod." [1]

McLeod had used the term " Laik " in place of " Pa " because he thought the two were interchangeable and could be used indiscriminately. According to Burmese custom လိုက် (Laik) is used by a superior to an inferior. The addition of ပါ (လိုက်ပါ Laik pa) would have made the message polite and friendly. McLeod, however, decided not to take notice of the action of the Ministers. [2]

The Rangoon Woondouk was a man of peace. He well understood the serious damage war would do to his country, and his great object was to strive for peace. He was, however, afraid that Tharrawaddy's attitude might bring about open hostilities with the British. He did not wish to be in charge of the Rangoon office in case of war, hence he requested the Ministers to recall him. Besides, he wanted to be at the capital, so as to support the peace party there, and disuade the King from plunging headlong into a war. In October, 1839, his resignation was accepted, [3] but he had to wait for two months

---

[1] *Ibid.* Vol. 26, pars. 912-914.
[2] *Ibid.* Vol. 26, pars. 912-914.
[3] *Ibid.* Consultations 30 October, 1839, McLeod's Letter, 8 October, 1839.

before the new Governor arrived to relieve him. On 31 October, 1839, McLeod wrote to his Government:— "The Woondouk is busy with the Pagoda Wall and is most anxious to get away; he is afraid of the King's committing himself before he gets away. The Woondouk will do his little all to keep matters quiet.........It is to me evident the Court will go on doing everything it can to annoy us, except invade us openly." [1]

Now that the friendly Woondouk was retiring, the question arose, whether McLeod should also withdraw from the Burmese country. The Government of India thought the opportunity had arrived to withdraw the Residency completely, but left the decision to the discretion of McLeod. "........as the Woondouk, who has been so urgent with you to remain for the sake of your cooperation in his endeavours to preserve peace, is about to retire, it occurs to His Honour-in-Council that you may be inclined to consider it a favourable opportuinty for withdrawing at the same time to Moulmein. On this point, however, you will be guided by circumstances. If the Woondouk still urges you to remain as a support to his endeavours at the Court to restrain the King and to avoid increasing in the public mind the expectation of war, and if his successor should manifest the same desire and be disposed to treat you with the consideration hitherto experienced, your continuance will be of course desirable. If on the other hand you have reason to think that an opposite course will be pursued, there can be no doubt of the expediency of your withdrawal, as when once your presence ceased to promote the end intended, it can in the actual state of things be productive of nothing but disadvantage." [2]

Auckland's view of the situation is contained in his letter 11 November, 1839:— "........it occurs to His Lordship that if he (the Rangoon Woondouk) has actually left Rangoon, one of the chief reasons........for Capt. McLeod's remaining will

---

[1] *Ibid.* Vol. 27, Consultations 6 November, 1839, No. 33.
[2] *Ibid.* Vol. 26, Consultations 30 October, 1839, No. 12.

have ceased to exist........as our relations now stand with the Court of Ava the continuance of a British officer in Capt. McLeod's position at Rangoon is not calculated to prevent the occurrence of disputes between the two Governments, that his departure will not increase the chances of a serious rupture, and that it is more consistent with the credit of this Government and our former declaration than to allow of his continuing longer in his present position." [1]

McLeod personally was anxious to retire. On 11 October, he wrote to Benson, " I only wish I was out of this place myself too, for I am heartily sick of such doings, and no consideration but duty would induce me to remain here........It is perfectly useless attempting to do anything with the Ministers; they are determined to have their own way." [2] For three reasons, however, McLeod decided to stay on for some time longer. First, the Woondouk most urgently entreated him not to depart, and said that his departure would in the people's eyes be tantamount to a declaration of war. Also the Woondouk promised that in Amarapura he would attempt to bring his master to a more healthy state of mind towards the British, and that it was possible the Residency might be honourably recalled to the capital. Second, the French Count was very important in desiring McLeod to retire. This roused McLeod's suspicions, and he feared his departure might open up the way for French influence into Burma. Third, by delaying his departure the British and Indian merchants would have time to make their arrangements to withdraw if they deemed it desirable. [3]

The Government of India entirely approved of the propriety of McLeod's decision to wait at Rangoon in order to give to the Woondouk the benefit of his presence and thus support him in his friendly policy at the capital. [4] The Governor-General,

---

[1] *Ibid.* Vol. 27, Consultations 27 November, 1839, No. 11.
[2] *Ibid.* Consultations 6 November, 1839, No. 33.
[3] *Ibid.* Vol. 33, Consultations 12 February, 1840, No. 94; McLeod's Journal, par. 1130; also No. 111.
[4] *Ibid.* No. 100.

however, was quite definite in the policy of withdrawing the Residency entirely, unless an honourable status was conceded to it at the caiptal. " You will however of course understand that the Government of India attaches no importance to your continuance at Rangoon on the footing which you have hitherto been acknowledged there, and though ready to admit that it would have been unwise to refuse the late Governor of Rangoon the support of your presence to which he attached so much importance, as a means of gaining over the Court to friendly and pacific courses, there can be no occasion for your remaining an instant after fulfilling to the letter the expressed or implied understanding in which he has proceeded to the Capital.

" If it should appear therefore that the late Woondouk Governor has aggravated the representation of his influence with the King, or if his party in the struggle for power proves the weaker, and measures indicate that a hostile and military spirit are still prosecuted, or if anything occur at Rangoon to alter in any respect your position for the worse, you will of course act upon the instructions received, and come away."[1]

The new Governor arrived in Rangoon on 28 November, accompanied by 1000 men. He entered the town in state. On 30 November, McLeod visited him, and was received " in a civil and cautious manner........; chairs were occupied by us and a neat dessert served up."[2]   The new Governor had been merely appointed as Myowoon of Hanthawaddy, and so did not possess the powers of an Ayé-bain.[3]   According to McLeod, he was a dull looking man, " but one who will obey implicitly the orders he receives from the capital." [4] He paid every deference to the Woondouk, called on him frequently, and always addressed him with the title of " Phaya." [4]

---

[1] *Ibid.* Vol. 33, Consultations 12 February, 1840, No. 100, Government dispatch
[2] *Ibid.* McLeod's Journal, pars. 1179, 1186, 1189.
[3] *Ibid.* McLeod's Letter, 5 December, 1839; His Journal, par. 1229.
[4] *Ibid.* McLeod's Journal, pars. 1191, 1209.
    Phaya is a Chinese word signifying a Buddha. . It is used as an honorific affix in addressing high personages.

On 3 December, the Woondouk paid a private visit to McLeod. He expressed his most sincere desire for peace and friendship. He entreated McLeod to keep matters quiet on the frontiers, and to recommend a policy of peace to the British Government.[1] On 14 December, the Woondouk left Rangoon much to the regret of the inhabitants.[2] He was undoubtedly an efficient and energetic officer, and understood the political situation better than most of his superiors at the capital.

After the departure of the Woondouk, the British Residency began to be looked upon by the people with greater disrespect than before. There were rumours that the King would open hostilities and not permit McLeod to leave the country. Under the circumstances, McLeod wrote to his Government:— " I cannot of course help viewing the position of the Residency and all the Europeans here with anxiety; and I most earnestly recommend, that a ship of war should be without delay sent down; and if the steamer could be spared to make a trip, it would be of the utmost importance, for by the time these vessels arrive, matters will have ripened so far as to enable me to decide what step to take, for unless I am strongly supported, I much doubt whether I should be permitted to leave this." [3]

McLeod's request for a warship was immediately complied with, and H. M. S. *Conway* arrived at Rangoon on 29th December.[4]

On 15 December, the French Count visited McLeod, and strongly advised him to leave Rangoon, for he feared the King would order a massacre of British subjects; or at least, he said, McLeod and his party would be seized and kept as hostages.[5] Besides rumours, McLeod was feeling concerned, because the Residency was situated in the heart of the town, and was exposed to the low abuse of the drunken followers of Burmese Chiefs as well as of insolent Burmese musketeers. McLeod,

---

[1] *Ibid.* pars. 1207, 1208.
[2] *Ibid.* McLeod's Letter, 14 December, 1839, No. 104.
[3] *Ibid.*
[4] *Ibid.* McLeod's Journal, par. 1364.
[5] *Ibid.* par. 1280.

therefore, decided to withdraw to Moulmein, and sent word to the Myowoon accordingly. The Myowoon requested him not to listen to reports, but wait for about two months more, within which period the Woondouk was expected to settle all matters at the capital. He also offered to McLeod the house, outside the town, once occupied by Burney and later by Bayfield. The offer was accepted, and on 25 December, the Residency was removed to more suitable quarters. McLeod also decided to wait and see what the Woondouk would accomplish at the capital.[1]

While McLeod was seriously considering the question of withdrawing from Rangoon, he heard that the Ministers had written to the Myowoon to say (1) that it was the King's determination to reconquer all the lost territory; (2) that foreigners would no longer be allowed to purchase from Burmans land for trade or for the purpose of building houses, without the King's permission; (3) that foreigners would not be allowed to hold Burmans as slaves: those already sold or pawned must be redeemed by their previous owners, and in case of their inability to do so would be redeemed by the King; (4) that the policy of Nga Dok Gyee, the late Woondouk of Rangoon was condemned by His Majesty, he being inclined to favour foreigners beyond measure.[2]

In obedience to the order concerning slaves, the Myowoon began to prepare a list of slaves under his jurisdiction; also a separate list of Burmese women who were living with foreigners. A few slaves belonging to certain Moghuls were also redeemed by the Governor, and Burmese women were ordered not to live with their husbands in their masters' compounds. There was a general alarm among European and other foreign residents of the city who owned slaves, and whose servants had married Burmese wives.[3] McLeod disapproved of this new regulation concerning slaves and servants, because, as he wrote, it made " an improper and invidious distinction be-

[1] *Ibid.* pars. 1340, 1345, 1350, 1353; McLeod's Letter, No. 113.
[2] *Ibid.* McLeod's Letters, Nos. 106, 110. Vide Appendix X.
[3] *Ibid.* McLeod's Journal, pars. 1338, 1357.

tween the Natives of this country and British subjects who are alike amenable to their courts of Justice and the Laws and Regulations of the country."[1]

McLeod sent a message to the Myowoon to say that the new regulation could not be viewed in any but the most unfriendly light. The Myowoon replied, "that the Royal order was there should be no *slaves,* which order only he was carrying into effect, that he did not intend to prevent servants residing with anybody, and that the servants above mentioned might of course reside in the master's compound, but their families could not be allowed to do so, as otherwise they could not keep the accounts of the people in each district."[2] McLeod's protest did produce some results. A few Armenians were allowed to manumit their slaves and then employ them as hired servants.[3] McLeod interested himself in this question, not that he favoured slavery, but, because as he explained, "the order did not appear to me to have been aimed at the foreigners generally, but especially against British subjects; but Burmese Mussulmans, whose parents have resided here for years, who have been born here and are in Government employ, Roman Catholics who belong to this place and whose relations have always lived here, and who are dressed in the Burmese costume, are not exempted."[3]

On 29 December, McLeod called on the Governor who received him civilly and made full professions of friendship. "I in strong terms," says McLeod, "remonstrated with him respecting the unjust and invidious line he was drawing between Burmese and foreigners respecting slaves. I pointed out that the foreigners had entered the country on the pledge of treaties, and with the full expectation that such as resided in it should be treated in every respect similar to the subjects of the King of Ava, that evenhanded justice should be dealt to them equally with those of the country."[4] In order not to be misunderstood,

[1] *Ibid.* McLeod's Letter, No. 111.
[2] *Ibid.* McLeod's Journal, pars. 1345, 1357.
[3] *Ibid.* par. 1361.
[4] *Ibid.* pars. 1368, 1370.

McLeod added, that the English nation had abolished slavery in their dominions, and would be glad if it was also done away with in Burma. The Myowoon said that he was simply carrying out the King's orders, and that soon things would relapse into the original condition, and all would be placed on the same footing as before. In other words, the Myowoon did not look upon this social reform measure of Tharrawaddy as being genuine. [1]

On 13 January, 1840, the Government of India dispatched instructions to McLeod sanctioning his remaining in Rangoon as long as he thought it advisable. He was also advised to abstain from complaining against the new slave regulations. It was definitely the policy of the Government of India to preserve peace with Burma at this particular time, not only because of the Afghan embroglio, but also because of the growing friction with China. " You will understand," says the letter of instructions, " that the state of things in China, and the resolution to make something more than a demonstration in that quarter, renders it more than ever expedient to avoid precipitating an unfavourable issue with the Burmese; without, therefore, yielding any points or entering into any new altercation, if by your remaining, relations can be maintained on their present footing, the Government will not be dissatisfied, and there can be no occasion to remove the Residency so long as the Rangoon authorities treat you with consideration, and regard its presence as an assurance of hostility not being meditated."[2] Even if it became necessary to withdraw the Residency, peaceful diplomatic relations were to be maintained with Burma. " The only reason," continues the letter, " that can warrant you withdrawing, while so treated, will be the conviction that your doing so will not embroil matters, and that from Moulmein the same policy of friendly intercourse with the Rangoon authorities can be equally maintained."

This change in the attitude of the Government of India, to be satisfied with Rangoon as the headquarters of the Resi-

[1] *Ibid.* par. 1370.
[2] *Ibid.* Vol. 33, Consultations 12 February, 1840, No. 116.

dent, was undoubtedly due to the desire, at much cost of prestige, to maintain peace at this particular time. A week before the instructions were penned, however, it became necessary for McLeod to quit Rangoon.

The Hon. Company's steamer, *Ganges,* was scheduled to depart for Calcutta early on the morning of 2 January, 1840. The Myowoon wished to send a follower of his by this steamer, and McLeod promised him passage, but the man failed to turn up in time, and the steamer sailed away at 3 a.m. This occurrence put the Myowoon out of humour,[1] and soon he furnished two causes which brought about the withdrawal of the Residency on 6 January, 1840.

McLeod made the following report concerning the change in the attitude of the Myowoon:— "......that since the departure of the Hon. Company's steamer *Ganges,* the Myowoon has thought proper to pursue a line of conduct totally in variance with the professions he formerly made, and also to form regulations respecting the closing of the stockade gates etc etc., which caused an unfriendly feeling and render my position here too humiliating to be submitted to.

"A few nights ago, Lt. Rodney and some officers of H. M. S. *Conway,* having been to visit some acquaintances within the stockade, found the gate shut when they wished to return on board the Frigate at 8-30, when the gatekeeper rudely pulled Lt. Rodney back in attempting to pass through the gate as usual. This he no doubt did from ignorance of that officer's person and rank. Mr. Edwards immediately waited on the Myowoon with a civil request that the gate might be opened for the officers, as the order that it should be closed at dark was not known to us. The Myowoon used most intemperate and even menacing language to Mr. Edwards, who almost expected personal violence. It was only after much firm and cool remonstrance on his part that he succeeded in pacifying the Myowoon and obtaining an order for the gate being opened; but even this

---

[1] *Ibid.* Vol. 34, Consultations 3 March, 1840, McLeod's Journal, pars. 1384, 1385.

was not permitted without an order to the gatekeeper that the party should be searched, a degrading order, which the guard, on Mr. Edward's remonstrance and threat of consequences, thought proper not to subject the gentlemen to."[1]

The next rebuff which acted as "the last straw" was a request from the Myowoon that McLeod should vacate the house occupied by him. This was too serious an insult to pocket, so that it was unhesitatingly decided to retire to Moulmein.[1]

McLeod requested J. Brown to hold charge of the Post Office and prevent British dispatches from falling into Burmese hands.[1] He addressed a circular letter to the British merchants of Rangoon, informing them that his departure was " in no way connected with any intended invasion of the country or other hostile act on the part of the British Government."[2] He also addressed a letter to the Myowoon " assuring him of the pacific and friendly disposition of the Government of India and recommending to his special care and protection all British merchants and subjects who may continue in the place."[2]

On the day (6 January) of his departure, McLeod wrote to the Ministers informing them of his impending retirement to Moulmein where he would await orders from his Government, and expressed the hope that there would be no impediment to the transaction of business between the two countries. He assured them of the pacific and friendly intentions of the British Government, and hoped the Burmese Government would recognize the footing on which the two governments had stood, evince a sincere desire to respect and strengthen the ties, and

---

[1] *Ibid.* No. 229. Edwards had served most acceptably as Interpreter and Clerk under Burney, Benson and McLeod successively. After the conquest of Lower Burma (1852) he was made Collector of Customs at Rangoon. *Fytche,* Burma Past and Present Vol. 1, p. 219. Edwards Street in Rangoon is named after him. Edwards also accompanied the Phayre Mission to Amarapura in 1855 as Interpreter. *Yule,* op. cit., p. 1. He also accompanied the three later missions to Mandalay in 1862, 1866, and 1867. The Journal of the Burma Research Society, Vol. XXVII, Part I, April 1937, article by *B. R. Pearn,* The Commercial Treaty of 1862.

[2] *Ibid.* The Circular Letter, No. 230.

protect British subjects in Burma.[1] McLeod was careful not to show any resentment publicly or officially, so that the Myowoon's attitude might not appear to be connected with his withdrawal.

On 6 January, at about 6 a.m. McLeod embarked with all his followers. When just on the point of moving off, a letter arrived from the Myowoon disapproving of his departure because, he said, it would prevent the Woondouk from winning over the King to a policy of peace. He also offered to erect a new house for the Resident without delay; finally, he opined, that " if you wish to depart, it would be proper as Chiefs to meet and greet each other."[2] The letter, however, failed to produce the desired effect, and on 7 January, at daylight, McLeod sailed away.[3]

There is no indication of any serious alarm among British merchants in Rangoon at the withdrawal of the Residency. They had much property at stake, so that they decided to stay on.[4] The Myowoon reported McLeod's departure to the Ministers, and made an accusation against him of having been concerned in smuggling money and women out of the country, and that alarmed at a threatened investigation into the business, he suddenly retired.[5]

The Ministers made the following reply to McLeod's letter of 6 January:—" Col. R. Benson arrived at the Golden City with a letter from the Woongyees of the English Ruler to the Royal Woongyees to the effect that the English Ruler being desirous that the two great countries should be peaceful and quiet, and that if there was any disturbance or disquiet in distant places on the frontier it might be easy to speak on the matter, had directed Col. R. Benson to reside at the Golden City, who, if there was any subject to discuss would write proper

[1] *Ibid.* No. 231, The Letter to the Ministers.
[2] *Ibid.* McLeod's Journal, par. 1424.
[3] *Ibid.* par. 1429.
[4] *Ibid.* McLeod's Letter, 6 January, 1840, No. 229.
[5] *Ibid.* Vol. 35, Consultations 16 March, 1840, Blundell to the Government of India, Moulmein, 19 February, 1840.

letters about it. Being arrived we met him at the "Youm-dau." He said he desired to enter the Palace (have an audience), we replied we would let him know on what day he might enter as customary with Envoys. After he went away he sent a letter to say he would wait 40 days without speaking or writing to us. Afterwards he informed us that he was ill and desired to go away leaving Capt. McLeod as his substitute. Though the English Ruler had sent no letter desiring Col. R. Benson to return, yet, there being a substitute and in accordance with friendship we sent him to Rangoon. Capt. McLeod was allowed to go in and out of the Palace. Capt. McLeod being ill, said, he desired to go to Rangoon for his recovery. We sent him there with boats and men complete. Now the Myowoon of Rangoon has written up to say that Capt. McLeod being ill, has gone to Moulmein, and has sent us Capt. McLeod's letter. In Capt. McLeod's letter he requests that protection may be afforded to foreign merchants. We will afford every assistance and protection to English merchants residing within the Kingdom. We request Capt. McLeod will let us know, after his arrival in Moulmein, whether he is better or worse in health." [1]

The British Resident had withdrawn without making any official protest against his treatment, the object being to avoid friction, which, it was feared, might lead to hostilities. The Burmese Government also pretended, as the Ministers' letter shows, that everything was right, that the Resident had been well treated in Burma, and that his withdrawal from Amarapura as well as from Rangoon was due to his ill health. Outward professions, however, did not remove mutual suspicions. Each government feared that the other would launch an attack, and so each continued to be on the guard; but neither of them desired war, at least not at this time.

In February, 1840, McLeod arrived in Calcutta. The Governor-General-in-Council approved of his action in withdrawing

---

[1] *Ibid.* The Letter from the Woongyees, no date, received at Moulmein by Blundell on 18 February, 1840, No. 75.

from Rangoon.[1] The Government also complimented him for his services in Burma. The Residency establishments were discharged on 31 March, 1840,[2] but the Residency was not officially abolished till on 10 August, 1840.[3] On 30 March, 1840, McLeod was informed by his Government that "as it is not the intention of Government longer to maintain establishment heretofore attached to the political mission in Ava, your services as Officiating Resident are no longer required, and you will be at liberty to rejoin your office in the Tenasserim Provinces."[4]

Before relinquishing his Burma office, McLeod suggested to his Government two lines of policy to choose from in the relations with Tharrawaddy: "one by the countenance of occasional friendly intercourse with the Court of Ava to keep the door open for re-establishing our influence over it should an opportunity occur at any future period; and the other to cut off all political intercourse at once by not replying to the Ministers' letter and thus leave affairs in a state of uncertainty bordering upon hostility."[5] The Governor-General directed McLeod to acknowledge the Ministers' letter, and in his reply to express his satisfaction at receiving friendly communications from them, "and that as you have ceased to hold the situation of representative of the British Government in Burmese Territories, it remains for you as an individual to express your good wishes and to bid your correspondents farewell."[6]

The Government of India now gave up the attempt to maintain a Resident in Burma. From the departure of McLeod up to the first visit of Commodore Lambert to Rangoon in 1852, there was no attempt at intercourse between the two governments. Mutual fears of invasion or attack were, however, by no means absent, so that each party endeavoured to remain on the guard.

[1] *Ibid.* Vol. 34, Consultations 2 March, 1840, No. 234.
[2] *Ibid.* Vol. 35, Consultations 30 March, 1840. No. 79.
[3] *Ibid.* Vol. 42, Consultations 10 August, 1840, No. 102.
[4] *Ibid.* Vol. 35, Consultations 30 March, 1840, No. 79.
[5] *Ibid.* McLeod's Letter, 21 March, 1840, No. 83.
[6] *Ibid.* Vol. 35, Consultations 30 March, 1840, No. 84.

J. Brown of Rangoon for some time kept the Government of India informed of developments in Burma. On 3 July, 1840, he reported that the late Woondouk of Rangoon had an audience of the King and was in favour, and that muskets by the thousand were being imported into the country from Singapore.[1] On 12 August, 1840, he reported that the coronation of Tharrawaddy took place on 8 July, and that the Rangoon Myowoon died on 10 August.[2] On 10 September, 1840, he wrote of the appointment of Maung Hmaee the Woon of Padown and the brother-in-law of the late Myowoon as the Governor of Rangoon.[3]

As early as December, 1839, there had been rumours that after his coronation Tharrawaddy would visit Rangoon. A site beyond the Shwe Dagon Pagoda was also selected by the Myowoon for the construction of a palace for His Majesty. There were also rumours that the King's object was the recovery of the lost territory. A year passed away and Tharrawaddy did not arrive. In December, 1840, again preparations were made on a large scale in Rangoon for the King's reception. He was expected to come with 100,000 followers.[4] Finally, in October, 1841, His Majesty arrived, and people thought he would attack the British in Tenasserim; but he was possessed of enough understanding not to embark upon so foolish and dangerous an enterprise. He left Rangoon in February, 1842, and was back again in Amarapura on 14 March.

The King's visit to Rangoon, however, produced one disturbing effect. For some time the Tenasserim frontier had not been troubled by Burmese dacoits. On 19 February, 1840, Blundell had reported "that this frontier continues free from acts of outrage and depredation on the part of the dacoits *known* to be assembled on the west bank of the Salween."[5]

[1] *Ibid.* Vol. 41, Consultations 20 July, 1840, J. Brown to Bayley, Asst. Secretary to the Government of India, 3 July, 1840, No. 62.
[2] *Ibid.* Vol. 43, Consultations 28 September, 1840, No. 86.
[3] *Ibid.* No. 87.
[4] *Ibid.* Vol. 51, Consultations 18 January, 1841, No. 76.
[5] *Ibid.* Vol. 35, Consultations 16 March, 1840, No. 73.

The King's visit encouraged these dacoits, and a good many cases of robbery and violence occurred at the expense of British subjects east of the Salween. Blundell advocated a more vigorous policy in order to put an end to these troubles. The Government of India, however, was not prepared to follow his advice, and informed him, " that His Lordship-in-Council is not prepared to consider the evil complained of as one, which you are to regard as calling for national satisfaction from the Burmese rulers; he looks upon it rather as a matter which may be corrected by constant vigour and activity in your police arrangements, and by prompt and exemplary punishment of the Burmese malefactors who may be apprehended and brought to justice." [1]

Although war was by all means to be avoided, every effort was also to be made to protect British subjects. The letter continues: " His Lordship-in-Council must hold you and your assistants responsible for the safety of the province from such marauders; you possess abundant means to maintain a constant command of the navigation of the Salween river and to protect our subjects from pillage by their neighbours, and if a striking example is made of all Burmese robbers apprehended and convicted of coming over the river to commit robbery in the British territory, a stop will soon be put to these vexatious incursions." [2]

A couple of days before the above instructions were dispatched, Blundell wrote as follows, giving his views on the political situation in the relations with Burma:— " I take this opportunity of briefly expressing for the information of the Right Hon. the Governor-General-of-India-in-Council my sentiments on our present position with respect to Burmah. The latest intelligence of the movements of the King lead us to conclude that he must now be in the neighbourhood of his capital. Once arrived he will probably disband his army and allow his men to revisit their homes, for whatever may be the effect on

[1] *Ibid.* Vol. 76, Consultations 7 March, 1842, Letter, 7 March, 1842. No. 40.
[2] *Ibid.*

him of the intelligence of our disasters in Afghanistan [1] grossly
exaggerated as it will no doubt be ere it reaches him, it is not
likely that after the heavy duty and the great mortality his men
have lately suffered, he will venture to keep them assembled
during the ensuing rains. I am of opinion that we have nothing
to apprehend from him till about next October, but as it would
be unwise to rely too confidently on this security, I beg to say
a few words on the measures I would recommend to be
adopted........

" I cannot but consider the true defence of Moulmein to
be in the adoption of early vigorous offensive measures on the
first appearance of evidently hostile designs on the part of the
Burmese. In such an event let a proclamation be issued pointing out the threatened hostilities of the Burmese and calling
on our people to assist towards their own defence. Let every
post on the Salween River be destroyed and everything in the
shape of boats be removed......

" There is not the slightest doubt in my mind that every
act of plunder committed on the Salween River is directly sanctioned and encouraged by the authorities of Martaban........
I am convinced that it is an object of the Burmese Government
to keep our people in a state of alarm and disquietude by
such acts, and consequently that no permanent check to them
can be hoped for so long as a safe refuge is insured to the per-
petrators by our *forbearance* to violate a foreign jurisdiction.
It is not that I desire to recommend this violation at the present moment, but merely to point out that such a measure will
alone relieve us as it immediately did in 1829 from these depredations on our people."[2]

---

[1] 2 November, 1841, murder of Sir Alexander Burnes.
23 November, 1841, the battle of Behmaroo lost.
11 December, 1841, the humiliating Treaty.
23 December, 1841, murder of Sir William Macnaghten.
6 January, 1842 to 13 January, 1842, retreat and annihilation of the
army; loss of 15,000 men.
[2] India Secret Consultations Vol. 76, 21 March, 1842, No. 145.

The Government of India did not act upon the suggestion of Blundell, and in spite of frontier incidents, peace between the two states was maintained up to 1852 when the Second War broke out. Relations between the two countries improved on the accession of Mindon in 1853, and although he refused to sign a treaty with the British, in 1862 he allowed the British Residency to be re-established at Mandalay his new capital city.

APPENDIX I

The Treaty of Peace concluded at Yandabo[1]

English Version

Treaty of Peace, between the Honourable the East India Company on the one part, and His Majesty the King of Ava on the other, settled by Major-General Sir Archibald Campbell, K. C. B. and K.C.T.S., commanding the expedition, and Senior Commissioner in Pegu and Ava, Thomas Campbell Robertson, Esq. Civil Commissioner, in Pegu and Ava, and Henry Dacie Chads, Esq. Captain commanding his Brittanic Majesty's and the Honourable Company's naval force on the Irawadi river, on the part of the Honourable Company, and Mengyee Maha-men-hlah-kyan-ten, Woongyee Lord of Laykaing and Mengyee-maha-men-hlah-thee-ha-thoo   Atwen - Woon, Lord of the Revenue on the part of the King of Ava, who have each communicated to the other their full powers ageed to, and executed at Yandaboo in the Kingdom of Ava, on this twenty-fourth day of February in the year of our Lord one thousand eight hundred and twenty six, corresponding with the fourth day of the decrease of the moon Taboung, in the year one thousand one hundred and eighty-seven, Guadama era.

Art. 1st.— There shall be perpetual peace and frendship between the Honourable Company on the one part, and His Majesty the King of Ava on the other.

Art. 2nd.— His Majesty the King of Ava renounces all claims upon, and will abstain from all future interference with, the principality of Assam and its dependencies, and also with the contiguous petty states of Cachar and Jyntea. With regard to Munnipore, it is stipulated that, should Gumbheer Singh desire to return to that country, he shall be recognized by the King of Ava as Rajah thereof.

Burmese Version

Treaty of Peace and Friendship, between the English Company's Governor-General of India and the King of Burma, made by the Chief General, the Noble Archibald Campbell, Commissioner, Robertson, Esq. Commissioner, and Chads Esq. Commander of the English war-vessels on the Irawadi river, appointed by the Governor-General, and Mengyee Maha-men-hla-kyan-ten, Woon-gyee, Lord of Lakaing and Mengyee Maha-men-hla-thee-ha-thu, Atwen-woon, Lord of the Revenue, appointed by the King of Burma, at Yan-da-bo, on the fourth of the decrease of Ta-boung, in the year 1187 (Feb. 24th, 1826).

Art. 1st.— Let there be perpetual peace and friendship between the Governor-General and the King of Burma.

Art. 2nd.— The King of Burma shall no more have dominion over, or the direction of, the towns and country of Assam, the country of Ak-ka-bat, (Cachar) and the country of Wa-tha-li (Jyntea). With regard to Munnipore, if Gan-bee-ra-shing desire to return to his country and remain ruler, the King of Burma shall not prevent or molest him, but let him remain.

---

[1] *Crawfurd,* op. cit. Vol. II, Appendix No. III.

Art. 3rd.— To prevent all future dispute respecting the boundary line between the two great nations, the British Government will retain the conquered provinces of Aracan, Ramree, Cheduba, and Sandowey; and His Majesty the King of Ava cedes all right thereto. The Amou-pectoumieu or Aracan mountains, (known in Aracan by the name of Yeoamatoung or Phokingtoun range), will henceforth form the boundary between the two great nations on that side. Any doubts regarding the said line of demarcation, will be settled by Commissioners appointed by the respective Governments for that purpose, such Commissioners from both Powers to be of suitable and corresponding rank.

Art. 3rd.— That there may be no cause of future dispute about the boundary between the two great countries, the English Government will retain the country of Aracan, that is, Aracan, Ramree, Man-oung (Cheduba) and Than-dwa, which they have conquered; and the King of Burma shall not have dominion. Let the Yo-ma and Bo-koung range of mountains, unto the Great Pagoda, on the Man-ten promontory (Cape Negrais) be the boundary. If hereafter there should be a dispute about the boundary, let men be appointed by the English and the Burmese Governments, to decide correctly, according to ancient limits. The men appointed, shall be respectable officers of Government.

Art. 4th.— His Majesty the King of Ava cedes to the British Government the conquered provinces of Yeh, Tavoy, Mergui, and Tenasserim, with the islands and dependencies thereunto appertaining, taking the Saluen river for the line of demarcation on that frontier. Any doubts regarding their boundaries will be settled as specified in the concluding part of Article Third.

Art. 4th.— The King of Burma cedes to the British Government the towns of Ye, Tavoy, Myik, (Mergui) and Tenasserim, with their territories, mountains, shores, and islands. The Salwen river shall be the boundary. If hereafter there should be a dispute about the boundary, let it be settled as specified above.

Art. 5th.— In proof of the sincere disposition of the Burmese Government to retain the relation of peace and amity between the two nations, and as part indemnification to the British Government, for the expenses of the war, his Majesty the King of Ava agrees to pay the sum of one crore of rupees.

Art. 5th.— The King of Burma, in order to make manifest his desire to preserve perpetual friendship between the two great countries, and to defray part of the expenses incurred by the British Government in the war, shall pay one crore of rupees.

Art. 6th.— No person whatever, whether native or foreign, is hereafter to be molested, by either party, on account of the part which he may have taken, or have been compelled to take, in the present war.

Art. 6th.— No person who has gone from one side to the other during the war, whether a Burmese subject who has joined the English, or an English subject who has joined the Burmese, whether voluntarily or by compulsion, shall be punished or molested on that account.

Art. 7th.— In order to cultivate and improve the relations of amity and peace hereby established between the two Governments, it is agreed that accredited Ministers, retaining an escort or safe-guard of fifty men, from each shall reside at the Durbar of the other, who shall be permitted to purchase or to build a suitable place of residence of permanent materials, and a Commercial Treaty upon principles of reciprocal advantage will be entered into by the two high contracting powers.

Art. 7th.— That the friendship now settled between the two great countries may be permanent, let one Government person be appointed by the British Government, with fifty attendants and arms complete, to reside in the royal city of Burma; and let one Government person, appointed by the Burman Government, with fifty attendants and arms complete, reside in the royal city of the Governor-General. And let the Burmese Governor, residing in the Ku-la country, and the Ku-la Governor residing in the Burmese country, purchase or build anew, as they may choose, a suitable house of wood or brick for their residence. And in order to promote the prosperity of the two nations, an additional Treaty shall be made, relative to opening the gold and silver (A Burman phrase) road and trading one with another.

Art. 8th.— All public and private debts contracted by either Government or by the subjects of either Government, with the others, previous to the war, to be recognized and liquidated, upon the same principles of honour and good faith, as if hostilities had not taken place between the two nations; and no advantage shall be taken by either party of the period that may have elapsed since the debts were incurred, or in consequence of the war; and according to the universal law of nations, it is farther stipulated, that the property of all British subjects who may die in the dominions of his Majesty the King of Ava, shall, in the absence of legal heirs, be placed in the hands of the British Resident or Consul, in the said dominions, who will dispose of the same according to the tenour of the British law. In like manner the property of Burmese subjects dying, under the same circumstances, in any part of the British dominions, shall be made over to the Minister or other Authority delegated by his Burmese Majesty to the Supreme Government of India.

Art. 8th.— All debts contracted previous to the war, by the Government people or common people, shall be completely liquidated, according to good faith. No one shall be suffered to excuse himself, saying, the war took place after the debt was contracted; nor shall either party confiscate the property of the other in consequence of the war. Moreover, when British subjects die in the Kingdom of Burma, and there be no heir, all the property left shall, according to the usages of white Ku-las, be delivered to the English Government person residing in Burma; and in like manner, when Burmese subjects die in the British Kingdom, and there be no heir, all the property left shall be delivered to the Burmese Government person residing there.

Art. 9th.— The King of Ava will abolish all exactions upon British ships or vessels in Burman ports, that are not required from Burman ships or vessels in British ports; nor shall ships or vessels, the property of British subjects, whether European or Indian, entering the Rangoon river, or other Burman ports, be required to land their guns, or unship their rudders, or to do any other act not required of Burmese ships or vessels in British ports.

Art. 10th.—The good and faithful ally of the British Government, his Majesty the King of Siam, having taken a part in the present war, will, to the fullest extent, as far as regards his Majesty and his subjects, be included in the above Treaty.

Art. 11th.—This Treaty to be ratified by the Burmese Authorities competent in like cases, and the ratification to be accompanied by all British, whether, European or Native, American, and other prisoners, who will be delivered over to the British Commissioners; the British Commissioners, on their part, engaging that the said Treaty shall be ratified by the Right Honourable the Governor-General in Council; and the ratification shall be delivered to his Majesty the King of Ava, in four months, or sooner if possible, and all the Burmese prisoners shall, in like manner, be delivered over to their own Government, as soon as they arrive from Bengal.

Art. 9th.— When British vessels come to Burmese ports, they shall remain without unshipping their rudders, or landing their guns, and be free from trouble and molestation, as Burmese vessels in British ports.

Art. 10th.— The King of Siam, the ally of the British Government, having taken part with the British in the war, shall be considered as included in the present Treaty.

Art. 11th.—This Treaty shall be ratified by Commissioners appointed by the King of Burma; and all English, American, and other black and white Ku-la prisoners shall be delivered to the British Commissioners. Also the Treaty, assented to and ratified by the Governor-General of India, shall be transmitted to the King of Burma within four months; and all Burmese prisoners shall be immediately called from Bengal, and delivered to the Burmese Government.

(L. S.)

Signatures of the British Commissioners

(Seal of the Hlutdau)

Signatures of the Burmese Commissioners

Additional Article

—The British Commissioners being most anxiously desirous to manifest the sincerity of their wish for peace, and to make the immediate execution of the fifth Article of this Treaty as little irksome or inconvenient as possible to His Majesty the King of Ava, consent to the following arrangement with respect to the division of the sum total, as specified in the Article above referred to, into instalments; *viz.* upon the payment of twenty-five lacs of rupees, or one quarter of the sum total, (the other Articles of the Treaty being executed), the army will retire to Rangoon. Upon the farther payment of a similar sum at that place within one hundred days from this date, with the proviso, as above, the army will evacuate the dominions of his Majesty the King of Ava with the least possible delay, leaving the remaining moiety of the sum total to be paid by equal annual instalments, in two years, from this twenty-fourth day of February, 1826, A.D. through the Consul or Resident in Ava or Pegu, on the part of the Honourable the East India Company.

Additional Article

—The British Commissioners, in order to manifest their desire for peace, and that the King of Burma may pay with ease the crore of rupees mentioned in the fifth Article, when he has paid eighteen and three quarters lacs of ticals, or one fourth part of the whole sum of seventy-five lacs of good silver, which is one crore of rupees, the English army will retire to Rangoon. Upon farther paying eighteen and three-quarters lacs of ticals, within one hundred days from this date, the English army shall speedily depart out of the Kingdom of Burma. In regard to the remaining two parts of the money, one part shall be paid within one year from this date, and the other within two years, to the English Government person residing in Burma.

APPENDIX II

Two Orders of the Hlutdaw

" Order regarding the purchase and Sale of Bundles of Rubies":—

"The Resident Major H. Burney having stated that he requires all the duties and customs regarding English Traders who come to Ava and purchase Bundles of Rubies to be properly fixed in order that orders may be attended to —

"If a Bundle of Rubies valued 1000 ticals are sold the Yabiad [1] shall examine and after having ascertained that there are no rubies suitable for the King 25 ticals will be taken as the usual royal duty, 25 ticals on account of the Yabiad, and 5 ticals for affixing the seal. To each of the Atwenwoons are to be given as usual when soliciting permission for the seal to be used one Piece of Book Muslin and one plate of sugar. Let only what is according to custom be given or taken. Let nothing in excess be taken.

"Year 1192 the 11th of the Waning Moon Tazoung Mhoun (10 November, 1830).

"Tsaben Menza Woonyendau Kyee Woon Mengyee, Myawadi Woongyee, Padein Mengyee, Nagarané Woongyee,[2] Kyouk Tshoung Woongyee, Tshan myoza Atwenwoon and Kyee Woon dau Maha Mengyan Yaza."

"Order regarding the money to be levied and received at the Kens or Chokies: —

"The Kyouk-ta-loun and Men-gwon-kenda chokies according to the ancient custom as may appear in the Records of the year 1145.

---

[1] Appraiser.

[2] Nagarané Woongyee: This was the Queen's Woongyee, also mentioned on pp. 74, 183, 235. There is no indication anywhere in Burmese history that there was such an officer as the Queen's Woongyee having a seat on the Hlutdaw. The records of this period, however, are most definite that such an officer did exist in the reign of Bagyidaw. On p. 235 Maung Wa is spoken of as the Nagarané or the Queen's Woongyee; also this Order of the Hlutdaw is signed by the Nagarané. On p. 74 the Queen's Woongyee is called by Burney the Min-ma-daw. It is possible that under the powerful influence of Queen Mai Nu, the favourite wife of Bagyidaw, this innovation was introduced and she came to have her representative on the Hlutdaw.

The meaning of the term Nagarané is obscure; but it might be suggested, that, Naga (meaning dragon, elephant, snake) was a title; rané is perhaps the Indian word for Queen: so that Nagarané would mean the officer appointed to protect the interests of the Queen; undoubtedly, therefore, he would sit on the Hlutdaw.

"Let the Kyouk-ta-loun Ken levy for each person in a boat one Moo of silver (10 Moos = 1 tical) and one pyee of rice (16 pyees = 1 basket); and the Men-gwon Ken levy for each person 1 Moo of silver. Merchants detected in carrying away to another country articles which are not exempt from criminal law, gold, silver, swords, spears, muskets or other articles not proper to be taken away, let the Ken Woon apprehend and after examining forward them (to the Hlutdau).

"Regarding the pass for leaving the City let the Ken Woon grant it as usual charging for a pass to leave the city as usual according to the breadth of the boat.

"Let three ticals be taken from a boat measuring from 5 to 14 cubits in breadth; 2 ticals from a boat measuring from 3 to 4½ cubits in breadth; and 1 tical from a boat measuring less than 3 cubits in breadth. Let nothing in excess be taken.

"Year 1192 (15 November, 1830)." (Bengal Secret and Political Consultations Vol. 360, Consultations 21 January, 1831, No. 8).

APPENDIX III

Burney's Observations on the Currency of Burma

Burney collected a good deal of information on this subject. Cox had done the same, but Burney says that the standard between Burmese silver and the Sicca rupees of the East India Company had since altered:—

"The late King of Ava, Men-dera-gyee,[1] attempted to introduce a coinage, and with this view coined a quantity of silver ticals and copper pice with the Mint machinery which was brought here by Capt. Cox.[2] The metallic purity of these coins was good, but the King changed a seigniorage of 66 ⅔ per cent on the silver and 315 per cent on the copper, ordering his coins to pass to that extent above their intrinsic value and prohibiting all other currency The consequence was that the inhabitants shut up their shops and there was no bazar or other commercial business for several weeks until the Woongyees persuaded the King to allow his subjects to continue the precious metals in the same manner as they had always done. The people can place no confidence in their government, and it would be difficult now to establish a regular coinage in this Kingdom." (Bengal Secret and Political Consultations Vol. 360, Consultations Fort William, 15 April, 1831, No. 12).

---

[1] Bodawpaya's name.
[2] in 1797.

APPENDIX IV

Translation of a Letter addressed by the Emperor of China to the King of Ava, and received at Ava in April, 1836

"Royal letter received from 'Tarup udi Men'[1] Emperor of China of the Eastern Empire of Gandalayit,[2] enclosed within a yellow bag marked with the figure of a dragon 12/3d cubit in length, the diameter of the tube containing the letter being 3 fingers. The letter is written in two languages the Chinese and Tartar upon yellow paper the breadth of which is 7 fingers and length 12/3 cubit, and it is marked according to Chinese custom with four seals. The following is a translation of the letter written in the Chinese language which consists of 51 lines and which the head merchants Nga Shwe-Yeh, Nga Lo-tsam, and Nga Lo-tauk residing in the Taroup Tangyeh long street occupied by the Chinese at Amarapoora were made to translate into the Burmese language at the Lhwottau on the 4th day of the waxing of the moon Katshown[3] in the Burmese year 1198 (18th April 1836).

"The Royal Elder brother Tauk Kwon (Tau Kwang)[4] Emperor of China who assisted by the Thagya[5] Nat rules over a multitude of umbrella wearing chiefs in the great Eastern Empire, affectionately addresses his Royal younger brother the sun descended King Lord of the Golden Palace who rules over a multitude of umbrella wearing chiefs in the Great Western Empire.

"In consequence of Elder brother studying to govern and perform all his duties with a view that the Empire which he rules over may continue firm and distinguished for 10000 years, he is

---

[1] Taroup or Tarup: in old Burmese it is Taruk which was the regular name for Chinaman, probably the same as Turk. *Vide* Burma census Report, 1931, Note by *G. H. Luce* on Taruk, pp. 300, 301. Udi or Ude or Udibwa: a term used for the Emperor of China; derived from the Pali Udaya, Lord of the sunrise.

[2] A term used for China, derived from the Gandhararaj of India. Gandhara was a mountainous kingdom to the north of India. In Burma it was taken to mean China.

[3] The Burmese month of Ka'son, April-May.

[4] Tao-Kuang, year name of the Manchu Emperor who reigned from 1821 to 1850. His immediate predecessor was Chia-ch'ing.

[5] Burney's Note: — "The Chinese Tien or Shang Tien, Lord of Heaven. The Burmese Thagya is the Hindu God Indra one of whose names is pronounced Thagya by the Burmese."

Thagya Nat = Sakra Natha, the Lord Indra of India.

Tien or Shang Tien = Heaven, the Upper Heaven, *i.e.* God.

exceedingly reverenced and considered as a father by the four and six ministers of state. To the principal queen, also all the inferior queens and concubines show the greatest respect and homage.

"Because the Royal Mother, also the great queen Koun-tshi-Khan-Yeng-an-tsheng twon Khuchuan tsho [1] possesses an excellent heart and acts always like the rain and wind (*i.e.* Her benevolence is as extensive and universal as the rain and wind which falls and blows alike upon all classes of beings) and bestows good instruction on the Queen and all the concubines and female attendants, the whole of the inmates of the palace are cheerful and happy. The Queen and all the concubines and female attendants have affectionately sought the protection of 'the Royal Mother in the same manner as all seek warmth from the Sun in winter, and in consequence of Elder brother listening to and following her advice the whole Empire is enjoying great happiness.

"On the 9th day of the increasing moon of Natdau (28 November, 1835) being the 15th anniversary of Elder brother's ascension to the throne, he together with all his queens, sons, daughters, relatives and officers did homage before the Royal Mother who abounds in such virtues and is now advanced to a great age and the title of Koun-tshi-Khan-Yeng-an-tsheng-tswon-Khue-shyo-shi-hwon-taik-ho [2] was conferred upon her in addition to her former name. The Royal Mother also having a view to future rewards has repaired the dilapidated stone vaults and graves constructed in the burying ground in which the different generations of the Emperors of China have been entered since the commencement of the world.

"Nobles and officers have been sent to the four quarters where the ocean is in order to perform worship with gold and silver coins and gold and silver candles, additional titles have been conferred upon the Royal Daughter as well as upon the wives and daughters of the Royal brothers, sons and officers. Appropriate titles and honorary distinctions have been conferred also upon the different officers in the city of Pekin and in the distant Provinces.

---

[1] and [2] The English transliteration is very defective: it is the work of Burney and his Interpreter Edwards from the Burmese rendering of the Chinese merchants from the Mandarin original. Mr. G. H. Luce has very kindly obtained for the author from the Rev. Bhikkhu S. Wan Hui the correct wording as well as the meaning of the title. It will be seen that the second title is an advance upon the first. This later title was conferred on the Dowager Empress in the winter (10th month) of the 15th year of Tao-Kuang, *i.e.* in 1835 A.D.: —

    Kung (reverent) — Tz'ŭ (compassionate) — K'ang (tranquil) — Yū (comfortable) — An (peaceful) — Ch'êng (perfect) — Chuang (sedate) — Hui (gracious) — Shou (long lived) — Hsi (joyous) — Huang-T'ai-Hou (Dowager Empress).

" To the soldiers of the city and those of the Royal body-guard one month's rations in addition to their usual allowances have been issued. To all Chinese and Tartars of more than 70 years of age 1 Roll of Satin, 1 piece of white cloth, 10 Viss of pork, and 1 basket of rice have been given, and to all those of more than 80 or 90 years of age double the quantity *viz.*, 2 rolls of Satin, 2 pieces of white cloth, 20 Viss of pork, and 2 baskets of rice have been given.

"The Temple and all the old and dilapidated bridges, wells, tanks and zayat (buildings for public accommodation) have been repaired with money issued from the Royal Treasury.

" Everything that occurs in Elder brother's Empire shall be made known to younger brother with respect to younger brother's Empire. It is not proper to allow the English after they have made War, and Peace has been settled to remain in the city. They are accustomed to act like the 'Pipal' Tree (wherever this plant takes root and particularly in old temples and buildings it spreads and takes such firm hold that it is scarcely possible to be removed or eradicated. I believe Pipal does not grow in the northern parts of China but the Burmese word Nyoung is applied to many species of Ficus). Let not Younger Brother therefore allow the English to remain in his country, and if anything happens Elder Brother will attack, take and give.

" This is affectionately addressed to Younger Brother the Son descended King and Lord of the Golden Palace."

" 18 April, 1836. The Menthagyee and Ministers, the Lords of Myawadi, Padein and Kyouk tshoung and the Royal Woondouk being assembled, the principal Chinese Merchants and Interpreters residing in the Taroup Tangyeh were made to translate the Royal Letter under the direction of the Awe-Youk-Tse-thu-zeya-gyo in front of the Lhwottau, and it was carried into the Levee room on the 19th April and delivered to the Royal Nakhan Naurathagyan and presented.

" The Engagement of the principal Chinese Merchants, 18th April, 1836. Engagement entered into by Nga Shwe-Yeh, Nga Lo-tsam, Nga Lo-tauk, and Nga Lo-Yeng principal merchants residing in the Taroup Tangyeh at Amarapoora. With respect to the order which we have received to translate the Royal Letter that has arrived from the Empire of Gandalayit there are two letters, and Tartar and one Chinese. We cannot translate the Tartar letter but can the Chinese and will accordingly do it fully. If it should hereafter appear that our translation is not correct and that something has been omitted or added we agree to suffer such punishment as may be suitable to our crime under which engagement the translation was made." (India Pol. Cons. Range 194, Vol. 23, Cons. 7 November, 1836, No. 51).

APPENDIX V

Credentials of Col. Richard Benson as Resident at Ava

"Whereas it has been judged proper to appoint a successor to Lt. Col. Burney as Resident on the part of this Government to the Court of His Majesty the King of Ava, We the Hon. The President and the Members of the Council of India, in virtue of the powers vested in us by the Queen and Parliament of Great Britain and Ireland and by the Hon. the East India Company to direct and control the political affairs of Her Majesty's Dominions and also of all the Company's settlements in India, relying in your fidelity and prudence and integrity, have in communication with the Governor-General appointed you our Resident at the Court of Ava; and in that capacity to do and to transact all such business as shall be given to you in charge by us, and we hereby invest you with full powers to that effect, declaring that we will confirm whatever you may transact with His Majesty the King of Ava and His Ministers in our name and in our behalf according to the instructions with which you have been furnished or shall hereafter be furnished for that purpose.

"And we hereby authorize you to receive complaints from all British subjects residing in the dominions of the King of Ava on the subject of injuries sustained by them from the Government or subjects of Ava, and to make such representations thereon to the King and Ministers as you may judge advisable; and we further authorize you to make requisitions regarding complaints preferred against them by the Court and subjects of Ava, to which requisitions they are hereby enjoined to reply, and to furnish proper explanations in every instance wherein the same may be required from them by you.

"Given under our hand and the seal of the Company at Fort William in Bengal this Twentieth Day of June 1838." (India Secret Consultations Vol. 10, Consultations 20 June, 1838, No. 14).

APPENDIX VI

Letter from The Council of India to King Tharrawaddy of Burma

" To His Most Excellent Majesty the King of Ava
From The Hon. Alex. Ross Esq. President
The Hon. Col. Wm. Morrison C.B., and
The Hon. Wm. Wilberforce Bird Esq.
Members of the Council of India at Calcutta.

" To His Most Excellent Majesty the King of Ava.

" In order to sustain the relations of peace and amity happily subsisting between Your Majesty and this Government, the Rt. Hon. Lord Auckland, Governor-General has, His Lordship's letter will separately announce, been pleased to appoint Col. Richard Benson to be his Resident at Ava in consequence of Lt. Col. Burney having departed from this country for Europe. We have taken necessary steps to carry this appointment which has our entire concurrence into complete execution and to forward Col. Benson to Your Majesty's Court with the usual escort and attendants.

" Col. Benson is directed to proceed to Your August Presence with all particular expedition, and is charged to convey the assurances of our adherence to solemn engagements, of our scrupulous observance of that good faith which is the well known characteristic of the British Government, and of our favourable disposition towards Your Majesty. He is enjoined also to express our desire to maintain the harmony and concord existing between the two great nations of Ava and British India, and our wish to improve by a friendly intercourse that amity and goodwill which it is the constant study of the British Government to promote.

" Regarding Your Majesty as taking interest in the welfare of Your friends, it yields us high satisfaction to inform you that under the fostering care of the British Government the extensive Empire of Hindostan enjoys profound peace; and it will afford us great gratification to learn that under the rule of Your Majesty the Empire of Ava is flourishing and prosperous. It is also our fervent hope, that the friendly disposition which animates the two governments of Ava and British India may diffuse itself through all ranks and classes of their subjects, and that the traffic so beneficial to both countries may increase and continue to flow through its usual channels.

" Col. Benson is charged with some articles of the manufacture of this country and of Europe which he will have the honor to present as a token of the consideration and respect entaintained for Your Majesty.

" We request Your Majesty will accept the assurance of our profound respect and esteem." Fort William, 20 June, 1838. (India Secret Consultations Vol. 10, Consultations 20 June, 1838, No. 15).

APPENDIX VII

Letter from the Secretary to the Government of India to the Woongyees of the King of Burma

"To The Ministers and Generals of the King of Ava,
From the Secretary of the Government of India.

"The Government of British India desires it may be announced to the Burmese Ministers of State that Lt. Col. Henry Burney having proceeded to Europe, the Rt. Hon. the Governor-General George Lord Auckland has been pleased in accordance with the Article of the Treaty of Yandaboo to appoint Col. Richard Benson to be British Resident at the Court of Ava, and the President-in-Council at Calcutta has taken all necessary steps to give effect to this appointment and to forward Col. Benson to the capital of the Burmese Empire.

"The Government of British India avails itself of this opportunity to repeat the assurance of the readiness of the Governor-General to receive any Burmese officer of rank and consideration whom His Majesty the King of Ava may be pleased to depute as the Burmese Resident.

"The experience of every civilized and enlightened nation has proved that the most efficacious mode of maintaining peace and amity, and of obviating distrust and misunderstanding is for the Rulers of great countries to have at the Court and near the presence of one another a public officer whose special duty it is to make explanations and afford information on all points thereby preventing the mischievous consequences of the false tales which ill disposed persons are apt to circulate. A further important part of such officer's duty it is to say and do all such things as may tend to promote mutual goodwill and to keep straight smooth and open the golden road of peace. Moreover the Burmese Ministers of state must be sensible, that in the absence of direct, certain, and immediate means of intercourse and correspondence between the King of Ava and the Governor-General of India, there is reason to apprehend that the subordinate officers on both sides, English and Burmese, may allow their local disputes to be reported to their superiors with much exaggeration whereby serious misunderstanding may be needlessly caused between the two nations.

"Col. Benson whom the Governor-General has selected to be his representative at the Court of Ava is an officer who has served many years in this division of the British Empire and who has recently returned from a visit to Europe. He was one of the trusty and esteemed secretaries of the late Governor-General Lord Wm. C. Bentinck and he possesses in an eminent degree the confidence of the Governor-General George Lord Auckland, and of all the Members of the Government of India.

"Col. Benson is empowered to communicate to the King of Ava and to the Burmese Ministers the views of the British Government upon any points that may need explanation, and to hear and write down and to report to the Governor-General and to the Government of India all that the King of Ava and the Ministers may desire at any time to be made known.

"The Governor-General trusts, that the King of Ava will treat Col. Benson with the courtesy and consideration which are due to him in his high office of Representative of the British Government and will evince towards him that regard and respect which will best beseem the dignity of both states, and secure for him every facility for maintaining a free and uninterrupted communication between the capitals of Ava and Calcutta.

"Col. Benson, will, soon it is hoped, by his early arrival at Ava have it in his power to reassure the Burmese Ministers that the British Government continues desirous to maintain peace and to improve commercial intercourse upon the principles established by the Treaty of Yandaboo, and further to satisfy them that he is prepared to discuss in a friendly spirit all questions and differences that may from time to time require adjustment.

"Col. Benson is the bearer of presents from the Governor-General to His Majesty the King of Ava. He has been appointed specifically for the purpose of maintaining the friendly relations of this Government with Ava upon the established footing on which account he is ordered to proceed to the Capital with his Assistant Capt. Mcleod who is already known to you as an officer of credit and intelligence with all practicable dispatch. Dr Bayfield will remain at Rangoon to communicate with the Local Officers of the King of Ava at that city and to settle under the orders of the Resident any questions that may arise with British Merchants and others. Any further information you may desire in respect to the arrangements and intentions of the British Resident I am directed to refer you to Col. Benson.

"I request you will accept the assurance of my high consideration and respect." (India Secret Consultations Vol. 10, Consultations 20 June, 1838, No. 16).

APPENDIX VIII

Establishments attached to the British and Burmese Residencies

(I) Under Burney at his departure in 1837: —

Monthly Salary

Mr. Edwards, Clerk and Interpreter	Rs. 300
Mr. Good, Sub-Assistant Surgeon	„ 100
One Burmese Writer	„ 30
One Burmese Munshi	„ 30
Four Peons at Rs. 10 each	„ 40
	Total Rs. 500

Boat Establishment: —

One Row Boat, one Serang and 14 Lascars	Rs. 174
One Gun Boat, one tindal and 14 Lascars	„ 169
One Bauleah,[1] one tindal and 13 Lascars	„ 158
	Total Rs. 501

Resident at Ava	Rs. 3000
Assistant to Resident at Ava	„ 700
	Total Rs. 3700

Grand Total Rs. 4701

(II) Under Benson: —

Mr. Edwards, Clerk and Interpreter	Rs. 300
Mr. Good, Sub-Assistant Surgeon	„ 185
One Burmese Writer	„ 30
One Burmese Munshi	„ 30
Four Peons	„ 40
	Total Rs. 585

One Row Boat and crew	Rs. 174
One Gun Boat and crew	„ 169
Part of Bauleah Crew or one Tindal and 8 Lascars	„ 103
	Total Rs. 446

Resident at Amarapura	Rs. 3000
1st Assistant at Amarapura	„ 750
	Total Rs. 3750

Total expenditure at Amarapura Rs. 4781

[1] Bholiah, row boat, covered over at one end.

With the Assistant at Rangoon:—

One Burmese Writer	..	..	..	Rs.	30
One Burmese Munshi	..	..	..	„	30
Two Peons	..	..	..	„	20
Five Lascars	..	..	..	„	55
Assistant to Resident	..	..	..	„	1000

Total Rs. 1135

Grand Total Rs. 5916

N.B.— Besides the above, Burney had an Escort consisting of One Indian Officer, Two Havaldars, Two Naiks, Two Drummers, and Thirty Sepoys. The Commander of the Escort was the Assistant Resident. Benson's Escort consisted of One Lieutenant, One Indian Officer, Five Non-Commissioned Officers, Two Drummers, and Forty-two Sepoys. Benson's Assistant at Rangoon had an Escort of 2 Non-Commissioned Officers and Eight Sepoys. (Bengal Secret and Political Consultations Vol. 357, 8 January, 1830, No. 32; India Secret Consultations, Vol. 11, 22 August, 1838, No. 66.)

(III) Establishment of the Burmese Resident in India, 1830-1833: —

Resident	..	..	1
Assistant Resident	..	..	1
Writers	..	..	2
Interpreters	..	..	2
Physician	..	..	1
Draftsman	..	..	1
Musketeers	..	..	20

Total Establishment .. 28

Other companions and followers: —

Resident's Son	..	..	1
Resident's Daughters	..	..	2
Resident's Wives	..	..	2
Resident's Son's wife	..	..	1
Asst. Resident's wife	..	..	1
Female Attendants	..	..	3
Male Attendants	..	..	46

Grand Total .. 84

(Bengal Secret and Political Vol. 358, Consultations 10 December, 1830, No. 7).

N.B.— The Burmese Mission of 1827 to Calcutta and then to Moulmein consisted of Two Officers and 100 armed followers. Bengal Secret and Political Vol. 348, Consultations 28 September, 1827, No. 62).

The Crawfurd Mission 1826, consisted of an establishment much more expensive than that of either Burney or Benson: — Crawfurd, Rs. 3000; Table expenses, limit Rs. 5000; Assistant to Envoy Rs. 750; Surgeon, Rs. 680; Interpreter (Judson), Rs. 400; Two Clerks, Rs. 250; Munshi, Rs. 30; Two Peons, Rs. 24: A total of Rs. 10,134 per month. The Escort consisted of Twenty-eight European and Fifteen Indian grenadiers. (*Ibid.* Vol. 357, Note to Bentinck's Minute, 30 December, 1829; *Crawfurd's Journal,* Vol. I, pp. 2, 3.)

APPENDIX IX

List of Principal British subjects in Burma, October, 1838

Names.	Country.	Character.	Where Residing.	Remarks.
13 Europeans				
Brown, John	Scotland	Good	Rangoon	
Biden, Wm. Henry	England	"	"	
Crisp, May Flower	"	"	"	Temporary.
Daniels	Scotland	"	"	
Dixon	"	"	"	
Hazelwood	"	Bad	Amarapoora	
Low, John	"	Good	Rangoon	
Roy, Wm.	"	"	Amarapoora	
Spears, Thos.	"	"	Rangoon	
Spiers, Hugh	"	"	"	
Spiers, Wm.	"	Bad	"	A very unprincipled man and of a very violent disposition.
Staig, David	"		"	
Trill, G. R.	England	Good	Rangoon	
3 Half-Castes				
Johnson, Peter	Madras	Bad	Rangoon	Receiver of stolen goods; keeps a grogshop.
McCalder	"	"	Amarapoora	
McCalder, James	"	"	Rangoon	
5 Armenians				
Abraham, Aratoon	British Born	Good	Rangoon	
Jacob, Isaac	"	"	"	
Lucas	"	Doubtful	"	
Manook	"		"	
Manook, Josa.	"	Good	"	Brother to Mr. Sarkies Manook who is not a British subject. Josa. Manook became one at the cession of the Tenasserim Provinces. His wife and family reside at Calcutta.

12 ¹ Parsees

Burjorjee Hormesjee	Bombay	Good	Rangoon
Byramjee Cowasjee	"	"	"
Edeljee	"	"	"
Framjee	"	"	"
Framjee Cowasjee	"	"	"
Jamashjee	"	"	"
Naserwanjee	"	"	"
Purunjee Jeeva Mehta	"	"	"
Rustomjee Hormesjee	"	"	"
Rustomjee Naserwanjee	"	"	"
Shapoorjee Cowasjee	"	"	"

7 Indians

Chokua	Madras	Good	Rangoon
Koola Moodeen	Bengal	"	"
Jawee Ally	Azeemabad	"	"
Phool Kassie	Bengal	"	"
Pooran Saib	Madras	"	"
Shaikh Mahomet	Bengal	"	"
Tittoo	"	"	"

A Grand total of 40.

Sd. R. Benson,
15th October, 1838,
Amarapoora

(India Secret Consultations Vol. 13, Consultations 21 November, 1838. No. 125).

¹ One name is missing.

APPENDIX X

Translation of a Letter from the Ministers of Tharrawaddy to the Rangoon Myowoon

Received at Rangoon about the middle of December, 1839

"The four Woongyees (titles given) to the Myowoon of Rangoon (title). In the reign of the late King the Officers of state were raised to eminence and received favors, but they reflected neither on the interests of the Kingdom nor of their sovereign. They considered only their own personal interests, petitioning unjustly as they chose, for the sake of bribes, not acting in the state affairs so that the Royal character might shine forth with lustre; having neither energy nor enterprise of spirit because deficient in courage and firmness; and tarnishing the fame of the National History.

"The King will destroy and retake all the Kingdoms that were established by his Royal Great Grandfather and Grandfather.

"Let not persons who come from other nations to the Port of Rangoon for the purposes of trade purchase or receive in power from Burman subjects land for building houses upon. Let them not build on unoccupied ground without having first obtained an order from the King. Let not foreigners hold Burmese as slaves, and referring to those already sold or pawned, let them be redeemed by the persons who sold or pawned them. If they are unable to do so, let them be redeemed with the Royal Money, taking an account of the same.

"Should there be any discussions with the Natives [1] of India, let not the customs and properties of great officers of state be departed from; they must be transacted with justice as a measure that is full.

"Nga-Dok-Gyee [2] who bears the title of Woondouk did not act in accordance with the customs of great officers; he destroyed the respect due to their rank and acted as if he harboured or took part with the Natives of India (i.e. Englishmen), and his orders were of no force or effect. If these things are again heard of, the Royal punishment will be decreed. We are directed strongly to impress these orders upon the Governor of Rangoon.

"On the 5th day of the increase of the moon Natta 1201, according as we have received upon our hands the Royal orders from the Princes of Mekkra, Prome, Pakhan, we record and repeat them.

"The King will destroy and retake all the Kingdoms founded by his Royal Great Grandfather and Grandfather.

---

[1] "This, I think, from the general tenor of the letter includes Englishmen also." (McLeod.)
[2] The Ayébain-Woondouk, Governor of Rangoon, who belonged to the peace party. Nga is used for him here as a term of disgrace.

"Let not the inhabitants of the Towns and Villages sell or pawn building land to the foreigners who come to the port of Rangoon for the purpose of trade. Let persons so wishing to build first obtain the Royal order and then let them build and remain.

"Let not foreigners hold Burmese as slaves, and with reference to those who have already been sold or pawned, let them be redeemed by the persons who sold or pawned them. If they possess not the means to do this, let them be redeemed by the Royal Money, an account being taken of the same. The Lord[1] of the Towns of Zeingu Nein and May Yein Za Ya in the district of Hanthawadee is deprived of his Towns.

"Nga-Dok-Gyee the person called Woondouk has not acted in the manner of a Royal officer. He destroyed the respect due to rank and his orders were of no force or effect. He has acted towards foreigners as if he took part with or harboured them. If such things are again heard of, the Royal punishment will be decreed." (India Secret Consultations Vol. 33, Consultations 12 February, 1840, No. 110).

[1] Mr. Sarkies Manook the Armenian. (McLeod.)

BIBLIOGRAPHY

I. Unpublished Documents

This is the main source of information. It lies in the Records of the Bengal and Indian Governments at the India Office. Details regarding these will be found in Foster's Guide to the India Office Records, 1600-1858:—

(i) Bengal Secret and Political Consultations. Vols. 339, 341, 344-348, 350-352, 354, 355, 357-363, 365-369, 371-377, 380.

(ii) India Political Consultations. Range 193: Vols. 55, 61-63, 67-69, 71, 74, 76, 77, 79, 81, 83, 85, 87, 89, 90.

Range 194: Vols. 1, 3, 5-10, 12, 13, 15, 16, 19, 20, 23, 24, 29, 31, 33, 35, 36, 41, 42, 46, 47, 58, 60, 61, 65.

Range 195: Vols. 3, 4.

(iii) India Secret Consultations. 1837-1842: Vols. 8, 10-13, 15-17, 19-23, 25-27, 33-35, 41, 43, 51, 76.

(iv) General Records: Home Miscellaneous. 1826-1837: Vols. 669, 674, 676, 680, 681.

(v) Bengal Military Service List.
Bengal, Room No. 204, Range No. 6, Shelf No. 27; Vols. 2, 3, 5.

II. Other Works

Aitchison, C. U. A Collection of Treaties, Engagements and Sanads relating to India and neighbouring countries. Vol. I. Calcutta.

Bayfield, G. T. See Pemberton, R. B.

Bigandet, An Outline of the History of the Catholic Burmese Mission, 1720-1887. Rangoon, 1887.

Brown, G. H. and Clark, F. The East India Register and Directory, London.

Cox. H. Journal of a Residence in the Burman Empire. London, 1821.

Crawfurd, J. Journal of an Embassy from the Governor-General of India to the Court of Ava in the year 1826, 2 Vols. London, 1829.

Dautremer, J. Burma under British Rule. London. Tr. by G. Scott.

Foster, Wm. A Guide to the India Office Records, 1600-1858. London, 1919.

Fytche, A. Burma Past and Present. 2 Vols. London, 1878.

Gait, E. A. A History of Assam. Calcutta, 1906.

Gouger, H. A Personal Narrative of Two Years' Imprisonment in Burmah. London, 1860.

Hall, D. G. E. Early English Intercourse with Burma, 1587-1743. London, 1928.

Harvey, G. E. History of Burma to 1824. London, 1925.

Johnstone, J. My Experiences in Manipur and the Naga Hills. London, 1896.

Laurie, W. F. B. Our Burmese Wars. London, 1880.

Lloyd, M. B. S. Gazetteer of the District of Rangoon, Pegu Province, 1868.

Malcolm, H. Travels in the Burman Empire. Edinburgh, 1840.

McLeod, W. C. Journal, of a Mission from Moulmein to the frontiers of China, 1836-37. London, 1869.

McLeod and Richardson's Journeys: East India to the frontiers of China, and the route of Richardson to the Shan Provinces of Burmah or extracts from the same. London, 1869.

McNeill, D. Report and Gazetteer of Burma, Native and British.

Nisbet, J. Burma under British Rule and before. 2 Vols. London, 1901.

Pemberton, R. B. Report on the Eastern Frontier of British India.... with a Supplement by G. T. Bayfield: Historical Review of the Political Relations between the British Government in India and the Empire of Ava....to the end of the year 1834. Calcutta, 1835.

Phayre, A. P. History of Burma. London, 1883.

Scott, J. G. and Hardiman. Gazetteer of Upper Burma. 5 Vols. Rangoon, 1900.

Snodgrass, J. J. Narrative of the Burmese War. London, 1827.

Spearman, H. The British Burma Gazetteer, 1880, 2 Vols.

Symes, M. An account of an Embassy to the Kingdom of Ava. London, 1827.

Trant, T. A. Two years in Ava (1824-1826). London, 1827.

Wayland, F. A Memoir of the Life and Labours of the Rev. Adoniram Judson, Vol. I, 1853.

White, W. A Political History of the extraordinary events which led to the Burmese War. London, 1827.

Yule, H. A Narrative of the Mission to the Court of Ava in 1855. London, 1858.

The Journal of the Burma Research Society. August 1936. Article in four chapters by W. S. Desai, History of the Burmese Mission to India, 1830-1833.

The World of Books, Rangoon. December 1935. Article by W. S. Desai, The First Burmese Mission to British India, 1827.

The Burma Census Report, 1931. Notes by G. H. Luce.

The Kone-baung-set Mahayazawin in Burmese, compiled by the State Chroniclers in the Royal Hmannan Palace, 1867, at the order of King Mindon (1853-1878). The Taing Press, Mandalay, 1905.

INDEX

Angus Calder